The GREAT TRAIN ROBBERY

The GREAT TRAIN ROBBERY

CRIME OF THE CENTURY

**Nick Russell-Pavier
& Stewart Richards**

WEIDENFELD & NICOLSON

LONDON

First published in Great Britain in 2012
by Weidenfeld & Nicolson

1 3 5 7 9 10 8 6 4 2

A CIP catalogue record for this book
is available from the British Library.

ISBN- 978 0 2978 6439 4

Typeset by Input Data Services Ltd, Bridgwater, Somerset

Printed and bound by CPI Group Ltd, Croydon, CR0 4YY

Weidenfeld & Nicolson

The Orion Publishing Group Ltd
Orion House
5 Upper Saint Martin's Lane
London, WC2H 9EA
www.orionbooks.co.uk

The Orion Publishing Group's policy is to use papers
that are natural, renewable and recyclable products and made
from wood grown in sustainable forests. The logging and
manufacturing processes are expected to conform to
the environmental regulations of the country of origin.

PREFACE

There have been many accounts, films, biographies, newspaper articles, television programmes and public records written over the last fifty years about 'The Great Train Robbery'. They have all, in their own way, contributed to the folklore that has evolved around the subject of the mail train ambush that took place in Buckinghamshire in the early hours of 8 August 1963.

The train was traversing a country that had more grocery shops than supermarkets and the nation's diet was limited and bland: pork luncheon meat, corned beef, eggs, overcooked meat and two veg. Few Britons would have ever tasted garlic or been on a foreign holiday. Men wore hats or flat caps, women headscarves sometimes with hair rollers underneath. The majority of adults smoked cigarettes. Houses had no central heating and in cold weather the air smelled of coal fires. Only 36 per cent of households owned a car, less than half had a washing machine. In the fading days of a vast empire, and attempts at socialist engineering following World War Two, much of the nation's land and wealth was still owned by successive generations of aristocrats and landed gentry. The British were a disparate island society divided by region, class and education. They remained culturally, intellectually and aesthetically distanced from their European neighbours by more than twenty-one miles of salt water. In a 1946 essay, George Orwell observed,

> During the war of 1914–18 the English working class were in contact with foreigners to an extent that is rarely possible. The result is that they brought back a hatred of all Europeans, except the Germans, whose courage they admired. In four years on French soil they did not even acquire a liking for wine.

By 1963, forty-five years and another war later, social values had shifted but the British outlook remained largely unchanged.

It is virtually impossible to read anything about England in the 1960s without it first being prefaced by the clichés of 'Beatlemania' and the 'Swinging Sixties', but for most of the nation, most of the time, that was only an incidental part of daily life. Britain in 1963 was a country riven by crime, in the grip of powerful trade unions and governed by an old-school establishment struggling to balance the crises of the Cold War with growing pressure for social reform.

In talking to the few surviving individuals who were part of the extraordinary 'Great Train Robbery' story as principal players or bystanders, what emerges is that no two stories agree. Each account invariably takes a particular viewpoint, whether it is that of the robbers, the police officers or other connected parties, and over time memory has a way of constructing unreliable narratives.

In the rich and complex mythology that has grown up since the 1963 mail-train raid, numerous versions and interpretations conspire against each other and it is now impossible to arrive at an account of the truth in an absolute sense. As a result, a book that claims to be definitive cannot reasonably be a statement of fact for a single viewpoint, a collective viewpoint or even try to arrive at a definitive conclusion. It can be definitive only by virtue of capturing and setting out the fascinating multiplicity of people, events, recorded statements, and contradictory viewpoints, past and present, that have created the myths and legends of 'The Great Train Robbery'. So there is room for the most likely to the absolutely barking mad.

Against the historical backdrop and enormous amount of money stolen, around £45 million in today's money, the heart of the story is surprisingly small, ordinary and human. In the true account that follows the legend is deconstructed and in the systematic dismantling I hope a clearer, more complete and intimate picture emerges of the events and people whose lives collided in the 8 August 1963 Royal Mail train robbery.

1962

1

'THE AIRPORT'
COMET HOUSE, WEST LONDON

Tuesday, 27 November 1962

Shortly before 10 a.m., in the top-floor Gents' toilet of Comet House, headquarters of the British state airline BOAC, at London Airport, four men in suits are looking out of the window. They are watching three guards escort a steel box measuring three feet by two to a security van four hundred yards away outside the Hatton Cross branch of Barclays Bank. Inside the strongbox are the cash wages for BOAC's airport staff: sixty-two thousand pounds, the equivalent of nearly one million in today's money.

In the ground-floor foyer of Comet House, three other men are waiting. One stands reading the *Financial Times*; he is wearing a tweed sports jacket, checked cap and has dyed black hair and a false moustache. The other two are dressed in dark charcoal-grey jackets, pinstriped trousers, and bowler hats. They are talking quietly to each other, holding furled umbrellas in which the stems have been removed and replaced by iron bars. In the car park outside, two young men in chauffeur's uniforms are chatting, standing by their gleaming 3.8 Mark 2 Jaguars.

In front of Barclays Bank, the steel wages box is loaded into the van and the doors are slammed shut. The guards get into a car in front and start the engine. The men in the Gents' at Comet House watch the security convoy begin the short drive towards them, followed by a wireless car.

A few minutes later, the van draws up outside the main entrance to BOAC headquarters. The heavy box is hauled out of the back of the van and placed on to a trolley. Following the regular Tuesday routine, the guards will escort their cargo in through the foyer and up to the cashier's office on the first floor.

On the top floor of Comet House, the men leave the Gents' toilet and walk down the corridor to the lift. One of them has gone ahead and has been keeping the lift ready by throwing the stop switch. All four men get inside and the button is pressed for the ground floor. As the doors slide shut, they pull out stocking masks from their pockets. From inside his jacket one man pulls out his lucky mascot: a foot long, inch-and-a-quarter-diameter length of pipe filled with lead and bound with cloth.

The radio car drives away as the security guards enter the Comet House foyer. They push the trolley across the polished linoleum floor towards the lift, passing the man in a sports jacket and checked cap, past the two gentlemen in city suits with umbrellas. As the guards press the call button for the lift they can already hear it descending. The man in the checked cap folds his newspaper and places it on a table. Along with the city gents, he walks nonchalantly in the direction of the lift.

When the doors glide open the four masked men explode from inside, screaming at the guards and lashing out. One guard is hit a glancing blow behind the ear and falls semi-conscious to the ground. Another starts to make a run for it but is caught by one of the city gents with a quick tap of his umbrella and crumples to the floor. The last guard collapses without being touched. The attackers spin the trolley round and wheel it back out through the entrance of the building to where the two chauffeur-driven Jags have just squealed to a halt outside. The five men throw the wages box into the boot of one of the Jags, jump into the getaway cars and take off at racing speed. The cars scream around the back of airport buildings, weaving between startled workmen and parked vehicles and turn out on to the airport's inner perimeter road. After a few hundred yards, they skid to a halt in front of a pair of locked, disused gates in the outer fence leading directly to the main A30 road. With dust and debris still swirling in the air, two men leap out of the leading car, cut a chain from the padlock on the gates with bolt cutters and swing the gates open. The Jags surge through the gap, stopping on the other side with engines revving.

A passer-by, driving west along the A30, spots the unusual activity up ahead. He pulls over and reverses his Austin in front of the two Jaguars, attempting to block the criminals' escape. However, the man's quick thinking heroics are in vain. The robbers with the bolt cutters are already in the back of the first Jag. Spinning their steering wheels to dodge the stationary Austin, both drivers floor their 3.8-litre engines, kicking up gravel, the squealing tyres leaving skid marks on the tarmac. One car clips the wing of the Austin as they swerve round it and the Jags roar away, accelerating hard down the Great West Road towards Central London. From start to finish the whole BOAC robbery has taken under three minutes.

Getaway driver Roy James, his lightning reactions honed on the motor-racing circuit, pulls across a major junction as the traffic lights turn to red, holding up crossing traffic, and the second Jag scorches through with three men in the back. They are quiet and collected. Everything has gone according to plan.

This is no ordinary wages snatch. This is a new type of crime, meticulously timed, stylish, executed with ruthless precision. The young criminals easing back into the red leather of the Jag's interior with smiles on their faces are wily and rakish Irishman Gordon Goody; Charlie Wilson, a good-looking South Londoner with a ready wit and Bruce Reynolds, who with his heavy-framed glasses looks the epitome of white-collar respectability and quite unlike the violent and seasoned criminal that he is. The portly man with a friendly smile riding up front is Ronald Edwards, known to his mates as 'Buster'. This job is something different and New Scotland Yard is about to receive a wake-up call.

Goody, Wilson, Edwards, James and Reynolds are the nucleus of a loose association of south-west London criminals who will go on to form a gang of sixteen for a mail-train robbery in Buckinghamshire the following year that will come to be known as 'the crime of the century'.

1963

2

'THE TRAIN'
BRIDEGO BRIDGE, BUCKINGHAMSHIRE

Thursday, 8 August 1963

At midnight, a diesel locomotive hauling twelve carriages rumbled through the quiet English countryside just outside Warrington, Cheshire. The Travelling Post Office was en route to London, a journey made by countless other TPOs every night for 125 years without incident. On board the maroon coaches, with their royal coat of arms and high slit windows, postal workers were sorting through the overnight mail. In the second carriage, where registered mail was kept, were forty-six white mailbags containing packets of banknotes. Due to the summer Bank Holiday, a large consignment of money was being sent south to various banks' head branches in the City of London. Most of the cash was surplus to the requirements of local banks but some of the payload was made up of old five-pound notes that were being withdrawn from circulation.

The TPO was scheduled to make seven stops before finally pulling into Euston. Along the way a total of 128 mailbags would be collected containing 636 packets of five-pound, one-pound and ten-shilling notes amounting to two million, five hundred and ninety-five thousand, nine hundred and ninety-seven pounds and ten shillings.

The 'Up Special' had left Glasgow Central station with five carriages the previous evening at 18.50. It had stopped at Carstairs, twenty-eight miles south of Glasgow, at 19.32 where four coaches were added from Aberdeen before departing at 19.45. At 20.54, it had arrived in Carlisle. There was a change of guard and sixty-one-year-old Thomas James Miller, of 83 Brent Terrace, London, N22, joined the train along with three further coaches making the full complement of twelve carriages. Miller had worked on the railways for forty-one years.

Before midnight, the train stopped twice more: 22.53 at Preston, departing 23.03 and 23.36 at Warrington, departing 23.43. With two more scheduled stops, the TPO was due to arrive at Euston station in London, after a nine-hour journey of 401 miles, at 03.59.

At Crewe station, the platforms were empty except for two men standing about in the balmy night air, chatting casually as they waited: train driver Jack Mills and his second man (sometimes referred to as the 'fireman' – a hangover from steam engines) David Whitby. At the age of twenty-six, Whitby had already been working on the railways for eleven years. He lived half a mile from the station at 154a Mill Street, Crewe. In fifteen minutes, Mills and Whitby were due to take over English Electric Class 40 locomotive, 'D326' and drive the mail train to its final destination. Fifty-seven-year-old Jack Mills lived about twenty-five minutes' walk from Crewe station at 35 Newdigate Street with his wife, Florence. They had a married son called John and their first grandchild, Stephen, was due to be christened that weekend. Jack Mills had lived in Crewe all his life and been driving trains for almost twenty-two years, so he was used to the routine of the night shift and he enjoyed the prestige that went with driving the TPO.

In a dilapidated farmhouse in Buckinghamshire, 138 miles south of Crewe, thirty-one-year-old Bruce Richard Reynolds was putting on the uniform of an army major. His SAS cap badge displayed the well-known motto of 'The Regiment' – *Who Dares Wins*. With fifteen other men he was about to engage in the biggest job of his criminal career. Known as a sharp dresser, Reynolds wore handmade suits, bought his shirts in Jermyn Street, drove an Aston Martin and was a regular at the Star Tavern in Belgravia. With his black, heavy-framed glasses, he looked the very image of Michael Caine's character Harry Palmer in the 1965 film *The Ipcress File*. Little did the boy from Battersea suspect that his image would influence future filmmakers. Reynolds had always wanted to be someone but for now, he was just a South London criminal no one had ever heard of about to take a chance with some mates.

In the sitting room below, thirty-three-year-old Gordon Goody was relaxed and chatting with the other members of the gang. Without Goody, none of them would have been there. Articulate, witty, well-respected and charismatic, his associates also knew that Goody could be ruthless and violent. With 'Hello Ireland' and 'Dear Mother' tattooed on his biceps, Gordon Goody's rough edges were plain to see. He had nine previous criminal convictions including robbery with violence and unauthorised possession of a firearm.

Outside in the farmyard, thirty-one-year-old Battersea-born Charlie Wilson, an easy-going joker with sharp blue eyes and a tangle of dark hair, was smoking a cigarette. Wilson and Reynolds had known each other since they were kids. Like most of the gang they had worked on a number of jobs together over the years; they trusted each other and the bond between them was strong. Wilson was talking to the youngest member of the gang: twenty-seven-year-old, five feet four inches tall, amateur racing driver Roy James who was feeding some stray cats.

A little way off across the moonlit yard, forty-three-year-old Jimmy White was checking over three vehicles. There was an ex-War Department, three-ton Austin Loadstar drop-side lorry that White had purchased for £300 on 23 July from motor dealer Stanley Phillip Dawkins of Mullard & Co. in Edgware, London. White gave his name and address as F. Blake, 272 Kenton Lane, Middlesex. The lorry now bore a set of new registration plates – BPA 260. That number was taken from a 1933 black Ford saloon that had been broken up for scrap by motor mechanic John Henry Charles Price two years earlier in May 1961. The remains of the car were in a yard behind the Black Dog Inn in Gloucester.

Displayed on the windscreen of the lorry was a road-fund licence relating to another lorry, VJD 35, belonging to James Edward Godfrey, a self-employed lorry driver of 5 Doric House, Cranbrook Estate, Old Ford Road, London, E2. The tax disc had been stolen from his vehicle when it was parked near his home between 19.30 on 29 July and 14.00 the following day when he reported it to police at Bethnal Green.

Also parked in the yard were two canvas-roofed Land Rovers, a Series One and a Series Two. The Series One had been advertised in *Exchange and Mart* and purchased by White (this time using the name Bentley) for £195 from Michael John Humphreys of Cross Country Vehicles, 45 Firs Park Gardens, Winchmore Hill, London, N21. Humphreys had acquired the vehicle for £145 in a sale of ex-government surplus stock at Ruddington, Nottinghamshire, on 2 July, re-sprayed it green and re-registered it with a civilian index number, BMG 757A. White had first looked at the Land Rover on 31 July, left a deposit of £155 and collected it on 3 August.

The Series Two Land Rover was purchased new by the owner, Anthony Biggins, in May 1963 and stolen between 19.30 and 23.00 on 21 July from Oxenden Street, London, SW1, by White and Reynolds. The vehicle, originally blue and white, had been repainted green by the gang to give it an army appearance. For some curious reason the two Land Rovers had both been fitted with the same BMG757A registration number.

A wiry, energetic man, with a high forehead and small eyes, Jimmy White was organised and thorough. He was in good physical shape for his age and moved with precision, looking the part in his thrown-together military uniform and neatly trimmed moustache. He had been a proud soldier in the Parachute Regiment until his discharge from the army, suffering from a duodenal ulcer, on 7 June 1944, the day after the D-Day landings in Normandy. But when White's army pension was subsequently reduced from eighteen shillings to nine shillings a week he felt betrayed by the country for which he had risked his life. Over the years that followed, White worked hard at a number of legitimate business ventures but the rewards were meagre until he turned his capable hands to 'ringing' stolen cars.

As the mail train pulled into Crewe station, Jack Mills slung his bag over his shoulder. In it was a thermos flask of tea and an old gas mask tin that he used as a lunch box, containing his favourite snack – an egg and bacon sandwich. Mills was unaware that the second carriage of his train, known as the High Value Package coach, or HVP, contained more money than he could imagine. In any case, it was not his job to worry about security. None of the train, or postal staff, was trained to think, or do, anything about that. It was taken for granted that the Royal Mail was something bigger than any of them, part of the unshakable establishment. This was an age when workers assumed their employers – their betters – took care of such things.

However, British Railways and the Post Office had not anticipated the danger of sending employees out into the night with large sums of money, to travel on a train through the dark, deserted countryside, unprotected. There were no guards, or transport police on board Royal

Mail trains. Aside from walking from carriage to carriage through the connecting doors, there was no means of communicating between the sections of the train, let alone with the outside world. There was no access from the locomotive to the first unmanned coach, and no access from coach one to coach two. The driver and his 'firemen' in their cab were completely cut off from the rest of the train behind them. Neither the banks, British Railways, the Post Office, the police, nor the men working on board, had considered they were vulnerable to attack and that from a criminal point of view, the Royal Mail train was an easy prize.

With Jack Mills and David Whitby now in the cab of their locomotive, the growling 2,000-horsepower engine of the Class 40 eased the train out of Crewe station. Meanwhile, the gang of sixteen, dressed in make-shift army uniforms, were getting ready to leave their Buckinghamshire hideout.

Leatherslade Farm was a run-down smallholding just outside Oakley, tucked out of sight up a long gravel track, away from of the road and prying eyes. It had been acquired by the gang, with the help of crooked solicitor's clerk Brian Field, three weeks earlier. In their planning, the bandits had decided they would need a place to convene undetected, somewhere to lie in wait beforehand and to hide out after the robbery. Having a base close to the scene of their intended crime seemed logical. Twenty-eight miles from Bridego Bridge, the gang had calculated that the farm was close enough to get to before the police could respond effectively, yet far enough from the scene of the crime not to arouse suspicion.

At 00.30, Reynolds' job was to check the gang members into the vehicles. Each man was given a number; Reynolds needed them to remember where they sat so they could easily be checked off later, for the return journey to make sure no one was left behind. Of the gang of sixteen, who carried out the robbery, four have never been identified. One was the back-up train driver who has often been referred to as Peter, or Stan. The others remain unnamed but came to be known as Mr One, Mr Two and Mr Three.

The vehicles started up, made their way slowly down the farm track and turned right out of the gate on to the B4011 Thame Road. Leading the convoy was the Series Two Land Rover driven by Mr Two. His passengers were Reynolds, Ronnie Biggs – a small-time crook and old friend of Reynolds; the train driver; John Daly – a sixteen-stone Irishman known as 'Paddy' and Reynolds' brother-in-law; and Roger Cordrey – florist, a compulsive gambler and leader of the South Coast Raiders gang, recruited for his expertise in doctoring railway signals. Behind them came the three-ton Austin lorry driven by Mr One, accompanied by Mr Three; Charlie Wilson; Buster Edwards – a former boxer, nightclub owner and long-time associate of Reynolds; Tommy Wisbey – a bookie, with a fine singing voice and well connected in the London underworld; Bob Welch – a former nightclub boss and gambler; and 'Big' Jim Hussey – a painter and decorator, who had served time for GBH. Last in the convoy, driving the Series One Land Rover was Roy James. James had beaten Jackie Stewart in the European Formula Junior Race at Phoenix Park in Ireland the week before. He also had a reputation as the best getaway driver around. His passengers were ex-soldier and café proprietor Jimmy White, and ladies hairdresser and bank robber Gordon Goody.

A few minutes into their journey, the convoy turned right off the B4011 up the Brill Road and passed a line of cottages. By chance, one of the occupants, Mrs Nappin, was up late and alerted by the sound of vehicles at the late hour, she looked out of the bedroom window as the convoy passed by. The gang was unaware that they had been noticed. Mrs Nappin thought nothing of it. But the image of the two Land Rovers and a lorry, loaded with men in army uniforms, stuck in her mind, as did the time she had seen them.

The small convoy drove through the sleeping village of Brill and headed east along quiet country lanes, avoiding major roads, skirting north of Aylesbury towards Leighton Buzzard. The order was to drive slowly. There was no need to rush. If spotted, they hoped to pass for an army unit from one of the camps in the area out on night exercise.

According to Reynolds, he had false papers in his pocket to produce in case they were stopped. To have obtained convincing official-looking documentation would have required both inside knowledge and the help of a printer. While the claim is theoretically possible, it seems more likely this is an example of the many later embellishments to 'The Great Train Robbery' mythology. Many such details have been added after the event feeding the misconception that the planning and execution of the 1963 mail-train robbery was something akin to the plot of an Alistair MacLean novel.

Given that military vehicles have special registration numbers and the gang's two Land Rovers had identical civilian numbers, the army charade was, at best, superficial. The equipment the men had with them was far from military; it consisted of: four walkie-talkies, an axe, coshes, pickaxe handles, a pair of handcuffs, some wire, eight six-volt batteries and a pair of black leather gloves. Each man had a dark balaclava and a boiler suit to put on over his army uniform.

By 01.00 the postal workers on board the mail train were well into a familiar routine in their noisy, closed-in world. It was mindless, repetitive work sorting post manually into ranks of wooden pigeonholes that ran the length of the carriages from waist height to ceiling. Over 98 per cent accuracy was expected, but the banter between the postmen and frequent cups of tea made the overnight work tolerable.

Frank Dewhurst, the man in charge of the HVP coach, had joined the train at Carlisle, along with Assistant Post Office Inspector Thomas Kett and Postman Higher Grade Leslie Penn. A stocky, taciturn forty-nine-year-old Londoner, Dewhurst was an old hand on the TPO. He had been doing the job for twelve years and was used to the routine. The only view of the outside world was through a line of slit windows, no more than eight inches in height, high up on one wall of each carriage. Not that there was much to see in the dead of night, apart from the occasional lights of towns flashing past as the TPO thundered south at between fifty and sixty miles an hour.

By contrast, the bandits' three-vehicle convoy was trundling along narrow Buckinghamshire lanes at half that speed. The men sat quietly, thinking about what was to come and what they had to do in the next few hours. Underpinning their reflective mood was the prospect that if everything went according to plan their lives would be transformed. By dawn they would not only all have become very rich men but every man for the first time in his life would have the chance to escape the dreary working-class world in which they had they grown up. And the start of that golden future was getting closer with each mile, with every bump in the road, as the minutes ticked by.

They had been driving for about twenty minutes when a lone figure loomed out of the darkness up ahead, picked out in the dimmed headlights, walking along the side of the road. The man turned as the vehicles approached and held out his thumb. He was dressed in RAF uniform, carrying a rucksack and appeared to be trying to hitch a lift. In the lead vehicle, several questions jolted the occupants from their thoughts. Would the hitchhiker recall seeing the convoy? Would he wonder which army base they were from? Would he remember the time and direction from which they had been coming? Would he catch sight of their uniforms and question why they had not stopped to give a fellow serviceman a lift? If asked later, would he recognise any of the men if he saw them again?

Reynolds raised his hand in acknowledgement, shielding his face as they passed. It was a casual gesture and did not give away what was running through his mind. There was not much they could do about it now. Other members of the gang had noticed the man too and it made them uneasy. Their plan was good but they could not predict every eventuality, particularly not small random incidents like this. And if they could not control that, how much else could go wrong in the next few hours? Sitting in the hot, confined space of the vehicles their coarse army uniforms made them itch and sweat. Pent up with nervous energy and anticipation, the hitchhiker had worried them.

At about 01.30 the convoy turned down a single-track lane that led to railway bridge 127, known as Bridego Bridge. The three vehicles drove up to the bridge and stopped just short on the verge by a pond frequented by local anglers. A quick check confirmed that there was no one night fishing, something the gang had considered when making their reconnaissance of the area. The moment they had seen the railway bridge, with a quiet narrow lane running under it, they knew it would be the perfect place – tucked away, surrounded by farmland with no houses anywhere nearby.

The vehicles turned around and parked ready to retrace their route when it was all over; the two Land Rovers nearest the pond and the Austin lorry nearest the bridge.

As the gang got out of their vehicles the moon was bright and nearly full, a white disc in a cloudless, star-dusted sky. The time had come to start putting their carefully laid plans into action. Wisecracks from Edwards and Wilson helped the men steady their nerves as they stood stretching cramped muscles in the warm summer night. There was little need for discussion about the job in hand as they pulled on their overalls. Each man knew what he had to do and where to take up his position.

James and Cordrey immediately set off to shin up a nearby telegraph pole and cut overhead wires. A fitness fanatic, Roy James could not have been more different in temperament and physique to the chain-smoking, obsessive gambler Roger Cordrey who reputedly had an encyclopaedic knowledge of Grand National winners. Whereas Cordrey often teetered on the edge of financial disaster, James was on the brink of success. He had bought a Brabham BT6 racing car with his share from 'The Airport' robbery and was a personal friend of Graham Hill. As well as being known for his driving skills, Roy James had earned a reputation as a good 'climber' from his younger days as a cat burglar.

Gordon Goody and some of the others clambered up the embankment and carefully paced out the position where a strip of white sheet was to be slung between two posts indicating the place where the train should be stopped for unloading. The gang's plan was to halt the TPO with a tampered red signal at Sears Crossing. But the signal was eleven-hundred yards north of the bridge where heavy mail sacks could be passed down the embankment to the road below. Having brought the train to a halt at Sears Crossing they would need to board the locomotive and uncouple the first unmanned carriage, known as the bogie brake van, and the HVP coach from the rest of the train. The locomotive and two carriages would then be driven the short distance to Bridego Bridge for the main event – the assault on the prized HVP coach.

With no part to play in the action until the TPO arrived, the gang's train driver stood back and lit his pipe. At sixty-three he was thirty years older than most of them and been given the nickname 'Pop'. Since arriving at the farm with Biggs two days earlier he had been the quietest member of the group clearly overwhelmed at the prospect of taking part in a major robbery.

While the gang ran through their preparations, the TPO made two further scheduled stops. The first was at Tamworth, Staffordshire where Dewhurst, Kett and Penn were joined in the HVP carriage by two sorters – twenty-one-year-old John William O'Connor and Joseph Henry

Ware aged fifty-five. Thirty miles later the train stopped at Rugby in Warwickshire to take on more mail. Both stations had minimum security. London-bound mail and high-value sacks were left sitting on the platform, ready to be loaded by TPO staff. Registered packages were placed in the HVP under Dewhurst's supervision. This was the quiet, unremarkable, reliable routine of overnight mail trains travelling up and down the country, immortalised in the 1936 poem 'Night Mail' by W.H. Auden. With Jack Mills at the controls, the train pulled out of Rugby at 02.16 with just under two hours to run.

At 02.20, fifty miles south of Rugby, the gang were still busy with their preparations. When James and Cordrey returned from their telephone line sabotage, James joined the rest of the team who began to make their way up the track to the signal gantry at Sears Crossing.

Reynolds, Daly and Cordrey climbed into one of the Land Rovers, started it up and headed north along the B488. In order to stop the train, Daly and Cordrey would need to rig two signals. The first, known in railway terminology as the 'Dwarf signal', would be set to amber and three hundred yards south of it the 'Home' signal on an overhead gantry at Sears Crossing, would be set to red.

A mile north of the bridge, Reynolds turned off the B488 up an unmarked track. On the far side of a moonlit field they could see the Dwarf signal by the railway line. A few yards down the track they stopped the Land Rover out of sight of the road. Cordrey took his bag from the cab and the three men made their way across the field and up the embankment.

Cordrey wasted no time in wiring up the Dwarf light – four Eveready six-volt batteries with leads, two crocodile clips and a switch that would illuminate the amber signal when the time came. He confirmed with Daly that all he had to do when Reynolds gave the word over his walkie-talkie was to cover the green light with a black leather glove and flick the switch. It was that simple.

Leaving Daly at the first signal, Cordrey and Reynolds walked back over the fields to the Land Rover. They drove south to Sears Crossing, situated about halfway between Daly's position and Bridego Bridge. Reynolds dropped off Cordrey near the overhead gantry across the railway where Cordrey was to follow the same tampering routine at the Home signal – a glove to cover the green light and four batteries, connecting wires and a switch to illuminate the red signal when he got the word from Reynolds over his radio that the TPO was in sight. This was to be the spot where Jack Mills and his train would be brought to a halt.

Meanwhile, on their way up the track towards Sears Crossing, the rest of the gang spotted a railway workman's hut. Perhaps because they were thieves by nature, or hoping to find something to assist them in their task, they broke into the hut to see what they could find.

Reynolds left Cordrey and took up his position as lookout at the track-side north of Daly. With binoculars, he could see Leighton Buzzard two miles away up the line and would be able to spot the train approaching. He lit a cigar, reputedly a Monte Cristo Number Two, and blew the heavy smoke into the night.

Reynolds was in his element, living out a misguided fantasy. In his imagination, his crimes were not just about ruthless, avaricious violence and easy money. They were daring escapades in which he cast himself as a romantic anti-hero in the mould of Raffles or more bizarrely, T.E. Lawrence who, as Reynolds later put it, 'stopped trains too'. He was undoubtedly a rarity in the drab black-and-white, working-class world from which he came. Fired by the notion of adventure since a boy, Reynolds was quixotic, self-absorbed, violent and determined. He revelled in the planning of his work, and if he could include a bit of theatre, so much the better. Dressing up in army uniforms and pretending to be a band of soldiers off on a daring mission was just his style.

In the distance to the south, a steam goods train was chugging north up the line. Presently, it passed the gang concealed either side of the track: Jimmy White, Roy James, Bob Welch, Buster Edwards, Mr One and Mr Three on the east side and Gordon Goody, Charlie Wilson, Tommy Wisbey, Jim Hussey, Mr Two, with Ronnie Biggs and 'Pop' the train driver on the west side. A cloud of smoke and steam enveloped Cordrey as the train went under the Sears Crossing gantry and on, passing Daly at the Dwarf signal, then Reynolds, who was standing back in the shadows at the most northerly point of the ambush.

Reynolds puffed on his cigar and checked his stainless-steel Omega wristwatch. The luminous hands glowed in the darkness. It was 02.50. Everyone was where they should be.

Unknown to the gang, a GPO engineer, Robert Hutchinson, had

received a call at 02.45 to look into a line faults noticed by the operator at Leighton Buzzard telephone exchange. The problems had arisen from the gang cutting the overhead telephone wires in the vicinity of Bridego Bridge. As will be seen during the course of the robbery, this was the first of a series of actions that were not fully considered by the gang and could have led to their carefully planned operation being compromised.

Eight long minutes ticked by during which three further goods trains hurtled past, heading north. At 02.58 the TPO thundered by No. 1 Signal Box at Leighton Buzzard. On duty was a lone signalman who went by the unusual and ironically apt name of Thomas Wyn-de-Bank.

Shortly before 03.00, Reynolds spotted approaching lights several miles away up the line against the background shimmer of Leighton Buzzard. He raised his binoculars, squinted into the darkness and adjusted the focus. He took his time, watching and listening, then bent down and touched the cool steel of the rail, checking for vibration. He could hear the deep, distant drone of a diesel engine now.

He looked at his watch again, pulled the walkie-talkie from his pocket and held it to his mouth. 'This is it. This is it. This is it,' he said.

3

At this point in the unfolding story of 'The Great Train Robbery' several relatively minor, but connected, things occurred that threatened the success of the ambush, prompting questions about the planning and execution of 'the crime of the century'.

Stopping the mail train with tampered signals created the possibility of collision with other trains travelling on the fast 'up line' into London. There was a danger that with the signals behind the TPO set to green, a following train might run into the back of the stationary one. Reynolds later dismissed the concern by saying that he followed railway procedure and placed safety detonators on the rails behind the TPO. The purpose of this under normal circumstances was to alert a driver to problems up ahead, such as a broken-down train. However, not only would specialist detonators have to have been obtained by the gang, but more crucially Reynolds would have had to place them sufficiently far back from the rear of the stationary TPO to give a following train driver enough distance to stop. Railway procedure stipulates up to a mile on a fast line. However prudent that precaution would undoubtedly have been, Reynolds did not have time for such a safeguard given the timetable of the raid.

The gang had decided to take no longer than thirty minutes to execute the robbery, as they had no way of knowing exactly how much time they would have before someone raised the alarm. It was impossible to estimate how long it would be before someone realised something was amiss with the normally impeccable schedule of the Glasgow to London mail train.

In the event, not only did the gang draw attention to the area by indiscriminately cutting overhead telephone lines, but a second unforeseen problem came into play shortly before 03.00. For reasons that remain unclear, John Daly, who had been instructed by Roger Cordrey in his method for falsifying the Dwarf signal – placing a black leather glove over the green light and switching on the battery power to illuminate the amber – did not follow the procedure that had been explained carefully to him.

Seconds after Reynolds announced over the radio that the mail train was approaching, a bell sounded in No.1 signal box at Leighton Buzzard. It was a signal failure alarm and thirty-seven-year-old signalman Wyn-de-Bank was immediately alerted by it.

Cordrey's method of using a glove to cover the green lamp was devised with exactly this technicality in mind but he had clearly failed to impress upon Daly the critical importance of not deviating from the procedure. The alarm that went off in the Leighton Buzzard signal box was because Daly had not placed a glove over the green light as instructed but instead had unscrewed the bulb. The discarded bulb, along with wire and a switch, was later found on the ground near the Dwarf signal by duty technician Frank Mead from the Signals and Telecommunications Department. Mead was called out by Wyn-de-Bank shortly after 03.00 to investigate what he assumed to be a failed signal near Sears Crossing.

Whatever Daly's reasons, whether he had dropped or misplaced the glove, or simply thought it did not mask the green light sufficiently, he could not have known that the signalman would be alerted by his improvisation. Daly's blunder was one of a number of critical errors during the raid that illustrate the gang's lack of technical knowledge and the consequences they set in motion.

The light-failure alert that was ringing in signal box No. 1 under Wyn-de-Bank's watchful gaze shortly after 03.00 could have been the gang's undoing before the raid on the mail train had even begun. If duty technician Frank Mead had arrived on the scene more promptly than he did, he would have discovered the truth about the signal problems at Sears Crossing. Had he arrived while the raid was in progress, he could have driven off and raised the alarm. The fact that he did not owed nothing to the gang's foresight and planning. It was simply a matter of chance.

Initially, Wyn-de-Bank had no immediate concern about the safety of the TPO. Railway procedure stipulated that if a train was held up at a signal and it appeared to be out of order the second man, or 'fireman', would climb down from the cab and call the signalman from the trackside phone, informing him of the defect and ask for clearance to proceed. But in the gang's efforts to ensure no one could raise the alarm they had cut the wires from the phone located on the leg of the Home signal gantry. The logic of that is undeniable. But with the signalman alerted to a problem with the signal, when he received no call from the TPO it would increase his concerns about what was happening at Sears Crossing, compounding Daly's error.

While the possible causes of the failed signal were running through Wyn-de-Bank's mind, Jack Mills was applying the brakes in the cab of his locomotive. Just beyond the bridge under the A4146, Mills had seen the amber light of the Dwarf signal doctored by Daly. From there the track runs straight as a ruler for the three and a half miles to Cheddington station and a couple of miles beyond. Approaching the amber light Mills could see the Home signal was set to red on the gantry at Sears Crossing beyond two smaller bridges (numbered 130 and 129) three hundred yards ahead, requiring him to stop his train. There was plenty of distance to bring the 368 tons of speeding locomotive and twelve carriages to a halt and time too for fireman Dave Whitby and his phlegmatic, more experienced driver to spot an anomaly and discuss what might have caused it.

What Mills and Whitby were looking at and wondering about as the brakes squealed and their train slowed just after 03.00 was why further down the track towards Cheddington they could see a green signal. With the signal at Sears Crossing showing red, they would have expected signals in the section ahead to be displaying a red light too. Applying the logic of railway signalling, the distant green light did not make sense. It suggested the track was clear and the red light was a fault.

From their respective seats in the cab, Mills on the left and Whitby on the right, they had a clear view of the track in front but the Class 40 windows gave a restricted field of vision. Despite the moonlit night, they could not see Cordrey concealed above them on the gantry. And as the train finally came to a halt at 03.03, Mills and Whitby could not see that just a few feet below them either side, men were lurking in the darkness, watching and waiting.

There was little need for further discussion. Whitby crossed the cab and pushed behind Mills' seat. Sliding the left side door of the locomotive open, he climbed down metal steps on to the stone ballast.

The firemen of a train held at a red light would normally wait a statutory three minutes and then call the signalman from a telephone mounted at the foot of the signal. But David Whitby never did wait the regulation three minutes and in any case, it appeared the Sears Crossing signal was faulty.

Time at this point becomes elastic in the various versions of what happened next.

In a BBC interview, filmed three days after the robbery, Mills was sitting in a chair at home with a large white bandage around his head and a deep bruise under his right eye. His deadpan delivery and native Crewe accent gave little hint of the drama of that night as he told the reporter, 'My mate went down to telephone, which is the usual custom. And he said these telephone wires have been cut – I didn't realise it was a trap, even then.'

As Mills watched Whitby walk back towards the engine, he said he saw two men coming from the east side embankment and assumed they were 'company linesmen'.

Even allowing for their assumption that the men at the trackside were railway workers neither Mills nor Whitby appeared to think it odd or alarming that the telephone wires to the signal box had been cut. Although the railway line was undergoing electrification work at the time, this did not normally involve holding up mail trains and would not have required cutting or disconnecting wires to the trackside phone, which was a vital piece of operational safety equipment.

Mills said that at this rather key moment he turned back to the controls of his engine, assuming an explanation for the delay was at hand and they would be told they could proceed.

Whitby's account of these initial events is slightly different. He said he walked the few yards to the telephone on the gantry. It took him a moment to get there, open the phone box and, in the headlights of the locomotive, spot that the wires to the handset had been cut. Whitby said that he went back to the cab to tell Mills and then saw a man looking in between the second and third coaches. The man was wearing bib and braces and Whitby thought he was a railway worker. Passing the open door of the engine he called up to Mills, 'I'll go and see what's wrong.'

Whitby walked towards the lone man standing between coaches two and three and said, 'What's up, mate?'

The man beckoned him over to the side of the track saying, 'Come here.'

As David Whitby got to him, the man seized him by the arm and pushed him down the embankment into the hands of two other men. One man rolled on top of him put his hand over Whitby's mouth, and held a cosh to his face.

'If you shout, I'll kill you,' he hissed.

A terrified Whitby, understandably keen to placate his attackers, replied, 'You're all right, mate. I'm on your side.'

All the while, Mills remained in his driver's seat in the cab, unaware that his fireman had been attacked and was pinned down on the embankment a few yards away.

These minor variations are seemingly inconsequential but they illustrate how the accounts of individuals deviate, create inconsistencies and ripples in the story. In many instances, the different versions pose questions about what actually took place. For example, there were two British Railways telephones mounted on the Sears Crossing signal gantry, one for northbound trains and one for trains heading south, but Mills and Whitby only mention trying one telephone and finding the wires cut.

At the rear of the train, the TPO's guard, Tom Miller, noted the train stopped at 03.03. Two minutes later, at 03.05, Miller noticed something else that becomes a critical technical detail in understanding what happens a little later. In the guard's van, sometimes referred to as the brake van, there was a large brass dial indicating the vacuum pressure in the train's braking system. The brakes had a failsafe mechanism. In order for them to be released, and remain in the off position, vacuum had to be maintained in the system. The vacuum pressure was created by a pump operated from the locomotive and the system ran through the entire length of the train from front to back, with each carriage connected in a daisy chain by flexible hoses with an airtight seal. If the vacuum system leaked or a hose became disconnected all the brakes on the train would automatically lock on.

Miller stated that at 03.05 he saw the vacuum gauge in his guard's van 'drop from twenty to zero' indicating that the train's brake system had lost pressure. A few minutes later he walked through to coach nine and spoke to the train's Post Office Inspector, forty-nine-year-old Frank Fuggle.

Reynolds, oblivious to any of the unfolding problems, had made his way back to his Land Rover, picked up Daly from the Dwarf signal and driven south along the B488, which ran parallel to the railway line, and about a hundred and fifty yards away. According to Reynolds, he pulled over on the verge and turned off the engine. Lights from the train spilled across the dark fields as the TPO stood motionless on the raised embankment under the clear night sky. Daly and Reynolds could hear the deep rumble of the engine's massive diesel engine ticking over and intermittent sounds of clanking metal.

Reynolds would no doubt have enjoyed the perspective. The distance between him and the action may have allowed him to project a romantic interpretation on the criminal events taking place not far away across the open farmland. Although Reynolds looked the part of a commander in his fake major's uniform and SAS cap badge, there is a paradox about the self-proclaimed leader of the gang he later claimed to be, not engaged in the field of battle, not leading his men, but voyeuristically observing them and the jeopardy of others from a safe distance.

Crouched between coaches two and three, in the grimy pressure and heat of the moment, Jimmy White and Roy James were uncoupling the engine and first two carriages from the rest of the train.

In the engine, Jack Mills stood up to stretch his legs and heard someone coming up the metal steps of the cab. He turned expecting to see Whitby. It must have taken him a few seconds to register the sinister dark figure entering the cab was not his fireman. The man dressed in a blue boiler suit and green balaclava with only his eyes visible was Buster Edwards and he was carrying a bar described by Mills as being about eighteen inches to two feet in length and wrapped in white cloth.

Mills then made the move of a brave and proud man – a move that was to cost him dearly. Unaware that he was up against a gang of determined criminals, and not a lone attacker, he grappled with the intruder, trying to force him off the footplate and almost succeeded. But as Mills was fending off Edwards at one door, a second masked bandit climbed through the opposite door on the other side of the cab and grabbed Mills from behind. The next thing Mills knew he was on his knees and the cab was filled with men in boiler suits wielding pipes and clubs.

With blood running into his eyes, Mills was put in his driver's seat while Wilson wiped his face with a rag. He was then manhandled into the narrow passageway of the engine room behind the cab.

The serious injuries sustained by Mills during the assault on the cab was a tipping point of the robbery. What happened in those vital seconds was subsequently reported and framed in various ways both in the press and in court. Peta Fordham (wife of one of the defence barristers) in her 1965 book *The Robbers' Tale* quotes Mills as saying that, although he was struck by the robbers, his main injury was sustained by hitting his head as he fell. It is possible. There are several protruding metal edges in the cab of a Class 40. However, if the initial blow had rendered Mills semi-conscious for a moment he would not have remembered falling. In the BBC television interview just days after the event Mills said, 'I don't remember anything after the first blow. I sank to my knees. The next thing I remember I was on my knees on the floor and I could see all these legs all around me.'

That he later allegedly made the statement quoted by Fordham that he gashed his head as he was falling creates some confusion in understanding what Mills did remember and exactly what took place. It might seem that the precise manner in which driver Mills sustained head injuries that later required fourteen stitches is academic. But much has been made over the years of this 'aggravated' aspect of the robbery and it has often been misreported.

It is true that Mills would have sustained no injury at all if the robbery had never taken place. However, there is a distinction to be made between deliberately inflicting a vicious injury on another human intending grievous harm and an accident resulting from a struggle with less violent intent. Mills' surviving family understandably have strong views on the subject, but that cannot entirely negate the need to be impartially clear about what happened.

In Piers Paul Read's 1978 book, *The Train Robbers*, Edwards was attributed with the assault on Mills. But that revelation was devised as a selling point by the recently released train robbers for the new version of their story. In other accounts Mr Three is blamed. He was reputedly a member of the South Coast raiders. It has been claimed that Mr Three was a childhood friend of Wisbey and also became good friends with

Hussey. In an interview for a 1994 BBC Television documentary series entitled. *The Underworld,* broadcast shortly before his suicide, Edwards had this to say about the injuries inflicted on Mills:

> I admitted to hitting him but I couldn't have, he was above me. Anyway, the person who hit him, you know, I know who it is, everyone knows who it is, but he don't want to admit to hitting people so, let's leave it at that.

The expression on Edwards' face as he makes the comment is telling. He appears resentful that the truth had never come out. The implication was that Mills' assailant was one of the men known to have taken part in the robbery, and not one of those who has never been named.

On hearing about the attack on Mills, Terry Hogan, one of the 1962 London Airport gang and a long-time criminal associate and close friend of Bruce Reynolds, said that he assumed it was Reynolds who had struck Mills. But in all the many accounts of the robbery by gang members, Reynolds is always placed elsewhere and so there is nothing concrete to support Hogan's comment. Nevertheless, Hogan's understanding of Reynolds was based a long associaton. In many ways, Reynolds based his persona on Hogan – his love of smart clothes and of Hemingway and his wider intellectual ambitions and sensibilities. In 1957, Hogan and Reynolds had robbed a bookmaker of £500 and the resulting charges against them included grievous bodily harm. On 16 January 1958, at the Central Criminal Court, Reynolds was found guilty of malicious wounding with intent and assaulting a police officer and sent to prison for three and a half years.

Writing for *Stern* magazine, German journalist, Henry Kolarz, who claimed to have interviewed several people closely connected with the robbery, offered another theory, suggesting that Gordon Goody was the man who hit Mills. In his statement Mills said his attacker had 'piercing eyes' which was something often said about Goody. It was also true of Wilson.

Two days after Jim Hussey died aged seventy-nine, on Monday, 12 November 2012, the *Sun* newspaper carried an article headlined: *'Great Train Robber admits: It was me who coshed driver.'* The report said that Hussey had confessed shortly before he died of cancer at St Christopher's

Hospice in Sydenham, South London. Although the dramatic deathbed revelation made the headlines forty-nine years later, there is no independent way of corroborating it. And, as will be explored later in the story, there may have been other motives behind Hussey's departing declaration.

A common misconception is that the attack on Mills was an isolated act of violence. It has been portrayed as a single mistake or as a heat-of-the moment aberration by the gang. However, the Great Train Robbery raid was peppered with acts of violence and it is only remarkable that other victims were not more seriously injured.

As far as it is possible to ascertain, the assault team on the cab consisted of Buster Edwards, who made the initial attempt that Mills tried to thwart, Gordon Goody, Jim Hussey, Tommy Wisbey, Mr Three and Charlie Wilson, who wiped the blood from Mills' head. It is of course possible that Reynolds was present too and not where he said he was. But there were at least six men crammed into the confined space of the Class 40 cab.

Shortly after Mills had been put in the hot narrow passageway next to the engine he was joined by Whitby who had been brought up by his captors from the embankment. Edwards climbed down from the cab and summond Biggs and 'Pop' who had been waiting at the trackside.

Biggs later claimed that Jack Mills was only hit once and sustained his worst injury as he fell against the cabin wall. Although this corroborates Fordham's account of Mills' off-the-record remark, it is questionable how much Biggs could have seen from where he stood some distance away, well below the level of the cab. And as with the rest of the gang, it was in Biggs' interests to play down the assault on Mills.

With Whitby joining Mills in the passageway and Biggs and 'Pop' in the cab, the total number in the locomotive had grown to at least nine, or possibly ten if Buster had got back on board. In some reports Welch was also there. Mills said he thought there were eight or nine.

With 'Pop' in the driver's seat, there was a long pause while he fiddled nervously with the controls. Goody, whose edgy personality was further hyped up by the situation, yelled at him impatiently to 'move it'. But the train did not move. In the crowded cab there was a sudden lull in the fraught activity and the seconds must have felt endless, more for the old train driver than anyone. He had been brought on to the job to drive the engine just eleven-hundred yards to Bridego Bridge so the enormous cash prize could be taken and unloaded into the waiting vehicles. But without moving the train the gang would achieve nothing.

More long seconds stretched out with nine anxious raiders breathing heavily and becoming ever more tense and hot. From the still hotter and more airless passageway next to the engine, Mills and Whitby could hear angry voices.

What none of the gang realised was that James and White had failed to properly seal the brake connecting pipe while uncoupling coach two from the rest of the train.

This critical oversight is another example of the gang's lack of technical understanding, both in the planning of the raid and vital details of its execution. The problem with the brakes resulting from James' and White's mishandled uncoupling of the coaches was bad enough, but there was another unexpected factor the gang had overlooked which made things worse. Despite Pop's long service on the railways, he had spent his entire career working on the Southern Region as a 'shunter' which used an air-brake system and so he had no experience of vacuum brakes or the English Electric Class 40 locomotives used for long-haul routes on other lines. The gang later claimed that ten days before the robbery on 29 July they had carried out a dress rehearsal in the train marshalling yards at Stewarts Lane depot near Nine Elms in Battersea. But their preparations had clearly been inadequate when it came to uncoupling carriages and they had recruited a driver who had no working knowledge of the type of train they intended to hold up. In an already highly charged situation, surrounded by violent criminals, the pressure on Pop was mounting as he fumbled with the unfamiliar controls. There is no way of knowing whether the elderly train driver had realised there was a problem with the brakes and was trying to rectify the situation but it was taking up precious time. And with each passing moment it was becoming increasingly obvious to everyone in the cab that the entire success of the robbery now rested in old Pop's trembling hands.

4

The touch-and-go situation aboard the locomotive on the night of the robbery was conspicuously absent from an article in *The Times* on 12 August 1963, which included a statement attributed to Mills: 'The raid went like a military operation. No orders were given. Everyone had their own station and knew their particular jobs.'

Mills is also credited with saying that the gang, which he estimated to be between twenty and thirty men, did not speak among themselves. It is debatable whether Mills actually made those statements, or at least not in quite that way. In the days after the robbery, the events of that night were being turned into a good story and the seeds of myth and legend were already being sown.

Back in the confined and intense situation aboard the locomotive, Mills and Whitby could hear the tense exchanges of the gang members as Pop's attempts to move the train were proving useless. Infuriated, Goody demanded that Pop be removed and told Welch to 'fetch the driver'. The moment of crisis had brought the robbery to a standstill and put the chances of its success into real doubt.

Despite Mills' nasty head injuries and very shaky condition, his engine-driving know-how had not deserted him and he quickly realised the brakes were not releasing. Mills later said that he 'opened up the large ejector as I thought they had not put the stopper on the back' to clear air from the vacuum pipes.

In an account later given to *Stern* magazine by Jimmy White he recalled:

> I saw the railway engine driver sitting at the controls with a bandage around his forehead. He started to operate the controls but the engine only moved a few feet, shuddered and stopped, then did the same again as the driver worked the controls. I at once dropped back on to the track and raced off along to the rear of the Security Coach where I discovered the air pressure valve was not fully closed. I kicked

it into the shut position and ran back and jumped on to the rear of the engine as it moved off. I heard one of our team shout, 'We're in business, boys, we're in business.'

With Mills' hand on the control lever, D326's massive diesel engine roared and the locomotive began to creep slowly ahead. One of his attackers said menacingly, 'Don't look up or you'll get some more.'

Ironically, Jack Mills had become both the principal victim of the robbery and the key to its success.

But as the engine drew away, taking the unmanned bogie brake van and HVP coach with it, yet another problem arose.

Inside the HVP coach, Assistant Post Office Inspector Thomas Kett heard steam escaping from the rear of his coach and thought that the coupling had broken.

In addition to the flexible hoses connecting the brake vacuum system, there was a second series of pipes that conveyed steam generated by the engine from carriage to carriage through the train's heating system. White and James had not disconnected the steam pipe so when coaches two and three parted company the link ruptured as the train corridor pulled apart.

The postal workers in the HVP carriage were unaware of the technical details, but seeing the corridor bellows separate and hearing the steam pipe burst it was obvious that something was wrong. Someone pulled the communication cord, others shouted through the window trying to attract the attention of the driver.

In the third coach of the train – first of the ten carriages left behind – were four Post Office employees: thirty-six-year-old, Stanley Edward Hall, who had joined the TPO at Carlisle, Dennis Ronald Jeffries, aged forty-two, who had boarded at Crewe and two colleagues, Leonard Ernest Lotts, aged thirty and forty-one-year-old Joseph O'Connell.

Hall said in a statement that several minutes after the train stopped at Sears Crossing, he opened the nearside door and saw a man of about five foot six (probably James), wearing blue overalls and a railwayman's cap standing between his coach and the HVP. After a few seconds, another man (probably White) came from underneath the joining bellows of the two coaches and said, 'Well, that's OK. That is all right.' The two men then walked towards the engine. Hall assumed they were railwaymen who had effected a repair of some sort. He did not see either of the men's faces, neither did he notice that just yards away, Dave Whitby was pinned down on the embankment below him.

Three or four minutes later, as Hall was walking across the carriage towards the connecting door to the HVP coach, there was a loud noise. The corridor pulled apart and the HVP and coach three slowly separated. Hall said his vision was impaired by a cloud of vapour from the broken steam pipe.

Dennis Jeffries looked out of the sliding door and saw the engine and first two coaches move off down the track. As the steam began to clear, Hall saw one of the Post Office employees inside the HVP van closing the connecting door, which was now open to the night. He also noticed that the signal on the overhead gantry was red.

Extraordinarily, the men in coach three remained unperturbed. Hall later reported that he did not think 'anything was seriously wrong' although he did admit to being 'puzzled'. Lotts walked through the carriages to coach five where Post Office Inspector Fuggle was located and told him what had happened. Fuggle accompanied Lotts back to the third coach to see for himself, and then made his way back down the train to speak to the guard, Tom Miller. This sequence of events is different from those in Miller's statement.

At 03.10, forty-two-year-old Len Kinchen, the signalman from Cheddington signal box, telephoned Wyn-de-Bank at Leighton Buzzard to ask where the TPO was. Wyn-de-Bank told Kinchen that the train had entered his section but he suspected there had been a signal failure at Sears Crossing. Five minutes later, Wyn-de-Bank noticed on his track indicator that the train had passed the signals at Sears Crossing. He could also see from his instruments that the approach to the signal was still engaged, which suggested that either a section of a train had become detached, or there was a track indicator failure as well as a signal fault.

Wyn-de-Bank advised the Control Office at Euston and his colleague Len Kinchen in the signal box at Cheddington of the situation, adding that he had arranged for Frank Mead to go to Sears Crossing to investigate. Aware of the possible dangers the stationary train presented, Wyn-de-Bank closed the 'Up fast line' to any further trains. He then hailed a parcels train heading into London on the slow line and asked the driver, whose name was Cooper, to stop at Sears Crossing and report the position of the TPO.

Back on the B488, Reynolds started the Land Rover and pulled away and he and Daly watched the slow progress of the train as they drove back to Bridego Bridge. Arriving ahead of the train they clambered up the embankment in time to guide it to a stop at the white marker they had erected earlier.

In all the numerous statements, newspaper articles, accounts, biographies and interviews given by the robbers there is no mention of any member of the gang remaining with the vehicles at the bridge. The account given to Piers Paul Read by at least seven of the gang in *The Train Robbers* states that, after cutting phone lines and placing the white marker on the track, 'they all started walking up towards the gantry'.

This was more than a technical error, it was a glaring oversight in the plan. If someone had driven down that quiet lane, or if a police patrol car had come along, they might have wondered what a lorry and Land Rover were doing, parked by the pond. They could also have spotted the strip of white sheet between two posts up on the railway line above. Curiosity might have prompted them to stop, get out and look around. They would have noticed a stationary train, waiting at the signal, seen it pull away leaving some of its carriages behind. With all the unusual activity in the middle of the deserted countryside in the early hours of Thursday morning even the sleepiest passer-by or policeman would have paused and wondered what the hell was going on.

Had British Railways technician Frank Mead, or duty GPO engineer Robert Hutchinson arrived at Bridego Bridge while the gang was storming the train half a mile up the track at Sears Crossing, the robbers would not have known about it if they had not posted a lookout – an elementary part of any schoolboy prank.

'Marvellous, just marvellous', was how Reynolds described the sight of the engine coming towards him with what he called 'members of the firm' hanging off it, waving their arms and shouting instructions about where the locomotive was to stop.

As the train slowed, the firm jumped down and prepared to go into action on the HVP coach. The assault team was made up of seasoned hard man Charlie Wilson; his childhood friend the huge Jim Hussey; Gordon Goody, a powerful and vicious villain who had a look that terrified his victims into submission; Bob Welch, an intelligent man of great strength who gambled most of his money away; Buster Edwards, one of the core team who had been the crucial link to Roger Cordrey and his 'South Coast Raiders' and Tommy Wisbey who came as part of the Cordrey package. Although Wisbey was a minor member of the mail train gang, he had associations with all the major London criminals. The godfather of his daughter, Marilyn, was Freddie Foreman, who worked for the infamous Kray brothers, and later served ten years for helping clean up after Jack 'The Hat' McVitie was murdered by Reggie Kray in 1967. Marilyn Wisbey later had a long-standing affair with 'Mad' Frankie Fraser. In his day, Fraser was one of the most feared men in the London underworld. During the course of his long career, he spent a total of forty years in prison including ten years for his part in the Richardson torture case and five years for leading the 1970 Parkhurst Prison riots. Tommy Wisbey's father-in-law was the cousin of another notorious London gangster, Billy Hill.

Along with Messrs One, Two and Three this formidable pack of young criminals converged on the isolated HVP coach. Only a set of bolted timber doors, a few panes of glass and a handful of frightened postal workers stood between them and a fortune in used banknotes. This was the part they had all been waiting for. All they had to do now was take the money and drive away.

Assistant Post Office Inspector Kett was in the HVP coach with Dewhurst, Ware, O'Connor and Penn. Kett's account stated that all doors and windows in the coach were closed and fastened. That was not strictly accurate: the connecting rear door was closed but not locked as the catch was bent. Not that it would have made any difference; a few bolts and locks were no obstacle for the gang of determined, ruthless criminals.

At 03.15 Charlie Wilson smashed the window of the HVP carriage with a pickaxe handle, hurling himself through.

Hearing the glass explode Kett shouted, 'It's a raid.' In an attempt to hold back the raiders, some of the postal workers piled mailbags against the sliding doors while others ran to doors and windows to make sure they were bolted.

A voice outside shouted, 'They're barricading the doors. Get the guns' – although this was later refuted by the gang. Concerned that a threat of firearms escalated their crime, they claimed that someone had shouted 'Get the cunts!'

Another window shattered and two masked men climbed in waving coshes. Other raiders kicked at the doors while men in stocking masks burst through the rear gangway screaming at the postmen to get back. One of the bandits was waving an axe.

According to Kett's statement, 'Within seconds between six and eight unauthorised men had entered the HVP coach, with other men shouting outside.'

One man hit Kett on the arm with a cosh as he tried protect himself and shouted, 'Who was the bastard that bolted the doors?' He then hit Dewhurst several times, yelling, 'Get some more men up here!' Penn turned away from the man with the axe and was struck across the shoulders by another raider who had climbed through the window wielding an iron bar.

The terrified HVP crew were herded to the front of the coach. Penn said, 'I was struck a second time and I went down. Mr Dewhurst was hit just in front of me by the same person. He went down right away.'

They were guarded by a tall man who lashed out again at Kett and Dewhurst, hitting Kett again on the head. Dewhurst said he was hit five or six times. The postmen were ordered to lie down and close their eyes. Kett said there was a lot of shouting and while the mailbags were being unloaded someone yelled from outside, 'We want some more help out here, guvnor.'

Interviewed in 1994 for the BBC Television programme *The Underworld*, Buster Edwards summed up the situation: 'We were the cream. We were all tops at what we were doing. You've got to be prepared for violence. You go on business to expect violence, to use violence. It's not a softy sort of thing really. If it's got to be used, it's got to be used.'

In the cab Mills and Whitby, who had been handcuffed together, were told to get out. The injured train driver with blood still streaming from his head wounds and his terrified fireman were manhandled along the embankment and ordered to lie face down on the grass.

Taking Mills and Whitby out of the cab where they could not see what was happening and leading them along the side of the train in full view of the robbery in progress was an odd piece of choreography.

Although they were told not to look up, it only took a fraction of a second for them to take in what was going on. While stumbling down the embankment to where they were held, Whitby saw the chain of men passing mailbags down to the road below and loading them into 'an army type lorry'. His observations compromised the gang's carefully devised anonymity and were to prove pivotal for the police in the days that followed.

Moving 120 mailbags weighing a total of two and a half tons down a steep railway embankment in a hurry was hard work but none of the gang complained or stopped for a breather. Bag after bag came out of the HVP coach and passed down the chain of eager hands to be dumped unceremoniously in the back of the old Austin lorry.

But not all the robbers were upbeat and exuberant. In the second Land Rover, parked by the pond, the elderly train driver sat pale and exhausted with his minder, Biggs. As they watched the bags of money coming down the embankment they must have felt relieved but also pretty stupid. Pop had never had any illusions about being a major criminal. The train raid was his first and last job. With a small but vital part to play, he had failed and jeopardised the entire plan.

Apart from Reynolds, most of the gang had been reluctant to have Biggs on the job. His contribution of a back-up train driver had been a fiasco and Biggs must have been dreading what the rest of the gang would say and do when it was all over.

At 03.30, Reynolds checked his watch and called time. The gang had decided in advance that they would leave no later than thirty minutes after stopping the train. Charlie Wilson shouted down that there were only a few bags left in the HVP coach, but Reynolds was insistent and the discipline of their plan held firm. One by one the men stopped what they were doing, clambered down the embankment and made their way to their allotted seats in the vehicles.

Mills and Whitby were led to the HVP carriage. As they struggled to climb in, Mills said, 'I can't get in, I'm handcuffed to my mate.' Someone caught Mills' legs and as they were bundled into the coach a masked robber said to Whitby, 'Now, David, don't say anything to any of them. There are some right bastards in this lot who will kill you.'

Mills, still bleeding and handcuffed to his fireman, was pushed down on the floor alongside the HVP crew. One of the raiders warned them not to move for half an hour, adding that they would be hurt if they did.

Down on the road below everyone was back in the vehicles. Reynolds did a head count and gave the signal to go. There was little noise or haste as the lorry and two Land Rovers started up and moved off down the narrow moonlit lane.

In the HVP coach Mills, Whitby, Kett, Penn, O'Connor and Dewhurst heard the sound of the gang driving away but they were wary of the order not to move. All still frightened and shaken they had no way of knowing if the warning that the robbers were leaving two men behind to stand guard was true. In calmer circumstances, they might have worked out that it was a bluff, a way for the gang to buy time to make their escape. It would not have made sense to leave gang members behind. Even if they were armed, the risk of someone raising the alarm was increasing with every minute. Besides, no one would have volunteered to stay while the rest of the gang disappeared into the night taking the stolen fortune with them.

As the dawn of Thursday morning crept over the eastern horizon, the scene at Bridego Bridge was eerily still and quiet. Just seven sacks remained on board in the open high-value package cupboards and a solitary white mailbag lay discarded at the trackside. With their faces to the floor, Mills, Whitby, Kett, Penn, O'Connor, Ware and Dewhurst heard the grinding gears of the old army lorry and two Land Rovers turning at the bottom of the lane and fading away in the direction of Mentmore.

With sidelights dimmed, the three-vehicle convoy began to retrace their route back to Leatherslade Farm. It had been a nerve-racking, frantic thirty minutes. But the gang was intoxicated and united in the belief that as a result of their endeavours they had said goodbye for ever to the hard, drab, working-class life that their parents and grandparents had endured. Not for them the long hours and relentless years of hard graft, only to end up just as poor at the end of it.

The robbers were old enough to remember how hard times had been during the war, eighteen years earlier. While men like Jimmy White risked their lives fighting, those who had remained at home struggled – many families separated, children evacuated, food and money in short supply. Moral boundaries were blurred as people did what they could to get through it and survive. For many Britons, being 'on the take' became a way of life; some did it to get a bit extra, others did it just to stay alive. By the end of the war and through the years of rationing that followed, the black market continued to thrive. Beating the system was endemic, an accepted part of everyday life.

With a new decade, the country finally seemed set to change for the better. 'The sixties' had a ring to it. For a new generation, free from the prospect of going to war, old ideas were being discarded and fresh democratic socialist values were taking root. There was a Welfare State and National Health and in December 1961 the Health Minister, Enoch Powell, announced that the contraceptive pill would be available 'to all'. Popular songs on the radio evoked another life. 1950s jazz bands, crooners and rock 'n' roll were being overtaken by earthy blues and skif-fle. Musicians looked different and sang with the voice of restless youth in changing times and sex, a natural part modern romance. American movies at local cinemas portrayed another way of life: flashy cars, nice clothes, emancipated girls who were not hardened and world-weary, old before their time. Somewhere out there was a less make-do-and-mend class-ridden 'lifestyle' where working people would not have to scrimp and save and watch every penny.

Yet not much seemed to have changed on the streets of London where honest working people would put in a forty-eight-hour week in exchange for as little as ten pounds.

These shifting factors, along with the fading influence of traditional religious and moral values, created a capital city that was plagued by crime. Breaking the law offered glamour and excitement and the chance of easy cash, even the possibility to get ahead. Many young men growing up in the poor fringes aspired to join the ranks of smartly dressed and stylish criminals. The names of London's notorious crime firms – the Richardson brothers south of the river and the Krays in East London – commanded respect, admiration and social standing. And for those at the top, that particularly empty preoccupation of modern times, celebrity. Decades before thug-inspired bling and the parlance of gangster rap became fashionable, gangster-chic was exerting its grip on the public imagination.

This was the provenance of the gang of young men that stopped the mail train at Sears Crossing. Through criminal enterprise they had been given glimpses of prosperity. But all too soon, the money would be spent and they would find themselves facing the choice of slipping back or doing another job.

It had all changed in less than an hour in the early hours of 8 August 1963. The mail train robbers had made the transformation from 'have not' to 'have'. And suddenly they found themselves confronting a problem they had never encountered before. Once you have a fortune, you have something to lose and that changes everything.

The more thoughtful among the bandits may have reflected on how lucky they had been to pull off the robbery. But once the sweat on them had dried, how far down those quiet country lanes had they gone before some of them started thinking about the questions that must follow. Were they going to get away with it? And now they had all that money, would they be able to hang on to it?

5

Through the smashed windows and wide-open doors of the HVP carriage, came the low steady throb of D326's diesel engine ticking over and the sounds of the early morning Buckinghamshire countryside stirring. Jack Mills and David Whitby lay handcuffed together, while Kett, Penn, O'Connor and Dewhurst whispered to each other, debating whether the warning the robbers had given them was true. Dare one of them make a move towards the open door?

Back at Sears Crossing, the TPO's guard Tom Miller had made his way to the front of coach three and discovered that the engine and first two carriages were missing. Miller was heard to say something along the lines of, 'What are the driver and fireman playing at? They should have informed me there was a problem.' Clearly, at this stage he was still under the impression the missing engine and carriages were the result of mechanical failure.

Miller then dashed back through the train, 'looking like a ghost' and saying that there was 'a flier' (a fast train) at their backs and he needed to lay safety detonators. He was unaware that just two miles north, signalman Wyn-de-Bank had already closed the fast 'Up' line.

In his statement, Miller reported that the train stopped at 03.03; two minutes later the vacuum gauge in the guard's van dropped to zero and he heard the brakes engage. He made his way towards the front of the train, reaching carriage three at 03.09 to discover that the engine, bogie brake van and HVP coach had vanished. He said he could not hear or see any sign of them.

There are several things about Miller's statement which do not add up. To begin with, his timing is questionable. He claims to have arrived at the front of the uncoupled carriages at 03.09, six minutes after the train stopped. Bearing in mind that after the ambush and uncoupling, the gang's driver made several abortive attempts to get the train moving before Mills was finally brought to the cab, there's no way the engine and HVP could have been eleven hundred yards away and stationary at the bridge by 03.09.

Various witness accounts agree that the attack on the HVP coach took place at 03.15. Before it travelled eleven hundred yards to Bridego Bridge, Mills initially made a false start and then drove the engine very slowly; even at around ten miles per hour, it would have taken him three to four minutes to cover the distance. So at 03.09, six minutes before the HVP assault, the engine and two carriages would have still been at, or very close to, Sears Crossing.

Furthermore, Miller claims to have been unaware that the engine and two coaches were missing until he got to the front of the train. For that to be so, the locomotive would have to have been out of earshot while he was walking down the train. The 2,000-horsepower diesel engine of an English Electric Class 40 locomotive had a loud, distinctive growl and high-pitched whine when revving and under way. The sound would have reverberated for some considerable distance in all directions across the quiet Buckinghamshire countryside. Why was it not audible to Miller?

The only way Miller could have failed to hear the missing locomotive and coaches is if he arrived at the front of the train some time later, around 03.15 or 03.20, by which time the locomotive and HVP would have completed their eleven-hundred-yard journey to the bridge and been standing stationary with the engine ticking over.

What remains a mystery, however, is how Miller could have failed to see the HVP with its windows smashed and the doors opened wide for unloading. As he stood looking over flat ground, with no other obstacles or background lights from other sources nearby, scanning down that straight section of railway track, it's odd that he could not detect the spill of electric light from the HVP carriage or the familiar shape of the missing engine and two coaches. In the stillness of that moonlit night, with a clear, uninterrupted line of sight, Miller says he saw nothing. And he did not hear the bangs and crashes of the gang breaking in, their shouted threats and orders, or the cries of his frightened colleagues as they were being attacked. According to the HVP staff, the attack was noisy and violent and that sound would have carried across the silent farmland.

Another witness, Francis John Ronald, reported: 'All I could see at that time were the signals on the near gantry at red and in the distance two white lights.' But it is unclear whether 'at the time' refers to 3.09 or some time later.

Perhaps Miller's eyesight and hearing were poor. Maybe he had the time wrong and got to the front of the train later than 03.09. But if that were the case, another set of problems arises because he would have had less time to accomplish all the other things he said he did next.

Having discovered the engine and first coaches missing, Miller says he tried the trackside phone and found the wires cut. Realising the situation was potentially hazardous he followed standard railway safety regulations. He dashed back through the train, collected detonators from his guard's van and then walked north, back up the track, placing them at statutory quarter-mile, half-mile and one-mile intervals behind the stranded coaches.

While Miller went to lay detonators, Fuggle told the sorters in the rear carriages to move towards the front of the train as a precaution against collision from the express train, which Miller had warned was following close behind.

When Miller returned, he told Fuggle he was going for help and began to walk south along the track towards Bridego Bridge.

In the HVP coach at Bridego Bridge, Kett and Penn had crept out on to the track, and seeing no robbers standing guard, started walking north towards the rest of the train to report the raid to Inspector Fuggle.

There is a discrepancy between the account given by Miller and those given by Kett and Penn. The two postal workers say they came across the guard as they made their way back to the train and told him what had happened. Miller's statement, curiously, makes no mention of this encounter. He says that after walking about half a mile he discovered the missing engine and HVP coach with his shaken colleagues and the injured Mills inside. The men then informed him about the robbery and he told them he would go for assistance.

Hall, Jeffries, Lotts and O'Connell were standing in coach three when a breathless, grimy and shaken Tom Kett suddenly appeared at the open gangway door and said, 'We've been done. They've got the lot.'

The postmen helped Kett and Penn on board and they explained to Inspector Fuggle what had happened. Hearing the commotion, other postal workers gathered round. James Patrick O'Reilly, Postman Higher Grade, said in his statement that Penn was 'very shaken and obviously suffering from shock. We tried to persuade him to rest but he did not seem able to do so.' O'Reilly said someone produced a hip flask and gave Penn a tot of rum.

Lotts and another Postman Higher Grade, Frank Stockwell, volunteered to leave the train 'to try and make contact by telephone with the police and the Post Office Chief Superintendent, Mr Shiers'. Stockwell and Lotts climbed down on to the track and set off across the fields to the offside of the train, 'in the direction of a farmhouse, the outline of which we could see in the distance'.

Back at Bridego Bridge, Miller was heading south again in the direction of Cheddington. After a few hundred yards he flagged down a slow train going north, told the driver and fireman about the robbery and Mills' injuries, and asked them to stop at the bridge and administer first aid. Shortly afterwards, Miller flagged down a second slow train, this time going south, and again explained the situation. The driver, 'Mr Cooper', told Miller he had been asked 'to report on the TPO by Mr Wyn-de-Bank at Leighton Buzzard signal box'. Cooper instructed his fireman to take a first-aid box and walk back to Bridego Bridge to offer what help he could and then drive the locomotive and two coaches to Cheddington. Clearly it did not occur to Cooper that moving the train would mean disturbing and possibly destroying vital evidence of a major crime scene.

Driver Cooper set off for Cheddington station with Miller on board, and on arrival they informed signalman Len Kinchen about the robbery of the TPO and Kinchen immediately called Euston Control.

According to Miller's account, from finding the engine missing to being picked up and taken to Cheddington he would have walked over two and a half miles along the uneven railway track. At an average walking speed of three miles per hour, that works out at fifty minutes. Even if Miller had managed four miles per hour it would have taken him forty-five minutes to cover the distance. But whatever his walking speed, he did a number of additional tasks along the way which would have taken a good deal of additional time and slowed him down. Miller's statement has him starting his walk at 03.09; we know he had reached journey's end by 04.15, because that was the time on the log sheet at Euston of the call received from Cheddington. To have accomplished everything that Miller listed in his statement in one hour and four minutes is nothing short of miraculous for a sixty-one-year-old man in the dark.

Are these minute-by-minute details of the unfolding events at Sears Crossing significant? Does it add up to an accusation that Miller was asleep, slow to react or deliberately lying because he was in on the robbery and delayed his reaction time and the other stranded men? It is possible he was an accomplice, although not likely. However, the day after the robbery the Postmaster-General, The Right Honourable Reginald Bevins MP, was quoted in *The Times* as saying that the mail-train raid 'may have been an inside job' and calling for a 'full and urgent inquiry'.

The apparent lack of awareness of train staff, their initial failure to respond to the extraordinary circumstances, and the inconsistencies in their statements concerning events on the night of 8 August, provides the context in which it was possible for the mail-train robbers to perpetrate their crime and get away. To a significant degree, the success of the robbery hinged on the mail-train staff being slow to work out what was happening and do anything about it. Was it mental paralysis induced by the numbing routine of working nights for a nationalised public service?

The gang had no contingency for dealing with the eighty men on the train and that is a surprising oversight. The robbers may have had the element of surprise in their favour, but they were outnumbered five to one.

The deficiencies in basic security, the institutionalised complacency with which British Railways and the Royal Mail daily transported enormous consignments of cash up and down the country in an era when crime was epidemic, was all mitigated under the banner of 'the crime of the century'. As the idea caught the public's imagination, it created a convenient diversion to shift attention away from the shortcomings of the postal and railway authorities and on to the alleged skill, audacity and extraordinary brilliance of 'The Great Train Robbers'.

Days later, British Railways and the Post Office went to some lengths to explain the actions of the men on board the TPO. *The Times* on 9 August reported that the GPO claimed the postmen in the uncoupled portion of the train went on working, unaware of the robbery:

It was dark and they would be very busy sorting the mail. It is not unusual for the train to stop at a signal, and they would have no way of telling that the train had been uncoupled. It was not until a guard walked along the track and discovered that part of his train was missing that the alarm was raised.

However, the GPO statement contradicted the first-hand accounts of their employees Hall, Lotts, O'Connell, Jeffries and other post office staff who were on the mail train that night. Had *The Times* got it wrong, or was the GPO engaging in a cover-up in an effort to exonerate themselves?

In his 1965 autobiography, *The Greasy Pole*, Reginald Bevins devotes a chapter to 'The Great Train Robbery'.

First, let me say the obvious – it should never have happened. The odds against it happening were at least a million to one. It is easy to say, as Graham Greene said, that it was beautifully planned. Whether this is true or not, it could never have succeeded but for the slackness of British Railways and the ineptitude of certain Post Office officials. It was the combination of those factors that made the robbery possible.

In his book *The Train Robbers*, ex-Detective Superintendent of Buckinghamshire CID, Malcolm Fewtrell, a senior detective in the mail-train case, stated his views on the matter of mail-train security:

General laxity about protecting money and property from thieves makes it easy for unscrupulous men to plan large scale robberies in this country. It must have been perfectly simple for the robbers to find out that millions of pounds are regularly transported for the banks by the General Post Office and British Railways and that a good deal of this would be on the post-Bank Holiday Up Special mail train from Glasgow to Euston. This train keeps to a carefully respected time-table so that mails get through on time even if other trains do not. Punctuality and regularity always help the criminal. With a little research the robbers found out that the Post Office believed the safest place on the train for the high value package coach was the second coach from the front and it cannot have been difficult to get to know that this coach possessed no means of communication with the outside world.

Several months after the robbery, on 5 October 1963, *The Times* carried a report of the previous day's preliminary hearing at Aylesbury in the cases of twelve men and a woman who stood accused of involvement with the mail-train robbery:

POSITION OF MAIL TRAIN COACH NEVER VARIED

There was a gasp of surprise in the courtroom here today when a Post Office witness told the Magistrates hearing evidence about the £2,600,000 mail-train robbery that it was common knowledge that the high-value coach of a travelling post office was always in the same place. It was always the second coach from the engine.

Mr Thomas Kett, an Assistant Post Office Inspector, of Cuffley, Hertfordshire, agreed it was also common knowledge that all high-value packages went into that one coach.

As a result of recommendations made in 1961, the following improvements were made to three new HVP coaches brought into service in 1962:

1.   Mechanical Bandit Alarms fitted.
2.   New HVP cupboards built and locks fitted.
3.   Gangway doors and side doors fitted with 'throw catches'.
4.   Coach windows fitted with bars.

But the HVP coach in use on the overnight Glasgow to London mail train on 7/8 August was an old-style model, with no bars at the windows, no proper locks on the doors and no means of raising the alarm. It is staggering that the Royal Mail was so negligent about the countless thousands of high-value packages they had been entrusted to transport over the 125 years they had been in operation.

Although the Investigation Branch of the Post Office diligently pursued the possible involvement of GPO staff, the subsequent intense inquiry by the police and in court did not examine the actions of the

TPO staff, Post Office Inspector Frank Fuggle, or train guard Tom Miller with the kind of breadth, depth and scrutiny that should have followed the Postmaster General's call for a 'full and urgent' investigation into the biggest cash robbery in British history.

6

Seventeen miles from Bridego Bridge as the crow flies, Leatherslade Farm was a circuitous twenty-eight miles along the narrow bumpy lanes that the robbers took in order to stay off main roads. First the convoy headed west, skirting north of Aylesbury through the slumbering villages of Aston Abbots, Cublington, Whitchurch, and then south-west, passing Oving, Pitchcott, Quainton, Wescott and Wotton Underwood.

Reynolds' version of events has the gang members in the lorry singing along as Tony Bennett's 'The Good Life' blared out of their radio, loud enough that he could hear it in the leading Land Rover. The image sounds suspiciously typical of Reynolds' romanticised reminiscences, and bears a striking resemblance to a scene from *The League of Gentlemen*, a British crime film made in 1960. The imagery also conjures up an *Italian Job* scenario, with an unruly gang, already conspicuous by virtue of being the only vehicles on those deserted lanes, further drawing attention to themselves by conducting a raucous singalong at four o'clock in the morning. As no one in any of the villages they passed through ever reported hearing the gang's revelries, it must be assumed that Reynolds' story is either a fantasy or the residents of rural Buckinghamshire are unusually heavy sleepers.

From other accounts we know that there were two radios on board the convoy, a pair of Hitachi VHF receivers, both tuned in to police frequencies so the gang could monitor reports concerning the robbery. Despite their elation, it had been a nail-biting ride by the time the vehicles crept quietly through the village of Brill, bearing right at the war memorial and telephone box at The Square. From there it was just a mile and half to the junction with the B4011 Thame Road and a little less than a mile beyond that was the farm entrance.

Just under an hour after leaving Bridego Bridge, the gang finally returned to the seclusion and safety of their hideout. Despite their high spirits, there must have been huge relief as the convoy finally turned in and drove up the gravel track. But as the adrenalin began to ebb and the farmhouse came in sight the silent police radio frequencies suddenly burst into life.

'You're not going to believe this...' a young police officer's voice broke through the static: 'they've stolen a train!'

It invited the inevitable derision from the robbers as they clambered out of the vehicles. Roy James and Mr Two parked the two Land Rovers in sheds while Mr Three reversed the Austin lorry up to the farmhouse so the rest of the gang could start unloading. They passed the mailbags into the house and stacked them against the walls of the small sitting room. When they ran out of space, they lined the passageway with bags of money. For the second time that morning two million, five hundred and ninety-five thousand, nine hundred and ninety-seven pounds and ten shillings passed through eager hands.

When the unloading was done, Mr Two backed the Austin three-tonner into an outbuilding, covered the protruding bonnet with a green tarpaulin and went into the house.

With sixteen robbers and 120 mailbags, there was not much room to move. As they started opening the white sacks and piling up the parcels of banknotes, Goody, ever vigilant, checked the bags for homing devices. There were none.

Reynolds remembered it was Biggs' thirty-fourth birthday and wished him all the best. All about them, their fellow gang members joked around and set about ripping open packets. With over two and a half million in five-pound, one-pound and ten-shilling notes, the scale of the cash was overwhelming. Despite his pride at the success of the raid, Reynolds says he felt a deep 'emptiness'. But it was not a reaction to the danger the gang had faced, the possible consequences of their actions, worry about what the police were doing, or regret for the injuries they had inflicted on Jack Mills. Years later, looking back on that Thursday morning, Reynolds' abiding memory was the sense of anti-climax he felt, surrounded by his jubilant comrades, still wearing his fake army major's uniform and SAS cap badge with the '*Who Dares Wins*' motto. Only four and a half hours earlier, that phrase had seemed to sum up the entire enterprise. However, back in their tumbledown hideout, surrounded by more money than he had ever seen, or would ever see again, the illusion was over. Reynolds had dared, but what had he won? Maybe it was exhaustion and the come-down that followed the adrenalin rush. After the days of careful planning, the recces, the noise, the violence, and those touch-and-go moments when it looked as though the whole thing was falling apart, all they had to show for it was countless wads of old banknotes.

Ever since he was a boy, Reynolds had been driven by the promise of adventure. Even at the age of seventy-eight, he was still pursuing the same tantalising images of a golden future, his own personal 'El Dorado', that elusive lost city of the Spanish Conquistadors. For him the mail-train robbery had been about attaining the ultimate treasure, a prize of infinite possibility. Nothing real could ever live up to that promise. At what should have been the crowning moment of his criminal career, all he could think was, 'So we've done it. What do I do now?'

And so, while his fellow criminals opened a seven-pint can of ale, Reynolds slipped quietly upstairs, telling Edwards that he was going to get some sleep. Maybe he just wanted to escape into his dreams.

Twenty-five minutes after leaving the third carriage to go and find a phone, Stockwell and Lotts arrived at Redborough Farm and woke the occupant, Cecil Rawlings, only to find his phone was out of order. Rawlings offered the young men a lady's bicycle and gave them directions to the police station at Linslade, a small town on the Buckinghamshire side of the River Ouzel, three and a half miles north of Sears Crossing. With Frank Stockwell on the bicycle and Leonard Lotts running beside him, they made their way along unlit, unfamiliar lanes. After a few miles, the men split up. Stockwell continued in the direction of Linslade while Lotts set off for some cottages that had just become visible across the fields in the pale dawn light.

In the meantime, Miller had reached Cheddington and alerted signalman Len Kinchen. Considering the information the guard had been given about the attack on the train and the injuries to the driver, it's surprising that the call placed at 04.15 from Cheddington signal box was not to the local police or ambulance service, but to British Railways' Euston office forty miles away in London. Perhaps Miller and Kinchen were nervous of overstepping the mark in the entrenched hierarchy of the monolithic British Railways organisation, and thought it best to refer such a serious incident to a higher authority.

The call was taken by a Mr Prentice in the main control office at
Euston. Nine minutes later, at 04.24, he telephoned the New Scotland
Yard incident room. Prentice's entry in the control office log offers no
explanation for the nine-minute delay in calling the police, nor does it
indicate why he called New Scotland Yard rather than Aylesbury Police
HQ. The information he wrote in his handwritten log is scant:

MESSAGE:
CHEDDINGTON STATION BUCKS
BREAK IN
REQUEST FOR POLICE AND AMBULANCE
INFO FROM SIGNALMAN
RAILWAY POLICE INFORMED
RESULTS OR REMARKS: AYLESBURY DEALING & SENDING
AMBULANCE.

At 04.25, details of an incident at Cheddington were phoned through
to the Information Room at Buckinghamshire Police HQ in Aylesbury,
which was manned that night by Sergeant Maydon, PC Whiteman, PC
Bell and an unnamed civilian. Constables Atkins and Milne in patrol
car HB5 were duly instructed to attend 'an incident' at Cheddington
railway station, along with patrol car HB3. It may have been this communication that the robbers heard on their radio at around 04.30 as
they pulled into the farm.

Sergeant Maydon immediately set about notifying the rest of Aylesbury division, and issued instructions for the sergeant at Linslade to
be contacted, as he was closest geographically. The scale of the police
response suggests that Prentice's call to New Scotland Yard had provided
more significant details than the terse entry in the Euston log book.

At 04.35 Detective Superintendent Malcolm Fewtrell, Head of
Buckinghamshire CID, was woken by his telephone ringing. Born in
a police station, with a CID man for a father, three brothers on the
force, and thirty-three years' service behind him, Fewtrell knew before
he opened his eyes that a phone call at that time of the morning meant
something serious had occurred. Seven weeks short of his fifty-fourth
birthday, he was looking forward to early retirement and an end to
being dragged out of bed in the small hours. Little did he know that

this particular call – delivering the succinct message 'There's been a train robbery at Cheddington, sir' – would herald the start of an investigation into the largest cash robbery ever to have taken place, and that the hunt for those responsible, followed by the longest criminal trial in British history, would consume him far beyond his planned retirement date. It would be an intense and exhausting eight months before Fewtrell was finally free of the case and able to reclaim his life.

By the time Frank Stockwell had completed his convoluted relay race and cycled the three and a half miles from Redborough Farm to Linslade police station on Farmer Rawlings' ladies' bicycle, news of the mail-train raid had beaten him. When he arrived at 04.36 the local sergeant was just climbing out of patrol car HB31. The post office worker's story provided extraordinary and shocking details of the ambushed train, stranded carriages and seventy colleagues marooned at Sears Crossing. The report was deemed alarming enough to warrant getting Sub-Divisional Inspector Mellows, who lived at Lindslade police station, out of bed.

Just after 04.36, Constables Atkins and Milne arrived at Cheddington in patrol car HB5. The village station had closed as usual at around ten o'clock the previous evening after the last train. The two country policemen were surprised to see a large Class 40 locomotive with two maroon Royal Mail carriages attached standing at the London platform. Even more bemusing was the group of shaken men who came forward with their story of an ambushed mail train at Sears Crossing and the violent raid on their HVP coach at Bridego Bridge.

An hour and eight minutes after the robbers had departed Bridego Bridge, news of the train robbery was finally beginning to reach neighbouring constabularies. At 04.38 Bedfordshire Police were informed by Aylesbury HQ and immediately set up road checks at Ampthill and on the A5. By that time the gang were already back at Leatherslade Farm, unpacking the loot.

While Fewtrell was making his way to Aylesbury Police HQ in his white convertible Triumph Herald, Constables Atkins and Milne at Cheddington were taking statements from Kett, Penn, Ware, Dewhurst and O'Connor, and administering first aid to Jack Mills, who was still handcuffed to David Whitby.

Four minutes later, at 04.45, Frank Mead, the British Railways signals and communications technician, arrived at Sears Crossing to be confronted with the startling sight of ten abandoned carriages and over seventy bewildered postal workers. Mead immediately made his way to the signal, where he found all four wires had been cut on the trackside telephone. He then climbed the gantry and discovered the red light, powered by four Eveready dry-cell batteries, and the green light covered by a man's black leather glove.

Meanwhile in Buckinghamshire two further roadblocks were set up at 04.47. Given the ambition and scale of the robbery, it was probable the gang came from a metropolitan area. The closest city and most obvious contender was the capital, less than forty miles away to the south-east. With the most direct routes from the crime scene being the A5, A41 or M1/A41, and Cheddington, lying north-east of Aylesbury, it was a strange decision on the part of Buckinghamshire Police to position a roadblock at the junction of the A40 and A4010, which lies south-west of Cheddington and the other side of Aylesbury. Hertfordshire Police also set up a roadblock, but there is no record of where or when that was.

At 04.48 the Information Room at Aylesbury received a request for a hacksaw from Constables Atkins and Milne at Cheddington. They reported that Mills and Whitby were manacled with 'American-style' handcuffs, for which the officers had no key.

By 04.50, Fewtrell had arrived at Aylesbury HQ. Buckinghamshire Police had emergency plans in place for dealing with major incidents and Fewtrell spent the next ten minutes 'getting things organised', as he puts it in his 1964 book on the robbery. By this time Assistant Chief Constable George Wilkinson had been contacted and was making his way to headquarters.

It is interesting to note that no police officers had yet been to the scene of the crime, even though two of the county's most senior policemen had been got out of bed and summoned to HQ. Perhaps the fact that the information had come via New Scotland Yard increased the level of response from Sergeant Maydon in the Aylesbury Information Room. The duty officers must have concluded that a serious crime had been committed, even though the only thing they had to go on at that stage was the initial report to Euston.

At 04.55 Mills, still handcuffed to Whitby, was taken by ambulance to the Royal Buckinghamshire Hospital, a twenty-minute drive from Cheddington. Constables Atkins and Milne remained at the station, diligently piecing together the sequence of events with Dewhurst, Kett, Penn, O'Conner and Miller.

By 05.00 Inspector Mellows from Linslade division had set off for Sears Crossing where, with no policemen in attendance, Frank Mead was trying to restore the signals. Meanwhile at Aylesbury HQ, Fewtrell and Wilkinson set about deciding how best to coordinate Buckinghamshire Constabulary's response.

Back at Leatherslade Farm, behind the makeshift blackout material covering the windows, the robbers were enthusiastically engaged in the enormous task of working out how much they had stolen. Faced with 636 packets of banknotes in 120 mailbags, it was taking time to unpack the bundles of money, let alone sort it into various denominations and count it. Outside, the undulating Buckinghamshire countryside was in semi-darkness and all was quiet; in one of the bedrooms above, Reynolds was stretched out on a camp bed, fast asleep.

7

There has been much speculation about who masterminded the mail-train robbery. The first book on the subject, published in June 1964, was *The Great Train Robbery* by ex-Superintendent John Gosling, a former head of Scotland Yard's 'Ghost Squad' undercover team, and his co-writer, Dennis Craig. Given their access to Gosling's former colleagues at the Yard at a time when the case was fresh in everyone's minds, the authors present a surprisingly poor account of the raid and subsequent investigation. While there was clearly no doubt in Gosling's mind that there had been a mastermind behind the heist, his speculations on the subject are rather vague and inconclusive.

Other published theories conjure up a fiendish supremo not unlike an Ian Fleming villain (no doubt sitting on a private island somewhere with a white cat à la Bond's adversary Ernst Stavro Blofeld). Peta Fordham, in *The Robbers' Tale*, describes the mastermind as 'a highly intelligent man who is an uncrowned intellectual king of the underworld'. She concludes her proposition: 'I do not know his present name.' Sadly, Fordham offers no suggestions for his past names either.

In his 1978 book *The Train Robbers* (confusingly the same title as Malcolm Fewtrell's 1964 book on the subject), Piers Paul Read promised to uncover for the first time the true story of the men behind the robbery, including their mysterious German financier. In Read's otherwise lucid account, based mainly on information supplied by the robbers and their families, he draws an exotic connection between the mail-train robbery and a former SS officer called Otto Skorzeny.

Skorzeny was certainly real enough; in 1943 he had been personally selected by Adolf Hitler to carry out a daring raid to rescue the deposed Italian dictator, Benito Mussolini, from prison. Read was told that Skorzeny and his German associates had put up £80,000 to finance the train robbery, and that in return they received a £1,000,000 share of the proceeds. There was no possibility of Skorzeny verifying the story; he died in 1975, from prostate cancer.

It would seem too fantastic to be true, but like all good lies, there was a grain of truth in it. After the robbery, when he was on the run in Europe, Buster Edwards had a passing encounter with Skorzeny and his wife concerning 'investment opportunities' in Spain. The German must have made quite an impression; later, when the gang were trying to come up with a fresh angle to reawaken interest in the flagging Great Train Robbery myth, they seized upon Otto Skorzeny, complete with a dramatic fencing scar on his left cheek, to step into the role of Mr Big.

The background to the robbery is broadly agreed by robbers, biographers and official investigators alike. As with so many major crimes, it began with an encounter between a criminal and someone with inside knowledge of routines and vulnerabilities. In this instance, the intermediary was twenty-eight-year-old Brian Field, a solicitor's clerk at a firm called James and Wheater. Field was charming, clever and ambitious. He had been nurturing his criminal clients and contacts for some years and the rewards came in different ways. There were the legal fees of course, but what began to interest Field more was brokering information.

According to Reynolds, Field first became known to his group of associates in 1959 when Buster Edwards was accused of stealing a car. Thanks to Field doing 'some work behind the scenes', Buster stayed out of jail. He later helped Goody and Wilson during their defence for the 1962 BOAC wages snatch, and subsequently became friends with Goody. Early in 1963, Field contacted Goody and offered to introduce him to a man who had some interesting information. A rendezvous was duly arranged at a bench in Finsbury Park between Goody, Edwards and Field's contact.

The man Goody and Edwards met was a middle-aged, slightly balding man from Northern Ireland. Goody had grown up there, and that gave the two men an instant connection. The contact said that his brother-in-law (or, according to some sources, his brother or stepbrother) worked on the railways and had told him about overnight mail trains from Glasgow to London that carried a large number of mailbags containing used banknotes. He said that the sums transported often amounted to as much as six million.

'Are you interested?' he asked.

Reynolds says that the informant then explained the route, the timetable, the whole set-up with the HVP coach, where it was placed in the order of carriages and how many men worked on the train. It is unlikely however, that he gave away all his valuable inside knowledge in this first meeting with a pair of complete strangers. Nevertheless, Edwards and Goody left Finsbury Park with enough information to outline the idea over a drink with Reynolds. They all agreed that it was better than any of the other possibilities they had been working on and was worth developing.

On 31 July, Goody met the contact again on a warm afternoon in Kensington Gardens. The man never gave them his name, but at one point he got up to buy a cup of tea leaving his jacket on a chair with a spectacle case sticking out of the pocket. According to Goody, he looked inside the case and found a label with a name and address. Sewn on the inside pocket of the jacket was the name of an Ulster tailor. From then on, the informant was nicknamed 'The Ulsterman'.

The men parted company with a deal agreed. Now Goody had more detailed inside knowledge of the large amounts of money being transported, plus the schedules and working practices of TPOs. He and his associates – Buster Edwards, Bruce Reynolds, Charlie Wilson, Roy James, Jimmy White, Jim Hussey and Messrs One and Two could now set about planning exactly how the robbery could be done. The most obvious challenge was they needed someone with the know-how to stop a train and an associate of Edwards suggested Roger Cordrey. Along with his fellow 'South Coast Raiders' – Bob Welch, Tommy Wisbey and the unnamed 'Mr Three' – Cordrey had carried out a number of successful if unspectacular heists on the south coast London to Brighton line. The vital link with the 'South Coast Raiders' provided by Edwards was Tommy Wisbey whom he had known since the mid-fifties, when they were both part of Freddie Foreman's gang.

The method Cordrey had devised for doctoring railway signals – using four six-volt batteries, lengths of wire, crocodile clips, a switch, and the all-important black leather glove – was simple enough to be worthy of an Enid Blyton 'Famous Five' caper. When Daly and Reynolds watched Cordrey wire up the Dwarf signal they might have questioned whether they had really needed his expertise.

The choice of location for the train raid was, in many ways, excellent. Cordrey had suggested they needed a location that was near to London,

yet isolated, with no inhabited buildings nearby. The other requirements were a set of signals, and access to a road.

In his 1995 biography, Reynolds claims to have been the first to spot
the potential of Bridego Bridge, which he saw from a train as he jour-
neyed up and down the line looking for possible sites. In Piers Paul
Read's *The Train Robbers*, Wisbey and Edwards take the credit. Scouting
for a suitable place for the ambush, they first drove to a location about
a mile north-east of Tring in Hertfordshire that they had previously
visited in connection with another plan – to rob the Irish Express.
However, the site proved unsuitable for the prospective mail-train raid
as the road crossed over the railway line, which was in a deep cutting,
and it would be impractical to carry a large number of heavy mailbags
up to the road.

When they returned to London, Edwards and Goody studied
Ordnance Survey maps covering the route taken by the Glasgow to
London line. South of Leighton Buzzard the quiet B488 road ran close
and parallel to the track. Two miles north of Cheddington there was a
road junction, two hundred and fifty yards from a railway bridge where
a narrow lane led west towards Ledburn.

The first reconnaissance was carried out by Goody, Edwards and
Reynolds. They found the isolated lane that passed under the railway
bridge number 127 and discovered there were no inhabited buildings nearby. Here it would be possible to unload mailbags down the
embankment to the road and under cover of darkness they would be
well concealed.

When Cordrey was taken to the location the following day he confirmed that Bridego Bridge would be perfect, but for the fact that the
signals were eleven hundred yards north of the bridge. This introduced
a complication: having stopped the train, they would need to move it
down to the bridge to unload it. After discussion it was decided they
could work round this and use it to their advantage. If they uncoupled
the locomotive and the HVP and then moved them to the bridge, it
would isolate the seventy postal workers in the remaining carriages,
leaving the gang only the driver, his mate and a handful of men in the
HVP to contend with.

Once they had identified a viable location, it threw up other logistics
of the robbery that would have to be tackled. There were considerable

challenges in carrying out an assault on a mail train in the middle of the night, deep in the Buckinghamshire countryside. Aside from getting vehicles and men to the location without attracting attention, they needed to devise an exit strategy that could cope with two and a half tons in used banknotes. Previous big money jobs had been done in Greater London where within a few streets it was easy to disperse and blend into the hubbub of familiar territory. But in rural Buckinghamshire the gang were venturing into the unknown where sixteen men travelling at night in two Land Rovers and a lorry would be conspicuous.

Terry Hogan, Reynolds' friend and regular partner in crime, declined to go on the job because he said it was too complicated and there were too many men involved. He had also been disillusioned after the BOAC robbery, where they had expected a much bigger prize. Perhaps he was also less seduced by the idea than Reynolds. Shrewdly, Hogan made sure that he was on holiday in the South of France when the robbery took place to avoid being implicated.

The story of how and why the gang came to be holed up at Leatherslade Farm goes back to the initial reconnaissance of sites for the robbery early in the summer of 1963. After the gang decided upon Bridego Bridge, Roy James drove up from London in his Mini Cooper to look at possible getaway routes. He came up with various ways they could make a dash for the city using fast cars modified to take both the men and stolen money. Taking the A41, they could cover the distance of about forty-five miles to South London, where most of them lived, in around an hour and twenty minutes. An alternative route would be the A5; originally a Roman road, it ran as straight as the ancient engineers could make it from Admiralty Arch in Holyhead, Anglesey, to Marble Arch in London. A third option was the M1, Britain's only motorway at the time; opened in 1959, by 1963 the M1 only extended as far south as Watford where it joined the A41. The motorway section offered two advantages over any other route: the police were not permitted to put up roadblocks on the motorway, and there was no speed limit.

Surprisingly, after weighing up all the factors the gang concluded that a straight drive back to London after the raid 'didn't appear feasible'. According to Reynolds, James was the only dissenter and the plan was settled by a majority vote.

It was a strange decision on the face of it. Using fast cars, the gang could have split up and taken different routes, merging undetected with early morning traffic heading south for the capital. Even if the robbers had driven at an average of fifty miles an hour, by the time Aylesbury Police HQ were first informed of the robbery at 04.25 the gang would have been at Marble Arch. They could have been safely on their home turf in South London before the police had begun to piece together what had happened, let alone taken any action.

Fewtrell later suggested the gang could have used a tanker to hide and transport their loot. It was a neat idea and more inventive and practical than the old lorry the gang acquired for the job. A couple of the gang could have stayed with the money and taken a roundabout route and then have slipped back into London days, weeks or even months afterwards.

So why did the mail-train gang choose to plant themselves in a hideout located in an isolated rural community, where a group of strangers would inevitably attract attention, rather than losing themselves in the metropolitan sprawl of the capital? Reynolds later claimed that they were worried about roadblocks. But when it came to deciding the best exit plan after the robbery the need to avoid getting stopped was an important factor but not the key one, so far as the gang were concerned. The overriding reason the gang chose to acquire a local hideout over all other options was the fact that none of the gang trusted their comrades enough to let the mailbags out of their sight until they had counted out the contents and everyone had their share.

Two months before the mail-train raid, on 27 June 1963, the Midland Mart estate agency in Bicester received a telephone call enquiring about properties for sale. There were a handful of houses on the market and the particulars were given to the caller.

One of these properties was Leatherslade Farm, home of Bernard Rixon, his common-law wife, Lily Elsie Rixon, and Mr Rixon's parents. A man introducing himself as a London solicitor with the firm James and Wheater later telephoned the farm and spoke to Lily Rixon, arranging to view the property the next day.

The following afternoon, two men drove up the quarter-mile dirt track to the farmhouse in a gleaming dark blue 3.8 Jaguar. Solicitor's clerk Brian Field had brought with him a man called Leonard Field, no relation, who was to pose as the prospective buyer. In reality, Leonard was a thirty-one-year-old merchant seaman working as a steward for P&O. His brother, Harry, had initially been represented by James and Wheater on a charge of horse-doping, and more recently when he was accused of robbing a bank in Stoke. Facing the prospect of a long custodial sentence, Harry had given his brother power of attorney. Thus Leonard had come to Brian Field's notice as a potential frontman. Not only was he easy to manipulate and, by virtue of his job, difficult to trace, but the power of attorney gave him another useful quality: access to ready cash.

They must have looked, if not unlikely purchasers, at least out of place. With Field's expensive suit and his companion's London accent, the men were clearly not local. Perhaps the sight of the Jaguar convinced Lily Rixon that her visitors had money and she enthusiastically showed them round the place.

The property had been advertised as

A smallholding between Bicester and Thame. Valuable freehold holding of five acres, elevated position, well set off the road, detached four bedroomed house, two reception and large kitchen, bathroom, adjoining two bedroomed cottage, main water, septic tank drainage, useful outbuildings. Price £5,500.

Like most estate agents' details they were optimistic, to say the least. In reality the farmhouse was a run-down, unprepossessing building. The windows were metal casements, cheap and functional. Two-thirds of the front elevation was rendered with discolouring sand and cement. There was a two-storey brick extension on one side and a brick box stuck on the back, which formed a separate annexe where Rixon's parents lived. The outbuildings included a dilapidated wooden shed with a corrugated tin roof, housing the generator – the only source of electricity for the property. Behind the house was another ramshackle outbuilding with a rusting tin roof about forty feet by fifteen with two wooden garages to one side. A third building was almost completely overgrown and had no roof at all. The surrounding shrubs and five-acre grounds were scrubby and unkempt. Mrs Rixon must have done a double-take when the smartly dressed man with the Jag said they were interested. The men had hardly looked in the house and seemed more interested in the outbuildings.

As a hideout, the smallholding had a lot to offer, at least when viewed through the eyes of a couple of men from the city. It was screened by trees and not visible from the road, despite being on top of an incline. From the upstairs rooms there was a 360-degree view of the undulating countryside. And it was about an hour's drive along winding country lanes from Bridego Bridge.

When the two men were leaving, Mrs Rixon asked them what they intended to do with the farm. Leonard Field put his arm around her and said, 'Can you imagine this place with nice gardens all round and a swimming pool?'

'Yes,' she said.

'If your husband lets us have the contract,' he told her, 'you can start digging a hole.'

As the Jag kicked up dust on its way along the bumpy farm track back to the road, Brian Field knew he had found exactly what the gang were looking for. When Mrs Rixon later told them that someone else had shown an interest in buying the farm, they put in an increased offer of £5,750 which the Rixons eagerly accepted. The Rixons' solicitor, Mr Meirion-Williams of Marshall and Eldridge, also agreed that on payment of a 10 per cent deposit of £550, access would be granted to the farm ahead of completion in order to carry out much-needed repairs and redecoration.

Some commentators have attached significance to the fact that Leatherslade Farm did not appear on Ordnance Survey maps of Buckinghamshire. The inference being that the gang had been extraordinarily clever in selecting the only property for miles around that was not on a map. In reality, though the Rixons' smallholding was not labelled Leatherslade Farm, the buildings were marked and could be readily identified as a dwelling. The fact was there were few properties for sale in the area at that time, and Leatherslade Farm was the only one that suited the gang's purpose. One of the first requirements of a robber's hideout was that it should be tucked away from prying eyes, however, unbeknown to the gang, Leatherslade Farm had a public bridleway running up the track and along one side of the house, which meant there was a possibility of passing walkers and riders observing the gang's comings and goings. At the entrance to the track which led up to the smallholding was a collection of farm buildings and a dairy parlour belonging to another farm. What at first appeared to be a secluded property to men brought up in the city was in reality all the more conspicuous because of its isolation. And with rural communities being what they are, it was not long before the gang found that out.

With the exception of Goody, the gang convened at the farm by the afternoon of Tuesday, 6 August. The following morning a neighbouring farmer, Mr Wyatt, came to the farmhouse. Reynolds spoke to him. Wyatt enquired if he could continue renting an adjoining field, as he had done under Bernard Rixon. Reynolds informed him that he was not the new owner but part of a team of builders getting the property ready. He said a Mr Fielding of Aylesbury had bought the place, and assured Wyatt he would pass on the request and put in a good word for him. The farmer went on his way without having seen how many men were there, or that they had no tools, or ladders, or decorating materials.

Wyatt was not the only local inhabitant to be curious about the new occupants of Leatherslade Farm.

For a number of reasons using Leatherslade Farm as a hideout was a fatal decision. Whether the gang knew that it was not marked on the local Ordnance Survey map was of no consequence. That omission neither protected them nor did it hinder or prevent the eventual discovery of the farm by the police.

In the weeks leading up to the raid the gang, now totalling fourteen, had been preoccupied by another consideration. If the mail-train driver refused to cooperate and move the train to the bridge, the plan would fail. The problem was debated at length. Roy James studied a Railwayman's Handbook and, passing himself off as a schoolteacher, persuaded a train driver to take him out in his cab. Afterwards, James said he was pretty sure that he could master the controls. Reynolds and Goody climbed into a North London marshalling yard one night and inspected parked diesel engines to see if they could understand the controls. When they later discussed what they had learned, they each felt fairly confident they could drive a locomotive, but not certain. Realising that this was too crucial to be left to chance, the gang decided to recruit a train driver to come on the raid with them.

Six weeks before the robbery, Reynolds received a phone call from Ronnie Biggs. The two men were old friends, having first met in

Wandsworth Prison in 1949 when Biggs was twenty-one and Reynolds nineteen. Convictions for a variety of petty offences saw Biggs return to prison again and again over the next ten years, until in 1960 he married and promised to go straight; a year later he set up a small building and decorating firm near Redhill in Surrey. When he telephoned Reynolds in 1963, it was to ask for a £500 loan. During their conversation he mentioned that he was currently decorating a house that belonged to a train driver. Reynolds could not believe his luck and suggested that Biggs ask the man if he would be interested in helping him with a job, and the possibility of the gang acquiring their own train driver suddenly fell into place.

So it was that Biggs and 'Pop' came to be recruited late in the day to make up the final gang of sixteen. Biggs had the prospect of obtaining a great deal more money than he had asked for, and the gang had their train driver. The irony was that the day before Biggs left home to take part in the mail-train robbery he won £510 at Brighton races.

With only weeks to go, the gang had resolved what they had long felt was the one possible weakness. The final plan was now complete.

8

In his book, *The Train Robbers*, Malcolm Fewtrell describes arriving at the crime scene on the morning of the robbery:

> At about 5 a.m., in the first light, we saw the abandoned coaches at Sears Crossing, with dozens of weary postman staring lugubriously into the dawn light. I took in the scenery, saw that the signal had been rigged red with a battery circuit and went off to Bridego Bridge to have a look at the business end of the train.

It is an evocative, visual and literary description – and entirely false. According to the Aylesbury Information Room log, Fewtrell did not arrive at the scene until over an hour later, and he went first to Cheddington station, not Sears Crossing. At 05.00 Fewtrell was still at Aylesbury HQ 'getting things organised' and awaiting the arrival of Assistant Chief Constable George Wilkinson. And while there were ten abandoned carriages, over seventy weary postal workers, and a rigged red signal at Sears Crossing at that time, if Detective Superintendent Fewtrell had walked the half-mile south to Bridego Bridge he would have found nothing but empty track and a strip of white sheet between two posts. He would have known, both on 8 August 1963 and in the summer of 1964 when he was writing his book, that the 'business end of the train' was not at Bridego Bridge but at Cheddington station – which was why Fewtrell made his way there at 06.17.

The critique of Fewtrell's account might seem pedantic, but such inaccuracy by a senior policeman who was intimately involved with the mail-train case from beginning to end is surprising. It begs the question: did Fewtrell not remember the extraordinary events of that morning, or was he simply making it up for the purpose of his narrative?

Fewtrell was not alone in his unreliable reporting. It is a common theme in the numerous public documents and published accounts of the robbery and investigation. Even the most straightforward details from seemingly knowledgeable sources, whether reported in official statements, the press, the court or in various biographies published after the event, when subjected to scrutiny and comparison prove to be inaccurate. Some result from poor memory, or differing perspectives; some arise from the natural human inclination to embroider anecdotes; but other accounts are complete fabrication, born of self-interest and vanity in an effort to gloss over errors, shift blame, or claim credit. Cumulatively, they create confusion about exactly what happened and why. The discrepancies create distortions in the picture, obscuring clarity and cloaking events in apparent mystery, giving rise to all manner of fanciful stories and theories. These myriad perspectives, inaccuracies and narrative inventions, both at the time and in the years that followed, have conspired to spawn a mythology that continues to obscure the real people and events of 'The Great Train Robbery'.

The first policeman to arrive at Sears Crossing was not Fewtrell but Inspector Mellows from Linslade, who got there at around 05.00. Apart from the men in coach three who had seen the train separate, none of the other marooned postal workers he spoke to, including Post Office Inspector Fuggle, had seen or heard anything of the raid. They said that they had been completely unaware of it taking place.

At this point, signal technician Frank Mead was heading north up the track on foot to inspect the Dwarf signal that had been doctored by John Daly, so Inspector Mellows had not yet had a chance to speak to him about the tampered lights. Even so, the rural policeman quickly grasped the serious nature of the crime. At 05.08 he radioed Aylesbury HQ for 'every possible assistance'; requesting that they 'turn the lot out' – meaning the entire Buckinghamshire constabulary, senior officers included – he asked for roadblocks to be set up, neighbouring police authorities to be informed and dogs to join the hunt.

Though he had no experience of major crime, Mellows displayed a shrewd insight into the criminals' strategy, correctly guessing that they might still be close by and recommending that isolated farms and buildings in the area be searched. Had Inspector Mellows' instructions been followed, the protracted investigation that tied up hundreds of police officers at vast public expense for many years would have been concluded within days if not hours.

At 05.10 Eric William Sidebottom, a British Railways technician, arrived to assist Frank Mead in repairing the signals. Up at the Dwarf signal, Mead found the missing bulb from the green 'aspect' (signal) lying on the ground next to the track. He also picked up a brown switch. Hanging over the open door at the back of the signal were some wires with two crocodile clips attached. Although he could find no batteries and no glove by the Dwarf signal, Mead assumed the robbers had used the same technique as at the red Home signal on the gantry.

Around this time, Detective Sergeant Fairweather showed up at Sears Crossing. He was the first member of Aylesbury CID on site, and the most senior detective available at the time, the Detective Inspector being away on leave. Fairweather 'immediately began to make inquiries of the train staff', even though Inspector Mellows had already done so and reported his conclusions to HQ. It is odd, given that Mellows was in attendance, that DS Fairweather went first to Sears Crossing rather than heading to Cheddington, where the section of the train that had been robbed was located, along with the principal witnesses who had been violently assaulted by the criminals. Although that would have seemed the most promising place for CID to begin their work, the job of taking statements and gathering evidence had been left to the two constables who first arrived at the scene.

By 05.15 Mills and Whitby, still handcuffed together, had arrived at the Casualty department of the Royal Buckinghamshire Hospital. Mills' injuries were examined by Dr Syed Masud, who reported:

> He had lacerated injuries to the back of the skull and I found one two inches long and half an inch deep and another one an inch long and a quarter of an inch deep in front of his right ear. There was another laceration at the back of the skull an inch long and a quarter of an inch deep and two smaller lacerations to the skull. I cleaned the wounds, and dressed them having inserted fourteen stitches. Mr Mills was detained as an in-patient.

From Dr Masud's report it is clear that, contrary to some accounts of the assault, Jack Mills sustained at least five separate injuries to the head. Although shaken and groggy, Mills was lucid and his short-term memory appeared to be functioning normally as he gave an account of the attack on him. Dr Masud decided to admit him for observation.

During Jack Mills' time in the Royal Buckinghamshire Hospital it was not recorded whether Dr Masud delved any deeper into his condition. In 1963, CT and MRI technology had not been developed so any neurological assessment would have been confined to checking reflexes and pupil size for signs of concussion and asking questions to test basic mental faculties.

As Fewtrell's memoirs and the statement's of men on board the mail train have shown, personal recollections of the robbery are frequently rife with inaccuracies. When it comes to the robbers' accounts, any details that cannot be corroborated by independent evidence should be treated with a degree of suspicion. Not only are criminals more inclined to be dishonest, exaggerating their deeds for the sake of bravado or downplaying their violent actions, but the gang's version of events was published fifteen years after the fact. Reynolds openly admitted that in old age he often finds it difficult to distinguish between his own memory and the received story – 'the product' as he calls it.

Despite the extravagant claim on the flyleaf that 'through her unique contacts she was able to obtain direct and extraordinary information', Peta Fordham's *The Robbers' Tale*, published a year after the trial, failed to take advantage of the unprecedented access to key participants that the author had enjoyed by virtue of being married to defence barrister Wilfred Fordham. The flyleaf concludes that the 'extraordinary information' to which she was privy was 'far too dangerous to print'.

It was not until 1976 that the robbers decided to tell their tale. In April of that year a man called Gary van Dyk arrived at the offices of London publisher W.H. Allen, touting the 'confessions' of the notorious Great Train Robbers. A lunch later took place in the top-floor penthouse flat of the publishers, attended by author Piers Paul Read and seven of the robbers.

In his introduction to *The Train Robbers*, Read describes his initial reaction: 'there was little to be made of them: some were tall, some short and most of indeterminate middle-age'. None of the men looked anything like their images on the wanted posters the police had released to the press in 1963. Only one man struck Read as 'slightly sinister' – a tall, well-dressed man with a South African accent. The others seemed amiable, and pre-lunch conversation was stilted but good-humoured as

Read worked his way round the room, mentally checking off each gang member. Goody was the easiest to identify, sitting on a black leather sofa observing the gathering from behind dark glasses. Also present were Edwards, White, James, Cordrey, Hussey and Wisbey. Finally, by process of elimination, Read realised that the rather sinister-looking man was not in fact one of the convicted train robbers but their literary agent, Gary van Dyk.

Aside from the aforementioned 'revelation' about Otto Skorzeny and associates, *The Train Robbers* offered some plausible details and fresh insights into the gang's activities. There is a description of the gang unpacking mailbags in semi-darkness on the morning of the robbery. Leatherslade Farm's electricity was supplied by a diesel-powered DC generator located in a shed at the side of the house; fearing that the throb of the engine would be heard for miles, the robbers worked by the light of candles, torches and bulbs rigged to car batteries, with make-shift blackout curtains covering the windows. Despite the gloomy conditions and having had little or no sleep, they worked tirelessly, counting out and stacking £2,500 bundles of five-pound notes, £500 bundles of one-pound notes, and £250 bundles of ten-shilling notes. Scottish and Irish currency, regardless of denomination, was put in a separate pile.

Also included in the haul were some of the old-style five-pound notes. Although officially withdrawn on 13 March 1961, the old 'White Fiver' hadn't completely disappeared from circulation. The design was essentially unchanged since the note was first issued in 1793, during the French Revolution, to replace gold coin. The smallest denomination banknote prior to that had been worth ten pounds. In 1957 the 'Series B' five-pound note – multicoloured but predominantly dark blue, bearing the image of Britannia – was introduced, but on 21 February 1963 these too were phased out to make way for the 'Series C': the first five-pound note to feature an image of the reigning monarch, Queen Elizabeth II.

Shortly before 05.30 Inspector G. Matheson arrived to take charge of the Information Room at Aylesbury HQ. Fewtrell, having dispatched PC Whiteman to the hospital with a handcuff key to release Whitby and Mills, set off for the crime scene accompanied by Assistant Chief

Constable George Wilkinson. Detective Sergeant Gaunt of the photography and fingerprint branch was instructed to meet them at Cheddington.

At around the same time, GPO engineer Robert Hutchinson, having received a call from Leighton Buzzard telephone exchange at 02.45, had been slowly working his way around the Bridego Bridge area, checking for faults. Hutchinson discovered two pairs of overhead wires cut fifteen inches from the insulators. At nearby Whaddon Farm he found the wires had been cut 'both sides of the pole'. Four dwellings in the immediate vicinity had been affected:

Leighton Buzzard 2274 – Mrs Ruth King at Rowden Farm;
Leighton Buzzard 2174 – Miss Nellie Maitland, Housekeeper to Lord Rosebury, Mentmore Towers;
Leighton Buzzard 3294 – John Ringrose, Assistant Farm Manager, Whaddon Farm Cottage, Slapton;
Leighton Buzzard 3283 – Mrs Eleanor Rott, Whaddon Farm, Slapton.

The residents had all been asleep when James and Cordrey cut the telephone lines at around 02.30, so the fault would have gone undiscovered until morning had those four houses been the only ones disconnected. But in an effort to prevent anyone on the ambushed train finding a working telephone in the area, the gang had indiscriminately severed the main overhead cables, thus attracting the attention of operators at the Leighton Buzzard exchange almost half an hour before the robbery had even started.

At 05.45 Detective Constable Gerald Lake arrived at Royal Bucks Hospital with a hacksaw and after two and a half hours shackled together, Mills and Whitby were finally parted and shortly afterwards, Whitby's cuff was unlocked. Unsurprisingly, the brief police report states that both Mills' and Whitby's wrists were swollen.

The handcuffs used by the gang were unusual, being American and the very latest design. This detail offered another potentially useful clue, yet there is no mention in the early stages of the investigation of detectives trying to trace the origin of the cuffs.

When Fewtrell and Wilkinson reached Cheddington at 06.17 they found a number of CID officers had begun to assemble and, with the benefit of daylight, a search was under way along the track. Fewtrell sums up their initial impressions in his book *The Train Robbers*: 'for the first time we realised just how carefully the robbery must have been planned and saw how remarkably little solid evidence remained of the raid two hours ago'. He does not elaborate on the kind of evidence he might have expected to find after a large-scale robbery but goes on to list a number of clues worthy of an Agatha Christie novel: a bloodstained cloth, a piece of string, a man's black leather glove, a railwayman's cap, a broken piece of train coupling, the iron crowbar, Eveready batteries, wires, two metal posts and the strip of white cloth the gang had tied between two posts to indicate where the train should stop. Fewtrell concludes: 'putting aside our doubts we took refuge in routine'. He appointed Detective Constable Keith Milner as Exhibits Officer, to take charge of the meagre collection and set about listing the finds. During the course of the investigation, Milner's list was to grow to over a thousand items.

Back at the farm, Reynolds, who recalls having 'slept deeply for two hours', was woken at around six in the morning by Buster Edwards.

'Two and a half million, mate,' he announced.

It was an unprecedented haul – 'staggering', in Reynolds' words – and the fact the gang were the first criminals ever to achieve such a feat was 'the stuff of dreams', giving him more pleasure than the actual figure. If Reynolds had realised just how famous the robbery was going to make him he would have thought that his dreams had indeed come true. However, had he known what that three-and-a-half-hour round trip to Bridego Bridge was going to cost him, he might have felt very differently.

Police photographers took 315 photographs of the crime scene and associated locations such as Cheddington railway station, Sears Crossing and Bridego Bridge. Over the course of the ensuing investigation and the series of trials that followed, police and press photographers were on hand to capture each new development. These images provide a window into the past, revealing things that written statements and records cannot adequately convey.

Very few of those first police photographs were released to the press, but there is one black-and-white image that has featured again and again in accounts of 'The Great Train Robbery', evoking as it does a sense of the determination of the investigators and the drama of the situation. The photographer is positioned north of Bridego Bridge, between the slow and fast 'Up' lines. In the far distance to the south, the four sets of tracks, two up lines and two down, converge into a hazy vanishing point in the direction of Cheddington. One man in plain clothes is purposefully stepping over the slow 'Up' line rail into the 'six foot', railway slang for the stony ground between pairs of tracks. Movement renders his image a little blurred, and his hand is indistinct as he reaches down for a slightly bent and pitted iron bar, about three foot long and an inch and a half in diameter, that is lying on the stones in the foreground. Behind him are three young men holding cameras. One wears a white shirt and tie, the others are in dark suits; all three stand with shoulders hunched, intense expressions on their faces. The man in the white shirt is taking a photo of the man retrieving the crowbar. Just visible behind the group, about twenty feet away beside the railings of Bridego Bridge, a uniformed policeman stands looking the other way, in conversation with a shorter man in a cloth cap.

It appears to have been taken early on the morning of 8 August as police searched the tracks between Bridego Bridge and Sears Crossing, and is often accompanied by some variation of the caption *Detectives retrieve crowbar used in the robbery* – a fleeting glimpse of a significant discovery in the early stages of the investigation.

That is the popular interpretation. But police records mention only two Buckinghamshire policemen assigned to photography and fingerprints: Detective Sergeant Gaunt and Constable John Bailey, who arrived at 06.00. Yet the photograph features three men with cameras, plus the photographer behind the lens. It is probable, therefore, that the bar is not a genuine piece of evidence, that the man reaching down for it is not a detective, that the photograph was taken some time later in the day, and that none of the young men with cameras are police officers. The likelihood is, they are all press photographers and the famous photo was staged.

This is one small example of how an intricate mosaic of facts and images has been built up over time with each piece contributing to the grand tableau of 'The Great Train Robbery' legend.

*

In the Aylesbury Control Room log there is a four-word entry at 06.16 that would pose a significant problem for the gang over the next thirty-six hours: 'believed army truck used'. The information had come from Whitby, speaking to one of the police officers who went to the Royal Buckinghamshire Hospital to try and release him and Mills from their handcuffs. The fireman had caught a glimpse of the army lorry down on the road below when he and Mills were ordered out of the engine at Bridego Bridge and made to walk back along the track to the railway embankment.

It is not clear why Whitby and Mills were moved from the cab. Given that the two men were handcuffed together, they could simply have been left where they were until the raid was over. Unlike the earlier slip-ups that undermined their plans in various ways, the gang were not going to get away with this one. Allowing Whitby to see the truck proved a foolish and critical error.

The robbers weren't the only ones to make mistakes. Crucial evidence had already been compromised when train driver Cooper instructed his fireman to move the train from Bridego Bridge to Cheddington. This was excusable: Cooper had no knowledge of police procedures; he was merely doing his best to cope with an emergency. However, before Fewtrell and Wilkinson arrived at the crime scene, Detective Superintendent Francis Ward of British Railways Transport Police began to set up an independent investigation HQ at Cheddington station. Without waiting for fingerprint or forensic experts to examine the engine and HVP, DS Ward authorised the removal of the engine, bogie brake van and HVP to Cheddington sidings.

That a senior police officer should sanction moving the train again was one of many blunders on that first day arising from lack of communication, coordination and basic common sense. In *The Train Robbers*, Fewtrell's frustration with this state of affairs is evident: 'Uniformed men were needed too. They had to make sure that nobody disturbed things on the train before they had been expertly examined. In fact the mobility of this part of the scene made things more difficult.'

At 06.30 Detective Sergeant Gaunt and Detective Constable Bailey arrived with a fingerprint kit and some statement forms. While examining the attacked portion of the train in Cheddington sidings the officers were called to Sears Crossing signal gantry to inspect the tampered signals, along with the pieces of wire and batteries that the gang had left behind, which promised to provide vital insights into how the robbery had been executed. But everything at the scene had been handled by British Railways engineer Frank Mead an hour and a half earlier. It did not occur to Mead that he should not touch or move things; his job was to repair signals, so that was what he set about doing. At the Dwarf signal he picked up a switch from the track and the bulb Daly had discarded. And he was not wearing gloves.

The same was true of telephone engineer Robert Hutchinson, dispatched to the area to inspect telegraph poles and restore the local telephone cables. He too was inadvertently compromising key evidence.

When DS Gaunt returned to Cheddington station he was informed by Fewtrell that Scotland Yard was going to be called in and there was no need for him do any further fingerprinting of the engine and HVP. Gaunt reminded Fewtrell that his initial examination of the train had not been completed. He was instructed to simply photograph everything, including the evidence found at the trackside.

At around 07.30 linesman Frederick Sinfield reported that the 'Ganger's Hut' near Bridego Bridge had been broken into. Sinfield and another British Railways worker, Arthur Boarder, noticed several articles missing from the hut including a railwayman's cap, which was found on the track. He also found a non-British-Rail-issue pickaxe handle leaning against Bridego Bridge, and a crowbar that had been taken from the hut was discovered on the 'six foot' between the 'Up' and 'Down' fast lines at the bridge. In addition to confirming that the photograph of detectives retrieving the crowbar used in the robbery was staged, this begs the question why were railway employees allowed to wander around the scene of a major crime, apparently unsupervised and unchallenged, picking up valuable evidence.

At Leatherslade Farm the robbers continued to eavesdrop on police activity via their portable VHF radios. As far as the gang knew the only local who was aware there was anyone staying at Leatherslade Farm was Mr Wyatt, the neighbouring farmer who had called to ask about renting a field. With a good supply of food and an excellent view of the surrounding area, they felt upbeat, in control and secure in their hideout.

But as the day progressed the scale of the mail-train raid was slowly dawning and bigger wheels began to turn. In London C.G. Osmond, the Controller of the GPO's Investigation Branch, having been informed that New Scotland Yard were aware of the robbery but had not yet been called in, telephoned Brigadier John Cheney, Chief Constable of Buckinghamshire. The two men agreed that an emergency meeting of 'all interested parties' should be held at GPO Headquarters that afternoon at 15.00.

There were now three investigating units, all working independently: the local Buckinghamshire police based in Aylesbury, led by Fewtrell; British Transport Police, led by Detective Superintendent Francis John Ward, operating out of an incident room at Cheddington station; and the GPO Investigation Branch in London headed by Osmond.

Two hours elapsed before Scotland Yard were contacted by Buckinghamshire police, during which time Fewtrell was seen showing Cheney over the crime scene. There may have been an element of professional pride in their reluctance to immediately call in outside help, or it may simply have been a side effect of the general shock and confusion. Whatever the reason, it was not until 10.33 that a telex was finally sent out from Aylesbury HQ:

> To: New Scotland Yard; the CCs (Chief Constables) of Bedfordshire, Hertfordshire, Oxfordshire, and Northamptonshire. At approx 2.45 hours today a mail-train robbery occurred between Leighton Buzzard and Cheddington, Bucks. 120 mail bags containing a very considerable sum of money are missing. It is thought that the persons responsible may have hidden up and attempted to get away by mingling with morning traffic. Observation and frequent spot checks of traffic vehicles is requested.

Cheney then telephoned Commander Hatherill at New Scotland Yard and invited him to the meeting at GPO HQ that afternoon. It is unclear how much detail Hatherill had already been given. Though the Yard were the first police agency to be notified – at 04.24 by Prentice of British Railways' Euston Control room – Hatherill had apparently not been contacted. He later said that the first he heard of the robbery was 'on the wireless that morning'.

An incident room was set up inside the rather nondescript new building housing Buckinghamshire Police HQ in Aylesbury. Ten miles from Cheddington and with 'modern facilities' including the conference-cum-incident room equipped with two telephone lines, one external and one internal, the new HQ proved woefully inadequate. The building's designers had failed to anticipate the demands on telephones in the aftermath of a major incident. The following day three additional lines were installed in the switchboard with one direct line connected to the incident room. However, in the twenty-four hours following the robbery it was virtually impossible to get through to the incident room because the line was permanently engaged. It was no easier for staff to call out. But the ongoing police work was only partly responsible for the heavy telephone traffic. Causing more chaos than anything else and hampering the investigation was the overwhelming number of calls coming into Aylesbury HQ from radio and TV reporters and members of the press.

9

On the afternoon of 8 August 1963, shortly before 15.00, the good and the great of crime investigation began to assemble at King Edward Building, GPO Headquarters, Newgate Street, in the City of London. The majestic, neo-Baroque, grey Portland stone building was designed by Sir Henry Tanner of the Office of Works, 1907–1911. Being architecturally related to the Central Criminal Courts at the Old Bailey and just two hundred yards away, GPO HQ must have provided some sense of solidity to those high-ranking officials shaken by the extraordinary events of the last twelve hours.

C.G. Osmond of the GPO's Investigation Branch chaired the meeting. There were about thirty people present, the most senior of whom was Commander George Hatherill of New Scotland Yard, a polyglot with seventeen solved murder cases to his credit. He was accompanied by Detective Superintendent R. A. Anderson, Detective Superintendent Gerald McArthur and numerous other officers of the Metropolitan Police. Detective Superintendent Malcolm Fewtrell was present, along with Brigadier John Cheney, Chief Constable of Buckinghamshire. British Transport Police was represented by Chief Constable William Owen Gay and Brigadier Holmes. Several other officers attended from the Travelling Post Office section. There were also heads of departments of the Post Office and British Rail security along with senior officials from both organisations.

Although no minutes of the meeting were taken, Fewtrell recalls that he began by outlining the facts of the robbery as far as Buckinghamshire police had been able to establish.

According to Fewtrell, Hatherill expressed the opinion that 'this was a crime planned in London by London criminals' and the fact that it had occurred in Buckinghamshire was incidental. Hatherill proposed that roadblocks be organised and a systematic search of the surrounding area undertaken. He assumed, of course, that something of the sort was already in place and that it should be extended after the meeting.

It was decided that local searches should concentrate on isolated farms and buildings.

In the smoke-filled room there was a great deal of debate and theorising about the raid and the Scotland Yard detectives suggested names of criminals capable of planning and organising such a robbery.

As is so often in crisis meetings following an event in which major failings in operating systems have been exposed, the heads of the organisations involved seemed intent on marking out their territory while being careful not to take responsibility for the problem.

No representatives of the eight banks – the Bank of Scotland, National Commercial Bank of Scotland, British Linen Bank, Midland Bank, National Provincial Bank, Westminster Bank, Isle of Man Bank and Barclays Bank – who had suffered losses, or their insurers, were invited to attend. A surprising oversight, given that in their absence there was no one who could shed light on one vital aspect of the robbery. As Fewtrell put it in his book the following year: 'The great irony was that this tense gathering had no idea about how much money the robbers had made off with.'

It was initially suggested that the figure might be close to a million. Frank Cooke, a senior Post Office investigator, disagreed. He calculated that the amount might be closer to three and a half million. Cooke's astounding figure only served to increase anxiety among his colleagues, who were already bracing themselves for the outcry from journalists, the public and Members of Parliament, not to mention the banks whose money had been stolen.

In a BBC interview filmed the day of the robbery, Postmaster General Reginald Bevins was asked: 'The people who have lost money, how are they going to get their money back?'

Bevins replied, 'They will be compensated to a very limited extent by the GPO because the maximum compensation is about twenty pounds for each registered packet. But I think you can take it for granted that most people who send large sums of money by registered mail make their own private insurance arrangements.'

The 120 stolen mailbags had contained 636 packets of banknotes from numerous branches of at least eight different banks. It transpired that the Midland Bank, who had lost about half a million pounds, were not insured. They were very sanguine about it and said in a press statement that their losses were well covered by the savings they had made by not taking out insurance over the years.

But the Midland Bank was a bit slapdash with their arithmetic too. It would have cost them sixpence per thousand pounds, or £12.10s. to have insured the £500,000 stolen that night and 40,000 uninsured trips to offset the half a million loss. Even if they transported that amount on mail trains seven days a week, fifty-two weeks a year, it would take one hundred and nine years and six months to recoup the equivalent value of the money stolen through not paying insurance.

Meanwhile at Leatherslade Farm the gang continued to monitor Buckinghamshire police radio frequencies as well as listening to national radio broadcasts. Beyond that, the robbers' activities can only be pieced together from various accounts they gave after the event and to a limited degree, there is some supporting evidence.

The sound of hammering had been echoing across the fields all morning as Jimmy White and Mr One spent their time working on the old Austin lorry, modifying a false floor in which to transport some of the money. Piers Paul Read's book has Roger Cordrey getting up in the afternoon, washing and changing into a jacket and trousers, taking £3,000 from his share and going downstairs. Biggs had lit the stove and was burning various pieces of incriminating evidence (a neighbour later reported seeing smoke coming from the farmhouse chimney). Cordrey handed Biggs the clothes he had worn for the raid and proceeded to make a cup of tea and a boiled egg. This may simply be picture-painting by Read, but more significant matters had been brewing while Cordrey was upstairs asleep.

While Cordrey had been dreaming of better things, the midday news on the radio reported that an estimated million pounds had been stolen and it was thought the robbers had used several army-type vehicles. Not surprisingly this news caused if not panic at least some urgent questions and intense conversation between the gang members. Had the hitchhiking airman they had passed on the way to Bridego Bridge (according to Reynolds) reported seeing the convoy of army vehicles shortly after midnight? Had the information come from Mr Wyatt, the neighbouring farmer who had called at the farm two days earlier to enquire about renting a field? Had he seen 'army-type vehicles' parked in the outbuildings when he drove up to the house? Had somebody else seen the convoy on the road as they were driving to or from the robbery?

Whatever the source of the information, the radio broadcast shook the gang's confidence and created a serious problem. The majority of the robbers had planned to leave the farm the same way as they had arrived. Once the initial post-robbery police activity had died down they had intended to return to London using the two Land Rovers and the lorry to transport them and their ill-gotten gains.

Pragmatic as ever, White's response had been to start painting the cab of the lorry with some yellow paint he had found lying around. But there was not enough paint to cover the original dark green and the finished result looked unconvincing. Meanwhile other fears were raised. Had the person who saw the convoy also made a note of the registration numbers? Having heard the radio reports, there was no way the gang could risk using their vehicles again.

According to Read's book an alternative means of transport was on its way: an associate, Joey Gray, was apparently due to arrive on Sunday with a horsebox. However, the story is peculiar to Read's account. Neither Reynolds nor Fordham mentions a man called Gray or a horsebox.

One thing was clear. The news reports on the radio had scuppered the gang's exit plans. The only other means of transport the sixteen men now had between them was a bicycle Cordrey had brought along.

While the other gang members were still discussing what to do, Cordrey got on his bike and cycled to Oxford. It must have taken him about an hour – Brill to Oxford is over ten miles. But Cordrey was not simply pedalling away from the problem and deserting his fellow gang members. Before he left, he agreed to contact Brian Field and ask for his help with transport. He also called Mary Manson, a close friend of Reynolds who lived in Wimbledon, and arranged for her and a friend, Rene, to drive to Buckinghamshire the following morning and meet Reynolds in Thame, six and a half miles south-east of Leatherslade Farm.

While senior police officers from Buckinghamshire and Scotland Yard were hunched around a table in tense discussion with GPO and British Rail investigators in London, the gang set to work cleaning up. White lit a bonfire and started burning shoes, balaclavas, the army uniforms and overalls worn for the raid. When someone threw one of the white mail sacks on to the flames it started billowing black smoke, due to the material being impregnated with wax waterproofing. Concerned that the smoke would attract attention, the gang doused the fire and decided not to burn any other sacks.

In the garden, in the long, uncut grass between clumps of Michaelmas daisies about fifteen feet from the farmhouse, Reynolds started digging a large pit in which to bury other evidence. Read describes the elderly train driver nervously watching the digging in the garden out of the window. He had so nearly brought the robbery to a halt before it had properly got under way by failing to drive the train at Sears Crossing and now he became anxious that the gang planned to do away with him and that Reynolds was digging his grave.

Reynolds corroborates the account in Read's book of the great lengths that the gang went to in cleaning up the inside of the farmhouse, specifically to eradicate fingerprints and other traces that would prove they had been there. All of the gang, apart from the train driver, had criminal records. Their fingerprints were on file at the Criminal Records Office and that would connect individuals to the farm. It was absolutely vital to remove any evidence, such as clothes, mail sacks, or money wrappers that would link the farm to the mail train. While all this seems a common-sense precaution, it was carried out in an un-methodical, uncoordinated fashion.

There has been an enormous amount of conjecture and debate about the clean-up at the farm. With the benefit of hindsight, there are only two logical interpretations and these will be explored in full later in the investigation timeline, but it is worth noting at this point that all the various accounts given by the robbers agree in one respect: a concerted effort was made to erase all traces of their fingerprints before they left.

The robbers had started 8 August with organisation, discipline and promise. They had stopped the mail train as planned and carried out the biggest cash robbery in British history. Despite the callous assault on Mills, several slip-ups and oversights, they had got away with over two and a half million pounds in used banknotes. However, as the day drew to a close and the gang found themselves faced with unforeseen problems, they lost focus, made hurried decisions and their actions were to result in catastrophic errors.

*

By 17.30 GPO telephone engineer Robert Hutchinson had repaired the sabotaged overhead cables and restored the four disconnected telephone lines near Sears Crossing and Bridego Bridge. It had taken in him best part of twelve hours.

At 18.00 the following message was received at Buckinghamshire HQ from Linslade sub-division:

> Re: Mail-train robbery. About 1.20 a.m. 8 August, three vehicles were seen on the Cublington to Aston Abbots road, travelling towards Aston Abbots. All three vehicles were in close convoy. They are described as a small vehicle, an army lorry, large wheels exposed and a light Land Rover. The persons giving this information were seen and statements taken.

When the thirty men eventually emerged from the meeting at GPO Headquarters, the London evening papers were headlining the story of the mail-train robbery. There had been radio news bulletins throughout the day and television news screened the interview with the Postmaster General. There was an initial quote in the papers from Mr Bevins, who had abandoned his summer holiday to return to London: 'I feel as uncomfortable as anyone in my position would.'

As part of the plan of action agreed in the meeting Commander Hatherill dispatched Detective Superintendent Gerald McArthur and Detective Sergeant Jack Pritchard to Aylesbury to assist Buckinghamshire police with the investigation. It is unclear why Hatherill offered so little assistance at this point. A two-man detective team would be the kind of support Scotland Yard provided for a murder in the provinces. Given the obvious magnitude of the train robbery, the amount stolen and number of criminals involved, the secondment of two detectives was at best a token gesture.

Fewtrell described McArthur and Pritchard as 'both philosophic and calm men'. McArthur had flown with Coastal Command during the war and Pritchard was an ex-Commando. When it came to matters of 'military precision' the two men from Scotland Yard were well qualified. It provided some reassurance for Cheney and Fewtrell as they set off for Aylesbury that evening followed by the men from the Yard.

Fewtrell recalled: 'Apart from the glamour value of the words Scotland Yard, detectives from it have the advantage of the experience and the resources of a big organisation. They get prompt service at the Central Criminal Record Office which keeps fingerprints and photographs and case histories of past offenders.'

Although the CRO was a good place to start, there was another line of inquiry that is central to any criminal investigation. The Flying Squad and London Criminal Investigation Department had many contacts in the underworld. They kept tabs on where known villains were, who had been drinking with whom and who was out of town. And if they did not know themselves, they knew people who would. That was always a vital complement to the more mundane and sometimes unrewarding task of piecing together hard evidence and trying to work it out. This unofficial, often shady side of detective work with money passing in both directions was very much the style of the times and continued without much scrutiny until a major shake-up of police practice was undertaken in the early 1970s following corruption scandals.

As a result of the urgent telephone call from Roger Cordrey on Thursday afternoon, Brian Field and his wife Karin drove to the farm in their dark blue Jaguar, arriving as daylight was fading.

Field told the gang about the unprecedented publicity surrounding the mail-train raid. He also had more reassuring news: he had passed no police roadblocks on the way to the farm or seen any evidence of police activity in the immediate area.

It was hurriedly decided that the Fields would take Roy James to London to organise alternative transport. They duly set off, and later that evening dropped James off at an address in Pembridge Square, Bayswater.

It was 22.20 by the time Detective Superintendent McArthur and Detective Sergeant Pritchard from Scotland Yard arrived at Aylesbury HQ. From now on Fewtrell, McArthur and Pritchard would be working together. McArthur was effectively in charge, though officially he was just an advisor. The men from the Yard – Mac and Jack, as they came to be known – had brought some information with them from Detective Superintendent John Cummings, head of C11, the intelligence branch at New Scotland Yard. As a result of 'information received' four names had been put forward, one of which was Robert Welch.

As far as the police were concerned, Welch did not fit the profile of the type of criminal they were looking for. An intelligent man, he had earned good money running the New Crown Club near the Elephant and Castle, until March 1963, when it was closed down for selling alcohol outside the permitted hours. Apart from a charge for breaching the licensing laws, Welch's only previous conviction was for receiving stolen goods in 1958. The Scotland Yard detectives considered Welch small fry. It is a surprising oversight and presumably the result of poor communication, as Welch was known to be part of the South Coast Raiders gang and connected to Roger Cordrey. Cordrey had been under observation by the GPO Investigation Branch in connection with theft of mail from trains since 1961.

McArthur and Pritchard suggested road checks should be carried out the next day to stop early morning traffic in the hope that they might jog the memory of regular commuters. Had anyone seen an army convoy or army-type vehicles heading for London the previous day?

As the detectives discussed what each of them would have done if they were planning the robbery, theories ranged from the gang driving straight back to London along any of the main roads and blending in with morning rush-hour traffic, to a dash down the M1. The other alternative they had been considering was the gang using a disused barn, or even a barge on the nearby canal to hide the money for later collection and distribution. It was decided to identify possible local farms and outlying buildings, ex-army and RAF bases that could have provided the robbers with somewhere to hide the considerable quantity of mailbags and possibly even conceal themselves and lie low for a few days.

For Fewtrell it had been a gruelling start to the investigation that had begun nearly twenty hours earlier when the telephone beside his bed had rung at 04.35. Accommodation arrangements had been made for McArthur and Pritchard at the Bull in Aylesbury and the three detectives decided to call it a day.

10

*N*ow – *the angry questions, IT MAY TOP £2,500,000!* was the front-page headline of the *Daily Express* on Friday, 9 August 1963. The article began predictably with the question 'How could it have happened?' with a small inset picture of a tense-looking Postmaster General Bevins at London Airport after curtailing his summer holiday. In the third paragraph the article claimed that Scotland Yard was mounting 'a fantastic manhunt'. While the editorial team at the *Express* had obtained an impressively accurate estimate of the amount of money stolen, their information about the scale of the Yard's contribution was something of an overstatement, given that Commander Hatherill had assigned only two men to the investigation.

Mr Bevins was quoted as saying that he was 'disturbed'. 'I want to find out why the precautions taken were not adequate,' he said.

There appears to have been no follow-up question as to what those precautions were. And Bevins would have struggled to provide a convincing answer, given that security precautions for the TPO were non-existent.

The subject was touched on when Bevins was interviewed by *The Times*. Asked whether there was an alarm system in place between the engine and carriages, the Postmaster General said that he would rather not answer, adding, 'It would help these people.'

But the criminals did not require any further help from Mr Bevins; they had already helped themselves to the contents of the mail train. Bevins went on to say that after a sixty-minute discussion with security chiefs at the GPO Headquarters he was 'uncomfortable' because 'clearly our security arrangements have not been satisfactory'.

Early on Friday morning, Fewtrell returned to the scene of the crime with McArthur while Pritchard remained at Aylesbury Police HQ to help organise the incident room. Fewtrell's and McArthur's working relationship must have got off to an uncertain start when the

Buckinghamshire Detective Superintendent walked on to the platform at Cheddington station with his esteemed colleague from Scotland Yard to find the locomotive and parcel van had vanished. All they saw in the sidings, surrounded by the gently waving stalks of overgrown grass, was the battered old HVP carriage with its roof felt cracked and peeling.

Having already made one grave error of judgement in moving the locomotive and parcel van to Cheddington sidings before the fingerprint experts arrived on the day of the robbery, Detective Superintendent Ward of British Transport Police had subsequently decided, in consultation with Detective Sergeant Fairweather of Buckinghamshire CID, that the engine and parcel carriage could be released. When he was asked for an explanation, Ward said that he was 'anxious the locomotive and parcel van got back into service'. In a surprising misjudgement, the senior British Transport Police Detective-Superintendent had hampered the chances of the Scotland Yard forensics specialists finding anything useful on board the mobile crime scene.

After incensed telephone calls from Buckinghamshire police the English Electric Class 40 locomotive D326 was eventually located in Crewe. The parcel van had ended up at Windermere. Both were returned to Cheddington the following day.

In the meantime Fewtrell showed McArthur over the HVP coach. They examined the broken couplings and pipes, the cupboards in which the mailbags had been stored. At Bridego Bridge the detectives walked the track and looked at the two signals that had been rigged at Sears Crossing. For the first time the man from Scotland Yard faced the stark reality of what the robbery had entailed and the hard evidence there was to work with.

Back at Aylesbury the detectives discussed what they had seen, what they knew, what witnesses had said and what they could deduce from it. In his memoir, Fewtrell recalls Pritchard picking up on the warning one of the robbers had given to Mills, Whitby, Penn, Kett, O'Connor and Dewhurst – 'Don't move for half an hour.' If the gang had gone to earth somewhere locally, Pritchard surmised, was that a clue to how far they needed to travel?

In national news broadcasts on the morning of Friday, 9 August 1963 it was announced that the search would encompass a thirty-mile radius of the crime scene, with special focus on all isolated farms and buildings. Members of the public were asked to be on the lookout and to report anything suspicious.

Hearing this latest information on the BBC Radio news, the robbers felt more precarious than ever in their hideaway. How long would it be before Buckinghamshire police came up the track to Leatherslade Farm? Isolated in the middle of unfamiliar country, the gang of sixteen men was stranded, with over two and half million in stolen banknotes to transport and no means of escape.

A year after the robbery the *Sunday Telegraph* published an article with the headline *How We Caught the Train Robbers*, written by retired Detective Superintendent Malcolm Fewtrell with the help of the newspaper's reporter on the case, Ronald Payne. Serialised over two weeks, the first instalment appeared on Sunday, 19 April 1964, and featured Fewtrell's claim that he was responsible for announcing the search area to the press. He went on to explain:

> Probably the robbers listened to the radio, for criminals always want to know what the police are doing and they must have felt that everybody was against them. By co-operating with reporters who gathered in Aylesbury we launched a psychological warfare campaign against the villains. It made them nervous and forced them to act more quickly than they had planned.

Fewtrell's claim had a logic to it but it seems strange that a policeman would want the men he is hunting to know what he is doing, where and how he is going to look for them. It was not like flushing an animal from its lair and catching it as it attempted to make an escape. That would depend on having some idea of where the quarry had gone to earth.

In a Home Office report into the mail-train robbery, commissioned by Sir Edward Dodd, Chief Inspector of Constabulary, and delivered to the Home Secretary on 6 October 1964, Fewtrell's assertion that releasing information to the press had been key to the police investigation was called into question:

> In an endeavour to flush the thieves from their hideout the press were

informed that the investigating officers had reason to believe that the thieves and loot were concealed within a thirty-mile radius of the scene of the crime. Nevertheless, no action was taken to set up road-blocks and checkpoints so that the thieves might be intercepted if they did endeavour to move.

Under recommendations for the future the report concluded:

Before publicity is given to a particular aspect of criminal investigation, the officer in charge of the investigation should ensure that he has made adequate arrangements to deal with any possible results from the release of such information.

Radio news broadcasts in the twenty-four hours following the robbery undoubtedly prompted the gang to evacuate the farm earlier than originally planned. Had Fewtrell not released details of the search area it's more than likely that the thieves would have stuck to their original timetable and stayed at the farm, waiting for things to die down, secure in the belief that their hideout was safe. The police would then have had a real chance of capturing them before they bolted.

At 05.08 on Thursday, 8 August, just over an hour and a half after the robbery, the quick-thinking Inspector Mellows from Linslade had suggested that arrangements be made to search isolated farms and buildings. Had Buckinghamshire detectives pursued this line of investigation they might have checked with local estate agents such as Midland Mart in Market Square, Bicester, for farm properties that had been let or sold in recent weeks. Leatherslade Farm would then have featured as a possible contender for the robbers' hideaway. Further investigation in the locality would have established that there was a group of recently arrived strangers in residence, and the police could have surrounded the farm, arrested the whole gang and recovered all the stolen money.

While hindsight is a wonderful thing, it would have required no more than straightforward detective work. In the pre-property boom, rural Buckinghamshire of 1963, people were less transient; there were fewer property transactions and fewer estate agents. To telephone every agent in the locality would have taken no more than an hour or two.

Had the police focused on this simple line of inquiry, the case would have been solved by the weekend.

Fewtrell's desire to tell his story and 'set the record straight' did not end with the newspaper article. His book, *The Train Robbers* – also published under *Sunday Telegraph* copyright and drawing on the 'help and guidance' of reporter Ronald Payne – continued the theme. The detective was later criticised in a Home Office report, which pointed out that since Fewtrell officially retired on 11 April, only eight days before the first instalment of his 50,000-word account was published in the *Telegraph*, 'at the time of writing the article he was a serving police officer'.

Thirty-six years later, at the age of ninety, Fewtrell corrected his claim about the thirty-mile search area in an interview for a 1999 Channel 4 television series, *Secret History*. He said that in the 1963 press conference what he had actually said was that he believed the gang to be concealed thirty minutes' drive from the crime scene. This was based on the warning of the departing robbers. But when his statement was reported it was misquoted as him saying the police believed the gang were within thirty miles – not minutes – of the crime scene. And thirty miles was what the gang heard on the radio. Given Fewtrell's correction, the misreporting was an extraordinary piece of luck for the police as the gang's hideout was actually over an hour's drive from the crime scene but it was twenty-eight miles away – just within the reported thirty-mile search area.

In the aftermath of the news broadcast that Friday morning, various gang members embarked on a spending spree, acquiring an odd assortment of vehicles in a manner reminiscent of an Ealing Comedy. It began with Cordrey purchasing a second-hand Wolseley in Oxford. He then drove it back to the farm, collected his 'whack' (share) and returned to Oxford with Jimmy White. Their first port of call was 28 Edith Road, the lodgings Cordrey had arranged before the robbery with Mrs Ida Louise Pope. White helped unload two suitcases containing Cordrey's whack into the ground-floor front room of the house.

Cordrey and White then drove to the nearby village of Black Bourton to see a car that had been advertised for sale in a local paper at £370. According to a statement later made by the vendor, John Steven

Bridego Bridge
(National Archive/Buckinghamshire Police)

HVP coach interior
(National Archive/ Buckinghamshire Police)

HVP coach at
Cheddington Station,
8 August 1963
(Getty Images)

Fewtrell and
McArthur
inspecting
broken coupling
and vacuum pipe,
August 1963
(Mirror Pix)

Crowbar found on track (staged press photo – note photographers), 8 August 1963
(Getty Images)

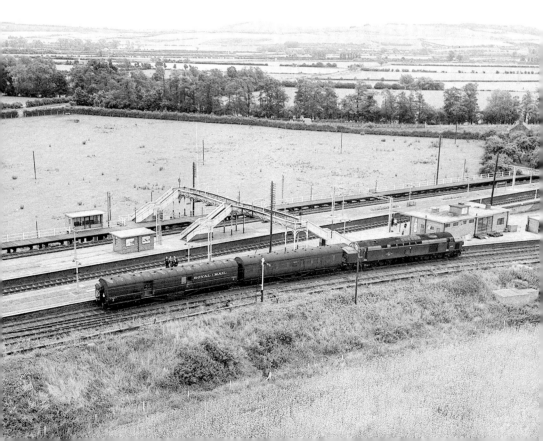

Engine 'D326', Bogie brake van and HVP coach at Cheddington Station, 8 August 1963
(Mirror Pix)

Ronald Biggs
(Press Association)

Roger Cordrey
(Press Association)

John Daly
(Press Association)

Buster Edwards
(Press Association)

Brian Field
(Getty Images)

Leonard Field
(Getty Images)

Gordon Goody
(Getty Images)

James Hussey
(Press Association)

Roy James
(Popperfoto/Getty Images)

Bruce Reynolds
(Popperfoto/Getty Images)

Robert Welch
(Daily Telegraph)

John Wheater
(Daily Telegraph)

James White
(Popperfoto/Getty Images)

Charles Wilson
(Daily Telegraph)

Thomas Wisbey
(Popperfoto/Getty Images)

William Boal
(Press Association)

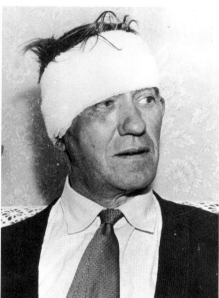

Jack Mills
(Getty Images)

David Whitby
(Mirror Pix)

Malcolm Fewtrell (left)
Gerald McArthur (right)
(Getty Images)

Tommy Butler
(Mirror Pix)

Commander George Hath-
erill (Getty Images)

Ernie Millen
(Associated Newspapers/Rex Features)

Frank Williams
(Getty Images)

Peter Vibart
(Daily Mail/Solo Syndication)

Jack Slipper
(Getty Images)

Furnival, Cordrey arrived at about 11.15 with another man who was wearing dark glasses and did not get out of the car. Cordrey seemed nervous and after a test drive in the vehicle – a blue and grey Rover 105R, registration number TLX 279 – he made an offer of £360. Furnival accepted but said he didn't have the log book to hand and would have to forward it later. Cordrey gave his name as Mr A.E. Tomkins and his address as 23 Burnthwaite Road, Fulham, SW6. It was the home of his forty-nine-year-old friend William Boal, whom he later telephoned to ask for help.

Jimmy White then returned to the farm in the Wolseley, collected Mr One, and set off for London taking their share of the money with them. Why White departed with only one passenger is not known. Perhaps he felt that more than two men in the car might arouse suspicion.

Only Reynolds recounts his own improvised departure from Leatherslade Farm in any detail. He says that early on Friday morning he left the farm and started walking into Thame, which lies six and a half miles to the south-east. He was dressed respectably and claims to have been offered a lift from a couple of 'Colonel types' as he was walking along the B4011 Thame Road. In the town he met with Manson and her friend Rene who, after receiving the telephone phone call from Cordrey the previous day, had driven up from Wimbledon early that morning in a van with some furniture in the back.

Leaving Manson and Rene in town, Reynolds drove the van back to the farm, collected Daly, loaded up their 'whacks' and returned to Thame. Manson then drove the van back to London while Reynolds and Daly caught a Greenline bus to Victoria coach station in London. From there they took a taxi to Manson's house in Wimbledon. They collected the van, delivered their loot to a lock-up garage Reynolds had recently rented and hid it behind piles of furniture.

At 13.00 Cordrey met Boal, a short, red-faced man with a Durham accent and thick tortoiseshell glasses, at the Public Library in Oxford. According to Piers Paul Read's book, Cordrey had said on the telephone that if Boal came to Oxford he would repay the £650 he owed him. Boal was short of money due to a recent illness and therefore keen to collect the debt.

They returned to Mrs Pope's modest Victorian terraced house in Edith Road, where Cordrey showed Boal the two suitcases he had unloaded earlier with White. Apparently he did not divulge the contents but simply told Boal that he needed to stash them somewhere safe and if Boal helped him he would be in a position to repay the £650.

While it is certain that Boal did go to Oxford that day to meet up with Cordrey, it is questionable why Boal would have agreed to go all that way without some kind of explanation. Nevertheless, Boal's claimed ignorance of Cordrey's involvement with the train robbery is hard to disprove.

Meanwhile Reynolds was busy in London. According to car salesman Dennis Kenneth St John, at 16.00 that Friday afternoon Reynolds called at the Chequered Flag Garage in Chiswick. After taking a brief test drive in a black Austin Healey, registration number 222NFC, Reynolds agreed to buy the sports car for £835 and said he would return later to collect it. At 18.30 he duly arrived with Mary Manson, who paid for the car in five-pound notes. Manson gave the salesman her real name but supplied her previous address: 209 Mitcham Lane, Streatham, London, SW16. The couple made arrangements to bring the car back the following day to be serviced, as Reynolds said they were planning a trip to Europe. They never did return.

Having reached London in the Wolseley with Mr One at 17.30, Jimmy White purchased another Austin Healey, registration number REN22, for £900 from Allery & Bernard at 372/4 Kings Road, Chelsea. White gave his name as John Steward of Rock House, Chaunston Road, Taunton, Somerset. Like Manson, he paid the entire sum in five-pound notes.

When Postmaster General Bevins was interviewed again by the BBC his growing discomfort was clear. Despite the sociolinguistic fashion of the time for Received Pronunciation, when under pressure traces of his Liverpool origins became evident in his vowels. In the close-up black-and-white interview, Bevins' deeply lined brow appears shiny and his rather jumpy delivery of the previous day is further augmented by his animated eyebrows, bouts of rapid blinking and looking off to the side. Questioned about mail-train security, he says:

I think you've got to look at this against the background that these trains have made thousands and thousands of journeys without the slightest mishap, without the slightest loss of money over the last a hundred and twenty years. This is the first time it's happened.

It seems not to have occurred to the Postmaster General, or anyone one else in his organisation, that effective security requires anticipation and crime prevention rather than waiting for things to go wrong before doing something about it.

Commenting on the subject of these shortcomings, authors of *The Great Train Robbery* John Gosling and Dennis Craig are unequivo-cal: 'The fact that this was the first robbery was more a reflection on the enterprise of past generations of criminals than on the difficulties placed in their way by Post Office Security.'

It would be unfair to single out Reginald Bevins. His attitude was typical of the atrophied thinking in the establishment at the time. It certainly did little to stem the burgeoning crime rate during the two decades following World War Two. To borrow the title of Donald Thomas' 2005 book on crime in Britain during the fifties and early sixties, the country had become a *Villains' Paradise*.

The unseen BBC interviewer, in a relaxed and courteous baritone reminiscent of a Bird and Fortune comedy sketch, challenged Bevins: 'Did the railway and the Post Office authorities on this occasion know that there was two and a half million pounds on this train?'

Bevins' eyes visibly flinch as the sum is mentioned. Realising where this line of questioning is heading, his tongue darts in and out between dry lips revealing heavily tobacco-stained lower teeth before he replies, 'Not with precision. No.'

The interviewer then asks, 'Well, isn't this rather extraordinary, if you are taking this amount of money about, that you don't *know* how much you've got?'

Bevins' tongue darts again and he gazes into the middle distance, hurriedly formulating his reply. 'No, there's nothing extraordinary in that at all. We know that on these overnight trains, we're constantly carrying very large sums of money, perhaps a million one night, two million the next, three million the next, but there are no means within the Post Office, or indeed with our customers, of collating the actual totals that travel on any particular train.'

Before Bevins' final sentence is complete the film cuts to the interviewer, an earnest blond young man in a striped shirt, who looks too young to be the owner of a voice with such assured authority: 'Well, are you blaming British Railways?'

The Postmaster General's chin drops and he gives a sheepish look. 'No, I'm not saying that at the moment.' After a fleeting grimace his face relaxes and the hint of a lopsided smile forms as it dawns on him that someone else could be held to blame. Bevins appears to take further comfort in the next question, shifting the focus away from the open door through which the horse had so obviously bolted (an idiom used earlier in the interview):

'Are you more convinced than you were yesterday that this may be an inside job?'

Looking down into his lap for the first half of his reply, Bevins says cagily, 'Well, when I was asked the question yesterday I said I did not rule out the possibility of it being an inside job. I don't rule that out now.'

The short film clip ends on that typical politician's fudge, the sound cutting out a few seconds before the vision, denying viewers the chance of hearing the qualifying statement that followed.

Bevins' initial public statements, like those of the police, were largely true. But the emphasis on the extraordinary nature of the train ambush helped to mask the underlying circumstances that had allowed it to happen and the liabilities of those responsible. The press didn't delve too deeply; they were happy with the headlines it gave them and created the world's first media crime.

The nation was captivated, not simply by the scale of the robbery, but by the real-life cops-and-robbers story unfolding hour by hour. Extensive reporting in the newspapers, radio and television was providing a level of detail, immediacy and intimacy which was new and fascinating. The mail-train robbery was the centre of discussion at work, in pubs, and at home, and the Great British Public could hardly wait for the next exciting instalment.

11

A t some point during Friday, 9 August there was an about-turn in police policy with the press. A report on BBC Television later that day had a very different tone to earlier broadcasts. The film begins with three establishing shots. The first features Detectives Fewtrell, McArthur and Pritchard awkwardly stepping through long summer grass at Cheddington railway sidings, walking away from the HVP. Fewtrell is identifiable by his full head of white hair; McArthur looks rather formal by today's standards, with a crisp white handkerchief in the breast pocket of his dark suit jacket and, despite it being August, a trilby. Also in a suit is Detective Sergeant Pritchard, following close behind. In the second shot, taken at Bridego Bridge, three young men in suits are looking earnest and a little bewildered. The third opens with two men in brown cotton coats carrying cameras, one hand-held and the other on a tripod, at a service bridge linking farmland near Sears Crossing. The TV shot pans left to reveal the Buckinghamshire police Austin A55 photography van in the background. By the open rear door of the van a Jack Russell terrier looks inquisitively into the lens of the film camera.

The BBC reporter, standing beside neatly manicured flowerbeds at the featureless entrance to the new Buckinghamshire Police HQ, informs viewers:

> At a press conference here at the headquarters of the Buckinghamshire county police, the police spokesmen haven't been giving very much away. Detective Superintendent Gerry McArthur of Scotland Yard said that they had been concentrating their inquiries at the scene of the crime. They were trying to get as much information as they could as to how the job had been done. He said he didn't like discussing theories. They were fighting a gang that was obviously well organised and it would be ridiculous for him to tell them what he was doing. The Detective Superintendent said that everybody who could help had

been called in. Members of the public had come forward with a great deal of information which was being sifted and he appealed again for anybody who thought they could help the police to come forward and do so. He was asked if he thought the gang or the money had got out of the country. Mr McArthur said that even if the gang had got out of the country he didn't think that the money had. But he wasn't saying of course that the gang had in any case. He said there was no truth at all in the rumour that the police had had a tip-off that the raid was going to take place on the mail train.

Far from having left the country, most of the gang were engaged in trying to get out of Buckinghamshire. Unsurprisingly, there are several conflicting accounts of what took place during their final exit from Leatherslade Farm.

During the course of Friday evening a series of vehicles converged on the farm. One of these was a Commer van driven by Brian Field, who arrived in convoy with his wife, Karin, driving their Jaguar. Field has never revealed his precise involvement in the mail-train robbery. Beyond his proven collusion in the acquisition of Leatherslade Farm, we must rely on the robbers' account that it was Field who first approached Gordon Goody saying that he knew a man with inside information about mail trains. That places Field as the instigator of the crime. It is probable that he never intended to get closely involved with the actual robbery, but his trip to the farm on the evening of Friday, 9 August with a van acquired by means unknown implies that his direct assistance had become vital to his co-conspirators. If Field was to avoid being implicated, he had no choice but to make sure the gang evaded capture.

Despite using Leonard Field as a front for the purchase, Brian had not seriously considered the possibility that the farm might be discovered and connected to the robbery. The negotiations and correspondence had left a paper trail which led straight to his employer, James and Wheater, and there was already a link through the law firm's defence of Goody and Wilson following the BOAC wages robbery the previous year.

In May 1964, Brian Field's German wife, Karin, was behind the publication of a series of articles in the magazine *Stern* written by journalist Henry Kolarz. Kolarz later went on to write the screenplay for a hugely popular German television series entitled *Die Gentlemen bitten zur Kasse*, a much-romanticised account of the mail-train raid starring Horst Tappert.

The Kolarz articles in *Stern*, based on information provided by Karin, went under the title '*Das Super Ding* [The Super Crime] – *The Great Train Robbery*'. The second of the *Stern* instalments, published on 17 May 1964, contained many details unique to Karin's account.

In her version of events, Brian received a phone call at their home that Friday evening from a man he did not know, requesting that he go to Leatherslade Farm as soon as possible. This was followed at 23.30 by the arrival of two men, whom neither Karin nor her husband knew. While Brian stayed at home, too shaken by the prospect of getting so closely involved to participate, Karin was coerced into driving their Jaguar to the farm, accompanied by Maxi, her black miniature poodle, and one of the men.

Karin describes being told to stop at the entrance. Roy James then climbed into the back of the car and asked her to drive him to Thame station. Finding that there were no late trains, Karin took James all the way to Pembridge Square, Bayswater. On the way they passed several checkpoints but were waved through as the police were only stopping vans and lorries. Having dropped James, Karin drove back to the farm alone, arriving just before 02.00.

On her return to Leatherslade Farm she was given a walkie-talkie and told to retrace the route to her home, keeping a lookout for police and roadblocks. In convoy behind her were two vans containing eight of the gang – Goody, Edwards, Wilson, Welch, Hussey, Wisbey, plus two other men whom she calls George and John – along with their loot.

Leaving aside whether Brian Field was part of this escapade – Karin goes out of her way to minimise her husband's involvement in the conspiracy and robbery – the major inconsistency in the *Stern* account is that the events are said to take place on Thursday evening rather than Friday, with the gang having miraculously obtained two vans. Alternative accounts, in which Brian Field takes James to London and is thus instrumental in organising transport for the gang, seem more plausible.

Furthermore, while under oath in court, Karin Field stated that she and her husband had no visitors between 7 and 11 August. Yet in the *Stern* articles, published a matter of weeks after her appearance in the witness box, she admits that eight of the gang came to her house on the night of Friday, 9 August. The reason for this impromptu visit by eight wanted criminals was apparently because they were alarmed by the news that all farms within a thirty-mile radius of the robbery were to be searched. Despite this astonishing and flagrant admission of her involvement, Karin Field was never charged with perjury, or aiding and abetting the mail-train robbers.

Another, more credible, version of the Friday-evening escape plan has Reynolds returning to the farm in his newly acquired Austin Healey, along with Manson in her black Ford Cortina, and Daly behind the wheel of a second van. Leaving the van at the farm for others to use, Daly and Old Pop the train driver departed with Mary Manson in her Cortina, while Biggs went with Reynolds. The Austin Healey did not offer the most practical or inconspicuous alternative transport as they made their exit through the rural roads of Buckinghamshire, but that seems to have been beyond Reynolds' foresight.

One detail the accounts of the robbers all agree on is that a group of eight – consisting of Goody, Edwards, Wilson, Welch, Hussey, Wisbey, Mr Two and Mr Three – set off from the farm on Friday evening in two vans and travelled to the Fields' house, 'Kabri' (the name was a composite of Karin and Brian), in Bridle Road, Whitchurch Hill, near Reading. This neat, 1960s detached home, overlooking woods and tucked away up an unmade track among a scattering of other cottages and houses, was around forty minutes' drive from Leatherslade Farm. On the face of it, Kabri offered the advantage of seclusion. But as with Leatherslade Farm, the privacy of the rural setting was an illusion. Rural communities notice comings and goings that are out of the ordinary.

In statements later taken by the police, the Fields' neighbours reported they could not sleep owing to a number of vehicles arriving at Kabri late that Friday night. A blue Commer Dormobile (camper van) was seen in the garage, another van in the driveway, while the Fields' Jaguar was left parked in the narrow lane outside.

In Read's book the robbers describe how they backed one van into the garage, parked the other in the drive and unloaded the money into the house. The eight men then bedded down on sofas and armchairs, apart from the smooth-talking Goody, who already knew Brian and Karin Field and commandeered their spare bedroom.

*

Headlines and articles about the mail-train robbery dominated the newspapers, radio and television reports throughout that Friday. In addition to a £10,000 reward offered by the Postmaster General, the insurance loss adjusters for the banks, Hart and Company Adjusters & Valuers, put up a further £25,000.

The *Daily Mirror* was quick to work out that the 'red light trick' had been used in November 1960, to stop a London-bound train, and again in March 1961, to hold up a Waterloo to Teddington train – *this was the ninth major train robbery in the south-east of England in the past three years*. This statistic is not mentioned in the report commissioned by HM Chief Inspector of Constabulary at the Home Office, but given the spate of robberies on trains at the time it seems all the more extraordinary that mail trains were left unprotected. Although Bevins had been keen to point out that a mail train had never been robbed before, the frequency of trains being ambushed by bandits in southern England was only rivalled by the exploits of the Jesse James gang in the Wild West.

Page four of the *Daily Express* featured a large cartoon by Cummings. It depicted a train coming off the tracks, railway workers gagged and bound at the trackside, and the engine driver reading a newspaper with the headline *Great Train Robbery Big Haul*. The caption read: '*Pah – that's nothing compared with the Great Beeching railway robbery ...*' Dr Richard Beeching had been the main author of an unpopular report, 'The Reshaping of British Railways', which made cost-saving suggestions that over the following decade would result in the closure of more than 4,000 miles of railway and 3,000 stations, a reduction of 25 per cent of rail track and 50 per cent of stations.

On page two of the *Daily Express* was a speculative piece headed *Mastermind with rule of silence* that expounded: 'It is almost certain that one man plotted the raid.' After setting out an elaborate scenario as to how the gang's leader obtained inside information and recruited suitable manpower, the author finally concludes that the men's loyalty and commitment would have been secured through a substantial down payment: 'Afterwards, raiders go their own ways knowing the haul will not be touched and distributed for several weeks.'

If the hypothesis of that *Express* journalist had been correct, the mail-train robbery would have been executed with wider perspective and the long-term consequences in mind. Most critically, the robbers' exit once they had carried out the robbery would have been a very different story. With a single mastermind behind it, the plan for what happened after the robbery would have been as carefully orchestrated rather than dictated by individual concerns, knee-jerk responses and self-interest. With two disused RAF airfields close to the crime scene the entire gang and their haul could theoretically have been airborne before the alarm was raised. How difficult would it have been in those hard-up times, in a country still struggling in the shadow of war, to have found a broke and disenchanted ex-serviceman like Jimmy White to fly a plane? With former War Department aircraft still littering the country, it would have been easy to buy or steal one rather than relying on an old ex-MOD lorry. Given the ease with which fifteen determined criminals were able to raid the mail train and drive off with over two and a half million pounds in banknotes, in all probability, with a Mastermind behind it, the gang could all have got clean away.

Interviewing Reynolds in 2009, I asked him about why the Land Rovers had identical registration numbers. His reply was that one of them had a valid road fund licence so they first drove one to the farm and then used the tax disc on the other vehicle. It was a revealing insight into the level of financial and intellectual investment the gang made in their preparations for 'the crime of the century'.

By midnight on Friday 9 August 1963, the sixteen men who had held up and robbed the mail train were out of the thirty-mile search area along with their loot. But their premature departure had meant they had to hurry and leave things behind. Nevertheless, the two Land Rovers were out of sight, padlocked in garages. In a shed the Austin lorry, now looking less like the 'army-type lorry' the police were looking for with its cab painted yellow, was covered with a green tarpaulin. If the police came up the drive in the next few days they would simply find an empty house. With a huge search area to cover and hundreds of farms they would have no immediate reason to connect Leatherslade Farm to the mail-train robbery twenty-eight miles away. And anyway, even if they did, what could they do? The bandits and their stolen money were gone.

12

In a 1999 interview for the Channel 4 documentary series *Secret History*, John Cummings, Head of Scotland Yard's Intelligence branch in 1963, said that within twelve hours of the robbery he spoke to a regular informant he calls 'Mickie'. Mickie, himself an armed robber, apparently gave Cummings the names of six men who he said were involved in the mail-train raid: Hussey, Wisbey, Welch, Wilson, Reynolds and Daly. The programme suggested that Mickie could have been a man called Michael David Kehoe. At the time Kehoe was certainly a known member of the South London underworld. His legitimate business was 'car hirer' and he was living at Barry Road, East Dulwich. In the *Secret History* programme Freddie Foreman dismissed the suggestion, as did Gordon Goody, but another notorious 1960s armed robber, John McVicar, said that he thought it was possible Mickie Kehoe had supplied Cummings with information about the mail-train raid. McVicar believed Kehoe had once informed on him after an armed robbery in which the two of them had participated. While McVicar was convicted, Kehoe, though arrested, was never charged.

In Oxford, William Boal had come up with a suggestion. He told Cordrey that he had friends in Bournemouth who might be able to help. Boal stayed Friday night in an upstairs room at Mrs Ida Pope's lodgings at 28 Edith Road and the following morning he and Cordrey set off for Bournemouth in Cordrey's Rover, leaving the two suitcases containing Cordrey's whack at Edith Road.

It was ninety miles from Oxford to Bournemouth and took over two hours. According to the account in Read's book, the two men then spent a further hour trying to find the house where Boal's friends lived. When they finally located it, Cordrey stayed out of sight in the car while Boal went to the house.

Despite nationwide publicity in the press, on TV and radio, and police appeals for help from the public, it did not occur to the former owner of Leatherslade Farm, Bernard Rixon, or his family that there could be a connection between the buyers and the mail-train robbery.

All the while, the eight members of the gang who had bunked down at the Fields' house in Whitchurch Hill were making plans for the next stage of their getaway. Brian and Karin Field were keen to get the fugitives and their loot out of their respectable home. Karin's account in *Stern* magazine describes wives and girlfriends arriving during the course of Saturday. Not surprisingly, all the unusual comings and goings over the weekend attracted further attention of the Fields' neighbours.

The robbers' version of events has Field driving some of the gang into Reading on Saturday morning. There they bought two more second-hand vehicles, a car and a van, and some suitcases. On their return to Kabri, they loaded up their vehicles and Welch and Wisbey then set off for the south coast.

Edwards was collected by a friend. His wife June was in the car with their daughter Nicolette. Buster, 'as jovial as ever', loaded his loot into the boot and they drove to a friend's house in Kingston-upon-Thames. Roy James turned up at Kabri in his Mini Cooper to collect Charlie Wilson. Having prepared Wilson's 'stow' in the East End, James returned later in the day to collect their money.

Goody was the only member of the gang who remained behind. He was later joined by his fiancée, nineteen-year-old Pat Cooper. They spent a further night at Kabri before finally departing on Sunday morning.

Gordon Goody was one of only two members of the gang who had prepared any kind of alibi. With the robbery originally planned for the early hours of Wednesday, 7 August, Goody travelled to Ireland on Friday, 2 August with his mother and a man called Knowles who bore a strong resemblance to Goody. Under the name McGonegal, Goody subsequently returned to England alone on Tuesday, 6 August, having arranged that his mother and Knowles, who now travelled in Goody's name, would return to England one day later. Thus it would appear that Goody was in Ireland with his mother at the time of the robbery. It may not have been a cast-iron alibi, but it was at least an attempt at one.

The rest of the gang had already gathered at Leatherslade Farm by Tuesday afternoon. By early evening, there was still no sign of Goody and they were getting edgy, wondering if he was going to show up and bring final confirmation that the job was on.

There was great relief when Goody finally arrived at 23.00 clutching a bottle of Jameson's whiskey, having been given a lift by Brian Field. But the mood quickly turned when Goody gave them the news that when the Ulsterman had telephoned him at Field's house, as arranged, he'd said the robbery should be postponed for twenty-four hours because the anticipated large consignment of money was not due to be transported until the following night.

The gang were all hyped up and ready to go. The last-minute change of plan severely tested them and their faith in the information on which the robbery had been planned and on which they were all about to risk their liberty.

When Goody had first heard the news he must have been more sickened than the rest. His carefully laid alibi was now effectively useless. But Goody had plenty of nerve. He was clever and resourceful. Once over the initial disappointment that the raid was to be delayed, he still had guile and ingenuity on his side.

Peta Fordham, who seems to have been rather seduced by Goody (not literally), describes him as wolfish and draws a favourable portrait of him in her book, *The Robbers' Tale*. Goody was certainly known as a ladies' man but there was a contradiction about him. The playboy image with a taste for expensive restaurants and stylish living was undermined by the fact that the smooth-talking Gordon Goody lived in a small cottage at Commondale in Putney with his mum.

In his biography, Reynolds gives an illustration of Goody's nature, good luck and bravado. In 1962 Goody had been arrested and charged for his part in the £62,000 BOAC wages snatch at London Airport. When his case came to trial there were several things stacked against him. The bolt cutters used to cut the chain across the perimeter gate at the airport were found in one of the abandoned getaway cars and subsequently traced back to him. The alibi that Brian Field had helped him to construct sounded less than convincing when challenged by the prosecution. A witness had identified Goody as one of the assailants and said he had been wearing a checked cap. A cap had been found in the foyer of Comet House after the robbery, having fallen from Goody's head in the struggle and been forgotten as he made a quick exit.

Undeterred, Goody still managed to get bail. He followed a member of the jury home and the next morning intercepted him on his way to court. His instincts about the man he had observed in the courtroom proved correct. The juryman was sympathetic to Goody's appeal and even refused the payment he was offered. At the end of the trial the jury was unable to agree a verdict and, despite his best efforts to resolve it, the judge was forced to order a retrial.

Next time around Goody decided to skew the evidence more in his favour. A £200 bribe was sufficient inducement for a police officer to swap an identical checked cap that Goody provided with the original one that had been found at the crime scene. As further insurance, Goody took Wilson and Edwards with him to Harrow to visit the witness who had identified him. By what means can only be guessed at, but the witness was persuaded to agree that when giving evidence he would ask to see Goody in the cap to confirm his identification of him. In court the next day when Goody was asked to step forward and put the cap on his head, it was several sizes too big and comically came down over his ears and eyes.

As Goody walked from the dock having been acquitted, he passed the prosecution barrister, who smiled knowingly and congratulated him. On the bench was the chain that had been cut from the airport gate. Before the robbery, the gang had replaced the original chain with one of their own, which had a special link that could be easily pulled apart by hand. However, in the heat of the escape the raiders had not been able to find the magic link and had cut the chain. Goody stopped at the prosecution bench, picked up the chain, casually undid the link, placed it in front of the prosecution counsel and walked out of court. Although the anecdote may have been embellished, Goody was acquitted for his part in the airport robbery despite the evidence against him and having stood trial twice.

When Ronnie Biggs had arrived home at 37 Alpine Road, Redhill, Surrey, with a suitcase full of money he had a lot of explaining to do. Before they married, his wife had made Biggs promise that he would go straight.

A headmaster's daughter, Charmian had met her future husband on a commuter train to London Bridge. Biggs had boarded the train two stops after her. Charmian later said that she was swept along by the attention. What she did not know about the charming and good-looking young man she met on the way to work was that he was already living with another woman. Biggs was twenty-eight at the time and his live-in lover was in her forties. When the older woman found out that he was seeing Charmian she went to the police. She asked them to inform Charmian's father that his daughter was going out with a criminal.

Charmian's family tried to intervene but, much to her parents' despair, she ignored their warnings and the couple ran away. It was at that point in their relationship that Charmian made Biggs promise her that after they were married he would 'never engage in any criminal activity again'. She believed that with her love and the stability of family life Biggs could be reformed.

Under the influence of his more honest and devoted wife, Biggs started a small building business in Redhill. After the birth of their first child the family moved into a rented house in Alpine Road. When the chance to buy their home presented itself Charmian saw it as the next step towards building a respectable, stable and secure future. But in order to make this happen, Biggs would need to find five hundred pounds' deposit, a sum he could not hope to raise from his fledgling business. He told Charmian that he might be able to borrow the money and made the fateful telephone call to his old friend Bruce Reynolds. Biggs' decision to take part in the mail-train robbery turned out to be a point of no return for the small-time thief, setting his and his family's lives spiralling into one of the most extraordinary stories in British criminal history.

Before leaving for the robbery, Biggs told Charmian that he was going on a tree-felling job in Wiltshire to raise money towards the deposit for the house. When news of the mail-train raid broke, Charmian had no reason to connect it with her husband. In any case, she had been preoccupied with trying to contact him about the untimely death of his brother, Jack, who had died aged fifty of a heart attack while Biggs was away.

Charmian had been so frantic she innocently called the local police, saying she needed to inform her husband of his brother's death. Wiltshire police were contacted and asked to try and locate Biggs, but they later reported back saying that despite extensive searches and inquiries across the county they had been unable to find him.

When Ronnie Biggs walked through the door of his house and found a distressed Charmian he faced several conflicting emotions: the sad news of Jack's death; Charmian's revelation that she had tried in vain to contact him and called the police, and that he had just returned home with over £130,000 in used banknotes in his suitcase.

Telling Charmian that he was going tree-felling in Wiltshire was never an alibi in the proper sense, as there was no independent witness who could vouch for his whereabouts. It was an excuse constructed for his wife's benefit rather than a defence against police inquiries, but it might nonetheless have served both purposes had it not been for his brother's death. On returning home Biggs was faced with having to explain to his wife where he had really been, and that he had earned considerably more than the £500 deposit they needed. Whatever slant the conversation took, Charmian's desire that she and her husband would live a good and honest life was to be shattered and subverted in ways that she could never have imagined when she first started talking to a handsome young man on the train to London Bridge.

In Bournemouth, on Saturday, 10 August, the developing farce involving Boal and Cordrey deepened. Having driven ninety miles and then spent a further hour trying to find the right house, Boal returned to the car where Cordrey was waiting and broke the news that his friends no longer lived there. They had moved away several years before. There is no record of what Cordrey said, but he decided to cut his losses and find somewhere else to stay.

Some time later that afternoon, Mr Henry Stewart Moulds of 69 Castle Lane, Bournemouth, received a telephone call in response to an advertisement for a three-bedroom holiday flat above his florist's shop at 935 Wimborne Road, Moordown, Bournemouth. At 16.00 Moulds met a man at the property who introduced himself as Mr Thompson from Slough. Thompson agreed to rent the flat and paid Moulds a month's rent in advance – £58.16s. in five-pound and one-pound notes. Mr Thompson was later identified as William Boal.

With his friend's help, Cordrey had secured a new place to lie low, but he still needed to retrieve his money from 28 Edith Road. As the master criminal drove his sidekick to Winchester station to catch a train home to London, he gave him his instructions for the following day.

13

B ritish newspapers weren't the only ones running the mail-train robbery story. The front page of Saturday's *New York Times* carried the headline *The Great British Train Robbery*. The article began:

Not even the most jaded viewer of television crime epics is likely to yawn at yesterday's great English train robbery. We hope the imperturbable James Bond has been put on the case; undoubtedly Goldfinger or Dr. No is behind this incredibly efficient bit of larceny.

How pallid our own crime syndicates are made to look, how wanting in imagination. After all, we hold the copyright on train robbery. We even put them on film half a century ago in the first movie with a fully developed plot 'The Great Train Robbery', yet now the best we can say about this updating of Jesse James is that we supplied the cultural inspiration.

The know-how is distinctly British. Or were some enterprising members of the American underworld there in a patriotic effort to help even out our balance of international payments?

The plan to rob the Glasgow to London mail train was certainly more ambitious than anything any British criminal had previously attempted, involving more men and requiring a higher level of planning and organisation. It was a significant step up from even the most notorious raids carried out by London's gangs in the post-war years.

Eleven years before the mail-train raid, on Wednesday, 21 May 1952, the Eastcastle Street robbery, planned by London villain Billy Hill, assisted by Terry Hogan, was the first of a new type of crime. It had been well thought out and executed with precision and speed. The robbers sandwiched a Post Office van between two cars. The first car pulled out of a side street causing the van to slow down and a second car pulled up behind. The GPO driver and his two colleagues were dragged out and coshed and the van was driven away by Hogan. The

Post Office vehicle was later found near Regent's Park with eighteen of the original thirty-one mailbags missing. They had contained £287,000. The gang responsible included Billy Hill, George 'Taters' Chatham and Bruce Reynolds' close friend and associate Terry Hogan. The Prime Minister, Winston Churchill, called for daily updates on the investigation and the Postmaster General, Earl De La Warr, was asked to report to Parliament on what had gone wrong. Despite the best efforts of over a thousand police officers at the height of the investigation, none of the gang was ever apprehended or prosecuted.

Freddie Foreman's firm had been involved in an ambitious gold bullion heist on 24 May 1963. The gold was being delivered from Rothschild's Bank to bullion brokers Sharps Pixley & Co. at Paul Street in the City of London. The gang staked out Sharps Pixley for several weeks in order to time the job when fewest employees would be there. The raid involved just a handful of men and a Bedford van, and was executed in a matter of minutes. Foreman and his firm drove away with forty gold bars weighing twenty-seven pounds, each worth over fifteen million pounds at present gold prices. It remains one of the biggest gold thefts in London's history.

Those smash-and-grab raids were as much about nerve as planning and relied on poor security, intimidation, the element of surprise and speed. In a 2004 television programme entitled *Freddie Foreman – A Life of Crime*, Foreman described how easy blowing safes had been: '... the old black and tan safes, they were like a bit of butter to get into, you know, by today's standards. Security wasn't like it is today. They'd been there since the year dot. They hadn't changed. But when we started caning them open they soon changed then. It was a race against time.'

Commenting on the mail-train robbery, Foreman said he had declined an offer to go on the job and take part in the physical side of the raid. 'But they did manage quite well without us. It was very successful,' he said and paused before adding with a wry smile, 'up to a point.'

Another young London criminal who was just emerging at the time was armed-robber-turned-'super grass' Don Barrett. In a 1994 BBC Television documentary, *Underworld*, he talked about robbing security vans loaded with cash wages:

I have to admit in the early days we were rather like cowboys. We'd be six- or seven-handed and arrive in a van. It wasn't nice but, I can almost say, a foolproof way of getting the bag because it didn't matter how big he was or how tough he was, if someone hit you hard or sprayed ammonia on you, you was in very bad pain.

Robert Alles King was only twenty-two in 1963, but he was already quite clear about his career options. King was attracted to the lifestyle enjoyed by his criminal friends:

The other guys had really sharp cars, really nice suits, good-looking girlfriends, much more attractive lifestyle. So quite consciously I thought, I'd rather have some of that than some of this. And that's what started it off, I suppose. Ego came a lot into it because of the prestige it gave you. When you went out and pulled a girl you felt good 'cos you knew you had a tasty motor, you had a tasty whistle [suit], you had money and for many working-class women this was very attractive. It didn't matter if you were as ugly as sin with nil personality, you suddenly became a more attractive proposition. And that sort of feeling of being something gave you this more confident air.

We found robbing an ordinary bank a really easy place to rob but it didn't really have much of a pay-off because all you would get is what was in the counters and that was six, seven, eight, if you were very luck nine grand and we were three- or four-handed. You was just really wasting your time because you knew you was going to get ten or twelve years if you got caught for it. So it had to be a lot more.

But a bigger plan required bigger thinking and the mail-train gang did not give enough thought to what lay beyond the initial prize. What every one of the gang failed to comprehend is that money in any quantity never was going to be an end in itself.

Being wealthy was going to provide greater choice and control not only over the present but, more significantly, over their future. For the young working-class criminals brought up in a hand-to-mouth culture, that concept was alien. Despite the aspiration for a better life, 'the good life', driving the gang, it was the more abstract longer-term prospects after the robbery that seem to have been beyond their vision.

Reynolds told the story that shortly after the raid when the gang were discussing what they would each do with their money he said he was going to put his son's name down for Harrow: 'Winston Churchill had been to Harrow and that was good enough for my boy.'

Was the underlying motive for Reynolds' long record of theft and violence – the reason he bought his handmade suits in Savile Row, his shirts and shoes in Jermyn Street, smoked Monte Cristo cigars, and drove an Aston Martin – the dream that he and his family could one day be 'one of them'? This is in direct contrast to a comment Reynolds made in a 2001 interview for the ITV series *Real Crime*: '... the way I looked at it, society didn't care much for me and I didn't care much for society.' In later years both Foreman and Reynolds have said the way they saw it was they were stealing in order to get enough money to go straight.

Across the British press, there was speculation about the train having been sabotaged. It had become known that the HVP coach used in the mail train on the night of the robbery, serial number POSV 30204, was old rolling stock. There were three HVP coaches of a newer design in service, but in early August they were all out of action for maintenance.

The *Daily Mirror* devoted its front page to the suggestion of sabotage, claiming that the information had been 'revealed in London yesterday by Postmaster General, Reginald Bevins'. He was quoted as saying, 'I don't rule out the possibility that the vans were tampered with.'

The *Daily Express* revealed that the remark printed in the *Daily Mirror* was only a partial quote, and reported the Postmaster General's comment in full: 'I don't rule out the possibility that the vans were tampered with although I think it is unlikely.' But the article went on to speculate that the new-style HVP coaches had been sabotaged by the gang, reproducing another quote from Bevins, who was clearly hedging his bets: 'To say the least', Mr Bevins said, 'it is rather mysterious and coincidental that these three have broken down.'

While the Postmaster General's statements were ambiguous, a spokesman for British Railways made his position quite clear: 'There is no question of sabotage to any of the security coaches.'

Nevertheless, this latest debate in the press only served to fuel public perception that the mail-trail thieves really had thought of everything.

In his 1964 book *The Train Robbers*, Malcolm Fewtrell took the sabotage question from another angle: 'It seems to me that the robbers would have had little more difficulty with the newer model than with the old.'

A more significant insight into the state of the ongoing investigation came at the end of the *Daily Mirror* article: the reward on offer for information leading to the apprehension of the mail-train raiders and recovery of the stolen money was now £260,000. Hart and Company, the loss adjusters, had increased their reward from £20,000 to £200,000. The uninsured Midland Bank (the article makes no mention of that fact) had added a further £50,000, and finally there was the original £10,000 put up by Bevins. It was a staggering figure in 1963 and equivalent to 10 per cent of the total amount stolen. Moreover £260,000 was considerably larger than any gang member's individual 'whack'.

'Squealers Bait' was how the *Daily Express* described the reward on their front page. At the top of the page was a graphic illustrating that £260,000 would buy a yacht (£40,000), a Rolls-Royce (£8,000), a house in the country (£30,000), a world cruise (£1,000), two thousand bottles of Champagne (£4,000), a private plane (£6,000). The *Express* suggested that the claimant should invest the remaining £171,000, which would produce £10,000 a year in interest to live off for life. If the robbers had read the *Daily Express* that day it might have given them some useful tips on how to invest their loot.

Away from the press hype and excitement about the crime and the police investigation, there was considerable manoeuvring going on. In a further effort to exonerate the GPO, Bevins said that Post Office employees would have been unable to provide detailed inside information. He told the press, 'It looks as though the robbers had a lucky night. Only the banks knew how much money would be going on that train. No one in the GPO could have given a tip-off.' Bevins had overlooked the fact that all anyone would have to do was count the number of white mailbags being loaded on to the HVP. More bags meant more money. What he could not have known when he made the remark was that the Ulsterman who provided the gang with their inside information had specifically stated that, following a Bank Holiday, TPOs carried more cash.

*

At his Putney home, Flat 1, 40 Putney Hill, London, SW15, Reynolds was reunited with his wife Franny. He describes hugging her and twirling her around so her feet left the floor. Unashamedly comparing the moment of homecoming to that of a conquering hero, in his 1995 biography he wrote: 'exactly four hundred years after Drake sailed home from Panama to Plymouth harbour with £50,000 he'd secured from the Nombre de Dois treasure trail ...' Despite the obvious differences between twentieth-century crime and sixteenth-century conquest, Drake could at least argue that he'd stolen from the Spanish silver train for Queen and country, instead of attacking and robbing his fellow countrymen for personal gain.

Fiction is often fed by true stories and conversely fiction sometimes influences the way real opinions are formed and real events are played out. In the British crime comedy *The League of Gentlemen* starring Jack Hawkins and Richard Attenborough a group of ex-servicemen are recruited to carry out a £1 million bank robbery. Hawkins plays the leader, Hyde, an ex-army major who has masterminded the details. The gang of eight men gather at his house in the country and billet down before the raid. In the initial briefing, which takes place in the private dining room of a fashionable London restaurant, Hyde explains that each man will get an equal share of the spoils. His principle is clear, 'the one sure way to disaster is for anyone to get greedy.'

In order to steal equipment needed in the robbery, *The League of Gentlemen* gang first carry out a raid on an army camp, dressing up in uniform for the purpose. They steal cars and an army truck and fit them with false number plates. The robbery is bloodless and precise. The loot is seized without mishap and the gentlemanly gang return to their country hideout for a celebration. Later, as they leave the house, the gang are all arrested. The police have traced them to the address with the help of a small boy who identified one of the vehicles used in the robbery.

While *The League of Gentlemen* is not a blueprint for the 1963 mail-train robbery, it has uncanny parallels and similarities. It is hard to imagine that consciously, or subconsciously, the fictitious robbery did not form part of the DNA of the real crime on the mail train, at least in Reynolds' mind.

*

Thirty-six hours after the biggest cash robbery in British history, Commander Hatherill, the man in charge at New Scotland Yard, woke up to the demands of the case and began dispatching officers to Buckinghamshire to join the investigation. On Saturday, 10 August, DS Maurice Ray of the Yard's fingerprint department, accompanied by two London detectives and a police photographer, arrived to examine the engine and parcel van, which had finally been returned to the sidings at Cheddington. They were later joined by Dr Ian Holden and Detective Inspector Faber of the Metropolitan Police Forensic Science Laboratory. In addition to going over the mail-train itself, the Yard team scrutinised the tampered signals and the scene of the robbery.

Despite their best efforts, the signals and HVP van yielded no fingerprint evidence and there was nothing useful to be found on the engine either. The fact that D326 had been removed from the crime scene, taken to Crewe and returned thirty-six hours later meant that a good deal of additional work, inquiries and comparisons had to be carried out to eliminate fingerprints and traces that had nothing to do with the robbery.

But there would be other avenues to follow in the long and complex police investigation that would eventually all piece together. Also on 10 August an application was received by London County Council for a twelve-month road tax licence on a grey Austin Healey registration number REN22 – the car Jimmy White had purchased the day before in Chelsea. The application included a change of registered owner in the name of James Edward Patton, 36 Tetbury Court, Clapham Common, London, SW4.

Just over a thousand miles away in Cattolica, on Italy's northern Adriatic coast, Detective Inspector Frank Williams was on holiday with his family. The Italian press was giving extensive coverage to a mail-train robbery in England and it was the main talking point in the Royal Hotel where Williams was staying and in bars and restaurants all over town. The ever-vigilant detective managed to find an English newspaper and sat reading it on the beach.

A tough, balding, moody-looking man, Williams was in charge of Number Five squad, one of eight teams that made up Scotland Yard's revered Flying Squad. Having begun his career in South London – an area so notorious that even the Kray twins referred to it as 'Indian country' – his methods sometimes deviated from those of his colleagues and superiors. According to Freddie Foreman, Williams was not averse to doing deals of one sort or another. Certainly he was regularly to be seen mixing and drinking with known criminals and getting to know their friends, haunts and associates.

With the hot Italian sun beating down, Williams read of the uproar back in England. Gazing out over the lazy azure water, he began to run through criminals he knew who would be capable of such a crime. It occurred to him that some of the raiders might have come from a group of South London criminals that he and his team had been monitoring for several months. But sitting in his swimming trunks far from home, detective work was going to have to wait until he got back and talked to his underworld contacts.

Jack Mills, having been discharged from the Royal Hospital on Saturday morning, returned home to Crewe with a blackened right eye and a large white bandage encircling his bludgeoned head. His first grandson, Stephen, had been born six weeks earlier and was due to be christened the following day, but Mills told his wife that he did not feel well enough to attend the service.

Mills was later interviewed at his house by BBC Television. The interviewer asked, 'Did any of them speak to you?'

Mills' reply was groggy: 'Yes, three of them.'

'What did they say?'

'The only thing was they threatened me. One man kept wiping in front of my eyes. And afterwards, one of the men, when I was lying on the grass, he said, "If you hadn't grappled with me I wouldn't have hit you."'

'But you felt you had to?'

'Well, I wanted to save my train if possible. I thought there was only two bandits. Now of course I know different.'

In the small hours of Sunday, 11 August, three officers from Scotland Yard's Criminal Intelligence unit, C11, paid a visit to Buckinghamshire Police HQ. Detective Chief Inspector Walker, Detective Inspector Trodd and Detective Sergeant Cummings had travelled to Aylesbury after one of Walker's informants told him that a farm about twenty minutes' drive from the town was being used by the thieves and should be searched within forty-eight hours.

During the late night meeting with Fewtrell and McArthur, DCI Walker also passed on a tip that Robert Alfred Welch was one of the mail-train gang. This was the second time Welch's name had come up and the Flying Squad had made some preliminary inquiries and discovered that he was missing from home. His wife, Mary, said that her husband was away and she expected him back in two or three days. Before leaving London the C11 detectives set up round-the-clock observation on Welch's house, as well as the homes of his known associates. One of these was Jean Iris Steel of 83 Ivanhoe Road, Camberwell, whom Welch was reported to have been visiting on a daily basis for the past eighteen months, regularly spending the night.

Unfortunately, Walker's informants had not been sufficiently 'in the know' to supply the name or address of the farm, or the fact that the gang had already fled. Fewtrell and McArthur worked through the night studying Ordnance Survey maps in an effort to identify which local farms and smallholdings to search. It was not an easy task. The area around Aylesbury was mainly agricultural and there were hundreds of likely places. At one point the detectives considered asking the army for assistance but decided against it because it was the middle of the weekend and help from the military would take time to organise.

Given the police manpower at his disposal, it's hard to see why Fewtrell would have considered calling the army in. The 1964 report to the Home Office noted that the neighbouring constabularies of Oxfordshire, Bedfordshire and Hertfordshire had offered their assistance along with their workforce. As early as 09.30 on the morning of the robbery a senior Oxfordshire officer – Detective Inspector Densham, head of the county's CID – had contacted his Buckinghamshire colleagues, even though at that time he'd received no official information about the raid. Densham's offer of uniformed officers and CID detectives was reiterated later that day by the Chief Constable of Oxfordshire. The offer was never taken up.

At 09.00 on Sunday morning, eighty uniformed and criminal investigation officers from both Buckinghamshire and Hertfordshire constabularies reported to Aylesbury HQ. They were briefed that Fewtrell's team had narrowed the search for the thieves' hideout to a total of thirteen likely premises.

14

As instructed, early on Sunday morning William Boal arrived at Oxford railway station accompanied by his wife, Renee, and their three children, David, Debbie and Tony. Cordrey picked them up and drove to Ida Pope's lodgings, where he had spent the night. On the pretext of taking his friends on a family outing to the seaside, he loaded the two suitcases and a kitbag into the boot, placed a third case in the back of the Rover. He handed back his keys to Mrs Pope and she watched the laden car with Cordrey, Boal, his wife and three children, drive away down the street.

By midday in Buckinghamshire the police had completed their search of the remote properties on Fewtrell's list, as well as several others that had come to light in the course of their hunt. Disappointingly, they'd drawn a blank.

Bob Welch, who had left Kabri with Jim Hussey and Tommy Wisbey the previous day and spent the night in Pevensey Bay, East Sussex, decided to stop off at a telephone box on his way back in to London and call his wife, Mary. When he told her that he'd be home in ten minutes, she replied, 'Bob, can you bring some of that ointment? Bruno's feet are bad again.'

This was a pre-arranged signal that the police were there. When Welch drove past the end of his street on the Elmington Estate to check, he spotted what looked like three Flying Squad cars parked a short distance from his home.

At the Reynolds' home, the family were hurriedly packing their suitcases, not knowing when they would return. Although he had avoided prosecution for the London Airport robbery, Reynolds knew that his record and reputation meant he was likely to be in the frame for the mail-train robbery. However, surprisingly he had not planned an alibi in advance. Reynolds later said his strategy was simply that in the event the police came to his Putney flat to talk to him, he was not going to be there. He does not seem to have considered that not being at home, or in his usual haunts, would inevitably serve to increase police suspicion that he was involved in the train robbery.

While his son Nick went to stay with Reynolds' father and step-mother in Dagenham, Bruce and Franny moved in with a long-time friend known as 'The Captain' who had a mansion flat in Queensway, Bayswater. According to Reynolds, the Captain, whose real name was Alan, 'lived in a fantasy land of role playing and skulduggery', having been a street photographer and an extra in the Richard Burton and Elizabeth Taylor epic, *Cleopatra*. But Reynolds clearly trusted him and there can't have been many friends he could rely on not to be tempted by the £260,000 reward money.

Having arrived in Bournemouth, Cordrey's 'family outing' went to the beach to drop off Boal's wife and three children then continued to the flat at 935 Wimborne Road Boal had rented the previous day. After unloading Cordrey's luggage the two men re-joined Renee Boal and the children and at a seafront café. Cordrey pulled out a brown paper package, handed it to Renee and asked her to deliver it to his sister 'Maisie' at the Buttonhole florist's shop in Molesey. He also gave her £100 in a roll of notes. After their meal they drove to Bournemouth station, where Renee and the children boarded a London train. Boal later said that he wanted to leave with his family but Cordrey threatened him so he stayed.

Jimmy White had also decided to get out of London. Using the name Ballard, he had purchased a caravan at Clovelly Caravan Site in Tedworth, just outside of Dorking, Surrey.

Biggs, having somehow managed to smooth things over with Charmian, persuaded her to join him for a Sunday night out in London's West End.

Goody turned up at the Windmill public house, Blackfriars, where the landlord, Charles Alexander, had often let him stay overnight at a moment's notice. Goody told Alexander that he expected to be hounded by the police and press in connection with the recent mail-train robbery. Alexander later said he asked Goody if he had anything to do with the raid and Goody assured him that he had not. It was agreed that Goody could stay at the Windmill until the police found the culprits. In the evening Goody's fiancée, Pat Cooper, arrived at the pub and the two of them went out to dinner.

Detective Inspector Densham of Oxfordshire CID spent his Sunday evening at a golf club in Oxford, in conversation with a man who suggested the police should take a look at a smallholding he called 'Rixon's place', off the Thame Road near Oakley. Densham's informant knew Rixon as they shared an interest in motorcycling. He told the detective that Rixon had moved out, having sold his home for a lot of money, and suggested the recently vacated property would be a likely hideout.

On Monday, 12 August, *The Times* published an account of the robbery given by Jack Mills at his home in Crewe. The *Daily Mirror*'s front page also featured Mills, reporting that he was to go to a British Railways convalescent home in Devon. Mills was quoted as saying, 'I don't know whether I'll ever be fit enough to drive again.'

The *Mirror* report included an update on the police investigation: '... detectives seeking the gang's hideout have started checking on all house agents around Sears Crossing. They are listing everybody who has bought or rented a house in the last few months within getaway distance of the ambush.' According to the report, the handcuffs used to manacle Mills and Whitby also looked likely to yield clues to the identity of the robbers. The handcuffs had been traced to a Birmingham supplier which claimed to have a complete record of sales.

All the national newspapers carried the police appeal for information on remote farms and buildings within a thirty-mile radius of the robbery that the gang could be using as a hideout. Readers were also asked to report any sightings in the early hours of Thursday morning of a convoy of three vehicles including a three-ton army-type lorry and a Land Rover.

Calls from members of the public eager to claim the £260,000 reward were flooding into the incident room at Aylesbury Police HQ. At 09.00 PC Peter Collins logged a call from thirty-three-year-old John Alfred Maris of Glencoe House, Little London, Oakley. Maris, a local herdsman, said he suspected that Leatherslade Farm might be the hideout the police were seeking.

After reading in the morning newspaper that the police were interested in isolated buildings, Maris began to wonder about a neighbouring farm that had until recently belonged to Bernard Rixon. After early morning milking in the sheds at the entrance to Leatherslade Farm,

Maris had driven his tractor up the track to Rixon's place to have a look around. Walking through the yard he noticed sacking hanging in all the farmhouse windows and in one of the sheds was a yellow lorry which he had never seen before.

PC Collins handed the message concerning John Maris' telephone call to Fewtrell, but it was not followed up.

Meanwhile in Bournemouth, Cordrey and Boal walked into Broadway Car Sales and approached salesman Percival Walker to enquire about one of the vehicles offered for sale, a Ford Anglia, registration number RHJ383. Boal said he wanted to buy the Ford and paid £73.14s. deposit, saying he would return to pay the £200 balance and collect the car the following day. He gave his correct name and address in Fulham while Cordrey, wearing sunglasses and a panama hat, loitered in the background. Cordrey then stepped forward and gave his name as John Edward Thomas in order to be put on the car insurance.

Miss Ruby Margaret Saunders had a garage advertised to let at her home in Ensbury Avenue, Bournemouth. Two men called at her house enquiring about it. The arrangements were agreed and the men left taking the garage key with them.

Throughout Monday Fewtrell's search teams had continued to comb the area west of Cheddington, but they had found nothing of interest. At 21.27 on Monday evening a message was sent out from Aylesbury HQ to all Buckinghamshire divisions as well as the constabularies in the neighbouring counties:

> Attention of all foot and mobile patrols is drawn to the fact that the money may be moved at night either in bulk or in part.

At 22.30 Fewtrell, having returned from a meeting in Hatfield with Detective Chief Superintendent Elwell of Hertfordshire Police, issued the following request to all Buckinghamshire divisions as well as the constabularies in the neighbouring counties:

> Reference to mail-train robbery.
> Bearing in mind that premises might have been specifically purchased or rented for use for the immediate concealment of the stolen property

and its transport, please have enquiries made of estate agents and obtain information of transactions during the past six months involving likely premises within 30 miles of Cheddington, particularly farms and derelict houses, etc. Please follow up where appropriate.

The 1964 Home Office report into the robbery states that it was Detective Chief Superintendent Elwell who suggested during the course of the Hatfield meeting that estate agents in the area should be contacted. But several hours before that meeting took place the *Daily Mirror* had reported on its morning front page that detectives were 'checking on all house agents'. This is yet another example of anomalies that come to light when scrutiny is applied to the chronology of reported 'facts', even from the most reputable sources, about the robbery and the subsequent investigation.

Oxfordshire CID had spent much of the day checking the tip-off Detective Inspector Densham had received at an Oxford golf club on Sunday evening about a possible location for the robbers' hideout at Oakley. They had learned that the previous owner, Bernard Rixon, mentioned by the informant, had a criminal record and had moved to Dunsdon, Berkshire at the end of July. Densham telephoned the following message to Aylesbury at 23.47 on Monday night, which was noted by PC78 Lewis in the incident room:

Whilst making enquiries at Wheatley, Oxfordshire, re mail-train robbery, information was received that the premises at Leatherslade Farm, Brill, Bucks were on the market for some time with no prospective purchaser. The premises were purchased a few weeks ago for a large sum of money. The informant suggested that this may be of interest to the robbery.

Over the coming days, a seemingly endless number of informants would emerge, lured by the promise of a £260,000 reward. Tuesday's edition of the *Daily Mirror* featured an article on page 6 about the insurance loss adjusters Hart and Co. It gave the telephone number, City 3266, with six lines manned by staff at their offices on the third floor of Blossom Inn, Lawrence Lane, London, EC2. However, the *Daily Mirror* reporter went on to explain that it appeared that some would-be informants had already worked out where Hart and Co. was:

> Up the stairs and in the lifts of the company's offices, came a pro-
> cession of callers with private business. There were shifty-eyed men,
> City-type gents and women who could not be mistaken for anything
> but boarding-house keepers with a look which said; 'I knew that man
> wasn't Mr Smith when he booked in.'

At 09.05 on Tuesday, 13 August, Sergeant Ronald Blackman of Waddesdon received a telephone call from Aylesbury HQ asking if he knew anything about Leatherslade Farm, Brill, as they had received a message the night before that it had recently been sold for a high price. Blackman had never heard of the place and contacted PC545 John Woolley, the village constable at Brill, who said he thought he knew the smallholding but would need to check where it was and phone him back.

While he was waiting for Woolley to call, Blackman was contacted again by Aylesbury HQ, passing on the information provided by local herdsman, John Maris, regarding Rixon's smallholding.

Having examined the map of his beat on the police station wall, twenty-five-year-old Woolley informed Sergeant Blackman that he had identified the property in question. They agreed to meet at Brill police station at 10.30 to go and take a look at Leatherslade Farm.

It was one of the many ironies of the mail-train-robbery story that the tip which prompted Buckinghamshire police to check Leatherslade Farm came from Oxfordshire's Head of CID, Detective Inspector Densham – the same man whose offer of assistance on the morning of the robbery had been ignored by Aylesbury HQ.

Leatherslade Farm was not pinpointed as a result of McArthur's and Fewtrell's late-night examination of maps, or the mass searches by police officers, or thanks to the input of the mighty forces of New Scotland Yard. And although John Maris had come forward as a result of reading one of the police appeals that had appeared in the national newspapers, his telephone call to Aylesbury HQ on Monday morning had been overlooked in the avalanche of reports coming into the incident room. The information which, over nine hours later, was finally acted upon, had come from a policeman who was not directly involved in the investigation but had nonetheless applied the good old-fashioned principle of getting out into the community and talking to your contacts. When Aylesbury police moved into action at 09.05 on Tuesday, 13 August, it was entirely due to Densham's call late the previous evening.

Here was a significant lead. After five days of searching and head-scratching and speculating over the hideout it was possible that in Leatherslade Farm, or 'Rixon's Place' as it was known locally, they had finally found the place where the mail-train robbers had concealed themselves, along with their unprecedented haul of over two and a half million pounds.

To say that Aylesbury police moved into action is overstating it. Out of seven hundred officers in the Buckinghamshire constabulary, only two uniformed policemen, Sergeant Blackman and Constable Woolley, were actively engaged in this critical part of the investigation. The men in charge of the hunt, Detective Superintendents McArthur and Fewtrell, were busy back at Aylesbury HQ in a meeting with Commander George Hatherill, who had grown concerned about the way the investigation was going and driven up from Scotland Yard that morning, accompanied by Detective Chief Superintendent Ernie Millen, head of the Flying Squad.

With no back-up, no weapons and not even a radio between them, Blackman and Woolley arrived at Leatherslade Farm on Blackman's standard-issue Triumph 250cc police motorcycle. If this was indeed the robbers' local hideout there was every chance the bandits could still be there. The two country policemen stood at the farm gate and peered up the long, unmade track to the smallholding, not knowing how many men might be lurking in the house or whether their every move was being watched.

15

It was a *Dad's Army* kind of bravery, or foolishness, and a *Dad's Army* kind of imagery too. With Blackman driving his motorbike and Woolley riding pillion, the two country policemen in their peaked white police crash helmets with chin straps made their way in uncertain fashion over the uneven, bumpy track that led the quarter-mile to the farmhouse. It could only have happened in England. If Bruce Reynolds, Jimmy White, Charlie Wilson, John Daly, Buster Edwards, Roger Cordrey, Roy James, Gordon Goody, Jim Hussey, Tommy Wisbey, Bob Welch, Ronnie Biggs, Mr One, Mr Two and Mr Three had still been at the farm, they would have looked out of the window in utter amazement. The national radio broadcasts that had panicked the gang into making a hasty exit had led them to believe there was an army of well-organised police officers scouring the Buckinghamshire countryside. In reality, two local policemen on a motorbike would have been no match for the fifteen ruthless mail-train robbers. It was extremely lucky for Blackman and Woolley that the gang had already fled, and also fortunate for the gang. Put to the test, they would surely have escalated the seriousness of their crime in order to avoid capture.

In his 1981 biography, *Slipper of the Yard*, ex-Detective Chief Superintendent Jack Slipper was quite clear about how dangerous the situation might have been.

> But they were no Robin Hoods, and I've always been convinced that it was only by chance that there wasn't more violence. If, for example, there had been a tip off and the police had cornered them at Leatherslade Farm, I'm quite certain there would have been little evidence of unarmed gentlemen robbers ... they had £2.6 million inside the farm. I don't doubt there would have been a blood bath.

On entering the farmyard, the first thing the two policemen spotted was the sacking hanging in the windows of the house. Without first checking to see if anyone was in the farmhouse Woolley and Blackman had a look around the yard. They found the remnants of a bonfire and in the ashes were the charred remains of food tins, some pieces of clothing and metal fittings. Poking out of a ramshackle shed, partially covered by a green tarpaulin, was the bonnet of an Austin lorry which had been hand-painted yellow. In two smaller sheds, which were padlocked, they could see two Land Rovers and noticed that both had the same registration number. There was also an assorted collection of motorcycle bric-a-brac strewn about the place, which had been left behind by Bernard Rixon.

The officers went to the pale blue front door of the farmhouse and knocked on it. There was no response. Apparently not considering that it was unlikely a gang of violent criminals hiding inside would answer the door, Blackman and Woolley walked around the outside of the house. On the far side, in the scrubby uncut grass behind a line of neglected runner beans, was a newly dug pit with a spade stuck into the earth. Sergeant Blackman then noticed an upstairs window was ajar.

The two policemen found an old door in one of the sheds and propped it up against the wall. PC Woolley, being the younger and more agile of the two officers, climbed up and clambered through the window. In the semi-darkness of the upstairs room were several sleeping bags, air mattresses and recent newspapers scattered around. With no electric light and all the windows covered, Woolley fumbled his way downstairs and let in Sergeant Blackman.

In the kitchen they found a two-ring, Calor gas camping burner, a collection of cutlery, plates and mugs, and a larder full of tins of baked beans, corned beef, pork luncheon meat and soup. There were dozens of eggs, toilet rolls and several seven-pint pipkins of ale. It was clear a large number of people were being catered for.

In the passage next to the kitchen Woolley spotted a trapdoor half-hidden under a sack of potatoes and some crates of fruit and vegetables. He dragged the sack away, pulled the hatch open and climbed down. In the dark cellar he could make out several bulging bags. At first he thought they might contain the missing mail-train money but having pulled one bag up into the light the constable discovered it was full of banknote wrappers. It was immediately obvious to Blackman and Woolley that they had found the robbers' hideout. They dragged other mailbags up from the cellar and searched through them; there were more wrappers, some clothing, and one bag contained several wads of Scottish banknotes.

Since they had no means of communication, Blackman told Woolley to stand guard at the farm while he rode off on the motorbike to the nearest telephone box to alert Aylesbury HQ. In a 2010 interview John Woolley recalled how he was left alone standing in the yard. He said he began to worry that the bandits might return or perhaps they were hiding and watching, concealed in the surrounding undergrowth, waiting for a chance to attack.

At 11.45 Buckinghamshire Police HQ logged a call from Blackman informing them of the discovery of the mail-train robbers' hideout.

By 13.30 the big guns had arrived at Leatherslade Farm in the form of Chief Constable Cheney, Detective Superintendent Fewtrell, Commander Hatherill and his fellow Scotland Yard detectives Millen, McArthur and Pritchard. More uniformed police arrived in minibuses shortly after and a cordon was set up around the farm. Leaving strict instructions that nothing further was to be touched, Commander Hatherill went to Brill police station where he personally telephoned Scotland Yard and made arrangements for experts from the fingerprint department and Forensic Science Laboratory to attend. On his return to Aylesbury, Hatherill set about overhauling the structure of the on-going police investigation.

From hereon four detectives from the Metropolitan Police would take over the running of the incident room. McArthur was put in charge of 'processing reports and paperwork', while the Flying Squad's renowned Detective Superintendent Tommy Butler was placed in overall charge of the investigation, assisted by Detective Chief Inspector Peter Vibart. Butler handpicked a special train robbery team.

However, the crack London detectives had their reputations, oddities and shortcomings. Detective Superintendent Tommy Butler was known as 'the Grey Fox'; a fitting nickname for the small, fifty-four-year-old detective whose dark eyebrows, receding hair and thin pointed nose gave him a strong resemblance to Mr Punch. Butler was a London policeman through and through. Born in Shepherd's Bush, he had joined the Metropolitan Police at the age of twenty-two. After serving fifteen years with CID he was promoted to the Flying Squad. In recognition of a distinguished career during which he had been commended thirty-two times, he was promoted to Chief Superintendent in July 1963, only a month before taking over the mail-train investigation. Now approaching retirement, Butler was undoubtedly a brilliant detective, but even his close colleagues said he was a remote, obsessively secretive character. In fact, Tommy Butler did not have close colleagues. He was not that sort of man. A bachelor, he lived with his mother and regularly worked late into the night, seven days a week, living off canteen food. Whenever he was driven home to West London in a police vehicle he would insist that they dropped him several streets away from where he lived.

In his biography, Freddie Foreman relates an anecdote about an encounter he had with Butler's assistant, Chief Inspector Vibart. One night Foreman had been out 'looking at some business' with a colleague he calls Alf. The two of them were driving home along the Embankment, with Alf asleep on the back seat, when Foreman noticed a car behind them. He woke Alf and warned him they were about to get a 'tug'. Slowing down for a red traffic light at Chelsea Bridge, Foreman locked his door and leaned over and locked the passenger side. As they stopped, three men got out of the car behind and started running towards them. Foreman took off, but one of the men managed to open the rear door and dive on to the back seat with Alf. According to Foreman, getting in the back with Alf was like getting in with a Rottweiler. As Foreman screeched away down the Embankment, Alf pinned the intruder against the door with his feet. All the while the man was yelling, 'I'm Chief Inspector Vibart!'

When they were finally pulled over by the squad car, Foreman and Alf protested indignantly. They said they had been scared out of their wits when a stranger jumped into the back of their car. After checking Foreman's vehicle was legitimate, Vibart had no alternative but to swallow his dented pride and let the two known criminals go.

It would be easy to jump to the conclusion that Hatherill's intervention, handing control to Butler and the Flying Squad, was a kick in the teeth for Fewtrell and McArthur. It was true there had been unfortunate omissions and errors made in the first critical hours and days. Certainly things could have been handled better, in terms of tighter focus on key lines of enquiry, organisation of police effort and the release of key information to the press. But with the discovery of the abandoned farm the police investigations were shifting away from Buckinghamshire to the capital. Scotland Yard had been working on the assumption that the mail-train criminals had come from London and the names being put forward by various informants confirmed that.

As well as calling in Tommy Butler and his team with their contacts and expertise in hunting down London's hardened criminals, Commander Hatherill was also concerned that in the first days of the investigation the press had been left free to roam around Aylesbury HQ more or less at will and aspects of the investigation had been compromised. Fewtrell argued that his relationship with the press had proved vital in finding the robbers' hideout but as far as Butler was concerned, talking to the press was always a bad idea and had probably resulted in the gang fleeing before the police found Leatherslade Farm.

The public's involvement had proved a double-edged sword. Britain had become fascinated by media accounts of the robbery. The courtship of the press by the senior members of the Aylesbury team in the early days of the investigation had the nation involved in a real-life game of Cluedo. Motivated by the size of the reward, all sorts of informants were coming forward with 'sightings' that had nothing to do with the mail-train robbery. The neighbours of one Buckinghamshire farmer reported suspicious activity after he was seen digging a hole in the corner of a field. When local police called to question the man, it turned out he had been burying a dead sheep.

The sheer volume of information flooding in was often overwhelming, which was why Maris' tip-off was initially overlooked even though the details he provided matched the kind of property the police were searching for.

Among the many leads being followed up by the police across the country, there were some whose significance only became apparent later. One such telephone call was made to Surrey police from Mary O'Rourke (45) who worked in Coronel ladies dress shop in Reigate. She and colleague Patricia Bemister (43) had become suspicious about a woman who entered their shop on 13 August. Miss O'Rourke told police that the woman bought clothing which she paid for with twenty-six one-pound notes and refused to give her address.

Finding this odd, Patricia Bemister and Mary O'Rourke watched the woman after she left the shop and saw her walk to a car and speak to a man. Mrs Bemister made a note of the registration number: REN22. The two shop assistants continued to observe as the woman then entered two other shops. The shop assistants agreed 'something was not quite right'.

At 14.30, Constables Donald Cooper and Gerald Bixley went to Church Street in response to Miss O'Rourke's telephone call. They located the Austin Healey 3000 sports car and questioned the driver. He produced a driving licence in the name of James Edward Patton of 36 Tetbury Court, Clapham Common, SW4, as well as a piece of paper with the address The Woodlands, Beulah Hill, London, SE19. The man said he ran a snack bar in Aldersgate Street in the City and was then joined by a woman, a baby and a white poodle. As everything seemed in order, the police constables allowed them to drive away.

Nevertheless Constables Cooper and Bixley were not quite satisfied and conducted further inquiries and discovered that the couple had been to a number of shops in Reigate that same day. Sales assistants Raymond Wilson, Eric Jones and Eric Hurst of Rhythm Agencies reported that they had sold a Perdio Portarama television set for £75 to a man called F. Rodgers of 27 The Parade, High Street, Barnet (which turned out to be a false address). The customer had paid in one-pound notes. Geoffrey Boorer, a sales assistant in another electrical shop in Reigate, told the police officers that he had sold a Decca transistor radio to a man called J. Ballard, who had given his address as Clovelly Caravan Site, Boxhill Road, near Dorking, Surrey. Boorer recalled that the man had paid with five five-pound notes and a one-pound note. While he was serving his customer, Boorer noticed the number Flaxman 1448 on the leather fob of the man's ignition key. This was later found to be the telephone number of Allery & Bernard motor dealers in Chelsea. Like the ladies in the dress shop, Boorer's extraordinarily sharp observations and suspicions were aroused by the man's odd behaviour and so Boorer recorded the make and registration number of his suspicious customer's car. It was an Austin Healey 3000, registration number REN22.

None of these names or activities linked the Reigate couple to the Buckinghamshire mail-train robbery, but Surrey police decided to continue following the trail of the Austin Healey. They too found it curious that the man and woman had paid for their many purchases in cash and had given a variety of names and addresses to local shopkeepers.

Jimmy White and his partner Sheree had been lucky that Constables Cooper and Bixley hadn't asked for a more detailed account of their activities when they were spotted in Church Street, Reigate. But White had a well-developed nose for trouble and was a master at covering his tracks.

The *Daily Mirror*'s main story on Tuesday, 13 August, went under the headline *Big Shock for Rail Gang*. The article stated that the haul from the train ambush 'may be too hot to handle' and that well over half the money stolen was in new notes, the serial numbers of which had been recorded (in reality, the numbers of only 1,400 notes were known). The report then went into detail about the make-up of the stolen money: some of the notes were being returned to head offices in London, being surplus to local banks' requirements; some were new and therefore identifiable through serial numbers; and some were old notes being withdrawn from circulation and destined to be destroyed.

The revelation confronted the thieves with a new dilemma. Were the banks bluffing? The original information supplied by the Ulsterman was that the bulk of the money carried on the TPO would be used, untraceable banknotes. Could the gang now distinguish between new notes and old, and would it be possible to identify which serial numbers had been recorded and which were untraceable? If the *Mirror* report was accurate and over half the stolen banknotes were traceable, given that there was no way of knowing which half was which, *all* of their money could be too hot to handle.

But although the robbers didn't know it, there were far more critical events about to confront them. Tuesday's morning newspapers had only reported that the search was on in earnest for a hideout within thirty miles of the scene of the robbery. And the news that Leatherslade Farm had been discovered by the police had not yet broken.

Over the last fifty years the gang members have given varying accounts where Leatherslade Farm is concerned. But on one thing they all agree: someone had been paid by the gang to go to their aban-doned hideout and remove all evidence of their ever having been there. The consensus that this clean-up was always part of the planning has persisted throughout the many versions of 'The Great Train Robbery' that have emerged over the decades. However, on closer examination there is a paradox. It is not possible to establish the incontrovertible truth, but by piecing all the known elements together an entirely different version of events emerges as the more likely scenario.

16

Leaving aside any possible evidence that New Scotland Yard's fingerprint department and Forensic Science Laboratory had been called in to examine at Leatherslade Farm by Commander Hatherill, there were a large number of items left behind by the gang that did not require Sherlock Holmes' acumen. Some of the artefacts critically linked the farm to the robbery and the provenance of other objects was not going to be hard to establish. And then there was the acquisition of the farm itself.

The three vehicles left in the outbuildings and sheds of the farm were the most obvious and easy to trace. Smaller items included a collection of clothing worn by the gang during the mail-train raid. One of the sacks found in the cellar had contained a lieutenant's jacket, a corporal's jacket, waterproof and cold-weather jackets, six khaki denim jackets, six khaki denim trousers, various blue denim overalls and jackets, blue denim trousers, a bib-and-brace overall, three black hoods with eyeholes, and a nylon stocking mask. In the remains of a bonfire was a half-burned balaclava helmet, pieces of a jacket and fragments of nylon stocking.

In the bedrooms were sleeping bags, inflatable mattresses, newspapers and magazines. There was a large assortment of utensils and provisions in the kitchen and other miscellaneous items lying around, including an instruction manual for American-style handcuffs of the type used to secure Whitby and Mills.

In the cellar Blackman and Woolley had discovered the most incriminating evidence of all in the form of thirty-five mailbags containing bank money wrappers and £627.10s. in Scottish banknotes. Although the vehicles and many other items were persuasive in constructing the case that Leatherslade Farm had been used as a hideout by the mail-train robbers, the mailbags and their contents were incontrovertible proof. For the gang to have left these mailbags and cash in the farmhouse seems an extraordinarily stupid mistake.

Though the robbers later claimed that they had arranged for some-one to go to the farm after they left to clean it up or even to burn the place down, given all the other factors that have emerged, that explana-tion seems both impractical and unlikely.

The first published version of the story about the gang's plan to dispose of evidence abandoned at Leatherslade Farm appears in *The Robbers' Tale*. Peta Fordham's postscript explains:

> It was only just before the manuscript went to the printers that I unravelled a vital piece of this inexplicable jigsaw. The truth was that a very close associate had originally been entrusted with the job, which he would have undoubtedly carried out faithfully. Unfortunately, a 'brush' with the police days before the robbery kept him tailed so closely that the robbers considered him too risky to use. They had, however, considered that they would have plenty of time themselves.

Fourteen years later, the robbers gave a rather different and more com-plex story to Piers Paul Read for his book *The Train Robbers*. In this version, Brian Field is the scapegoat. After calling Field on Monday, 12 August, to check that the evidence had been destroyed, Charlie Wilson was so concerned by Field's unconvincing response that he set up a meeting with Reynolds, Daly, James and Edwards outside Clapham North underground station to discuss the problem. They all agreed they must go back to the farm and make sure the job was done.

There is a revealing statement about James which provides an insight into the gang's plans for their hideout: 'Roy was particularly anxious because he had not worn gloves, never envisaging that the police would find the farm.' If true, this remark explains why James did not clean or destroy everything he had handled. It is also unlikely that James would not have been informed if there was a plan to remove or destroy evi-dence after they had all left the farm.

Wilson, Reynolds, Daly, James and Edwards then met with Field on Tuesday morning outside Holland Park underground station. It appar-ently became clear that the clean-up had not been carried out and the gang members decided to go to Leatherslade Farm that afternoon to remove anything that could link the farm to the mail-train robbery. Having arranged to meet later at Hanger Lane, West London, they all went home to change and make calls to round up other members of the gang to help with the operation.

As they made their way to the rendezvous, news came over the car radio that police had found Leatherslade Farm. With 'heavy hearts' they called off the plan. James is reported as saying, 'We're nicked.'

What Piers Paul Read's version overlooks is that, of all those involved in the robbery, Brian Field was the one most directly connected to Leatherslade Farm. He could be identified by Lily Rixon from that first visit to the property, and he had overseen negotiations for the purchase with Bernard Rixon's solicitors. All police investigators had to do was follow the paper trail back to Field's employers, James and Wheater.

Field had to have known that his position would be precarious in the event the farm was connected to the robbery. If disposing of the evidence left at the farm had been his responsibility, he would have had the strongest incentive to make absolutely sure it was done.

Reynolds' version of events, published in his 1995 memoir *The Autobiography of a Thief*, is similar to the one in Piers Paul Read's book but with a few notable variations. He attributes the identification of the gang's military vehicles to the RAF hitchhiker they passed on their way to Bridego Bridge. Later, after the gang had vacated the farm, Reynolds says that he became 'increasingly disturbed about the lack of confirmation that the farm had been cleaned up'. Curiously, given the insight and details he provides on less pivotal aspects of the crime, he glosses over the matter of who was supposed to have carried out the clean-up and provided the confirmation. There is no mention of Brian Field in this context. In Reynolds' version, he arranged to meet with Wilson, Edwards and James four days after he left the farm on the afternoon of Tuesday, 13 August, at a café on the North Circular Road in London. Over a cup of tea the robbers discussed what needed to be done 'in the absence of confirmation' – again no mention of how, from whom, or when this had been expected. For some unexplained reason Edwards then goes out to buy the afternoon newspaper. 'I saw from his face as he returned that something terrible had happened. Without a word, he placed the paper on the greasy table. "HIDEOUT DISCOVERED".'

Goody does not feature in either of these accounts, which is another oddity since Goody and Field were closely linked and central to the whole enterprise. If circumstances demanded any liaison with Field, Goody would have been the obvious choice.

And why, if the gang had an arrangement in place to pay someone to go to the farm and clean up after them, did they behave as they did in the final hours before they left? Why did Biggs set about burning things in the kitchen stove? Charred remains of incriminating items were found in the half-burned bonfire outside, not far from the spade left in the ground, marking the spot where a freshly dug pit had been prepared to bury other evidence. What was the point of attempting to bury and burn evidence when they knew all along that someone was coming to clean up after them?

The logical thing to do if a clean-up team was expected would have been to gather all their paraphernalia together in one place so nothing was overlooked and it could all be disposed of or destroyed in situ. For a team of experienced criminals, determined to ensure that no evidence remained, this would have been an essential strategy. Instead, the gang made disjointed attempts to destroy and hide some pieces of evidence, while leaving their food and utensils in the kitchen, sleeping bags, air mattresses and newspapers in the upstairs rooms and, most incriminating of all, the mailbags and money wrappers from the ambushed mail train piled in the cellar. The fact that the gang's detritus was strewn all over the property and grounds would have made any subsequent clean-up operation extremely difficult and time-consuming. Where were the keys to the vehicles and the padlocks for the sheds in which the two Land Rovers were left locked? The police forensic and fingerprint teams found no keys during their inch-by-inch search of the farmhouse and outbuildings.

Moreover, with or without Field's involvement, why would they have left themselves with no means of contacting 'the cleaners' to tell them how and where the evidence had been left? This would have given the gang no control and no guarantees, yet it was as critical as any other aspect of their crime. Such a vital part of the operation would never have been entrusted to a third party who was not known to the gang. There were plenty of tried-and-trusted members of their own close-knit criminal fraternity they could have recruited, so why leave this crucial aspect of the planning for Brian Field alone to organise? When viewed as a whole the omission of these critical components of the plan do not make sense.

The other questionable element of these stories is the timing. To have offered a solution to leaving evidence behind, the clean-up would need to have been carried out very soon after the gang left on Friday evening. After all, the reason for the gang's premature exit was their certainty that a visit from the police teams searching the area was imminent. But in both Read's account and Reynolds' version, the gang left it until Monday or Tuesday before enquiring whether the clean-up had gone ahead. Given all the incriminating evidence they knew they had left behind at the farm, they would have been chasing the clean-up team for confirmation immediately rather than waiting three or four days.

The manner in which the farm was left and later found by the police points to a hasty, improvised attempt to destroy and hide evidence before making a quick exit. There is nothing to suggest a clearly thought-out and preconceived strategy. John Gosling and Dennis Craig's 1964 book *The Great Train Robbery* offers a succinct opinion on post-robbery events: 'The complete story of carelessness and panic begins to unfold. The gang, so closely disciplined and trained for the actual raid had behaved like amateurs once the action was over.'

Nevertheless, the claim that a clean-up operation had always been part of the plan has survived and been perpetuated for fifty years. Individuals have come forward claiming that they, or their associates, or families were part of the failed cleaning team, offering various explanations as to why it did not happen. Not one of these accounts, however, presents a convincing scenario that fits in with the known facts and evidence found at Leatherslade Farm.

Although the versions in Read's and Reynolds' books are similar, it is conceivable that both are untrue since neither story quite adds up. If there ever was a plan for someone to clean or even, as some later claimed, to burn down the farm, the facts point to it being scrambled together as an afterthought. Clearly trying to set fire to the farmhouse and farm buildings would have attracted attention for miles around and not guaranteed that all the evidence was destroyed.

But leaving the apocalyptic claims to one side, perhaps the robbers did have a carefully devised plan and it simply went wrong. Following the known facts of the situation that unfolded in the immediate aftermath of the robbery, an alternative version of events suggests itself.

The first clue to the robbers' original plan is the agreed completion date for the purchase of Leatherslade Farm. This was set for Tuesday, 13 August – ironically, the day their hideout was discovered. This key fact is not mentioned in any previously published accounts.

The sequence of events concerning the acquisition of the farm was that on 17 July Brian Field's boss, John Wheater, asked Rixon's solicitors, Marshall and Eldrige, if his client could occupy the premises prior to completion. On 19 July, Marshall and Eldridge agreed that, once contracts had been exchanged, the property would be made available on the basis that Wheater's client would pay extra interest from date of occupation until completion. On 23 July Wheater handed over the 10 per cent deposit of £550 and on 24 July contracts were exchanged. The keys for Leatherslade Farm were collected from a neighbour, Mrs Lillian Brooks, on 29 July.

At this point the gang had two choices: they could either pay the remaining balance of £5,000 and complete the purchase of Leatherslade Farm as agreed on 13 August, or they could do a vanishing act and renege on the deal, forfeiting their £550 deposit. The sum would have had no significance, given their haul from the robbery, but withdrawing from the purchase in this manner would have risked arousing suspicion. With the nationwide publicity and searches of Buckinghamshire rural properties, the gang's temporary occupation of the farm as a party of 'builders and decorators' would, in all probability, have come to light.

A tangible indication of the gang's original intentions is the large quantity of unused stores discovered by the police at Leatherslade (see Appendix for complete itemised list). Presumably the robbers had done some basic calculations to work out how much food they would consume per day and how much toilet paper they would get through. When they vacated the farm that Friday evening, the gang left behind thirty-four toilet rolls. Was this a case of profligate overbuying or do those thirty-four toilet rolls, along with the numerous tins of soup, baked beans, pork luncheon meat, corned beef, pipkins of ale, a sack of potatoes, two hundred eggs and boxes of fruit and vegetables, provide clear proof that the gang had been prepared for a much longer stay?

In his biography, Reynolds states: 'We had enough food to last us for weeks if we found ourselves under siege. Every eventuality had been considered, I thought, but I was wrong.'

A few pages later, dealing with the issue of Brian Field's involvement, he says: 'He had always been a weak link, one that we had accepted in our confidence that the farm would never be associated with the robbery.'

In a 2001 interview for the ITV series *Real Crime*, Tommy Wisbey had this to say about Leatherslade Farm:

> Well, I thought the way it had been planned, they bought it on the sole reason they was gunna keep it 'cos it was thirty miles away from the actual crime so therefore there was no need to lose it. All it meant was someone being in the farm at the time to say that, if there was anybody coming round – 'cos this never happened till after the event, the radius of thirty miles and going round old outhouses and whatever – so then we decided if someone is there when we leave then they can just front the farm up. You know, we wouldn't be there, and it meant someone being there, saying if anyone was nosing around, 'Oh yes this our farm blah, blah, blah,' and they'd have gone away. But being as it was empty, the two policemen walked around it, found a window open and got in. But if someone had been there they wouldn't have been able to do it. Knocked on the door and that was it and then most probably gone away.

As the gang clearly had not anticipated a search of farms in the surrounding area it is possible that they originally intended to complete their purchase of Leatherslade Farm on 13 August. Given the size of the haul, £5,000 was a comparatively small amount, and in any case could be later redeemed legitimately if the farm was sold. They may have considered that purchasing the farm, once they had the money to do so, would also buy them time. Ownership of the farm would have allowed them to conceal themselves there for as long as they needed to and, more crucially, to take their time over destroying and disposing of evidence. This would explain why they went to all the trouble and additional expense of purchasing a hideout and the clear-up they undertook themselves before they left on Friday, 9 August was only cursory.

It was only as the post-robbery situation developed in unforeseen ways that the robbers abandoned their original plans. Instead of co-ordinating their efforts as a well-drilled team they panicked and started making hasty, spur-of-the-moment decisions driven by fear and self-preservation. As the gang made hurried, improvised escape plans, the focus was on staying one jump ahead of the law rather than worrying about what they were leaving behind. They may have still thought they would be able to return to the farm later, once the police activity had died down, and attend to the clean-up at their leisure. In the meantime, they might have envisaged that anyone calling at Leatherslade Farm would find the place unoccupied and assume the new owners had not yet moved in. With the gang's 'army-type' lorry now painted yellow, parked in a shed and no obvious evidence visible, the fleeing robbers may have hoped there was little to invite closer scrutiny.

It was only after the gang had escaped the claustrophobic confines of the farm that some of the more astute members began to worry that what they had left behind them was a time bomb.

Speculation aside, if the evidence at the farm had been dealt with effectively before the gang left that Friday, none of the mail-train robbers would ever have been successfully prosecuted. Given the available time and manpower, not to mention the gang's reputed criminal organisation, it would have taken only a modest amount of foresight, thought and work to have completely eliminated all the key evidence.

Whatever the explanation, Leatherslade Farm was the gang's most disastrous mistake and one from which the Great Train Robbers would never recover.

So why have the gang continued to promote the idea that the farm was to be meticulously cleared of evidence by a third party? The answer might be that, as authors of a robbery touted as 'the crime of the century', some of the robbers were keen to make their exploits fit the star billing. As I talked to Reynolds forty-eight years after the event, he told me, 'I never devalue the product.' For the members of the mail-train gang who were caught and sacrificed a decade of liberty, friends and family relationships, they had at least made their names and earned the lasting respect of not just the criminal world but many members of the British public. With the stolen money spent or mismanaged, reputation was all they had to show for it. That might have been too much to forfeit.

While the investigation in Buckinghamshire had focused on locating Leatherslade Farm, Scotland Yard detectives had been busy making discreet inquiries among their underworld informants. The names that had been supplied to C11 within days of the robbery – Robert Welch, John Daly, Gordon Goody, Roy James, Bruce Reynolds and Charles Wilson – were given particular attention.

By Wednesday, 14 August, the Flying Squad had sufficient information to make their move. Detective Inspector John Hensley, Sergeant Reid and other members of the squad got off to an early start, paying a 05.00 visit to Welch's home at 30 Benyon Road, London, N1. Welch's wife was at home to receive the search warrant, but he was not. Officers found nothing incriminating but took away a small quantity of cash, keys, a pair of shoes and a bill from the Flying Horse Hotel, Poultry, Nottingham. The hotel receipt, dated 23 May 1963, was for £19.7s. It showed that accommodation for five men had been charged to a Mr Richards.

Back at Leatherslade Farm, Wednesday morning saw the arrival of Detective Superintendent Maurice Ray and his team of fingerprint experts. A senior police photographer, plus two chief inspectors and four laboratory staff from the Forensic Science Laboratory also attended.

Fingerprint classification had changed little since Sir Edward Henry saw the potential for criminal investigation in fingerprint identification when he was an Inspector General of Police in India under British rule. Henry was later appointed Commissioner of the Metropolitan Police and in 1901 his Classification process became the cornerstone of Scotland Yard's first fingerprint department. The earliest use of fingerprint evidence in a criminal prosecution was in 1892, when it led to the conviction of an Argentine woman for a double murder. In the intervening years the retrieval of fingerprints had been honed to a fine art. By 1963, experts could not only lift prints from hard surfaces like glass and metal, they could also retrieve them from a wide variety of rougher surfaces, and even porous materials such as wood and paper. These developments were something the gang seem to have been unaware of in their haphazard attempt to clear traces of their occupation at Leatherslade Farm, and the resulting evidence would prove decisive in the criminal prosecutions of most of the robbers.

There was a huge quantity of fingerprint and forensic evidence to be gathered from the vehicles, farmhouse and outbuildings. The full list of items left in various places around the farmhouse was astonishing:

£627.10s. cash (Scottish banknotes)

A single man's leather glove

3 balaclavas

3 black hoods with eyeholes

A nylon stocking mask

Instructions on the use of handcuffs

6 sleeping bags

11 air beds

5 air cushions

13 blankets

20 towels

4 (6 volt) batteries – same size as those found on the gantry

40 torch batteries

A collection of games including Chess, Monopoly, Ludo and Snakes
    & Ladders

A lieutenant's jacket

A corporal's jacket

Waterproof and cold weather jackets

6 khaki denim jackets; 6 khaki denim trousers

Assorted blue denim overalls and jackets

A pair of blue denim trousers

A pair of bib-and-brace overalls

116 outer white mailbags

236 inner green mailbags

38 small white canvas bags

109 linen bags

43 canvas bank bags

13 bank belts from National Provincial and Midland banks

A collection of string and sealing wax

A large number of bank and GPO labels paper and wrappings

Various newspapers and magazines

In addition to fingerprinting and examining each of these items, the team were faced with the task of going over every inch of the farmhouse interior, along with the outbuildings, not to mention combing the surrounding grounds for evidence. The fingerprint and forensics experts were told to take as long as they needed to complete the job.

The forensics team weren't the only ones working at the farm that

Wednesday. To aid police communications, the GPO installed two telephone lines at the farm. Chief Inspector William John Knight of C10, the Stolen Car Squad, arrived and spent two hours examining the Land Rovers, both of which had been fitted with adhesive number plates, index number BMG757A. When Knight took a closer look at the Austin lorry he saw it had been originally dark green but had been crudely hand-painted with yellow. The lorry also had adhesive number plates, index number BPA260. Knight described these plates as the sort that would stick to any flat surface when dampened, the type normally used on sports cars or racing and rally cars. By cross-checking index numbers, engine and chassis numbers, C10 quickly established that the Austin lorry had been purchased recently, the older Series One Land Rover was originally registered 296POO and the newer Land Rover was stolen.

There was initially some suspicion about Bernard Rixon, as he had a criminal record. However, when Tommy Butler interviewed him he came to the conclusion that Rixon knew nothing of the plan to raid the mail train. Both Rixon and his solicitor were questioned about the sale of the farm and the relevant documents were passed to Detective Chief Inspector Mesher of C6, Scotland Yard's Fraud Squad, and he was instructed to make further inquiries.

Detective Superintendent Ray discovered that the single black leather glove found among the clothing left behind by the gang was identical to the one discovered at the trackside by British Railways signal technician Frank Mead on the morning of the robbery. During his initial examination of the farmhouse, Ray deduced that the surfaces and doors, particularly downstairs, had been 'wiped down'. Support for his theory came in the shape of two sponges left in the kitchen sink, which he was certain had been used to clean up.

The Wednesday, 14 August edition of the *Daily Express* carried the headline £14 *a week herdsman gave the tip on BANDIT FARM*. The accompanying article stated that if the discovery of the farm led to the arrest of the bandits, Maris could be in for the reward money. It was a cruel twist that, although Maris had been the first person to contact Aylesbury police about Leatherslade Farm, it had not been his telephone call that prompted the police to go there.

The *Express* reporter interviewed sixty-year-old Lily Brooks, whose home The Bungalow was on the Thame Road close to the farm. She explained that she had handed over the keys to a man she believed was the new owner. Mrs Brooks was quoted as saying, '... he was tall, fair and charming and said, "Good morning, I have come to collect the keys for Leatherslade." He was dressed in an expensive sports suit. He was not a countryman. He had a London accent.' She recalled saying, 'I hope you will be very happy,' to which he replied, 'I expect I shall be, very.'

The description sounded like Reynolds, although neither Mrs Brooks nor the reporter would have known that at the time. Clearly Mrs Brooks would be in a position to identify the man if she saw him again.

The Times carried the news that a grocer in Brill had put up a sign in his shop window – 'Old Bank notes accepted'.

Meanwhile a police vehicle toured the area around Brill broadcasting the following message over its public address system:

> Can you help the police? Can you give us any information about the recent occupants of Leatherslade Farm? Or about activities at the farm in the past two weeks? If so please call at Brill police station or telephone Brill 802.

The appeal was heard by Mrs Nappin, who lived in a cottage near the junction of Thame Road and Brill Road. Immediately recalling the convoy that had passed her home in the early hours of Thursday morning, she contacted the police. According to her statement, on 7 August she had gone to bed at about 22.00, but woke at midnight and could not get back to sleep. Looking out of her window, which faced the Thame Road, her attention was drawn to a bright light on a vehicle coming towards her. As it approached the headlights were dimmed. She saw three vehicles and heard a motorcycle turn right on to the Brill Road, and they passed in front of her house going in the direction of Brill. She woke again at about 04.00 and again could not get back to sleep. At around 04.30 she heard approaching vehicles and went to the window. A covered lorry and another vehicle were coming from the direction of Brill and again she thought she heard a motorcycle engine. They passed in front of her cottage, turned left on to Thame Road and drove off in the direction of Leatherslade Farm. They were showing only dim lights but she was certain they were the same vehicles she had seen earlier.

While the description of the vehicles was not an exact match for the configuration of the robber's convoy, the timing fitted perfectly. Mrs Nappin had witnessed the gang on their way to the robbery and on their return four hours later.

In London, Jimmy White dropped his Austin Healey 3000 off at Zenith Motors on Aldersgate, and asked the mechanic, William Phillips, to tune the engine, fit four new tyres and a new exhaust system. He told Phillips he lived above the café opposite the garage.

In Bournemouth it was a case of 'Groundhog Day'. Boal and Cordrey bought another vehicle, a grey Austin A35 van, registration number UEL937, from Robert Nabney at Northbourne service station. As before, Boal was the front man while Cordrey loitered in the background in his panama hat and sunglasses. Nabney had the car for sale at £225. Presumably to add to the charade, Boal negotiated the price down to £210 cash. He said the car was for the other man and gave Cordrey's details as Mr J. Gosdin, 23 Lyndale Road, Southbourne, West Sussex.

They now had three vehicles – and Boal could not drive. Their plan was to hide the money in two of the vehicles and use the Ford Anglia as a runabout. Next stop was the flat above the florist's shop in Wimborne Road, where they loaded some of the loot, packed in six suitcases, into the boot of the Rover then took it to the garage in Ensbury Avenue, rented the previous day from Ruby Saunders. Having safely deposited the Rover, the two men set off in search of a second garage to rent. They'd driven all over Bournemouth by the time Boal spotted an advertisement in a newsagent's window in Castle Road. He immediately rang the number.

At 20.15 that evening, Boal arrived at the home of sixty-seven-year-old Ethel Emily Clarke in Tweedale Road, Bournemouth. Mrs Clarke was initially reluctant, saying that she wanted to let the garage to someone who lived locally. Boal assured her that he would shortly be moving to the area and offered to pay more than she was asking. They agreed the rent and he paid three months in advance: £7.10s. cash, which he produced from a large roll of notes in his pocket. Mrs Clarke gave Boal the key to the garage and he said he would bring the car later that evening.

Maybe it was her 'Miss Marple' instincts, or perhaps the fact that her late husband had been a Hampshire police officer, but a few minutes after Boal left, Ethel Clarke telephoned the police.

17

At 20.40 on Wednesday, 14 August, Detective Sergeant Stanley Davies of Bournemouth CID was informed of Mrs Clarke's telephone call. He immediately drove to Tweedale Road accompanied by Detective Constable Charles Case. As the police officers made their way along the quiet cul-de-sac they spotted two men standing by the garage, located down the side of the semi-detached property.

Davies and Case then spoke to Mrs Clarke, who explained the men had just returned and put a car in the garage. While they were talking, Cordrey and Boal walked off down the road and Davies went after them.

Outside 9 Tweedale Road, Cordrey and Boal split up. Cordrey went into the front garden while Boal crossed the road and started walking back in the direction of Mrs Clarke's house. Davies followed Cordrey and asked him to accompany him to the police car. Back up the street, Boal was intercepted by Detective Constable Case and led to the car where Davies was talking to Cordrey. Davies told both men that he suspected them of breaking into houses in the area and cautioned them.

Despite having been seen talking with Cordrey at the garage only minutes earlier and walking off down the street with him, Boal protested, 'I have never seen this man in my life. I live here. I have a business in Wimborne.'

When Davies told Boal that he wanted to search him, Boal suddenly became violent and tried to get away. He had to be restrained and Davies radioed for assistance. After a struggle, both men were handcuffed and put into a police van.

Cordrey doubted that Boal's denial was going to work. Aside from having been seen together, they both had keys to the same flat. On arriving at Bournemouth police station, Cordrey asked to go the toilet and hid the flat key in his rectum.

Cordrey and Boal were separated and searched. Cordrey had on him several other keys and £159.3s.3d. in cash. Boal had a receipt for the

Austin A35 van, some keys, including one with a label attached showing the address of the garage they had rented from Miss Saunders in
Ensbury Avenue, £118.10s.½d. in cash, and a lady's right-hand glove.

Cordrey was put in a cell while Boal was taken to the charge room
and questioned. At this stage the police officers had no idea the two
men were connected with the mail-train raid, but their behaviour, particularly Boal's, was arousing suspicions.

Boal was calmer when questioned. He gave his correct name, date
of birth and address, 23 Burnthwaite Road, London, SW6. He said he
owned an engineering company called Precision Works at 43a Queens
Road, Sheen, London, SW14.

Sergeant Davies asked him about the vehicle he had parked in Mrs
Clarke's garage. Boal said that he had bought the Austin A35 van that
afternoon but would not explain why. When Davies pressed for an
answer, Boal suddenly lost control and shouted, 'I'm an honest, well-
known businessman and will not be interrogated in this way!'

Boal was then taken down to the cells and Cordrey was brought
up. He was asked where he had got the money that was found on him.
Cordrey said nothing and was taken back to his cell.

Boal and Cordrey had dug themselves into a hole. Their behaviour
had been odd and irrational, and they were now locked in separate
police cells, each trying to think how they could bluff their way out.
They had resisted the police officers' efforts to bring them in, but that
might be seen as understandable if the police had nothing on them.
After all, on the face of it, they had done nothing wrong.

While both men were brooding, Sergeant Davies returned to
Tweedale Road at 22.30. Using the keys found on Boal, and with Mrs
Clarke's permission, Davies unlocked the garage and searched the
Austin A35 van. In the back he saw a suitcase. In the suitcase was a
green canvas bag. To Davies' amazement, when he unzipped the bag he
found £56,047 in five- and one-pound notes.

Returning to Bournemouth police station at 23.00, Davies gave the
bag of money to his detective superintendent and the two officers discussed what to do next.

At 23.15 Boal was interviewed again.

Without mentioning the money discovered in the Austin garaged at
Tweedale Road Davies asked, 'Are there any other vehicles?'

Boal told him about the Ford Anglia, registration number RHJ383, which he said they had left in the car park of the Horse and Jockey Hotel in Wimborne Road.

It seemed a straightforward answer. But not all the keys the police had found on the men were accounted for.

Davies put a second question: 'Have you got any other vehicles in Bournemouth?'

Boal became agitated again and did not answer. Davies left the charge room for twenty minutes.

He returned at 23.35 with two other officers and asked Boal to remove his clothing, saying that it was needed for scientific examination. Boal was furious and refused.

As might be expected, there are two accounts of what followed.

Detective Sergeant Davies' story was that Boal waved his arms around and had to be restrained, but no punches were thrown by either side. He said Boal removed his own clothing. The bruise to his head had been sustained when he 'fell against the wall'.

Boal, on the other hand, claimed that the police officers forcibly removed his clothing and he was hit repeatedly. He said that one police officer grabbed hold of his feet, another took his legs, and his shoes and trousers were pulled off while Davies 'dragged his coat off backwards'. Davies asked him again about the keys and knocked him into the wall, at which point Boal started bleeding from his nose and mouth. The two officers then held him while Davies pummelled him in the stomach.

With Boal now in his shirt, socks and underpants, the officers left the interview room. Davies said they provided Boal with a blanket. Boal said they did not. It was certainly an undignified predicament for a man of forty-nine to find himself in. He was returned to his cell.

Cordrey was then brought up. He gave his correct name and supplied his address: 4 Hurst Road, East Molesey, Surrey. Asked about the money found in the car at Mrs Clarke's house, Cordrey said it was not his, it belonged to a man called Freddie he had met at Brighton Races. Davies asked what Cordrey was doing in Bournemouth. Cordrey said he was staying at an address in Wimborne Road.

Unconvinced by Cordrey's explanation about the money, Davies had him put back in his cell.

At 01.15 the Ford Anglia was found at the Horse and Jockey Hotel in Wimborne Road by Constables Archer and Webley. No money was found inside the vehicle.

At 01.45 other officers drove with Sergeant Davies to the address attached to one of the keys found on Boal. At Miss Saunders' house in Ensbury Avenue they unlocked the garage and found the Rover 105R, registration number TLX279. Using keys found on Boal they unlocked the Rover, searched the inside and the boot. In total there were six suitcases in the car containing £78,982 in used banknotes.

At 03.00 officers searching the flat above the florist's shop in Wimborne Road discovered two briefcases, one brown and one black. The brown briefcase contained £5,060 in five- and one-pound notes, and in the black case were several letters addressed to Boal, along with log books for the Rover and Ford Anglia, a notebook, and twenty-seven engineering blueprints. They found a further £840 under a pillow in one of the bedrooms.

Back at the police station the haul of cash had grown impressively: Boal had £118.18s.½d. on him when searched and Cordrey £160.3s.3d. This was now added to the £56,047 in the bag in the Austin A35 van found in Mrs Clarke's garage, a further £78,982 found in six suitcases in the Rover at Miss Saunders' garage. With the addition of £5,910 discovered at the flat, the cash totalled £141,218.1s.3½d.

Cordrey was brought up from the cells again. Davies went over what he had retrieved from the various locations. Cordrey admitted the money had come from the mail-train robbery. When questioned, Boal denied any involvement in the train raid, or any knowledge that was where the money had come from. He said he had been threatened by Cordrey and coerced into helping him. To try and extricate himself further, Boal contested the ownership of the keys each man had on him when searched. Both men refused to sign for the property found in their possession.

As soon as he'd realised that his suspects were probably a couple of train robbers, Davies had put through a call to the incident room in Aylesbury. At 05.50 on Thursday, 15 August, Fewtrell, Pritchard and McArthur arrived in Bournemouth to question Boal and Cordrey. It is not known whether the detectives were aware at this point that Roger Cordrey had been under observation by the Post Office Investigation

Branch since 1961 in connection with suspected offences including stealing mailbags from Southern Railways.

Boal continued to insist that he did not know 'that the money came from the railway job'. He was cautioned and then made a statement saying that he had been forced to stay in Bournemouth by Cordrey and that he had no part in the mail-train raid. When Cordrey was interviewed he refused to answer any of the questions put to him.

While the interviews continued, Detective Sergeant Peter Southey was sent to Northbourne service station. Robert Nabney confirmed that he had sold a grey Austin A35 van to Boal the previous day and handed over the thirty-four five-pound notes and forty-one one-pound notes he had received in payment.

During the long hours of searching, questioning and waiting, Cordrey began to grow increasingly concerned about the key he had concealed when he first arrived at Bournemouth police station. He had one further revelation to make to the officers: he could not retrieve it. The police doctor, Maxwell Saunders, was called out from his home and at 13.15 he extracted the second key for the flat in Wimborne Road from Cordrey's rectum.

Later that Thursday, Frances Reynolds called at the home of Bruce's father and stepmother at 113 Lindsey Road in Dagenham, Essex. She asked them to look after their grandson, Nick, for two or three days. It is not known whether Franny explained to her father-in-law the reasons why, but given that Thomas Richard Reynolds was a hardworking, honest man it is unlikely that he would have been happy to learn that his son was part of the mail-train gang.

Like Reynolds, Buster Edwards had decided that he, his wife, June and their daughter, Nicolette, should make themselves scarce, leave their flat at 214 St Margaret's Road, Twickenham and find alternative accommodation. Using the name Mr and Mrs Green, the Edwardses rented a house in Old Forge Crescent, Shepperton for twelve guineas a week. The area was respectable, suburban and middle-class, and June told neighbours they planned to be there for about a year. Whether this was just a cover story they had decided upon or they actually planned staying for that long is hard to tell, but the house at Old Forge Crescent was a strange choice of hideaway, being only eight miles from their old address, which was searched by police shortly after the Edwardses left.

In the Captain's Bayswater flat, Reynolds was following developments reported by the media. The involvement of the Flying Squad and the familiar names of Tommy Butler and Peter Vibart indicated that the police investigation had stepped up a gear. Another familiar name was that of fingerprint expert Detective Superintendent Maurice Ray. In his biography, Reynolds says that Ray frequented a pub called the Marlborough Arms where they both enjoyed after-hours drinking sessions. In conversation, Reynolds said that despite Ray's reputation he remained confident that nothing would be found by the forensic team – 'They'd find the same blank canvas as when they "printed" the locomotive and the coaches. We'd left nothing behind.'

The *Daily Express* headline on 15 August was *NINETEEN NAMES. Yard Files Dossier on the Train Robbers.* The article began: 'Scotland Yard's picture of the Train Gang built up last night into a rogue's gallery of 19 suspects. The problem was how to pick them up without losing the £2,500,000 loot.'

Members of the Flying Squad train-robbery team had been quick to respond to the arrests of Cordrey and Boal. Detective Inspector John Hensley, Detective Sergeant Nigel Reid and Detective Sergeant Marshall arrived at Boal's house in Fulham at 01.15 that morning. Renee Boal answered the door and invited the police officers into her home. When the officers explained that her husband had been arrested in Bournemouth, Renee led Hensley and Marshall upstairs to a bedroom where she produced £325 cash in five-pound notes from a chest of drawers and handed it to the detectives.

At 03.30 Detective Inspector Hensley and his team drew up outside 119 Bridge Road, East Molesey, Surrey. It was the home of Alfred William Pilgrim and his wife Florence May Pilgrim, Cordrey's sister. While searching the house, the officers found £850 in cash.

Renee Boal was arrested and taken to Rochester Row while the Pilgrims were transported to Cannon Row police station for questioning. Mrs Boal was later charged with receiving 65 five-pound notes. Alfred and May Pilgrim were charged with receiving 172 five-pound notes knowing or believing the money to be stolen.

*

At Leatherslade Farm police vehicles and officers came and went all day. The gateway was guarded by several uniformed constables who stood chatting with pressmen and bystanders. Up at the farmhouse, Scotland Yard's top forensic team spent a second day going over the building, vehicles and farmyard in minute detail.

BBC reporter Reginald Abbiss interviewed Lily Brooks who recounted a slightly more polished version of the interview she had given to the *Express* reporter about handing over the keys to Leatherslade Farm.

There was also an interview with a local boy whose hobby was collecting car numbers in a notebook. The boy explained with pride that the police had questioned him about vehicles he had seen and asked for the information he collected. Viewers familiar with *The League of Gentlemen* would no doubt have recalled the small boy in the film whose collection of registration numbers led to the capture of the fictional gang. It was another extraordinary example of the real-life robbery mimicking fiction.

The Fraud Squad meanwhile had been poring over the documents provided by Rixon's solicitor, Mr Meirion-Williams, concerning the sale of Leatherslade Farm. The names of Brian Field's boss, solicitor John Wheater, and Leonard Field, the man they had used to 'front' the transaction, were earmarked for further investigation.

At the end of a long session in Bournemouth, Fewtrell, McArthur and Pritchard had to borrow additional cars to transport Cordrey and Boal back to Aylesbury HQ along with seven suitcases of banknotes. A small crowd of press and onlookers had gathered to watch the five-car convoy's arrival at 21.30.

Shortly before midnight, Roger John Cordrey and William Alfred Boal were charged that 'On 8 August 1963, at Mentmore in the County of Buckinghamshire being concerned together and with other persons at present unknown armed with instruments robbed Frank Dewhurst of £2,631,784 in money the property of Her Majesty's Post Master General'.

The figure on the charge sheet was incorrect, but no one was in any mood to quibble.

18

The arrests of Cordrey and Boal gave the police 'new heart' according to ex-Detective Superintendent Malcolm Fewtrell. In his memoirs he wrote: '... in spite of careful planning and timing of the train raid the robbers had made mistakes. These two had rushed off after the raid without any clear idea of what to do ...' Fewtrell concludes '... if there were two clowns among the villains perhaps the raid planners had not been as clever as we thought they had'.

Seventy miles south of Aylesbury, early on the morning of Friday, 16 August 1963, forty-five-year-old John Ahern was going to work on his motorcycle with a fellow clerk, Mrs Nina Hargreaves, riding pillion. They stopped at 08.35 at some woods on Coldharbour Lane, Leith Hill, near Dorking, Surrey. The reason given by Ahern for the break in their journey was that the engine of his motorcycle was overheating and he needed to let it cool down.

While they were waiting, the couple decided to take a walk into the woods. When they got to a clearing, about twenty yards from the road, Ahern spotted three bags covered with polythene – a holdall, a camel-coloured bag and a briefcase. Opening one of the bags, he discovered it was full of banknotes. With all the recent publicity about the mail-train robbery, Ahern and his companion quickly surmised that the money could be connected. They ran back to the road and flagged down a passing car.

The driver, Bill Howard, was with his wife and their twenty-three-year-old daughter, Betty, whom he was giving a lift to work. Ahern and Mrs Hargreaves told the Howards what they had found and took them to see the bags. Nina Hargreaves was nervous that the criminals might be somewhere nearby and could return at any minute to collect their loot. Bill Howard volunteered to go and call the police and suggested that Ahern and Mrs Hargreaves wait by the roadside.

Minutes later the Howards arrived at a nearby cottage and the owner, Mrs Hinds, promptly telephoned Dorking police station.

When Detective Inspector Basil West arrived at the woods with another officer and a police dog, Ahern and Hargreaves were waiting at the roadside and led them to the bags they had discovered. West noted that, although the ground was wet and it had been raining overnight, the bags were quite dry. Searching the immediate area, the German shepherd, who went by the name of Mount Browne Kevin, and his handler found another suitcase seventy-five yards away. It too was full of money.

At Dorking police station West handed the four bags over to Inspector George Cork, who proceeded to unpack them and note the contents. There was so much money to deal with that Cork called in two local bank clerks to help count it. After several hours' diligent work, the clerks finally declared the cash from the camel-coloured bag totalled £36,500; in the holdall there was £7,000; the briefcase held £26,500 and the large suitcase £30,900. The grand total was £100,900.

Detective Constable Alexander Illing had been examining the bags for fingerprints. He found thirteen prints, and in the bottom of a zip pocket in the camel-coloured bag was a receipt for 358 marks and 40 pfennigs from the Café Pension Restaurant, Hotel Sonnenbichl, Hindelang, Germany, dated February 1963. At the top of the bill was written Herr and Frau Field.

The headline on the front page Friday's *Daily Express* was *MIDNIGHT CHARGES*. The *Daily Mirror* led with *5 HELD – THEN A BLACKOUT BY YARD*. *The Times* also reported the arrests of Boal and Cordrey (although *The Times* misspelled his name as Cowdrey). The good news was that nearly £150,000 of the stolen money had been recovered following the arrests of two men in Bournemouth and the subsequent arrests of a blonde woman in London and a couple from East Molesey. The report said that all five were to appear before Linslade Magistrates later that day.

The Pilgrims' friends and family in East Molesey were stunned by the news. In the *Express* a neighbour was quoted as saying, 'They're a lovely family. So hard-working. Very respected.' The Pilgrims' sons, Stephen and Terry, were left minding the business the family had run for the past ten years, Buttonhole florist's shop, with its green-and-white sunblind. Looking bewildered among the chrysanthemums, gladioli and carnations, when asked by a reporter for his comment Stephen said, 'I don't know what is going on.'

News of the arrests in Bournemouth had spread quickly. The *Daily Mirror* reported on events the previous night: 'Outside the police station in the narrow Exchange Street, Aylesbury, a crowd of 200 had been waiting for nearly two hours for the police convoy to arrive from Bournemouth. As the prisoners arrived they were cheered and clapped by some of the people in the crowd.'

The first car in the convoy was a black Jaguar with its blue roof light flashing, next came a grey Jaguar with Detective Superintendent Gerald McArthur in the front and a covered figure sandwiched between two officers in the back. The third car was another black Jaguar containing Detective Superintendent Malcolm Fewtrell and a man in the rear seat with an overcoat over his head.

Already locked in cells at the police station were Renee Boal and Alfred and May Pilgrim. And waiting patiently in the interview room to greet the new arrivals was the Grey Fox, Detective Superintendent Tommy Butler.

The police issued a statement, no doubt authored by Butler: 'We regret we cannot disclose to the public what we are doing or where our inquiries are taking us.'

At 11.00 on Friday, 16 August Detective Sergeant John Swain and Detective Sergeant Burdett of the Flying Squad knocked on the door of 6 Commondale, Putney, London, SW15. It was the home of Mrs Goody and her son Gordon. Getting no response, the officers waited a few minutes, stood back, looked up at the windows and knocked again. No one appeared to be in the house, so they drove away.

A crowd had gathered in the road outside Linslade Magistrates' Court near Cheddington in Buckinghamshire when shortly before noon a blue minibus carrying the accused drew up at the entrance. Two women covered their heads with a policewoman's cape and were led out of the side doors. Three men draped with dark-blue blankets were taken out of the back doors by uniformed police officers and escorted through the main entrance to the courthouse.

Inside the tiny courtroom the proceedings were brief. From the witness box Fewtrell outlined the sequence of events leading to the arrests of the three men and two women the police now held in custody. McArthur then gave his corroborating evidence.

All the while the accused stood in line in the cramped dock, listening to the litany of indictments against them. Mrs Boal and Mrs Pilgrim were next to each other in blue winter coats. The three men, Arthur Pilgrim, William Boal and Roger Cordrey, wore open-necked shirts. The accounts given by the policemen were simple, damning and conclusive. Cordrey and Boal had been found in possession of £141,218. Boal's wife, Renee, with £325; May and Alfred Pilgrim £850. All the confiscated cash was believed to have been stolen during the mail-train raid in the early morning of Thursday, 8 August. Little further evidence was needed to convince Linslade magistrates to remand all five in custody for a week.

Alfred Pilgrim, Boal and Cordrey were led from the courtroom handcuffed and under blankets and driven away to Bedford Prison. Renee Boal and May Pilgrim were taken to Holloway women's prison in London.

At New Scotland Yard, Robert Welch was interviewed by Flying Squad officers Roberts and Byers. He had contacted the police voluntarily after learning that inquiries were being made about him. Welch told the detectives he had never been to Aylesbury or any nearby towns. He made a statement that he was at his home with his wife on the night of 7/8 August and was told he was free to go.

At 16.00, Flying Squad detectives Swain and Burdett returned to 6 Commondale, Putney. Mrs Goody came to the door and the officers explained who they were. She told them her son was not at home. Swain said he had a search warrant and that they wished to search the house and garden. Without asking to see any documents, Mrs Goody invited the police officers into her home. The detectives spent some time going through the house but found nothing incriminating. Swain and Burdett thanked Mrs Goody and left.

It was fortunate for the investigation that nothing important was found at Goody's house as it transpired later that Swain was not in possession of a warrant when the search was made. Although Mrs Goody had invited them in, she did so in the belief that the officers had a warrant to search her house. In the circumstances, any evidence discovered on that visit would have been ruled inadmissible.

Reynolds later recalled that the news of Cordrey's and Boal's arrests 'dropped like a bombshell' and destroyed his confidence. However, there was the prospect of less pressure too, as he believed the focus of the investigation would shift to Cordrey and his South Coast Raiders gang.

Briefly abandoning his self-imposed incarceration in the Captain's flat, Reynolds decided to dispose of the black Austin Healey that he had bought at the Chequered Flag Garage in Chiswick the day after the robbery. He'd left it in the care of Terry Hogan, who had parked it in his garage at 10 Walpole Lodge, Cumlington Road, Ealing. Hogan's neighbour, James Bryning, subsequently reported to police that he had noticed the Healey parked outside Walpole Lodge on 13, 14 and 15 August, and seen Hogan garaging it behind the flats.

Reynolds drove the Healey to Cranford Hall Garage in Hayes, Middlesex, with Hogan following in his green Ford Zodiac. Reynolds told pump attendant John Leaby that he was leaving the car for a few days while he was away and he asked for the vehicle to be thoroughly cleaned inside and out. In the event the Healey was later found by the police, the proximity to London Airport was intended to suggest that Reynolds had left the country.

Over the weekend, crowds gathered outside Leatherslade Farm, parking their cars on the grass verges of the B4011 Thame Road near the entrance, hoping to get a glimpse of the notorious hideout. Also at the entrance was BBC Television reporter Reginald Abbiss:

Out here in the Buckinghamshire countryside it's been a case of destination robber's roost. All day scores of cars, motorcycles and bicycles have been arriving at the gates of Leatherslade Farm where the mail bandits hid with their loot for a few days after the train ambush. But the people here, and there have been quite a lot today, can't get any further than the main gates of the farm which are guarded by the police. Only official callers are welcome. While up at the farmhouse itself detectives have been continuing their painstaking search looking for fingerprints and who knows what else. The search will widen tomorrow when many more police officers will be called in to make another painstaking and minute search of the farmlands around the farmhouse itself.

Watching news reports about the discovery of Leatherslade Farm, solicitor John Wheater, realising the inevitable, had contacted the police the day after it was found. In an interview with Detective Sergeant Hughes, Field's boss stated that he had been acting on behalf of a client, Leonard Field, who was the prospective purchaser of Leatherslade Farm. Wheater gave his client's address as 150 Earls Court Road, London, W5.

On Monday, 19 August, Wheater was interviewed again, this time by McArthur and Pritchard. Wheater confirmed the information he had given in his statement, referring as he did so to his client's file, which appeared to have very little in it. McArthur asked to see the file. When he queried the absence of correspondence between Field and his solicitor, Wheater explained that it was because Leonard Field had been in the office almost daily in connection with other matters. McArthur took the file away with him.

At this stage, the police were still under the impression that John Wheater would help them find his client. In reality, Wheater was desperately trying to think of ways to throw them off the scent.

Flying Squad officers called at the address Wheater had given them for Leonard Field, a three-storey Victorian terraced house with peeling blue walls. The building was divided into a number of dingy bedsits. They spoke to a Mr Paplinski, who ran a members-only drinking club in the ground floor and basement, and were told that the house had been sold three months earlier. The ten bedsits on the upper floors were empty. Paplinski said he used to manage the building for the previous owner, the late Mr Rachman, but did not recall Leonard Field.

The Scotland Yard detectives knew all about Peter Rachman, a Polish Jew whose dubious business interests had made him notorious. He had ended up in Britain at the end of the Second World War after having joined the Polish army after his 1939 internment in a Soviet labour camp in Siberia. By the mid-1950s Rachman had established himself as a landlord, mainly in the Notting Hill area of London, where his exploitation of the Afro-Caribbean immigrants who made up the majority of his tenants was so blatant and unscrupulous that the word

'Rachmanism' entered the Oxford English Dictionary as a synonym for a greedy landlord.

John Wheater had no doubt come up with the idea of using 150 Earls Court Road as a bogus address for Leonard Field because his firm had acted for Rachman's widow in the mortgaging of the property. Given Rachman's notoriety, it was an injudicious association.

Wheater had probably been introduced to Rachman by Brian Field, whose wife Karin had encountered the infamous landlord during her time as a showgirl at Mayfair's Winston Club. In the *Stern* articles Karin describes how, after quitting her third job as an au pair, she found employment at the club: 'I was given a glittering costume with a few feathers on my head and on my bum and just very little at all elsewhere. It was pretty primitive but at least I earned £35 a week.' At the time, drag artist Danny La Rue was headlining at the Winston Club, which he did for seven years from 1957. There was a string of such clubs in the West End, including the Cabinet Club in Gerrard Street, Al Burnett's Stork Club and Tommy McCarthy's Log Cabin in Wardour Street. The potent cocktail of cabaret, late-night booze and hostesses attracted a mixed clientele of society types and the likes of the Kray twins, Freddie Foreman, Frankie Fraser and Billy Hill. According to Fraser, he and Hill got a 'pension' from the owner of Winston's, Bruce Brace. Clubs which were not run by gangsters paid protection.

This sleazy environment was a world away from Karin's staunchly religious, conservative German upbringing; her mother was a member of the synod in Hanover. The *Stern* series includes an account of her introduction to Peter Rachman at the Winston Club. She claims that he offered her a free apartment in Mayfair, a sports car, clothes and jewellery in return for being a hostess at his parties. Rachman's parties would later gain national notoriety when it became known that infamous call girls Christine Keeler and Mandy Rice-Davies had been his mistresses and he had owned the mews house in Marylebone from which they plied their trade. Karin declined, having found herself an admirer with more serious intentions; a young solicitor's clerk called Brian Field. How the relatively impoverished Field could afford to hang around in Mayfair clubs is open to question. At the time he was married to his first wife, Brenda, a secretary at John Wheater's law firm, but clearly Field had more exotic aspirations.

The Flying Squad officers searching for Leonard Field were initially unaware of the various connections between Rachman and solicitors James and Wheater. But meanwhile, following the Brian Field branch of the investigation, Detective Superintendent Malcolm Fewtrell had contacted Interpol and asked them to confirm the identity of Herr and Frau Field, on the hotel bill found in a zip pocket of one of the bags containing the money discovered in Dorking woods.

In Buckinghamshire, the police were contacted by Mr Wyatt, the farmer who had gone to Leatherslade Farm to enquire about renting a field. He told them he had called at the farmhouse at between 10.30 and 11.00 two days before the robbery, and reported seeing two men in the garden, one of them elderly, sitting in a deckchair 'enjoying the sun'. The younger man, whom Wyatt described as tall and between twenty-five and thirty, had told him they were decorating the house for the new owners.

Mr Wyatt wasn't the only one who'd been following the unfolding mail-train robbery story in the news. The police received a 999 call from Mrs Phyllis Evans, owner of Cranford Hall Garage in Hayes, Middlesex. Her suspicions had been aroused by a tall man in 'a blazer and thick glasses' who had called at the garage on Friday saying that he was taking a plane at nearby London Airport and wanted somewhere to park while he was away. The man asked for the car to be cleaned and said he would be returning on 7 September. Officers were immediately sent to inspect the car for fingerprints and it was subsequently removed to Aylesbury.

Still on the trail of the other Austin Healey and the suspicious couple who had been seen driving it and questioned in Reigate on Tuesday, 13 August, Surrey police were keeping the caravan that had been purchased by Mr Ballard under observation at the Clovelly Caravan Site, Boxhill Road, near Dorking.

On Sunday, 18 August a man arrived in a black Ford Cortina 692GLH and was stopped as he entered the caravan by Detective Inspector Basil West. The man gave his name as Harry John Brown and said he worked in W&M Regan betting shop at 38 Aldersgate Street, London, EC1. When asked why he was entering the caravan, Brown explained that a man called Jim Bollard [sic] who ran a café next door to the betting shop had offered the caravan to him and his family for a week's holiday. After further questioning, there were no grounds on which to detain Brown any longer. However, the names Bollard and Ballard obviously referred to the same man and now Inspector West had another address connected to the man and woman they had been investigating.

On Monday, 19 August, further inquiries into the identity of the couple yielded more information. The owner of Clovelly Caravan Site was sixty-nine-year-old Mrs Hetty Dunford. Her husband informed police that the caravan belonging to Mr Ballard had been bought by two men who told his wife they ran a coffee bar. 'The following day one of the men returned, accompanied by a woman and a baby girl. They had a white poodle with them in the car.'

A neighbour at the site, Mrs Vera Rukin, reported a lot of banging after the new owners arrived. 'It seemed rather odd,' she said, 'as there isn't a great deal of repair in a new caravan.'

Having discovered that the couple they had questioned were no longer occupying the address at Beulah Hill and no rent had been paid since 24 June, Surrey police decided the time had come to take a closer look at the cream-and-fawn four-berth caravan they had been watching. Behind the red-checked curtains of the caravan, officers got to work systematically removing the interior panelling. Their diligence was finally rewarded when a section above a window was removed and they discovered a large quantity of five-pound notes.

The manager and a clerk from the Dorking branch of Midland Bank were called in to count the cash. It totalled £30,440.

The caravan was later examined by Detective Sergeant Wright of Scotland Yard who lifted several prints which were identified as belonging to James Edward White and his partner Sheree. It was now clear that Patten, Ballard and James Edward White were one and the same man.

On Monday, broadcasting from the road outside Leatherslade Farm in buoyant Pathé Newsreel tones, the BBC's Reginald Abbiss had a further update for viewers:

Well, here they go, a police car leading the convoy to the county police headquarters at Aylesbury. The yellow-fronted truck, the three-ton lorry, which the police found at Leatherslade Farm, robber's roost, covered with a tarpaulin. And two field cars which the robbers also left. Away they go to be examined again.

In the old black-and-white archive film images it is possible to see that Jimmy White's attempts to cover the khaki paintwork of the Austin lorry were poor. Flanked by press photographers and members of the public standing at the gate, the Series One Land Rover with a canvas roof followed next, and last in the convoy was the Series Two SWB Land Rover with no roof at all.

By the end of Monday the police had withdrawn from Leatherslade Farm, taking with them everything the robbers had left behind.

The headline of the *Daily Mirror* on Tuesday, 20 August was *5s-A-PEEP PLAN FOR GANG FARM*. The article revealed Bernard Rixon's intention to turn the farmhouse into an 'exhibition', charging members of the public five shillings admission (half a crown for children) to the infamous robbers' hideout.

The police were keeping quiet about the possible forensic and fingerprint evidence found at the farm, but the obsessively secretive Tommy Butler and his Flying Squad colleagues were trying to persuade their superiors, Hatherill and Millen, to extend the embargo by not releasing photographs of suspects to the press.

Publishing images of individuals suspected of a crime would inevitably serve to prejudice a future jury. However, what concerned Butler and his team was that declaring exactly whom they were looking for would simply drive those individuals into hiding. The Grey Fox was tenacious and astute when it came to tracking down criminals, and his objections were a matter of common sense. Nevertheless, Hatherill was determined to go ahead and release the photos. He argued that the enormous reward on offer would not only encourage the public to be vigilant, it would tempt other criminals to provide information, thereby making it very difficult for the wanted men to find refuge anywhere.

19

Despite Reynolds' initial belief that the arrest of Cordrey would divert the investigation away from him and his associates, the observation and questioning of suspects was still continuing, hovering ominously around him and the rest of the gang. It wasn't only the mail-train gang whose movements were being hampered by the investigation; every criminal in London was keeping their head down. The early sixties London crime wave had not abated altogether, but there was a definite lull in activity.

Tommy Wisbey had been the first name to be put forward by a police informant but at that early stage of the investigation it had not been taken seriously. But with their knowledge of working links between London criminals and underworld contacts the Flying Squad team had let it be known they wanted to talk to Wisbey. On Tuesday, 20 August, he presented himself at Scotland Yard. Wisbey was interviewed by Detective Inspector Roberts and made a statement, not under caution. He told Roberts that he had been at a pub until 23.00 on the night of the robbery and the landlord would corroborate his story. He then went to his mother's house as, following a domestic argument, he was not living at home at the time.

The choice of alibi was simple but open to question. One of the Flying Squad aces, Detective Inspector Frank Williams, knew the landlord Wisbey had mentioned very well. For years Williams had made it his business to get to know the haunts and associates of South London criminals and that meant he also knew how to bring pressure to bear when he wanted something. But that line of inquiry would have to be worked on. Wisbey was released even though he said he was shortly going on holiday to Spain, which at the time had no extradition treaty with Britain.

On Wednesday, 21 August, the proprietor of Zenith Motors Ltd, 170 Aldersgate, London, EC1, informed the police that an Austin Healey registration number REN22 had not been collected by the owner.

White's Healey was later removed by PC Bartlett of the Stolen Car Squad and taken to Chalk Farm police garage. White's caravan was on its way to Aylesbury along with the £30,440 in five-pound notes recovered, but there was no further trace of him.

Page five of the *Daily Mirror* displayed three photographs released by police of the provisions and utensils found at Leatherslade Farm. Although there were still reports circulating in the press about the gang having consisted of twenty men, the inventory of plates, cups, knives and forks listed only fifteen or sixteen sets of each. Other, less obvious, inferences were made. The *Mirror* reported that the discovery of a tea-strainer among the items suggested that 'a woman was involved in the stocking up. Police believe that few men would think of such a thing.'

At noon, Detective Inspector Frank Williams and Chief Inspector William Baldock interviewed Mary Manson, whom Williams recognised as a woman known to him as Mrs MacDonald. She had presented herself at New Scotland Yard, accompanied by solicitor's clerk George Stanley of Lesser and Co., having seen reports in the press relating to the purchase of an Austin Healey at the Chequered Flag Garage. Manson had brought along a prepared statement explaining her involvement in the transaction. After reading her statement and questioning her, Williams remained unconvinced and asked Manson to accompany him to her flat at 4 Wimbledon Close, The Downs, Wimbledon.

Detective Sergeant Moore and Woman Detective Constable Willey searched the flat and found nothing incriminating, but Manson was duly charged with receiving £835 knowing it to be stolen, which she had used to buy the Austin Healey. She was kept in custody overnight to appear at Linslade Magistrates' Court the following day.

Another one of the aces in the forty-strong Flying Squad team hand-picked to investigate the mail-train robbery was thirty-nine-year-old Jack Slipper – a sleazy-looking man with receding, slicked-back hair, a small neat moustache and gaps between large tombstone teeth. Slipper of the Yard, as he came to be known, was flattered when he was informed that Butler had chosen him. In his 1981 biography Slipper wrote:

I knew Tommy's reputation and it was obvious that the investigation would demand long hours, but I didn't fully appreciate just what I was letting myself in for. But even if I had, I'd have wanted to be on that team. To be picked was a mark of professional respect and approval by a man whose opinion really mattered.

Slipper's first assignment was to trace and question Roy James. James was a conspicuous figure and already well known to the police, both as a villain and an amateur racing driver. Three weeks before the robbery he had won a junior formula race at Oulton Park motor-racing circuit.

By Thursday, 22 August Slipper was closing in. With the photographs of 'men wanted for questioning' due to be released to the media that evening, Slipper was keen to apprehend James before he saw them. Having heard there were practice sessions taking place that day at Goodwood, Slipper deduced that James' passion for racing might draw him out of hiding. The detective rang the racetrack and, posing as a friend of James, established that he was there. Slipper immediately called Sussex police and without explaining the connection with the mail-train robbery, he arranged for an officer to be dispatched to Goodwood as soon as possible.

Pursuing another line of inquiry, Detective Inspector Byers paid a visit to 45 Crescent Lane, Clapham, accompanied by Detective Sergeants David Dilley and Nigel Reid. It was 12.30 when the three officers arrived at the yellow front floor of Charlie Wilson's four-bedroom terraced house. His wife Pat was there with their two daughters, Cheryl and Tracy, but she said her husband was out. Reid waited at the house while Byers and Dilley went off to Penge on another matter.

Patricia Wilson later objected that while Reid was in her house the telephone rang and he told her not to answer it.

At 12.55 Charlie Wilson turned up in a maroon Rover 3.5 Coupé. He seemed unperturbed to find Reid in his house. The detective asked him to wait in the sitting room while he contacted Byers and Dilley.

Byers returned at 13.20 and told Wilson he was making inquiries about the mail-train robbery. Wilson's response was, 'I know what you mean. I've never been there.'

Reid then stayed with Wilson while Byers and Dilley searched the house and garden. At one point Wilson said to Reid, 'Can you tell me the strength of this?' But Reid said that he could not. Still fishing, Wilson asked, 'You are taking me in then? It must be strong for you to do that.' Reid said nothing.

Having searched the premises, Byers asked Wilson to accompany them to Cannon Row police station. It is not clear whether Wilson understood his rights. He had allowed police offers to search his home without a warrant, the officers had found nothing incriminating and he had not been placed under arrest or cautioned. This meant he was not obliged to go with them. Perhaps Wilson was ignorant of his legal position, although given his previous experience that seems unlikely. Maybe Charlie Wilson was just playing the helpful and innocent man.

As he was leaving the house, he said to his wife, 'Ring him, won't you?'

Mrs Wilson replied, 'You bet.'

On the way to Cannon Row, Wilson asked, 'What put you on to me?' The officers gave no response.

Despite not being under arrest, on arriving at the police station Wilson was fingerprinted. He was then taken to the charge room by Byers, Reid and Dilley. No further questions were asked of him and he was just sitting down when the door opened and in walked Chief Inspector Baldock followed by Tommy Butler. Byers, Reid and Dilley left the room.

Butler began by asking, 'Do you know Cheddington in Buckinghamshire?'

'No, I have never been there in my life,' Wilson replied.

'Do you know Leatherslade Farm?'

'No, I have never been there in my life.'

Butler then asked Wilson where he was on 8 August. Wilson said that he had left home at about 5 a.m. and gone to work in Spitalfields Market.

Before Charles Frederick Wilson was formally charged he was recorded as saying, 'I do not see how you can make it stick without the poppy [slang term for money], and you won't find that.'

Wilson was no doubt feeling confident because, after leaving Brian Field's house on 10 August he and James had driven to the East End of

London and hidden their 'whacks' in a lock-up garage Wilson used as his 'stow'.

Despite it not being recorded in an authorised statement, Butler also alleged that Wilson said, 'You obviously know a lot. I must have made a ricket [mistake] somewhere. I will have to take my chances.'

An hour after putting in his call to Sussex police, Jack Slipper heard from the detective sergeant who had gone to the racing circuit. He had missed James by a matter of minutes. By the time he arrived at Goodwood, James had packed up for the day and gone, having driven a record lap of 95.57 mph in his Brabham Ford racing car.

Undeterred, Slipper set his next snare. From the file the Yard had on James the detective knew he had a garage in Spicer Street, Battersea where he kept his racing car. Two local officers were sent there and asked to stay out of sight and keep watch.

When the car towing James' Brabham Ford on a trailer turned into his Battersea garage the officers were ready and waiting. But as the car drew up only mechanic Robert Pelham got out. There was no sign of Roy James. On the way back from Goodwood, James had heard of Wilson's arrest on the radio.

It was frustrating news for Slipper. The *Evening Standard* was now on London streets with images of three men wanted in connection with the mail-train robbery on the front page:

Bruce Richard Reynolds – 6'2". Glasses. Motor trader or antiques dealer with a quiet Cockney accent.

Charles Wilson – 6'. Scar on knuckle of first finger, left hand. Turf accountant. Cockney accent.

James E. White – 5'10". Recently removed small moustache. Possibly accompanied by partner Sheree, a baby approximately six months old and a white miniature poodle called 'Gigi'.

Reynolds meanwhile was scouting around the Midlands for a better place to lie low. Franny was in Bond Street, having her hair done at Vidal Sassoon. After leaving the hairdresser's she was walking past D.H. Evans in Oxford Street when she saw Reynolds' face on the front page of the afternoon edition of the *Evening Standard*. She quickly decided not to return to the Captain's Bayswater flat as the porter had seen both her and her husband coming and going. It was possible that he had seen the newspaper images too and had already called the police.

With his name and photograph in the papers, Reynolds recounts that he had a new worry on his mind. After Mary Manson had driven his and Daly's whacks back to London on Friday, 9 August they had gone to a garage he rented and hidden their stolen money behind piles of furniture. But Reynolds had rented the garage in his own name and his most pressing concern was that the letting agent would see the newspapers, remember his name and face and contact the police. Reynolds had been consumed with preserving his liberty but now he was also fretting about losing his share of the stolen money.

He contacted an old friend whom he refers to as Tony. He described him as 'straight as a dye'. Tony offered his help and his van; the two men drove to the garage. Still worrying that the police might be one jump ahead and keeping a watch on the lock-up, Tony – who was obviously not that straight – drove Reynolds round the area to make sure there were no police officers lying in wait. Having concluded that 'unless the police were very good at camouflage, we were all clear', they drew up at the garage and Reynolds jumped out and unlocked it. As he lifted the door and tunnelled his way through piles of furniture, it was still on his mind that the police might have got there before him. Against the back wall, just as he had left them, were the holdalls bulging with stolen mail-train money. He passed the bags back to Tony, who stacked them in his van and within a few minutes they had closed up the garage and were away with £300,000 in the back.

With his face 'drenched with sweat' Tony drove Reynolds to a friend's house in what Reynolds describes as 'the plush stockbroker belt of a Northern town'.

For the time being the money was safe but when he telephoned the Captain's flat Franny was not there. Had she been arrested or seen the papers and gone into hiding somewhere?

Reynolds called Terry Hogan, who told him everything was fine. Franny was staying with friends of friends and he had booked Reynolds in with another old associate in Wimbledon.

By the time Reynolds got to Wimbledon the news was out that Charlie Wilson had been arrested. Reynolds knew his new safe house could only be temporary. His host had been at their wedding. He was in photographs which had been left behind with other possessions in the Reynolds' Putney flat, and the police would have already been there and turned the place over looking for clues.

All the while Gordon Goody had been keeping himself successfully out of the way at the Windmill public house in Blackfriars. He may have drawn some comfort from the fact that the search of his mother's house in Putney had proved fruitless and his name was not among those released to the press.

Goody borrowed a Sunbeam Rapier sports car, registration number UUF726, from the Windmill's landlord. Goody had a date. Not with his fiancée Pat Cooper, but with Jean Perkins, a twenty-seven-year-old model who lived in Leicester.

With Miss Perkins on his mind, Goody's hundred-mile journey north up the M1 motorway was unexpectedly diverted when the car broke down and he was towed to Allan White & Son's garage at 121 High Street, Cranfield in Bedfordshire. A mechanic inspected the Sunbeam and told Goody that the big end bearings had gone and he would need a reconditioned engine, which would cost £75. Giving his name as C.F. Alexander, The Windmill, Upper Ground, Blackfriars, London, EC4, Goody spoke to Eric White, the owner of the garage, and asked if transport could be arranged. White said that his mechanic, Keith Wootton, would be happy to take him wherever he wanted to go. Goody first said Blackfriars, but then after making a telephone call, no doubt to Miss Perkins, he changed his mind and said he wanted to go to Leicester.

Rather later than planned, Goody arrived at the Grand Hotel, Leicester, accompanied by Jean Perkins at around nine o'clock. He checked in using the name Alexander. The hotel receptionist, Janet McIntyre, gave Goody a single room and the porter took his bags up to room 202. Goody and Miss Perkins then had a drink in the hotel cocktail bar.

Back in London, Slipper had little hope of Roy James returning to his flat at 907 Nell Gwynne House in Sloane Avenue, but he still had one last card to play. He decided to pay a visit to 456B Alexandra Avenue, near Rayners Lane underground station, the home of Mrs Violet James, Roy's mother. Detective Slipper spent the evening talking to Mrs James, but by the early hours of Friday morning her son had not shown up.

Slipper of the Yard knew he had been beaten this time. Not by the foresight of James, who earlier in the day had been driving his racing car, oblivious to the hunt, but by the news of Wilson's arrest and Commander Hatherill's decision to provide the press with key information.

Just as Butler had predicted, within hours of the images of Reynolds, Wilson and White appearing on newspaper front pages, Roy James and the other men wanted for questioning had gone to ground.

The life of a career criminal has its setbacks and complexities. By necessity there are constant lies, deception and half-truths that must be told and perpetuated. At times it must feel like a hall of mirrors. This was most vividly illustrated by the experience that befell Gordon Goody as he slept alone in his hotel bed after Jean Perkins had left in the early hours of Friday, 23 August 1963.

At 02.00 Detective Sergeant Henry James Strong and Detective Constable Brown of Leicester City Police arrived at the Grand Hotel. They went to room 202, woke Goody and asked him to identify himself. A half-asleep and bemused Goody said that he was Charles Frederick Alexander.

What Goody did not know was that police had already spoken to Alexander and confirmed that he was at the Windmill pub and not in Leicester.

When the officers said that Mr Alexander was in London, Goody replied, 'No, I am here.'

Goody was taken to Leicester police station where he was searched. Among his possessions was an address book, a five-pound note and a ten-shilling note. While officers were examining the five-pound note Goody said, 'I've got no worries about that one.' He then picked up his address book and defaced one of the entries.

Goody later said in a statement the name he had crossed out was Jean Perkins, but according to Piers Paul Read it was Jimmy White.

When asked why he had done it, Goody replied it was 'just a precaution'. The ever-shrewd Goody then asked if he could make a note of the number of the five-pound and ten-shilling notes, which he was allowed to do.

After further discussion it became clear to Goody that it was pointless trying to maintain the pretence that he was pub landlord Charles

Alexander. He told officers that he was Douglas Gordon Goody, explaining that he had been staying out of the way at the Windmill as a number of people he knew were wanted for questioning about the mail-train raid.

It was no surprise to Goody when he was later brought up from the cells to find Detective Chief Inspector Vibart and Detective Sergeant Reid waiting to talk to him. But he still couldn't figure out how he had ended up in the police station interview room. What had prompted the police to come to his hotel room to check his identity? How could they have known he was there?

In the course of further questioning about Goody's movements and his connection with Jean Perkins, Vibart finally provided the answer. The consummately charming Goody had bought flowers for his girl-friend at the Grand Hotel the previous evening. Mary Mason, the florist who had served him, had immediately recognised his companion because Miss Perkins' picture had been in the local paper in connection with a beauty contest. Other newspaper images had also stuck in Mrs Mason's mind, including the three men wanted for questioning about the mail-train raid. In a bizarre twist of fate and bad luck for Goody, Mrs Mason had telephoned the police and said that she thought she had just seen Bruce Reynolds in her shop.

20

S lowly the police investigation team were piecing together the story behind Leatherslade Farm. The file McArthur had obtained from solicitor John Wheater on 19 August contained scant information about Leonard Field, the client who engaged the firm to act on his behalf in the purchase of the farm. But the discovery of a Bavarian hotel bill made out to Herr and Frau Field in one of the bags of money found in the woods outside Dorking had thrown up another possible connection. One of the employees at James and Wheater was a clerk named Brian Field, and he had a German wife.

This presented the investigation team with a dilemma. They had established links between Field, Leatherslade Farm, the robbery and the recovered money, but it was a common name and there were two Fields implicated in the case.

At 06.20 on Friday, 23 August, Fewtrell, Pritchard and four other officers arrived at Whitchurch Hill, near Pangbourne in Berkshire. They parked in the lane and walked a little way up the unmade track to Brian Field's house, Kabri. At that hour of the morning the place was quiet and there were no signs of life. Two officers went round to the back of the house while Pritchard and Fewtrell approached the front door. With a search warrant in his jacket pocket, Fewtrell rang the bell and waited.

After several minutes, Brian Field opened the door in his dressing gown. He seemed at ease when he saw the two officers and Fewtrell told him they had a search warrant. Field smiled slightly and said he was only surprised they had not come sooner. He invited the officers in without asking to see the warrant. His relaxed and congenial manner made Fewtrell fairly certain that there was not going to be anything incriminating in the house, but they searched it anyway. Nothing was found.

Karin Field, who was six months pregnant at the time, was as calm and courteous as her husband. While the detectives went through her home she made coffee.

Pritchard and Fewtrell then joined the Fields in their sitting room overlooking the garden. Brian Field admitted going to visit the farm. He said Leonard Field had asked him to accompany him to have a look at the place. The explanation was simple and straightforward and there was little the police officers could challenge or disprove. Fewtrell then questioned him about Leonard Field, asking how the law firm of James and Wheater had come to be engaged to handle the purchase of Leatherslade Farm. Initially, Brian's response was that all the information was at the office. But then he said he did have a document in his briefcase. He got up and went to the garage to get the case from his car.

The document he produced was more useful than he supposed. It was a bank mandate, signed by Leonard Denis Field. Importantly it had Leonard's address on it. Not the Earls Court address Wheater had given the police, but 262 Green Lanes, London, N8.

As a formality, Fewtrell then asked to see Brian Field's passport. He nonchalantly flicked through the pages and asked about journeys Field had taken abroad. It was all a ruse to divert attention from the question he was leading to. When Fewtrell got to a stamp for West Germany dated February 1963, he asked about the trip. Brian and Karin Field talked enthusiastically about their skiing holiday and Fewtrell asked casually where they had stayed. The Fields told the detectives about the small Bavarian hotel, saying it was very comfortable and good value. The Fields were now ripe for the killer question and Fewtrell delivered it as if his interest was merely casual.

'What's the hotel called?'

Brian Field paused and thought about it for a moment. 'Hotel Sonnenbichl,' he replied, adding that the owners were friendly and helpful.

Fewtrell had got what he came for. With confirmation that Brian and Karin were the Herr and Frau Field on the receipt, he now had a definite link between Brian Field and the recovered money. But he wasn't giving anything away at this stage. The receipt alone was not going to be enough to prove Field's complicity in the mail-train raid. Nevertheless it was a good start.

As the detectives were leaving, Field told them that he and his wife were due to go on a business trip to Gibraltar for about a week. Fewtrell raised no objection.

Field was an articulate, clever and confident young man. Perhaps it was over-confidence, or maybe he had underestimated the police, but the smooth-talking, ambitious solicitor's clerk had made elementary and careless mistakes. The police now knew that Brian Field had been instrumental in the purchase of Leatherslade Farm and that one of the bags found in the woods near Dorking containing £100,900 belonged to him. Along with the hotel bill the police had also discovered finger-prints on the bag but with no criminal record there was no legitimate way of checking if they were Field's.

After thanking Brian and Karin Field for the coffee and their help, Fewtrell and Pritchard walked back up the lane to their car. They would take their time to secure further evidence against Field and when they were ready they would pay him another visit.

The front page of the *Daily Mirror* on Friday, 23 August had a photograph of a woman being led from Linslade Magistrates' Court. The accompa-nying article described how, head covered by a blanket, forty-year-old Mary Kazih Manson had been led into the little country courthouse the previous day. Faced with charges of receiving £835 of the stolen money, she took her place in the dock:

> She stood with her hands in the pockets of her black, fur-collared coat. She glanced across the courtroom and smiled at a red-haired woman. Another glance at the redhead. This time a wink too. Then the magis-trate, farmer Walter Leach, took his seat and the court was in session.

The evidence concerning Manson's involvement with the purchase of an Austin Healey at the Chequered Flag Garage in the company of an unidentified man was then presented. Twenty-four minutes later, it was all over.

Defence Counsel Wilfred Fordham (husband of Peta, author of *The Robbers' Tale*) fought to get Manson out on bail. 'This is not a woman on the run,' he argued. 'This woman went to Scotland Yard to face alle-gations made against her.' But Fordham's plea was unsuccessful and Manson was remanded in custody for two days and dispatched to Holloway Prison.

In Leicester, Detective Sergeant Strong went to Jean Perkins' home at 09.30 and carried out a search. She confirmed Goody's story that she had loaned him a five-pound note.

At Aylesbury HQ, Colin Charles, an inspector from the National Provincial Bank, carried out an examination of the various banknotes that had been recovered by the police. Charles identified the source of some of the notes by their serial numbers; bank records confirmed they had been part of the consignment stolen from the mail train. Some of the notes he identified had been part of the haul recovered from Cordrey and Boal in Bournemouth.

Friday morning was also a busy time at the Windmill pub in Blackfriars. The day began with a visit from two police officers who spent forty-five minutes going over the building. The landlord, Charles Alexander, was with them the whole time.

At 10.00 another police officer arrived, asking to see Alexander's registration and insurance documents for his Sunbeam Rapier.

Then at 15.00 Detective Sergeant Vaughan arrived in the company of the Yard's principal scientific officer, Dr Ian Holden. They asked to see where Goody had been staying and Alexander showed them to the room, which was normally occupied by his daughter, then left them to carry out their search alone. Vaughan found Goody's passport on top of the wardrobe under a doll's house. Holden picked up a pair of Tru-form suede shoes. After ninety minutes, the New Scotland Yard men left the Windmill pub taking the shoes and passport with them.

At 15.15 Vibart and Reid carried out a second interview with Gordon Goody in Leicester police station. Goody evaded questions about his movements on 8 August, but confirmed that the car he had been driving belonged to Alexander. He said he had stayed at the Windmill ever since his mother's house had been searched.

Finally he said, 'Look, I was away, out of it, over the water on the Green Isle, so you can't fit me in.'

Asked if he meant that he was in Ireland on 8 August, Goody replied, 'Yes. I was there all the time and out of it.'

Unconvinced, Vibart and Reid escorted Goody to their grey Jaguar and drove him back to Aylesbury HQ, arriving at 20.30 on Friday evening. Goody was then questioned by Tommy Butler in the presence of George Stanley, the clerk from Lesser and Co., Goody's solicitor. Goody told Butler the same story about having been in Ireland on the night of the robbery with his mother. He said that he had been lying low at the Windmill merely to avoid the press.

'I was going to stay away until things died down,' Goody said. 'Them blokes who are in all the papers are friends of mine and that puts me in it, according to you.'

He then complained to Butler that he was tired and had not had much sleep.

An hour earlier, at 19.30 that Friday evening, Roy James' twenty-six-year-old mechanic, Robert Pelham, had been questioned by Chief Inspector Baldock and Detective Sergeant Dilley. It had been reported that parked outside his home was an Austin Mini Cooper, registration number 293DBD, which was owned by James. The house, at 79 Lonsdale Road, Notting Hill, was searched and a brown paper parcel containing £545 in one-pound notes was found. Pelham was taken into custody, questioned further at Scotland Yard, and then informed that he would be taken to Aylesbury to be formally charged with receiving stolen money.

Friday's editions of the national newspapers had all carried photographs and descriptions of Reynolds, White and Wilson – two men still wanted, one already charged. On Saturday, 24 August, photographs of Roy James appeared in the press, accompanied by a description of the wanted man, which stated that he was 5'4", of slight build and nicknamed 'The Weasel'.

Frank Williams said in his 1973 biography that he was certain James had never been known as 'The Weasel' and the use of the nickname in the official press release was a mistake. He went on: 'although it was later corrected by Scotland Yard the name continued to be used.'

After a few hours much-needed sleep in his Aylesbury cell, Saturday morning began with another round of questioning for Gordon Goody with 'the terrible twins', Butler and Vibart. Again he was asked where he had been on the night of 7/8 August.

'I was in Ireland doing a bit of fishing and shooting,' he replied chirpily.

Goody denied knowing Leatherslade Farm other than through recent reports in the press. When Butler told Goody that they knew his mother and friend Knowles had returned to England on 7 August while he had returned a day earlier, Goody refused to say anything more until he had spoken to his solicitor.

Linslade Magistrates' Court was in session on Saturday, with Cordrey, Boal and Wilson standing in the dock on charges of robbery, while Alfred Pilgrim, Robert Pelham, Renee Boal, May Pilgrim and Mary Manson were charged with receiving. Detective Inspector Vincent Hankins of Aylesbury police made an application for remand, but indicated that he would not object to bail for those accused of receiving, particularly the women. After hearing the evidence, magistrates remanded all eight of the accused in custody until 2 September.

At 18.45 on Saturday evening Detective Inspector Morris and Detective Sergeant Church went to 37 Alpine Road, Redhill, Surrey, the home of Ronald Arthur Biggs. They told him they had come to see him following reports that his wife, Charmian, had been spending a lot of money recently. Biggs said that he had won £510 at Brighton races. The officers then asked Biggs if he knew Bruce Reynolds. He replied that he did and they had spent time in Wandsworth Prison together. When asked if he had seen Reynolds recently, Biggs replied that they met occasionally when Reynolds came to Redhill to visit a friend, Mrs Alkins in Malmstone Avenue, but he had not seen Reynolds for three years.

Goody had been in police custody for almost twenty-four hours and been interviewed at length by a series of interrogators. It was obviously suspicious that he had gone into hiding and that when first approached at the Grand Hotel by Detective Sergeant Strong and Detective Constable Brown of Leicester City Police he had pretended to be Charles Alexander. Some of the things he had said and done during the subsequent interviews had heightened suspicions of his involvement in the raid, particularly his false claim he was in Ireland on 7/8 August. Butler had quickly found out that this was not true. Still, circumstances and suspicion alone did not add up to much of a case. The astute Goody was all too aware that, without hard evidence, sooner or later Butler would have to release him.

An insight into Goody's nature is provided by a letter that he wrote shortly after his home was searched on Friday, 16 August by Flying Squad detectives Swain and Burdett. Addressed to Detective Superintendent Oxborne of Ealing CID, the letter was posted on 21 August. A transcript was later presented by Tommy Butler in court:

Dear sir,

No doubt you will be surprised to hear from me after my double trial at the Old Bailey for The London Airport Robbery. At the time of writing I am not living at my home address because it seems that I am a suspect in the recent train robbery. Two Flying Squad officers recently visited my home address whilst I was out and made a search of the premises, and honestly, Mr Oxborne, I am very worried that they connect me with this crime.

The Reason I write to you now is because you always treated me in a straightforward manner during the airport case. I will never forget how fair and just yourself and Mr Field were towards me. That case took nearly eight months to finish and every penny I had, and to become a suspect in this last big robbery is more than I can stand. So my intentions are to keep out of harm's way until the people concerned in the train robbery are found.

To some people this letter would seem like a sign of guilt but all I am interested in is keeping my freedom. Hoping these few lines find you and Mr Field in the best of health.

Gordon Goody

Fewtrell described the letter as 'bizarre'. He was convinced that Goody was one of the leaders of the mail-train robbery. His name had been suggested early on in the inquiries because of his long record of violent crime.

Why Goody wrote to Detective Superintendent Oxborne can only be guessed at. A hardened criminal seeking the support of a senior detective seems an odd alliance. But Gordon Goody had his reasons. He had encountered Oxborne when he was charged for the London Airport robbery. It's possible that he considered him an honest but gullible detective. On the other hand, Goody escaped conviction for the Airport robbery after bribing a police officer to swap the checked cap found at the scene for a substitute that was several sizes too large for him. Was the police officer he bribed on that occasion the man whose help he now sought in the letter – Detective Superintendent Oxborne?

Throughout his time in custody, both in Leicester and Aylesbury,

Goody had lied and dissembled and avoided answering certain questions put to him. He knew he had the right to refuse making any statement at all, but as a seasoned criminal he also knew that if he continued to appear relaxed and cooperative while giving as little away as possible, the police would eventually run out of questions and let him go.

Despite the best efforts of Butler and Vibart, there was nothing concrete to link Goody with the mail-train raid. At 00.15 on the morning of Sunday, 25 August, Goody was released from Aylesbury on police bail under Section 38 of the Magistrates' Court Act 1952. The condition of Goody's bail was that he must undertake to appear at three nominated police stations on certain days between his release date and 3 October. According to Piers Paul Read, Vibart and Butler then drove Goody all the way from Buckinghamshire to the corner of Commondale in Putney.

In the Forensic Science Laboratory, Dr Ian Holden made an important discovery on Monday, 26 August, while examining a jacket that had been removed from Boal's house. Hidden in the lining was a small brass winder. Close inspection revealed traces of yellow paint mixed with dirt in the grooves of the knurling.

Holden then turned his attention to a pair of suede shoes, retrieved from the room in the Windmill pub where Gordon Goody had been staying. First he compared the pattern on the sole of the shoe to the sample he had taken from an imprint found at Leatherslade Farm; there was no match and Goody's shoe was a different size. However, when Holden cleaned dirt from the bottom of the shoes he found a smudge of yellow paint under the instep of the right shoe and some circular patches underneath the toe of the left shoe.

Recalling the hurriedly painted lorry he had observed at Leatherslade Farm and the squashed tin of yellow paint lying discarded in one of the sheds, Holden's mind began to race. By subjecting the various samples to spectrographic analysis, he would be able to establish whether yellow paint on the lorry, in the tin, on the grooves of the brass winder found in Boal's jacket and on the sole of Goody's shoes had all come from the same source.

However, when he went through the inventory of all the numerous pieces evidence that had been removed from the farm by the police, there was no mention of the squashed yellow paint tin that Dr Holden had seen two weeks earlier in the shed.

21

During Monday and Tuesday the investigation continued grinding through the list of possible suspects who had yet to be tracked down and brought in for questioning. Detective Superintendent Tommy Butler, eager to follow up a lead on a man known only as 'Buster', put in a call to C11 at Scotland Yard. The intelligence branch came back with the name Ronald Christopher Edwards, a known villain born in Lambeth, 27 January 1931.

An article in Monday's edition of *The Times* offered an explanation as to why the accused were led into court with blankets over their heads. The report included a quote from Geoffrey Leach, the barrister representing the Boals, the Pilgrims and Cordrey, who had been asked by the newspaper to explain why, on entering the courthouse, Boal had melodramatically flung the blanket from his head:

> ... what the public do not seem to appreciate is that the placing of blankets over their heads is not that these people are afraid of being seen or anything of that nature, nor is it the case that the police want to invest the whole procedure with some Victorian melodrama and create a villainous atmosphere. The police do it to protect them from photographers and other sightseers in order that any question of identity should not be prejudiced by photographs taken in that way. Mr Boal most unfortunately misunderstood the situation and it was his desire to show to the world he had nothing to hide and is not scared of holding his head up high.

The Times did not pick up on the irony of Mr Leach's statement. With pictures of the men being sought for questioning plastered all over the national press, it begged the question why they too were not being 'protected' by the police against any resulting prejudice.

With the lifting of the police cordon on Leatherslade Farm, Bernard Rixon had been swift to invite the press into his old home. He posed, sitting in a chair in front of an empty fireplace, for a photograph that appeared on the front page of Tuesday's *Daily Express*. Despite the fact that it was commonly known Rixon no longer lived at the farm, having moved out in July to become a sub-postmaster at Dunsden, near Reading, the headline read *By his own fireside again*. Page two featured shots of the farmhouse kitchen, with Rixon emerging in rather sinister fashion from the trapdoor to the cellar.

While Rixon enjoyed his five minutes of fame the gang members continued to live in fear of being recognised. By Tuesday, Reynolds had moved from Wimbledon into a small flat in Clapham. When Franny called into the local butcher's she was greeted by a man behind the counter who used to work at the shop where she bought her meat in Putney. She rushed back to the flat and told her husband, already knowing what it meant. The butcher might not say anything, but with a £260,000 reward at stake there was every chance that he would. They were going to have to find a new hideout. And unbeknown to the Reynoldses, the police had learned that he was in possession of a white Lotus Cortina with a green flash down the side, registration number BMK723A.

Over two weeks after the mail-train raid in Buckinghamshire, stories about 'The Great Train Robbery' continued to dominate the press. For an indication of just how insular Britain was in the 1960s one need only look at the column inches generated by the train robbers and the coverage given to a speech made three thousand miles away at the Lincoln Memorial in Washington, an iconic moment which would make all other events of the summer of 1963 seem incidental and parochial.

On 28 August, the day Martin Luther King was making his evocative and poetic 'I have a dream' speech in front of an estimated audience of a quarter of a million, Bernard Rixon opened Leatherslade Farm to paying visitors. The police had left very little behind, but Rixon gathered together a few things he thought might be of interest to his visitors and brought them into the house for his 'exhibition'. The items on display included some meat and fruit tins, spent photographic flash bulbs that had been used by police photographers, and a few other odd remnants he had collected including a squashed tin of yellow paint. Before the day was out Rixon's rather dismal collection of exhibits was depleted when a police officer called and asked to take away the can of paint.

Scotland Yard released two new photographs of men wanted for questioning, an updated picture of Reynolds and another image of Roy James, still perpetuating the nickname 'The Weasel'. When Detective Sergeants Maidment and Marshall paid a visit to Reynolds' grandmother's flat at 38 Buckmaster Road in Battersea, where he was known to stay on occasion, they found nothing incriminating. They did, however, notice that in the spare bedroom there was a copy of the *Evening News* dated 13 August with a front-page article about 'The Great Train Robbery'.

Even those gang members whose photographs had yet to appear in the press were not taking any chances. After his interview at Scotland Yard on 16 August, Bob Welch had decided to leave London and hole up with some associates in a rented farmhouse in Beaford, not far from Bideford on the north coast of Devon.

John Daly and his twenty-two-year-old wife, Barbara, who was heavily pregnant, had been staying at the Endcliffe Hotel in Margate, Kent, since 14 August. At some point during 28 August he surfaced long enough to park his British racing green 3.8 Jaguar Mk2 at the Metropolis Garage, Olympia, London, W14.

A report in *The Times* illustrated the impact of the robbery on the fevered imagination of the general public:

Inquiries in Canada are being made to try and discover whether £500 in £5 notes found by demolition workers in a derelict shop in Bradford Yorkshire is connected with the Buckinghamshire train robbery. Police are trying to trace Mrs Farrell, believed to be in her seventies who recently left her home to visit her son in Canada. It is thought she may know something about the money.

The combination of police requests in the press for information, coupled with the enormous reward on offer, had unleashed a deluge of information. As the case of John Maris had shown, any crucial tip-offs that did come in were liable to go unnoticed by investigators who found themselves swamped with useless 'leads' that served no purpose but to waste police time. Nevertheless the Yard issued a statement thanking the public for their help: 'The response is appreciated although it is not possible to reply to letters individually.'

Flying Squad officers were taking out up to fifty search warrants a day. There were raids all over south-east England, from Essex to the Sussex coast. The increase in the Flying Squad's activity had brought serious crime in London to a virtual standstill.

Still working away diligently in the background, Dr Ian Holden of the Forensic Science Laboratory finally gained possession of the squashed tin of yellow paint. On Thursday, 29 August he ran tests on samples of paint taken from the tin itself and from the gang's Austin three-ton lorry. He also examined a sample of green paint from the Series One Land Rover that had previously been blue but re-sprayed green before it was bought by White from Cross Country Vehicles for £195 on 31 July.

In the fingerprint department, Detective Superintendent Maurice Ray had been going through all the finger and palm marks left on surfaces at Leatherslade Farm and lifted from various items he had recovered. During their time at the farm, Ray and his team had taken 243 photographs and collected 311 fingerprints and 56 palm prints. After eliminating prints that belonged to Rixon and his family, Ray set about painstakingly checking the prints against those held by his colleagues in the Criminal Records Office in the hope of identifying the robbers.

Of particular interest were prints found on the mailbags left at the farm. These had been carefully emptied and the contents scrutinised. Among the money wrappers in one bag was a green card and in another a number of Monopoly tokens. Detective Superintendent Ray and his team dusted them for prints and found marks on both the green card and on the tokens.

Eight of these prints were identified as belonging to John Daly, including those found on the green card and a Monopoly game. Fingerprint experts also matched two marks of Reynolds, and several belonging to Biggs on the Monopoly box, a blue-edged Pyrex plate and a bottle of Heinz Tomato Ketchup.

As a result of these findings, on Friday, 30 August, Detective Inspector Frank Williams called at the large detached house Daly occupied at 73 Burleigh Road, Sutton. Unsurprisingly, there was nobody home, although the state of the kitchen suggested someone had been there and left recently. Williams took away Daly's Irish passport and a letter dated 19 August. New Scotland Yard later released Daly's photograph to the press. In addition, posters of all the men wanted for questioning were circulated to every police station and post office in the country.

The front page of the *Daily Express* on 31 August led with an article on Daly and Reynolds, having made the connection that Daly's wife Barbara (née Allen) was the older sister of Reynolds' wife Frances. Daly and Reynolds were brothers-in-law.

What the *Express* reporter did not know – not that it had any major bearing on the ongoing mail-train investigation – was the complex web of connections between the Allen sisters, Reynolds, Mary Manson and her brother, Ernie Watts.

In the 1950s, before his marriage to Frances Allen, Bruce Reynolds had lived with her sister Rita – the eldest of the three Allen sisters. By 1957 Reynolds was serving a three-and-a-half-year prison sentence in Wandsworth (after a failed robbery with Terry Hogan, Reynolds had been charged with GBH and ABH on two policemen). While Reynolds was away, Rita moved into his grandmother's house in Battersea and began a relationship with Mary Manson's brother Ernie, a diabetic and obsessive gambler.

When he heard about Rita and Ernie, Reynolds became so incensed that he tried various drastic measures to secure an early release from Wandsworth so that he could take his revenge. In one attempt, Reynolds resorted to setting up an attack on himself and had to be hospitalised after being stabbed three times in the showers. The desperate plan failed; instead of releasing him on recovery, the prison authorities merely transferred him to Durham Prison. While serving out the remainder of his sentence Reynolds wrote Ernie Watts a threatening letter. Shortly afterwards, Watts was found dead from an insulin overdose and Rita disappeared to Canada.

There was also a connection between Daly and Manson that went unreported. Mary Manson's common-law husband was a man called James MacDonald, who employed Daly at Mac Antiques, a shop he owned on the Portobello Road.

On Monday, 2 September, Cordrey, Boal, his wife Renee, Cordrey's sister and brother-in-law appeared again before Linslade magistrates.

Pending further investigations, Boal and Cordrey were remanded in custody while Renee Boal and the Pilgrims were granted bail.

The next major development took place at 14.45 on Wednesday, 4 September, when Detective Inspector Williams and a team of officers went to 37 Alpine Road in Redhill, the home of Ronnie Biggs. Charmian came to the door and said her husband was at work. Williams told her he had a search warrant and the officers went over the house. According to Williams, when Biggs arrived home three and a half hours later at 18.20, the search was still going on.

When Biggs walked in Williams said, 'We are police officers. We are here in connection with the train robbery in Buckinghamshire and I am in the process of searching your house.'

'What, again?' Biggs said. 'The law turned me over some time ago about that. You haven't found anything have you?'

'No, nothing has been found,' Williams replied.

Biggs said, 'That's all right then.'

Williams took Biggs into the front room while the search was completed and said, 'It is proposed to take you to Scotland Yard in order that further inquiries may be made.'

Biggs answered, 'That don't sound too good. What are my chances of creeping out of this?'

Biggs was unaware that detectives Jim Nevill and Jack Slipper had been talking to the wife of his business partner, Raymond Stripp. First Mrs Stripp had told them the story they had already heard from Biggs about him being away tree-felling in Wiltshire at the time of the robbery. When she mentioned that Biggs had taken an axe with him, Slipper's interest grew. Axes had been used in the mail-train raid. Even so, it was still no more than a possible connection. But what Mrs Stripp said next was a gift. She told the detectives that Ronnie's brother had died while he was away and that in trying to find him Charmian had called the local police.

Nevill and Slipper went to Redhill police station and checked their Occurrence Book. There was an entry recording Charmian's call asking for help to trace her husband. This was followed by a list of the calls Redhill police had made to various police stations in Wiltshire. But despite extensive inquiries the Wiltshire police had no luck finding Biggs.

With the search of the house concluded, Williams escorted Biggs to a waiting police car for the drive back to London. On the way, Biggs said, 'I don't know how you have tied me in with that lot in the papers.'

'Do you know any of them?' Williams asked.

'Well, I have read all about it,' Biggs said, 'but I do not know any of them.'

'Are you sure?' Williams pressed.

'I know what you are getting at,' said Biggs. 'Yes, I know Reynolds. He'll want some catching.'

At New Scotland Yard Biggs was questioned by Butler before being formally charged and taken to Aylesbury.

Despite his delight at having been released on bail, having narrowly escaped the clutches of Vibart and Butler, Gordon Goody was a worried man. He knew there was a danger that members of the gang might view his release with suspicion, especially in light of the recent arrests. Having spoken to Pat Wilson, he decided to accompany her on a visit to her husband, who was being held in Bedford Prison. When they got there, Goody gave a false name. According to Read, the conversation between the two robbers began as follows:

'I wanted to reassure you, mate,' said Gordon. 'Because if I was you the same thoughts would have gone round in my head.'

'Don't be fucking ridiculous,' said Charlie. 'I ain't worried about any of our firm.'

Although it would have been understandable in the circumstances and entirely correct for any of the gang to assume that someone had talked, they did not know that the recent arrests and identification of men wanted for questioning had also been reinforced by the work of Chief Superintendent Maurice Ray and the fingerprint team.

On Thursday, 5 September thirty-four-year-old carpenter Ronald Arthur Biggs was the ninth person to appear before Linslade magistrates in connection with the mail-train robbery. Like the others, he entered the court concealed under a blanket. During the hearing Williams stated that, having answered a series of questions at Scotland

Yard, Biggs had turned uncooperative: 'At the conclusion of the questions he was asked to sign a document and refused to do it.'

Biggs had said, 'Get on with it. You'll have to prove it all the way. I'm not admitting nothing to you people.'

Wearing a blue-green check suit, red tie and suede shoes, Biggs told the court, 'It's all lies.'

Biggs, who told the court he earned £35 a week, was granted Legal Aid (then called poor person relief). Magistrates remanded him in custody until 10 September.

At 09.50 on Saturday, 7 September, Jim Hussey received a visit from Slipper and Nevill at his home in Dog Kennel Hill, London. They told him that they had a warrant to search his house.

Thirty-year-old Hussey, who was described by Slipper as 'a monster of a man', stood aside meekly. 'Help yourself,' he said. 'There's nothing here.'

The officers searched and found nothing, but told Hussey they were taking him to Scotland Yard. They arrived at the Yard at 10.45 and fifteen minutes later Hussey was in an interview room being grilled by Butler. Hussey denied knowing Buckinghamshire, Leatherslade Farm, or Brill and Oakley, and said he did not know anyone involved in the mail-train raid.

He agreed to having his palm prints taken, saying, 'I have no worries.'

Finally he signed his statement, giving his occupation as 'painter'.

Butler left the interview room and returned at 13.00. He asked Hussey if he had taken part in the purchase of a Land Rover from Mr Michael Humphreys at Winchmore Hill, London, N21 in July, or an Austin Lorry from Mullards of Kenton Lane, Middlesex. Hussey said he had not and signed another statement.

Butler then left the interview room again to talk to a forensics officer who had been comparing the palm prints just taken from Hussey with those found at the farm. There was a match.

Butler returned to the interview room again at 13.45 and told Hussey that he was to be taken to Aylesbury where he would be charged.

On being cautioned, Hussey said, 'In that case it looks as though it's on me. I want my solicitor here,' and gave the name Ellis Lincoln.

At 16.00 Williams went back to Hussey's house in East Dulwich, accompanied by Dr Ian Holden, and took away a pair of 'stained trousers' from his bedroom. The nature of the stains was not recorded.

In accordance with the conditions of his police bail, Goody duly showed up at Aylesbury police station on Saturday, 7 September and was given a lift home in police transport.

At 08.25 on Monday, 9 September Leonard Field left 262 Green Lanes, Haringey – the house he had shared for several years with his mother – and set off for Tilbury Docks. After half a mile, while he was stationary at traffic lights, a man leaned into his van, switched off the ignition and explained to Field that he was a police officer. Detective Inspector Harry Tappin of Scotland Yard then came to the van and told Field that they were taking him to Highbury Vale police station. At the time Tappin was in the company of Detective Sergeant Hyams, Detective Constable Simmons and a police driver. Field travelled with the other officers while Simmons got into his van and followed them to Highbury Vale. After dropping off the van, they continued on to Cannon Row police station.

At 09.55 Leonard Field was interviewed by Butler and Detective Chief Inspector Bradbury. He told the detectives that he did not know Oakley, or Brill, or Leatherslade Farm. He confirmed that he knew solicitor John Wheater, as he had handled his brother Harry's horse-doping case in Brighton and other affairs, including the sale of Harry's house in Colville Road. He said that he also knew the managing clerk at James and Wheater, Brian Field.

Butler put it to him that he had entered into negotiations to buy Leatherslade Farm on behalf of the criminals who had robbed the mail train.

Lennie Field denied all knowledge of it and said, 'Never in your life.'

He was asked if he had an address at 150 Earls Court Road, to which he replied, 'I know people there, but I do not live there.'

He denied having visited Leatherslade Farm, saying, 'You are making a mistake. It must have been somebody who looks like me. Did Brian Field say it was me?'

Field then refused to answer any further questions and asked for his solicitor. 'I am not going to say any more until you get Mr Wheater here,' he insisted.

Bradbury left the room. When he returned he told Field that Wheater was not currently available. Field was then escorted to a detention room.

Leonard Field had not been cautioned or charged and was at liberty to leave after his interview with Butler, but either he was hoping to bluff his way out by cooperating or he was unaware of his rights. This was a running theme with many of the suspects brought into police stations for questioning, asked to provide finger and palm prints and answer to questions, all without having been charged or cautioned. Under due process of British law, evidence gathered in this way is subject to scrutiny under 'Judges' Rules' in order to determine whether or not it is admissible in court.

It was midday by the time John Wheater arrived. Before he could see his client he was taken to Tommy Butler, who reminded him that on 19 August he had told Detective Superintendent Gerry McArthur that he had acted for Leonard Field in the purchase of Leatherslade Farm. Butler then asked Wheater if he had given Field a receipt for the deposit of £555 that had been paid to Rixon's solicitors.

'I can't remember,' Wheater said. 'I don't think I did.'

Leonard Field was then brought in and Wheater said to Butler that, in the circumstances, it was 'very awkward' for him to act for Field.

Leonard protested, 'I never purchased any farm, did I, Mr Wheater? You know I didn't.'

Wheater got up from his chair, went pale and loosened his collar. After a moment he said, 'I'm confused, I'm confused. I'm not sure now. I thought this was the man at first, but now I am not so certain.'

He turned to Butler and asked to see him alone. Once the two men had left the room, he told Butler, 'This puts me in a very embarrassing position. I'm not at all sure now that he is the man who entered into negotiations respecting the farm. I only saw him twice and although he is remarkably like the man, I cannot really say. There is a startling resemblance; he is the splitting image of the man who negotiated to buy the farm.'

Wheater then made a statement saying that he was currently selling a substantial property for Harry Field at 28 Colville Road, W11. Harry Field was currently serving five years for breaking into a bank and his brother Leonard had been given power of attorney. Wheater said that he had only met Leonard Field when he had been engaged by his brother to represent Harry on a charge of buggery.

It is not known if the Grey Fox's usual grim expression gave way to a smile on this occasion, but the detective let the matter rest there. No doubt he had a shrewd idea of what was going on. When first questioned about the farm, Wheater had given Detective Superintendent McArthur the name Leonard Field and an address in Earls Court that turned out to be false. When McArthur had asked why the Leatherslade Farm legal file contained no correspondence from Leonard Field, Wheater had said that Field had been in his office 'nearly every day'.

Only moments before, when Field had been brought into the interview room, he clearly had no difficulty in recognising Wheater and addressed him by name. And yet Wheater was now trying to convince Butler that it was all some kind of misunderstanding and a case of mistaken identity. Despite the absurdity of the charade, not even Tommy Butler could make anything of it in a court of law. He needed to gather more evidence before an arrest would be possible.

Much to Wheater's and Field's relief, Butler had no option but to release them both.

22

The Times on Monday, 9 September reported that James Hussey was due to appear at Linslade Magistrates' Court and reminded its readers that Hussey was the tenth person to be charged in connection with the mail-train raid and the fifth accused of robbery.

On Tuesday, 10 September there was a reshuffle at New Scotland Yard. Head of the Flying Squad Ernie Millen was promoted as Deputy Commander to George Hatherill and Chief Superintendent Butler was made the new head of the Flying Squad.

At 11.00 on Wednesday, 11 September Detective Inspector Frank Williams received a telephone call.

'I am Wisbey,' a voice said. 'I understand you want to see me?'

For years Williams had made himself a well-known figure among the South London underworld and knew many villains personally. Recently he had let it be known among his many contacts that he wanted to speak to several people, one of whom was Wisbey. Like some other members of the gang, Wisbey had remained confident that the police might have their suspicions but they could not pin anything on him in connection to the mail-train raid. He had already presented himself to Scotland Yard on Tuesday, 20 August and been interviewed by Detective Inspector Roberts. He had made a statement in which he said he was at a pub until 23.00 on the night of the robbery and then went home to his family. He had told Roberts the landlord would corroborate his story. By coming forward again voluntarily and cooperating further, Wisbey no doubt thought he could demonstrate that he had nothing to hide and an old hand like Williams would understand that.

In response to Wisbey's question on the telephone Williams said, 'I think you might be able to help me. Where are you now?'

Frank Williams was an astute if unorthodox operator. If he offered to meet Wisbey on his home ground, Wisbey would be less guarded, less suspicious that Williams was doing anything more than working through his list of usual suspects.

Wisbey replied, 'I'll be at my shop in half an hour.'

Williams called Butler in his office at the Yard. Butler thought the man on the telephone was most likely someone with a warped sense of humour pretending to be Wisbey. He told Williams to go ahead but said it was probably going to be a waste of time.

Just after 11.30 Williams and Sergeant Steve Moore drew up at Wisbey's betting shop at 1 Red Cross Way, London, SE1. Wisbey must have known it was less routine than he had thought when Williams walked in with another officer. But according to Williams, Wisbey greeted him like an old friend and seemed genuinely puzzled why he wanted to see him.

'I would like you to come to New Scotland Yard,' Williams said formally, 'where you will be questioned in connection with the train robbery in Buckinghamshire.'

Wisbey laughed and said he had thought Williams' visit must be about something else. He shrugged and said that he had 'nothing to worry about' and kept up a convincing pretence of being the innocent and helpful villain. 'OK then,' he replied, 'I will come now.'

At the Yard Wisbey's finger and palm prints were taken before he was interviewed by Butler. Butler may have been the newly appointed Head of the Flying Squad but he did not let that interrupt his detective work. Nothing was going to distract him from the task of tracking down the robbers of the mail train and putting every single one of them away.

In the presence of Williams and Detective Sergeant Moore, Butler ran through the usual list of pre-prepared questions. Wisbey denied knowing the villages of Brill and Oakley, or knowing Leatherslade Farm.

Butler asked, 'Do you know any of those charged with the robbery?'

'I only know Jimmy Hussey,' Wisbey replied. 'I have known him for years. I don't know the others.'

Wisbey repeated his alibi that he had been at a pub that Williams knew. It was ridiculous to suggest, Wisbey pointed out, that just a few hours later he was in Buckinghamshire taking part in a train robbery. At 12.05, having read through his statement, Wisbey signed it.

Butler then left. Ten minutes later at 12.15, Wisbey is recorded as making a second statement in the presence of Williams. It is not known how that added to or varied from the information he had already given.

Williams' relationship with his criminal contacts was sometimes ambiguous. Had he offered to help Wisbey in some way, or was he boxing him in further?

The next day Wisbey was the eleventh hooded figure to be guided by police officers through the doors of Linslade Magistrates' Court and, like all those that had gone before, he was remanded in custody.

Meanwhile Williams checked Wisbey's alibi. He first spoke to his family at his home at 27 Ayton House, Elmington Estate, London, SE5, who predictably stood by him. However, the landlord of the pub Wisbey had mentioned was more vulnerable to Williams' methods. Initially the landlord backed up what Wisbey had said. But Williams knew the man well, having helped him over an assault charge some years earlier; the two had been, as Williams puts it in his biography, 'on friendly terms' ever since.

After further questioning the landlord said that he did not know if Wisbey had been in the pub on the evening in question. But that was not quite what Williams was after and he turned up the pressure, saying that if the landlord was eventually found to be lying to the police he could lose his licence.

Williams left the pub with the confirmation he had been after. The landlord finally said that Wisbey was definitely not in the pub on the evening of 7 August and that Wisbey had later approached him and asked him to say that he was.

In his 1973 biography *No Fixed Address*, Williams questions why Tommy Wisbey tried to get away with his bluff and says that it remains a mystery to him. Certainly if Wisbey had not called and offered himself for questioning that day he could have quietly disappeared along with his share of the mail-train money.

Hidden away in his rented house in Shepperton, Buster Edwards had been growing increasingly alarmed by the Flying Squad's strike rate of arrests. He must also have been wondering how long it would be before his picture was plastered all over the front pages. To prepare for the eventuality, he had put himself on a strict diet to try and change his appearance. Other than that, all he could do for now was sit tight, keep his head down and hope.

On Thursday, 12 September, *The Times* reported that the police wished to interview Ronald Christopher Edwards, known as 'Buster', in connection with the mail-train robbery. The report also informed readers that it was believed Edwards was accompanied by his wife June, aged thirty-one, and their daughter Nicolette, aged two years, nine months.

Later that same day, Scotland Yard released photographs of a number of men they were looking for in connection with the mail-train robbery. They also issued photos of the men's wives and the images were shown on the television news that day.

Phones at Scotland Yard started ringing within minutes of the photographs being broadcast to millions of TV screens around the country. One call was from a man who lived in Old Forge Crescent, Shepperton. He said he had just seen the photographs of Edwards and his wife and they were identical to a couple he knew as Mr and Mrs Green who had recently moved in down the street at number six.

Local police were immediately dispatched to the address while detectives from Scotland Yard sped out from Central London. When they converged on the house they found no one in. Another neighbour informed the officers that the Green family had left home early that day in their Morris 1100. The Edwardses never returned.

On Friday, 13 September nothing particularly ominous happened. A report was circulated among the various investigating police departments that Edwards was thought to be in possession of a red Morris 1100, registration number 480GLM.

The whereabouts of the car was later reported to the police by Arthur Blake. On 12 September someone had left it parked outside his home at 14 Blandford Road in Ealing with the side lights on. The following morning the lights were still on, so Blake telephoned the police. The vehicle was examined and subsequently taken away by police officers.

It was discovered that the vehicle had been purchased from Raven Motor Company in Ealing on 12 August. The salesman, William Harrison, reported that two men and a woman had come to look at the Morris 1100 and the woman paid £659 in cash, giving her name as Mrs Green, 214 St Margaret's Road, Twickenham. Harrison described both men as being in their thirties, about 5'8", stocky, clean-shaven and well dressed. He said the woman was aged about twenty-four, heavily made up, well dressed but with a common-sounding London accent. On 22 August the ownership documents had been changed to Nicolette Wig

Fashions Ltd, a company owned by June Edwards with her business partner William Green.

Like everyone else in Britain, William Green had been following the unfolding news of the mail-train robbery. When he saw the picture of Buster and June Edwards in Thursday's evening papers and read about them being wanted for questioning, Green immediately called John Wheater and asked for his advice.

It is not clear how Wheater and Green knew each other, or why Green sought Wheater's advice rather than telephoning the police.

Wheater said he had to go north on business and suggested that Green come to his office on the following Monday, 16 September.

Given Wheater's claims of ignorance, it is worth noting that he had already been interviewed several times at this point, most recently by Butler at Scotland Yard on 9 September. So he was well aware of the importance of Green's telephone call, yet he did not pass the information to the police. Three days later, when he was again interviewed by detectives Butler, Williams and Van Dyck, Wheater failed to mention anything about Green having contacted him.

Now effectively homeless, Buster and June Edwards needed to act quickly. It was June who came up with an idea. A few weeks before the robbery they had looked at a house in Wraysbury, Middlesex. Although not far from London, the area was tucked away between a meandering stretch of the Thames that runs between Staines and Eton and the reservoirs and sewage works to the west of London Airport. The detached red-brick house with leaded windows was set back on a private road, hidden behind a copper beech tree, and at the rear the garden ran down to river. Edwards, being a keen angler, had been particularly keen on the place and June had spent some time talking to the owner about the rent. June's Nicolette Wig Fashions Ltd was a successful company supplying wigs for shop mannequins, but the Edwardses' financial resources at the time could not stretch to the £20 pounds a week being asked.

The owner of the house did not recognise June when she returned two months later wearing a blonde wig (from Nicolette Wigs) over her jet black hair. After looking over the house a second time, June said she would take it and gave her name as Mrs Green.

*

Following Butler's interview with John Wheater and Leonard Field on 9 September, the documents concerning the sale of Leatherslade Farm had been passed to Maurice Ray and his fingerprint team for examination. According to the paperwork, a deposit of £555 had been paid on 23 July and exchange of contracts had been arranged for 29 July. As is common practice in property conveyancing, Wheater had signed the contract on behalf of his client, Leonard Field. On a bank authority form with Leonard Field's signature at the bottom, Detective Superintendent Ray had found a fingerprint. If the signature proved genuine and the fingerprint could be verified as belonging to Leonard Field, it would prove that he was lying during his interview with Butler at Scotland Yard when he said he knew absolutely nothing about the farm.

On Saturday, 14 September, Metropolitan Police officers arrived at Lennie's home in Green Lanes, Haringey and arrested him in connection with the mail-train robbery. A day later, and they would have missed him; Lennie was due to join the P&O cruise liner SS *Canberra* as a steward when she sailed from Southampton. He was taken to Cannon Row police station where he was met by Tommy Butler.

Field's response was, 'You did not tell me all this the other day. You only said it was about buying the farm. I did not do no robbery. You can believe that.'

Butler now had the bit firmly between his teeth. With one Field already in custody, he was eager to add the second. Once Fewtrell had established that the Bavarian hotel receipt tucked inside one of the bags of money found in Dorking was issued to Brian Field and his wife, the fingerprint department were asked to determine whether any of the prints found on the bags belonged to Field. When Superintendent Ray declared there was a possibility that the prints were a match, that was good enough for Butler. On Sunday morning the seven-day-a-week detective set off for Whitchurch Hill accompanied by Detective Sergeant Van Dyck, Detective Constable Thorburn and Woman Police Constable James. The Flying Squad officers parked their cars at the bottom of Bridle Road then walked up the track and through a gate with the name 'Kabri' spelled out in wrought iron.

When Butler knocked on the front door, Field answered almost immediately. Butler introduced himself and announced the reason for his visit.

'Yes, I know about the case,' Field said in his usual easy and confident manner. 'I have already made a statement to your colleagues about it the other day.'

Butler was in no mood for social pleasantries. He never was. 'We have reason to believe you were involved,' he said. 'You are to be arrested and charged for it.'

'I didn't take part in the robbery,' Field replied truthfully. In his calculated response he was careful to avoid actually lying about his complicity. 'You are making a mistake,' he added lamely. 'I know that the firm and myself were involved in the business of the farm with Leonard Field, but that's not robbery.'

Again, Brian Field was not lying, but that made no difference to Butler. The Grey Fox knew better. He had his men search the house. In Field's wallet they found £110 in five-pound notes. There were no other significant discoveries.

Due to heavy traffic, the journey from Whitchurch Hill back to New Scotland Yard took nearly two and a half hours. Butler noted that Brian Field chatted away incessantly. Perhaps Field was trying to give the impression he had nothing to worry about and he was not the sort of man to be implicated in a major robbery. But under it all Field must have been a very worried man and that's the way Butler saw it.

When they finally arrived at the Yard, Butler went to fetch the hotel bill and leather case. He brought the items into the room separately. Field denied that the case belonged to him. He could not deny that the hotel bill was his, but expressed great surprise that it had been found in a case left in Dorking woods, as he had believed it was at home on his desk.

Leonard Field was then brought to the interview room. Butler pointed to him and said to Brian, 'This is the man who I am certain accompanied you to Leatherslade Farm posing as a potential buyer. What have you to say to that?'

Brian Field replied, 'It is decidedly like him, but this is not the man.'

His response was as bizarre as Wheater's had been when questioned on 9 September. Clearly both men were desperate, given the circumstances, but it is hard to believe that two intelligent men could have constructed such a flimsy excuse and seriously expected to fool the Flying Squad.

After answering further questions, Brian Arthur Field and Leonard

Denis Field were told that their fingerprints were to be taken and they would be driven to Aylesbury the next morning to be formally charged.

The following week there was a procession in and out of Linslade Magistrates' Court of the ten people who had been arrested and held in custody in connection with the mail-train robbery – Biggs, Boal, Cordrey, Brian Field, Leonard Field, Hussey, Mary Manson, Pelham, Wilson and Wisbey.

There were elaborate security precautions as the prisoners arrived at court in two police vans accompanied by three Jaguar police cars. The accused, shrouded in blankets, were handcuffed to prison officers and led into the courthouse through a cordon of a dozen uniformed police-men holding back a large and vocal crowd of press and onlookers.

Each of the accused was asked by the magistrate if they wanted to say anything.

Wisbey responded, 'No, sir.'

Boal said, 'Nothing at this stage.'

Mrs Boal said, 'Nothing to say,' as did Mr and Mrs Pilgrim.

Mary Manson said, 'I have already given my explanation and I am innocent.'

Wilson said, 'Nothing, on the advice of my solicitor.'

Pelham said, 'I absolutely deny the charge and I am completely innocent.'

Hussey said, 'No. I don't want to say anything.'

Biggs just said, 'No.'

When the same question was put to the two Fields, Brian Field said, 'Nothing to say except I am innocent of the charge.'

Leonard Field's response was, 'Definitely not guilty.'

The hearing lasted forty minutes and all those charged were remanded in custody until the preliminary committal proceedings on Thursday, 26 September.

This date was later than originally planned. That morning's edition of *The Times* had published a quote from one of the prosecution lawyers, M. Jardine, stating that as there had been two further arrests (Leonard Field and Brian Field) the opening of committal proceedings would have to be delayed to give the prosecution time to prepare their case.

23

On Thursday, 19 September, Dr Ian Holden of the Forensic Science Laboratory examined the Series Two Land Rover the gang had left behind at Leatherslade Farm. He found yellow paint on the clutch pedal, a smear on the pedal arm and a few specks on the brake and accelerator pedals. He took some samples of the yellow paint traces for analysis.

Leonard Field, now on remand in Aylesbury Prison, received a visit from Detective Sergeant Jack Pritchard on Monday, 23 September asking him to take part in an identity parade the following day.

The purpose of the exercise was to see whether Mrs Rixon could identify Leonard Field as one of the two men who had come to look over Leatherslade Farm with a view to buying it. There were eight men in the line-up. Originally there had been nine, but Leonard Field objected to one man on the extreme right of the line, presumably because he was too unlike himself. Field, who had his solicitor advising him, then raised another objection about a second man. But when Chief Inspector Reginald Ballinger, who was in charge of proceedings, explained that an identification parade had to be made up of no less than eight, the objection was withdrawn.

Pritchard, who was present as a representative of the detectives engaged in the mail-train investigation, was more concerned about Leonard Field's appearance than his objections. In an effort to make himself look different, Field had arrived with his hair slicked flat and parted in the middle, reminiscent of an Edwardian music hall act. His normal style up until then had been to wear his hair parted on the left and free of styling grease, which made it appear fairer.

Mrs Rixon was brought in and Ballinger carefully explained the procedure for making a positive identification. She listened attentively and as soon as Ballinger had finished Mrs Rixon walked straight over to Leonard Field, pointed at him and said, 'This is the gentleman.'

*

On Wednesday, 25 September the drama of 'The Great Train Robbery' was eclipsed as the nation turned its attention to the publication of a controversial report by senior judge Lord Denning. Such was the seduction of scandal, two thousand members of the press and public had queued from midnight to get their hands on a copy; Her Majesty's Stationery Office had a bestseller on its hands, priced seven shillings and sixpence. The *Daily Express* ran a cartoon by Giles depicting a classroom of children with their heads down, hard at work. As their grim-faced teacher stands at the front of the class studying a tome on his lectern, one boy whispers to another: 'Chalkie's not reading 'Omer – he's reading my confiscated Denning Report.'

The subject of Denning's report, though less epic and romantic than the liaison between Paris and Helen of Sparta, was as old as Homer. A man of political importance had allowed his carnal desires to get the better of him, and the ensuing uproar threatened to topple the ruling power.

The story first broke in 1962, when Harold Macmillan's Conservative Government had been rocked by what came to be known as 'The Profumo Affair'. The story sounded like the plot for a James Bond film, although the man at the centre of it did not have Sean Connery's looks. He was, after all, a politician.

Secretary of State for War John Profumo had met twenty-year-old call girl Christine Keeler at a house party at Cliveden, the home of Viscount Astor. The relationship only lasted a few weeks, but Keeler was also reputed to be the mistress, or perhaps more accurately the occasional bedfellow, of a Notting Hill drug dealer called Johnny Edgecombe and – more damaging from Profumo's point of view – a Russian spy named Yevgeny Ivanov.

On the face of it, Keeler's connection with Ivanov, a senior naval attaché at the Soviet Embassy in London, could have put Profumo in a vulnerable position. But it was not quite that simple. Ivanov and Profumo had met socially at that same house party at Cliveden. They even took part in a swimming race together.

But there were rumours about Keeler, her reckless lifestyle, her friend and 'promoter' Stephen Ward, a portrait painter and osteopath, whose clients included Winston Churchill, members of the Royal Family and movie star Elizabeth Taylor. Outside Ward's flat in Wimpole

Mews, drug dealer Johnny Edgecombe appeared one night with a gun and fired it when Keeler refused to let him in. The story began to leak out and once the press and satirists got hold of it they were not going to let it go.

When questioned about his affair with Keeler in the House of Commons, unsurprisingly, John Profumo had lied about it and although no actual damage had been done the whole 'what if' and moral debate had kept bouncing around like a ball on a roulette wheel. Three months later, in June 1963, he was forced to confess and resign.

On 22 July 1963, Stephen Ward stood trial for living off the immoral earnings of prostitution. Keeler and her friend Mandy Rice-Davies appeared as witnesses. Inevitably, members of the establishment, including Viscount Astor, found themselves implicated. As the trial was coming to a conclusion, Stephen Ward committed suicide, prompting yet another twist in the spiralling saga.

For the British public, Ward's trial served to confirm a growing perception that the establishment was threaded with double-standards, seedy associations, immorality and hypocrisy.

Nearly a year after Profumo's indiscretion, the ensuing outrage and repercussions had not gone away. The Denning Report threatened to reignite 'The Profumo Affair' which had shifted public opinion and was all part of why many chose to see 'The Great Train Robbery' as an anti-establishment act. The more public figures and pundits railed about the bandits 'striking at the heart of the nation' the more it seemed to encourage support from people across creed and class who quietly sniggered at the embarrassment. There was an appetite to see old-school institutions get their comeuppance and many people in Britain saw the train robbers as folk heroes who had stuck two fingers up at the establishment.

Critics of the Denning Report said it was a whitewash. The pressure for change was rising inexorably and the cliques of high authority were facing not just loss of face, but loss of confidence and political power.

While prosecution counsel grappled with the numerous bundles of legal documents, witness statements and exhibits that had to be organised, there was a more practical problem that threatened to prevent the mail-train robbery committal proceedings from starting on schedule.

For days workmen had been coming and going from the council

offices in Aylesbury. The building resonated to the sound of constant sawing and hammering. It was all because Linslade Magistrates' Court was a tiny rural courthouse and there was no possibility of the accused, plus counsel for prosecution and defence, court clerks and police officers, let alone members of the press and the public all squeezing in. As a result, it had been decided that a special courtroom would be created within the Rural District Council Chamber at 84 Walton Street, Aylesbury. Which was why the place was full of workmen, busily constructing a special dock and witness box, along with seating for fifty members of the public.

Another logistical problem was that the male prisoners were being held over an hour's drive away at Bedford Prison (where John Bunyan had written *Pilgrim's Progress* during his incarceration three hundred years earlier). It was therefore agreed by the prison authorities that the accused men should be lodged at HMP Aylesbury. Although it was a low-category prison, it would reduce travelling time and ease concerns about the security risks of a longer journey.

By Thursday, 26 September the scene was finally set for the next step in the process of bringing to justice the thirteen men and women accused of taking part in the mail-train raid of 8 August or knowingly receiving the proceeds. The purpose of the committal proceedings was not to prove their guilt beyond reasonable doubt, but simply to review all the evidence against them and then decide if there was a case to answer. Assuming there was, it would be referred to the Crown Court for a full trial by jury.

In the dock at the specially prepared courtroom in the Aylesbury Rural District Council Chamber were Roger Cordrey, William Gerard Boal, Renee Boal, Charles Frederick Wilson, Ronald Arthur Biggs, James Hussey, Thomas William Wisbey, Leonard Denis Field, Brian Arthur Field, Robert William Pelham, Mary Kazih Manson, Alfred Pilgrim and his wife Florence May Pilgrim.

Mr Howard Sabin for the prosecution opened, setting out his narrative of events that had led to the arrests of the accused. Sabin began with a rather confusing statement for anyone unfamiliar with the law and the details of the case. He said that at earlier hearings the theft of £2,631,000 had been cited but in the amended charges the total sum stolen was not mentioned. It was a neat piece of manoeuvring. The total sum stolen was most reliably calculated by the police in the Home Office report and the GPO Investigation Branch as £2,595,997.10s., but £2,631,684 is often quoted and sometimes £2,631,784. The exact figure remains open to debate.

Howard Sabin went on: 'The prosecution is not in fact proposing to prove the full amount of money that was on the train. It is quite clear there was an enormous sum of money in the high-value packets.'

On the face of it, his statements were rather odd and contradictory, but they were underpinned by a logic and expediency that had been determined at the highest level of the British criminal justice system. For the prosecution to prove the continuity of the money stolen, over a thousand witnesses from all over Scotland and the North of England would have to be called from the many banks who had made up the bundles of notes that had been sent to London. The time and cost involved was incalculable but clearly it would be enormous. Presenting each individual piece of the financial jigsaw cogently in court would also be complex and unwieldy. The contents of the 128 mailbags on the mail train had come from so many disparate sources it would be impossible collate them as a body of evidence and prove the total amount stolen.

For the purposes of the criminal prosecution it had been decided to simply charge the defendants with stealing mailbags from the Royal Mail train and from the man in whose care they had been placed, the man in charge of the HVP coach at the time of the robbery: Frank Dewhurst.

Sabin's opening speech was long and detailed, but it successfully wove together all the threads of the story and established how the thirteen people in the dock had come to be traced and arrested by police officers. Much of this was already familiar to the accused, but what was only just becoming clear to them was the weight of the forensic evidence amassed by the prosecution – Leonard Field had left a fingerprint on a bank transfer document that he had signed, both Hussey and Wisbey had left their palm prints in several places, Biggs' fingerprints had been found on the Monopoly box and other objects, Wilson's thumb print was on a drum of Saxa salt, his palm print on a window sill and on the cellophane wrapping of a Johnson's travel first-aid kit and Brian Field's on one of the bags discovered in Dorking woods.

Evidence was then heard from Mrs Rixon, who was questioned about the two men who had called at the farm. Once again she pointed out Leonard Field as being one of them.

At the end of the first day the hearing was adjourned for a week until Friday, 4 October. The bail of Alfred and May Pilgrim was renewed and Mary Manson was also released on bail. The other nine accused men were remanded in custody and returned to Aylesbury Prison.

On Thursday, 26 September, new charges of robbery of mailbags and receiving were brought against Boal, Wilson, Biggs, Hussey, Wisbey, Leonard Field and Brian Field.

Tommy Butler, Dr Ian Holden and police photographer John Bailey paid a visit to Leatherslade Farm on Saturday in connection with paint found on the instep of the shoes removed from Goody's room at the Windmill pub. Holden collected samples of gravel and yellow paint from a shed floor while Bailey photographed the area in question.

Pursuing a minor tributary of the mail-train investigation, Detective Sergeant Van Dyck and Detective Constable Thorburn went to search a flat at 17 Michaelson House, Bower Drive, Dulwich. It was the home of twenty-eight-year-old Martin Harvey who, other than by association, was unconnected with the mail-train robbers. During the course of their search, the officers discovered a brown paper packet containing £500 in banknotes and a further £18 on a mantelshelf. Van Dyck told Harvey he had reason to believe the £518 found came from the train robbery at Cheddington.

Harvey said, 'You are dead right. It is from the job, but I was not in it and that's gospel.'

The officers told him he would be arrested, to which he replied, 'Fair enough. I am not arguing.' He went on to say that he had been paid £200 for minding the money for 'someone'.

It was a large fee for looking after such a small sum and Harvey must have regretted it instantly. The following day he appeared in Linslade Magistrates' Court, the fourteenth person to be arrested in connection with the mail-train raid.

On Thursday, 3 October, in compliance with the conditions of his police bail, Gordon Goody got into his silver-grey Jaguar, registration number 9811UB, and drove the short distance from his home to Putney police station. When he arrived at the station 'the terrible twins', Butler and Vibart, were waiting for him.

Butler produced a pair of Tru-form suede shoes wrapped in brown paper and asked Goody if they were his. Goody said that they were and confirmed he had not loaned them to anyone. Butler asked Goody again when he had travelled back from Ireland and Goody asked to see his solicitor.

Detective Sergeant Nevill and Detective Sergeant Slipper went to Goody's house and were let in by his mother. This time the officers did have a search warrant and they were more determined than ever not to go away empty-handed.

After carrying out a very thorough search, the two detectives left with a pair of check slippers, a pair of suede boots, a diary, two letters, a notice of sale, two pairs of rubber boots and nine other assorted pairs of shoes. Dr Holden and his team had become obsessed with Goody's footwear and now they would have plenty to keep them busy.

When solicitor Raymond Allan Brown of Lesser & Co. arrived, he spoke to Goody and then informed Butler and Vibart that he had instructed his client not to say anything more. However, when Goody was later charged at Aylesbury he did speak again on the subject of the mail-train robbery.

'I know nothing about the matter,' he said. 'I am completely innocent.'

The grand total of fifteen suspects arrested looked impressive in the newspaper headlines. There was the unfortunate collection of family and associates – Bill Boal and his wife Renee, Alfred Pilgrim and his wife May, Robert James Pelham and Martin Harvey. There were two conspirators, Brian Field and to a lesser extent Leonard Field. But out of the gang of fifteen criminals, not including their train driver, who robbed the mail train in the early hours of 8 August only six had been detained – Ronnie Biggs, Roger Cordrey, James Hussey, Charlie Wilson, Thomas Wisbey and Gordon Goody.

John Daly, Buster Edwards, Roy James, Bruce Reynolds, Bob Welch, Jimmy White, Mr One, Mr Two and Mr Three were still at large. And they intended to keep it that way.

24

On Friday, 4 October committal proceedings continued in the Rural District Council Chamber at Aylesbury with the presentation of evidence against those who stood accused of taking part in the mail-train robbery or having been found in possession of the proceeds.

As part of the hearing, the case against Martin Harvey for receiving was introduced and he now made up the total of fifteen men and women seated in the dock:

Roger John Cordrey, aged 42 of Hurst Road, East Molesey, Surrey.

William Gerard Boal, aged 50, of Burnthwaite Road, Fulham, London, SW6.

Mrs Renee Boal, aged 52, of the same address.

Charles Frederick Wilson, aged 31, bookmaker, of Crescent Lane, Clapham, London, SW4.

Ronald Arthur Biggs, aged 34, carpenter, of Alpine Road, Redhill, Surrey.

James Hussey, aged 30, painter and decorator, of Eridge House, Dog Kennel Hill, East Dulwich, London, SE22.

Thomas William Wisbey, aged 33, bookmaker, of Ayton House, Camberwell, London, SE5.

Leonard Denis Field, aged 31, merchant seaman, of Green Lanes, Haringey, London, N8.

Brian Arthur Field, aged 29, managing clerk, of Kabri, Bridle Road, Whitchurch Hill, Oxfordshire.

Robert William Pelham, aged 26, motor mechanic, of Lonsdale Road, Notting Hill, London, W11.

Mary Kazih Manson, aged 42, of Wimbledon Close, The Downs, Wimbledon, London, SW19.

Alfred Pilgrim, aged 52, florist, of Bridge Road, East Molesey, Surrey.

Mrs Florence May Pilgrim, aged 49, of the same address.

Martin Harvey, aged 28, of Michaelson House, Bowen Drive, Dulwich, London, SE22.

Douglas Gordon Goody, aged 33, hairdresser, of Commondale, Putney, London, SW15.

The charges were as follows:

1. Cordrey, William Boal, Wilson, Biggs, Wisbey, Hussey, Leonard Field, Brian Field and Goody that between 1st May and 9th August 1963 in Buckinghamshire, conspired together with other persons unknown to stop a train with intent to rob the mail.
2. Cordrey, William Boal, Wilson, Biggs, Wisbey, Hussey, Leonard Field, Brian Field and Goody being armed with offensive weapons robbed Frank Dewhurst of 120 mailbags.
3. Cordrey and William Boal on a date unknown between 7th August and 15th August received £56,037, £79,120, £5,060 in money, the property of the Postmaster General knowing the same to have been stolen.
4. Brian Arthur Field on a date unknown between 7th August and 17th August received £100,900 in money, the property of the Postmaster General knowing the same to have been stolen.
5. Renee Boal on a date unknown between 9th August and 16th August received £325 in money, the property of the Postmaster General knowing the same to have been stolen.
6. Alfred and May Pilgrim on a date unknown between 9th August and 16th August received £860 in money, the property of the Postmaster General knowing the same to have been stolen.
7. Robert William Pelham on a date unknown between 9th August and 24th August received £545 in money, the property of the Postmaster General knowing the same to have been stolen.
8. Mary Kazih Manson on 9th August received £835 in money, the property of the Postmaster General knowing the same to have been stolen.
9. Martin Harvey on a date unknown between 8th August and 1st October received £518 in money, the property of the Postmaster General knowing the same to have been stolen.

The scene in the courtroom was sombre. The only splash of relief against the African hardwood panelling and dark suits of the men came from the three women in the dock. Mary Manson wore a bright-red outfit, Renee Boal a dainty white nylon hat with matching gloves, and May Pilgrim had chosen a green coat with fur-trimmed collar. Although it was August, it had been one of the most sunless, wet and gloomy summers on record.

All the while driver Jack Mills sat two feet from the huge polished pine dock studded with blunt metal spikes in which the fifteen accused were seated in two rows, surrounded by police officers.

When the ashen-faced Mills was called upon to speak, he told the court, 'I haven't been able to go back to work. It has affected my nerves very much.'

Both Mills and Whitby gave accounts of the ordeal they had suffered. Their stories were simple and straightforward, two railwaymen going about their honest work when their train was stopped in the dead of night and attacked by a large gang of violent, masked thieves. Their first-hand statement of what they could remember was in stark contrast to romantic notions of dare-devilry and Robin Hood images that had been evolving in the minds of some people.

Even so, their stories were not without humour or a sense of dark irony. Whitby told how one of the train robbers had said to him, 'I'll get your address when this is all over and send you a few quid.' Needless to say, that promise was never delivered – or at least, no one asked Whitby if he had received any money from the gang.

He described being held on the railway embankment while the gang formed a human chain, passing mailbags to the lorry. He had lit a cigarette and tried to give one to Mills. The robber standing over them said, 'I'll have one if you've got one to spare,' and borrowed the fireman's lighter to light it.

Shocking, traumatic and detailed though Mills' and Whitby's accounts of the robbery were, they were unable to identify or connect any of the accused in the dock to the raid. It was one thing for the prosecution to tell the story and produce witnesses to the events, but quite another to produce evidence that connected the individuals arrested to the crime.

GPO sorter Thomas Kett gave a statement which followed much the same lines. He had been hit, manhandled and terrified during the robbery, but the question remained: were the men in court who stood charged with these crimes the bandits who'd been on the track that night? It had yet to be proven if any of those in the dock had a case to answer.

Next, the prosecution set out to establish the connection between the robbery, the vehicles that had been used and Leatherslade Farm. In the specially constructed witness box Mrs Nappin repeated her report of vehicles passing under the window of her cottage on the Brill Road at just after midnight and again around four thirty on Friday morning.

All the newspapers on Monday, 7 October had pictures of 'Buster' Edwards and his 'raven-haired' wife June. In the new photographs, the fleshy face and cheerful, friendly smile of the seasoned and violent criminal beamed out at the British public, while his wife emerged looking like a character from the recently released gothic horror film, *Black Sabbath*, starring Boris Karloff.

The *Daily Express* let readers in on what it described as 'the most unusual trap ever devised':

Behind the trap is the belief that Edwards and his wife, June are in London. So the Yard last night asked the BBC and ITV to stay silent about the Edwardses and at the same time stepped up a great new hunt for them, issuing more pictures of the couple to newspapers. The Yard's hope is that before the Edwardses get hold of a newspaper and realise the heat is on again somebody will have remembered them and dialled 999.

The vital hours it is thought are between 6.30 a.m. and 9 a.m. when Britain is eating its breakfast. The Edwardses with no reason to get up will probably still be in bed during that time. The couple, who have a three-year-old daughter, Nicolette, have been reported seen in London in the past few days.

The Yard had certainly come up with an unusual ploy. But it was tenuous at best and clearly contrived by a man who had no experience of living with young children. Unless there was something unusual about three-year-old Nicolette, it was unlikely that her parents would be enjoying the luxury of sleeping in.

*

Committal proceedings at Aylesbury recommenced on Monday. Detective Sergeant Stanley Davies of Bournemouth police gave his account of the arrests of Cordrey and Boal. On the face of it, the evidence against those two defendants seemed fairly cut-and-dried. They had been found in possession of a great deal of money and Cordrey had admitted that it had come from the train ambush. However, when interviewed by detectives, Cordrey maintained that while he had been asked to provide the gang with information about stopping trains and later asked to 'look after' the proceeds, he had not taken part in the robbery.

The basis of Cordrey's and Boal's prosecution for the actual train robbery was at best circumstantial. Unlike some of the other accused, there was no fingerprint evidence to connect either man to Leatherslade Farm. Neither was there ever likely to be as far as Boal was concerned since he had never been there, despite Dr Holden's yet to be presented forensic analysis of paint found on a brass winder in Boal's jacket pocket.

Daly and Reynolds were finding life on the run expensive. Reynolds and his wife Franny, who had dyed her hair ginger, had moved to a small one-bedroom flat above a dry-cleaning shop at 71 Handcroft Road, Croydon. As Reynolds put it, he was being 'milked for readies' at every turn.

He got a message via Terry Hogan that Daly wanted to see him. Daly too had been suffering 'at the hands of the jackals'. When they met in Central London after convoluted, covert transport arrangements, Reynolds did not approve of Daly's investment plans or the company he was keeping but agreed to risk retrieving his whack.

In the meantime Daly's racing green 3.8 Jaguar Mk2 had been collected by the police from the Metropolis Garage, Olympia, and taken for forensic examination.

There was drama in Aylesbury courthouse on the morning of Tuesday, 8 October when Detective Sergeant Jack Pritchard mentioned, during the course of his evidence, conversations that had taken place at Bournemouth police station between one of the accused, Roger Cordrey, and detectives McArthur and Fewtrell.

Defence barrister Geoffrey Leach immediately sprang to his feet and said, 'I object to the whole of this verbal evidence, being in breach of Judges' Rules.'

There followed a lengthy legal discussion which was reported in *The Times* the following day. Even the headline was long: *Detective tells of interviews with two accused in mail raid case EVIDENCE 'IN CONTRAVENTION OF JUDGES' RULES'.*

The legal technicality Leach was presenting to the magistrates concerned police officers reporting in the witness box what suspects had said before being cautioned as opposed to what was contained in the formal statements they had made. This was a general practice of police investigation that continued unabated until the introduction of mandatory audio recordings of interviews, improved access to legal advice and a range of recommended codes of practice under the long-overdue 1984 Police and Criminal Evidence Act (PACE).

Despite the rather abstruse legal terms employed by Leach, most of the men in the dock got the gist of his objection to what, in their vernacular, was known as being 'verballed'. Real police methods were often a far cry from the Sherlock Holmes model of a detective painstakingly finding clues in order to deduce who the culprit was. The practice of verballing often involved the concoction of incriminating remarks or confessions alleged to have been made in the back of a police car or some other venue outside a formal interview under caution. It was all part of a culture based on the police deducing who was guilty and then finding or sometimes fabricating evidence to support it.

When presented as evidence at a trial, judges could admit or overrule these verbal reports at their discretion. Such evidence usually fell outside their rules of admissibility.

Geoffrey Leach's application was backed by fellow defence counsel Wilfred Fordham, who said that a greater part of the officer's evidence was 'in flat contravention' of Judges' Rules and at trial might well be ruled inadmissible. Fordham added that Leach was the oldest member of the bar in court and in his submission 'must be right on the matter'.

Leach continued to set out the case for some restriction of verbal evidence in the magistrates' court as it would not only be a matter for a judge to decide later but, he suggested, in the meantime the press would report what was said and that would be prejudicial to the later trial by jury, since the members of that jury would have formed opinions from reading the newspapers.

It was a valid argument and tossed back and forth between Geoffrey Leach for the defence, the magistrates' bench, and Sabin for the prosecution. In the end, the chairman of the magistrates' bench, Walter H. Leach, said that in the past there had been very few cases when magistrates had sat 'in camera' and there was the important principle, particularly in a case which was very much in the public eye, that justice should be seen to be done.

Geoffrey Leach repeated that it would be wrong for full publicity to be given to evidence which had not yet been ruled upon by a judge as to admissibility. He said that he was not asking for the case to be withdrawn from the public eye, only that police officers in giving evidence to the court should confine themselves to statements made under caution and not quote uncorroborated verbal asides.

To illustrate his point, Leach then produced a copy of *The Times* from the previous day and read the headline, *Man's alleged admission: Money came from the train robbery.* He pointed out that the remark came after the man concerned had been told that the money had been recovered from a car. If this was what the man had said at the time, it might amount to an admission that at some stage he had realised the money came from the robbery, but *The Times'* headline was an edited quote of a police officer's verbal evidence taken out of context and would be construed by readers as the suspect's admission of complicity in the whole train robbery.

After further consideration, the magistrates refused Leach's application for restrictions. There was a small concession that his point had not gone unrecognised when the magistrates asked the press to be considerate, 'only reporting what is absolutely necessary'.

Geoffrey Leach, clearly sceptical about the likely effectiveness of that warning, ended his appeal with a parting salvo to the press:

... if any part of this officer's evidence were reported in the press, BBC or television my instructing solicitors would not hesitate to report it to the Attorney General to see if he thought fit to bring proceedings for contempt of court to ensure these defendants had a fair trial and remedy the injustice already done to them.

Leach then resumed his questioning of Pritchard, drawing his attention to a passage concerning Judges' Rules:

> Rule three is not intended to encourage or authorise the questioning or cross examination of a person in custody after he has been cautioned on the subject of the crime for which he is in custody ... it has been the practice for the Judge not to allow any answer so improperly put to be given in evidence.

'You are aware of that?' Leach asked.

Pritchard replied, 'Oh, yes. I am.' Adding that in his opinion there was no breach of Judges' Rules.

Leach then asked, 'If there was a breach of the Judges' Rules, Superintendent McArthur is responsible?'

'If in the opinion of some later person there was a breach, yes,' Pritchard confirmed.

Next to give evidence was Dennis Kenneth St John, a salesman employed at the Chequered Flag Garage in Chiswick. He outlined the sequence of events that had led to the sale of a black Austin Healey 3000 on 9 August. The court was then adjourned until Thursday.

By Thursday, 10 October, Roy James had taken refuge in a mews house at 14 Ryder's Terrace in St John's Wood, where he learned from news reports that his prize possession, his Brabham Ford racing car, had been taken by officers from his garage in Spicer Street to Chalk Farm police garage. The news presented James with a further dilemma. His sudden and unexplained withdrawal from the motor racing scene and disappearance from his usual address had already made him look suspicious. His mechanic, Robert Pelham, had been charged with receiving stolen money. If James did not now contact the police and ask why they had taken his racing car it would confirm that he had gone into hiding. His suspected connection and complicity in the mail-train raid would then look all the more convincing.

Since he first heard of Wilson's arrest while driving back from Goodwood and decided to make himself scarce, things had slowly escalated and the problems were not going to die down or go away. Whether he realised it at the time or not, James had reached a point of no return.

He was on the run and was possibly going to have to stay on the run for the rest of his life if he was to avoid going to prison.

Also in the news that day was the resignation of Prime Minister Harold Macmillan. It may not have been a matter of immediate concern to Roy James, but events on the political stage would have significant influence on the eventual fate of the mail-train robbers.

A protégé of Winston Churchill, Macmillan had been nicknamed 'Supermac' for his pragmatism, unflappability and wit. Educated at Eton and Oxford, he had served with distinction during the First World War as a captain in the Grenadier Guards. Out of twenty-eight contemporaries at Balliol, Macmillan was one of only two to survive the war. During the Battle of the Somme he was wounded and spent an entire day lying in a trench with a bullet lodged in his pelvis reading the plays of Aeschylus in the original Classical Greek. As a result of his injuries, for the remainder of his life Supermac walked with a slight limp.

Macmillan was a survivor in every sense and he could no doubt have ridden out the storm of the Profumo Affair, but his decision to resign came shortly after he was told that he had inoperable prostate cancer. It was later found to be a misdiagnosis and Macmillan, 1st Earl of Stockton OM, PC, went on to live for another twenty-three years, dying at the age of ninety-two in 1986.

The Flying Squad continued its round-up of known associates. At 08.15 on 10 October, Detective Sergeant Jack Slipper, Detective Sergeant Moore and Detective Constable Thorburn went to 14 Linhale House, Murray Grove, Shoreditch. It was the home of bookmaker Walter Albert Smith and his wife Patricia. The officers searched the flat and, as might be expected in the home of a small-time bookmaker, they found various sums of money and postal orders. On the top shelf of the airing cupboard were several piles of one-pound notes.

According to the explanation Smith gave the police, a man had come round on Thursday last and asked him to change the money for him; as the notes were all wet he'd put them in the cupboard to dry out. He would not tell the officers who the owner of the money was, but admitted that it had come from the train robbery and said he had been offered a shilling in the pound for changing them. He explained that the man had given him two lots of money and he had already changed seven to eight thousand pound into postal orders. The detectives found an unused cheque book under the water tank in the airing cupboard, and further cash in Mrs Smith's coat and handbag. When Mrs Smith was asked if there was any more money, she said yes and patted her stomach. She then put her hand in the top of her skirt and produced several handfuls of one-pound notes, totalling £465. Mrs Smith said she had put them there when they heard the knock on the door. Both Mr and Mrs Smith were arrested and taken to Aylesbury, where they were charged with receiving money totalling £2,000. Both were granted bail when they appeared before Linslade magistrates the following day.

In the middle of all the public attention surrounding the mail-train robbery, the ongoing investigation, the arrests and legal technicalities of evidence against the accused, a smaller, more personal drama was unfolding. During Thursday's session of the committal proceedings at the Rural District Council Chamber, defence lawyer Ivor Richard announced that the Home Office had sanctioned that his client, Brian Arthur Field, should be allowed out of Aylesbury Prison under escort to visit his wife. The court had earlier given its approval for the visit after being told that the shock of her husband's arrest, combined with the strain of travelling back and forth to the prison and court at Aylesbury had caused Field's pregnant wife great distress. Karin Field had given birth to a daughter four months premature at their home at Whitchurch Hill.

That evening Field was driven to Kabri in handcuffs. When the police car pulled up at the gate, officers removed the handcuffs and Field immediately ran to the house and went upstairs to Karin. With police officers standing at the bedroom door, Field kissed his wife as she told him that she had feared she was going to lose the baby but their neighbour, Evelyn Bowsher, who fortunately for Karin was a midwife, had come to her aid. Having spotted that the child was breathing, the midwife enlisted the aid of local florist Brian Stanley, who had come to the house to make a delivery of fifteen gardenias from Karin's sister in Germany. While nurse Bowsher cradled baby Jacqueline, who weighed less than two pounds, Stanley made the five-mile trip to Battle Hospital at Reading in just over five minutes. The infant was immediately placed into an incubator in the maternity unit.

At the end of his half-hour visit, Brian Field was driven back to Aylesbury Prison leaving his wife alone in bed at their home and without seeing his newborn baby daughter, who was reported to be in a 'very weak' condition.

25

On 15 October 1963 there was a small column on page four of the *Daily Express* under the headline *DRIVER MILLS GETS REWARD*. The article reported that the previous day British Railways had formally thanked Jack Mills for his courage during the mail-train robbery.

Mr J. Royston, line manager at Crewe said, 'The Great Train Robbery will go down in history. Driver Mills played a big part in it. He proved a real railwayman. No one expected him to throw the raiders off the footplate; that would have needed a whole police force. Driver Mills is worthy of the highest commendation. He had a shocking time.'

Royston then presented Mills with a certificate for 'courage and resource' and a cheque for twenty-five guineas.

After accepting the accolade Mills said, 'I don't feel at all well. I only wish I did and could go back to the trains. I'm fed up with the sound of the great train robbery.'

On Wednesday, 16 October, Brian Field was again allowed leave from Aylesbury Prison. His elation at becoming a father had been dashed by the news that baby Jacqueline, born four months prematurely, had not survived. The funeral for the child he had never seen was held near his home in the Church of Saint John the Baptist at Whitchurch Hill.

At 07.30 on the morning of Thursday, 17 October, Chief Superintendent Tommy Butler, Chief Inspector Mesher from the Fraud Squad and Detective Sergeant Pritchard went to the home of John Wheater at Ottways Lane, Ashtead, Surrey. In the house were Wheater, his wife Angela, two daughters and a nursemaid.

As Jack Slipper would later say in his book *Slipper of the Yard*, his old boss Tommy Butler 'wasn't only very dedicated; he was also very serious and very, very thorough'. Wheater being a solicitor, the Grey Fox chose his words carefully. He informed Wheater that he had a warrant for his arrest for conspiring to rob the mail train on 8 August and also for being an accessory after the fact.

Wheater asked to read the warrant, which had nine names on it. 'I don't know any of these people,' he said, 'or at least only half of them.'

Butler said, 'It is alleged that you concealed the identity of the purchaser of the farm in that you gave the address of your client, Leonard Field as 150 Earls Court Road. Do you remember that?'

'Yes,' Wheater replied.

The detectives then entered Wheater's house. As they were conducting their search, Wheater said to Butler, 'This is a mistake, you know.' And with the news still sinking in, he added, 'This will ruin me.'

Once the search had been completed and a collection of papers and an address book had been seized, Wheater was driven to his offices in New Quebec Street. There a further search was carried out. The solicitor was then taken first to Scotland Yard and later to Aylesbury, where he was formally charged.

After being read the charges, Wheater said, 'I am completely innocent of both charges.'

He was detained overnight in the cells at Aylesbury police station. On Friday, 18 October, John Denby Wheater appeared before Lindslade magistrates. The forty-two-year-old solicitor had a courageous military record from the Second World War, but in peacetime he had struggled to find his place. He was described by Fewtrell as having 'a sad puffy face and copious moustache, looking very much like the ex-army officer busy adapting himself rather clumsily to life as a civilian'.

Ivor Richard, defence counsel for Wheater, added to the pathos by saying that his client wanted this whole thing to be cleared up as soon as possible. 'All he wants is to get his name cleared as quickly as possible and get back to his practice.'

Howard Sabin for the prosecution said he hoped to open the case against Wheater 'next Thursday', when the rest of the accused were due to appear again. Wheater was granted £5,000 bail.

Wheater's public humiliation was to be made more acute when the case against him opened with an account of his arrest by Detective Sergeant Pritchard. The detective reported to the court an alleged exchange that had taken place when Butler had told Wheater his house was to be searched.

Wheater had replied, 'Don't think I am being rude, but I would like to search you people first. I don't want anything put on me.'

Chief Superintendent Butler responded curtly, 'Surely you don't mean that. You must have been listening to too many fairy tales from your clients.'

As Pritchard read out the alleged remarks, there was laughter in the dock where Wheater was sitting with his fellow prisoners.

There was a serious aspect to Pritchard's reporting of the conversation, which was subsequently printed in the press. Following an objection by defence counsel Geoffrey Leach earlier in the proceedings about verbal evidence, the chairman of the magistrates' bench had asked the press to be considerate 'only reporting what is absolutely necessary'. But as the defence counsel had predicated, the warning had gone unheeded. Wheater's unfortunate remarks made good copy and they were later reported in full in the *Daily Mirror* under the headline *ACCUSED MAN WANTED TO SEARCH DETECTIVES*.

Wheater's involvement had not been at first obvious. He had been drawn into it by his quicker-witted clerk, Brian Field. By his own admission, Wheater was never much of a solicitor. But it was hard to believe he had no idea what was going on in his office or that he did not realise what he was being asked to do was criminal. The final case against him looked damning. To acquire the farm, the gang had needed the services of a solicitor. Unwittingly, perhaps, Wheater had been a lynchpin in the whole process. The prosecution had originally thought he would be a useful witness and shed light on the process by which the gang had obtained access to the farm, and even that he might help identify the organisers. But as the farcical relationship between Wheater and Leonard Field had slowly emerged, the investigators came to the conclusion that Wheater must not only have been complicit but a key component in planning the crime.

At 20.50 on Friday, 25 October in Railway Approach, SE1, just outside London Bridge railway station, Detective Inspector Frank Williams and Detective Sergeant Van Dyck had been waiting for some time when they spotted Robert Welch coming out of the station and meeting another man.

Williams had been on Welch's trail for several weeks, slowly gathering information. Though he had disappeared from his home and usual haunts, the resourceful detective learned from an informant that Welch was with four associates in a rented farmhouse in Beaford, on the north coast of Devon. With the help of local police this had been confirmed and covert observation was set up.

Williams had discussed the matter with Butler but the wily Flying Squad chief was not in favour of moving quickly. He argued that other members of the gang might turn up at the Devon farm and for the time being they should just keep watching and waiting.

As time went on Williams got reports of Welch and his associates spending freely in local bars, frequently buying drinks for every customer and taking supplies of beer back to the farm. The group had apparently even donated generously when the local vicar came collecting for church funds. The detective, relying on an intimate understanding of the criminal mindset, became convinced that no other members of the gang were going to join the party. Nevertheless Butler continued to insist they wait.

Then another informant told Williams that Welch was planning to travel to London to meet his brother. The rendezvous was due to take place outside London Bridge station at around nine o'clock on Friday evening.

As the appointed time approached, Williams and Van Dyck parked their unmarked car with a clear view of the station entrance. They posted two other officers in a second car and three on foot strolling casually around the station and the street outside.

When Welch walked out of the entrance, Williams spotted him immediately. He watched the suspect greet his brother and the two men started walking towards Williams. As they got to a parked car nearby, the detectives pounced. Welch stood motionless, looking stunned. It took him a moment to fully grasp what was going on as he tried to work out how the police officers had found him.

Williams described Welch as a pale, quiet and polite man. True to form, the man who had been recruited as one of the 'heavies' on the train robbery courteously confirmed his identity and seemed genuinely perplexed when Williams explained why he wanted to speak to him.

'Do you mean the train job?' he said. 'I don't know anything about that.'

When Williams told Welch he was to be taken to Scotland Yard, he still appeared dumbfounded but acquiesced and said nothing further.

Back at the Yard, Butler and Williams went through the pre-prepared questionnaire with Welch. He continued to be civil if terse in his responses, no doubt thinking that the police had little more than suspicion to connect him to the mail-train robbery. He did not attempt to deny that he was acquainted with Wisbey and Hussey, who were known associates, but said he did not know any of the other men in custody or wanted for questioning in connection with the robbery. When asked about Leatherslade Farm, Welch said he had never been there and denied any knowledge of the place. Welch's reply suited the detectives very well, as his prints had been found at the farm on one of the pipkins of ale.

Welch was taken to the cells at Cannon Row. When Williams offered to call his wife he replied, 'Don't trouble. It will only worry her, and in any event I'm in the dog house with her.'

At 15.00 the following day, 26 October, Robert Welch was driven to Aylesbury where he was formally charged. The farm he had been staying at in Beaford was later raided by Flying Squad detective Steve Moore with officers from the Devon Constabulary. No money or incriminating evidence was found.

The committal proceedings in Aylesbury resumed on Monday, 28 October with the additions in the dock of John Wheater and Robert Welch. Among witnesses giving evidence, magistrates heard from John Ahern, who had found the bags of money in the woods near Dorking, and the owner of Leatherslade Farm, Bernard or 'Tubby' Rixon as he was known locally.

As far as the press and public were concerned, interest in the story of 'The Great Train Robbery' was flagging, but for the detectives it was far from over. Half the gang had so far evaded capture and as time went on it was going to become harder to find and arrest them. The New Scotland Yard forensic and fingerprint teams were still comparing, matching and cataloguing the huge amount of evidence they had collected at the farm. It would all have to be presented convincingly in court in order to secure the prosecution's case. The mail-train robbery investigation was proving unprecedented, not only due to the number of criminals involved and huge amount of money stolen, but because the scale and complexity of linking all of the accused to the crime was growing exponentially. Although each element of the investigation and legal proceedings was vital to constructing a successful prosecution and conviction of the criminals, the process of doing so was not easily portrayed in newspaper headlines and far less compelling than the cops-and-robbers story that had been unfolding over the preceding weeks.

An example of the amount of arduous and unglamorous work that was being done behind the headlines was the thorough investigation into the provenance of the nine seven-pint pipkins of ale found at the farm. The batch number 723 on the pipkins was first traced to the Friary Meux Brewery at Guildford. That particular batch had been dispatched by 7 August. The exact distribution of all 2,574 cans was established and the relevant retailers were sent a questionnaire asking if any customer had purchased six or more pipkins in late July or early August.

The questionnaires were returned to local police stations and the painstaking business of going through them consumed men and time. The most promising lead was the fate of 108 pipkins with the 723 batch number that had been delivered to the Ind Coope depot in Oxfordshire. A dozen had been sent from there to an off-licence in Bicester, and the manager confirmed that a man had bought ten pipkins in July. But when later questioned by police he was unable to identify any of the suspects as the customer on that day. However likely it seemed that the pipkins found at the farm had been purchased at the Bicester shop, all the extensive tracing, interviewing and recording of this single aspect of the investigation was inconclusive.

The issue of identifications had been raised in the committal proceedings the previous week. When witnesses were asked to identify individuals in court from among the accused in the dock, Wilfred Fordham for the defence had raised an objection. He argued that firstly some of the accused were well known from photographs that had appeared in the press. Secondly, witnesses would naturally examine the men and women in the dock, and this did not constitute a proper means of identification. That could only be done outside the courtroom through the normal procedure of identity parades in which at least eight participants of similar appearance would be assembled. Mr Gavin for the defence was in support, saying there was 'small value in identification straight from the dock'. Howard Sabin for the prosecution replied that there was a great deal to be said for the objections if there were only one

person in a dock. But in this case there were so many and he intended
to call a number of witnesses concerned with identification.

Despite the obvious flaws in Mr Sabin's logic, the defence counsel
left the matter for the rest of the morning. But there was a surprising
U-turn by Sabin after the lunch break when he made the following
announcement:

> The prosecution are willing to accede to the requests that before the
> witnesses are called they should be asked to attend identity parades.
> The prosecution have been a little reluctant to arrange that because it
> means a very large number of identity parades and I have taken the
> view hitherto, in view of the number of persons in the dock, that iden-
> tification in court is fair.
>
> I am proposing to arrange that these identity parades shall take
> place at the beginning of next week. It is not very easy to arrange with
> such a large number. There will have to be at least nine and I am told it
> takes perhaps two or three hours to arrange each one.

The chairman of the magistrates' bench announced that after the
day's proceedings the court would be adjourned for a week to allow
time for identity parades to be organised.

On Wednesday, 20 November identity parades were duly set up.
Biggs, Wilson, Leonard Field, Brian Field, Goody and Welch were put
up in pairs with twelve others. Hussey, Wisbey, Boal and Cordrey were
each put up individually with eight other male volunteers.

Chief Inspector Reginald Ballinger of the Buckinghamshire
Constabulary was in charge of the identity parades. Brian Field
attended two parades and was not identified by any of the twelve witnesses. Goody was in two parades and not picked out, even though he
was very distinctive looking and 6'2". Wilson was on two parades and
never identified. Welch attended two parades, on 13 and 20 November,
and was not identified. William Boal was also put in two parades and
like all the others was not singled out.

The dry legal arguments and procedures of the committal proceedings in Aylesbury and rigours of the identity parades were a world away
from the life of the men still on the run. Jimmy White, his partner,

baby daughter and Gigi the poodle were still lying low. Their choices were limited and they had been forced to stay wherever they could find through White's associates in London. Like Reynolds, he was being fleeced for money at every turn, but he had no option but to pay. Everyone who offered help knew White had money and they all were quick to point out the risks they were taking and exploit it.

Buster Edwards, his wife June and toddler Nicolette were faring better, hunkered down in their rented house by the River Thames in Wraysbury. Bruce Reynolds and Franny were still in the one-bedroom flat above a dry-cleaning shop in Croydon. Roy James was in St John's Wood. John Daly and his heavily pregnant wife were in a small, £45-a-week flat in exclusive Eaton Square, Belgravia.

As far as Tommy Butler and his team were concerned, they were hoping it was only a matter of time before they either received another tip-off from an informant eager to claim the huge reward money, or one of the wanted men made a mistake. Based on the behaviour and lack of planning of the members of the mail-train gang already in custody, it was possible that those who were still at large had not gone very far. With their images firmly imprinted on the minds of the nation, and realising that most links to their former lives had been cut off, sooner or later those wanted for questioning would have to make a move.

In the meantime Frank Williams carried on talking to his contacts, while the other members of the Flying Squad team continued to make life very difficult for London's criminal underworld, and the careful, patient and obsessively secretive Tommy Butler kept on working alone in his office at New Scotland Yard late into the night.

26

Through the darkening weeks of November the committal proceedings at Aylesbury produced few surprises. On Wednesday, 12 November, the fourteenth day of the case, Dr Ian Holden, principal scientific officer at Scotland Yard, gave evidence concerning samples of paint he had found on the Austin lorry, a Land Rover, and on the gravel floor of a shed at Leatherslade Farm. The tall, slim, fair-haired, articulate Holden struck a different kind of figure from previous witnesses who had appeared at the converted courtroom in the Rural District Council Chamber. Not only did he have a PhD but the very title Forensic Science Laboratory carried an aura of alchemical mystery. In many ways, Dr Holden's words were turning the base elements of everyday objects such as paint particles into the gold dust of convincing criminal evidence.

Holden's methods and analysis were steeped in a long and illustrious history that stretched far beyond the scientific traditions in which he had been educated. In 250 BC the Ancient Greek physician Erasistratus had discovered that his patients' pulse rate increased when they were telling lies. In 1447 the missing teeth of the French Duke of Burgundy were used to identify his remains. In 1786 John Toms of Lancaster was convicted of murder on the basis of a torn wad of paper found in a pistol that matched a remaining piece in his pocket. In 1810 a test for a particular ink dye was applied to a document known as the Königin Handschrift in Germany. By the end of the nineteenth century, forensic science as a means of finding and convicting criminals was widely accepted and understood to such a degree that it featured in popular fiction. Among numerous forensic discoveries and elementary deductions, Conan Doyle's detective Sherlock Holmes attributed phosphorus to the demonic appearance of a murderous hound that roamed the remote, foggy expanses of Dartmoor in *The Hound of the Baskervilles*.

After Sir Edward Henry, Commissioner of the Metropolitan Police, set up Britain's first fingerprint department in 1901, forensic evidence soon became established as an indispensable part of criminal investigation. The first British forensic laboratory was established in Hendon in 1935. Identifying corpses through dental records began in the 1940s, and in 1950 Max Frei-Sulzer, founder of the first Swiss forensic science laboratory, developed methods for lifting trace evidence by using adhesive tape.

When Dr Holden said there was a match between the paint on vehicles used for the robbery and at Leatherslade Farm and traces later found on a pair of suede shoes belonging to Gordon Goody, it carried weight and authority. But that did not explain why Holden was convinced that the same paint was on a small brass winder that had been found in a jacket taken from William Boal's house in Fulham. Neither Boal, nor his jacket, nor the brass winder had ever been anywhere near the vehicles or Leatherslade Farm. The problem with alchemy is that it can be seductive.

The mail-train robbery investigation team continued to follow up information received and to pursue routine inquiries that might lead to the discovery of the eight remaining fugitives and the huge amount of stolen money still missing. An example of the collateral rewards that came to light during these investigations was a visit to a warehouse belonging to Arthur McGuire at Stonebridge Park, Willesden, London, NW10. McGuire was courteous when Detective Inspector Harry Tappin and other officers arrived at his premises and even showed them round. While the fifteen-strong police team were looking through a pile of cartons, they found a door leading to a secret room that contained a printing press, thirty-two litho plates, twenty-four tins of ink and eleven alloy sheets. They also discovered thirty photographic reproduction plates bearing the images of five-pound notes. During the subsequent hearing at the Old Bailey on 13 November, the prosecution was unable to prove McGuire was responsible for making the forgeries. He was, however, found guilty of concealing the crime and jailed for eighteen months.

On the morning of Friday, 22 November *The Times* reported on the account that had been given at the committal proceedings that week of the arrest of solicitor John Wheater. The downfall of a professional man had provided a new twist in the mail-train robbery story when the news first broke a month earlier. But many of the details had already been reported by other newspapers and *The Times'* article failed to inject fresh drama into the long-running story, which was now into its fourth month.

Later on Friday the death of two prominent literary figures offered more promising headlines for broadsheet journalists. Following health problems that had dogged him since 1961, the sixty-four-year-old Belfast-born author of *The Chronicles of Narnia,* C.S. Lewis, collapsed at 17.30 at his home and expired a few minutes later.

Earlier that day, Aldous Huxley, English intellectual and author of the iconic *Brave New World*, had died of cancer, aged sixty-nine, at his home in California. Huxley was bedridden and had become unable to speak. At 11.45 US Pacific Time that morning he had written a short note in a very shaky hand to his French wife, Laura, asking her to administer an intramuscular injection of 100 micrograms of LSD. A couple of hours later, while Huxley lay more peacefully than he had for weeks, Laura asked if she should give him a second injection and he squeezed her hand weakly.

At 17.20 on the afternoon of 22 November, Aldous Leonard Huxley finally passed away, leaving in his wake a remarkable literary legacy and many prophetic visions of the future.

During his lifetime Huxley had raised concerns about the potential power of mass media to unify and standardise the perceptions, thoughts and opinions of vast numbers of people. In many ways, the enormous media attention given to 'The Great Train Robbery' was a practical demonstration of Huxley's vision and was to be further illustrated in the way the story played out.

The significance of Huxley's life and work was initially overshadowed by a more unexpected and seismic event that seized the attention of the world. At 12.31 Central Standard Time, in Dealey Plaza, Dallas, Texas, the forty-six-year-old American President John Fitzgerald Kennedy was shot.

The time of the Kennedy shooting in Britain was 18.31. It had been a quiet and unremarkable day. BBC Television's *Six O'Clock News* had covered a by-election in Dundee and the departure of the newly crowned Miss World, Jamaican-born Carole Crawford. First on air with news of the Dallas shooting was northwest England's Granada

Television shortly before 19.00. At 19.04 BBC Television broadcast a newsflash read by John Roberts:

'News has just come in that President Kennedy has been shot. There's no news yet of his condition. It happened as the President was riding with his wife in an open car through the streets of Dallas, Texas. Several shots rang out and the President collapsed into the arms of his wife. One eye-witness said he saw blood on the President's head. The Governor of Texas, Mr John Connally, who was with him, was also shot down. The President was rushed to hospital, where there's still no word of his condition.' Millions of Britons stayed glued to their TV sets, anxious for more details. However, despite the enormity of the event, BBC Television returned to its usual Friday evening schedule. At 19.26 John Roberts read a second newsflash that concluded, 'We regret to announce that President Kennedy is dead.' For the next nineteen minutes all viewers of BBC Television saw was the black-and-white revolving globe of the network ident with occasional repeats of the newsflash. Like the BBC, ITV stopped broadcasting programmes and put up a static interlude card with periodic announcements on the shooting.

With nothing more to go on, a stunned British nation was left to draw their own conclusions. Kennedy's presidency had been beset by controversy, culminating in the Cuban Missile Crisis twelve months earlier, so it was inevitable that the assassination invited speculation.

In the days that followed, the shooting of President Kennedy, the arrest of his assassin, Lee Harvey Oswald, and the killing of Oswald by Jack Ruby two days later was made all the more compelling, immediate and intimate through television pictures and commentary, with live satellite reports direct from Dallas and Washington. The image of Jackie Kennedy reaching out over the long boot of the open-topped Lincoln presidential limousine to retrieve a blown-away piece of her husband's skull was indelible. And in a way that had not happened before, and just as Huxley had predicted, the power of mass media technology was having a profound influence on the perceptions and opinions of countless millions of people around the world.

For the mail-train robbers locked in their cells, and for others still on the run, it was hard to comprehend that the shooting of an American president could have any influence on their own fate. But beyond the practical and legal considerations of bringing the mail-train robbers to justice, Kennedy's assassination, along with the recent Profumo Affair and the resignation of Prime Minister Harold Macmillan, were all components in the political *zeitgeist*. With public opinion divided, shifting social values and epidemic crime rates, the old-school establishment in Britain was under siege. News of Kennedy's violent death in such a very public and shocking way served to intensify the government's concerns that subversive forces and anarchy were not far away. There was an echo of the assassination of Archduke Franz Ferdinand, heir apparent to the Austro-Hungarian throne and his wife, Sophie, while driving in an open-topped car through the Bosnian capital, Sarajevo. Forty-nine years earlier their deaths had triggered unrest that culminated in World War One.

With the shocking news of Kennedy's assassination still at the forefront of everyone's mind, the committal proceedings at Aylesbury sat for its final session on Monday, 2 December. Howard Sabin for the prosecution announced he had decided not to ask magistrates to commit Mary Manson for trial. He said that on reflection it was unfair to regard her association with Reynolds, who had not been arrested for the crimes, as significant. There was no evidence that any of the money she had used to pay for a car at the Chequered Flag Garage came from the train robbery. Sabin asked that Manson should be discharged, but that the other accused should be committed for trial at the higher court.

Mr Hawser, QC for the defence of Brian Field, submitted that his client had no case to answer on the charge of robbery and that the evidence produced by the police to support the charge of conspiracy was 'thin'. Hawser proposed that, in light of the evidence produced against him, Brian Field should be committed for trial only on charges of receiving some of the stolen money.

Hawser's appeal was a curious tactic. The evidence that had been given in court clearly implicated Brian Field in the purchase of Leatherslade Farm. Not only had his law firm handled the conveyancing but Field had been to visit the property with Leonard Field and then lied about their association to the police. Field had also been connected with the stolen money discovered in the woods near Dorking, both through a German hotel receipt found in one of the bags with his name on it and through fingerprint evidence.

Mr Mathew, acting for Charlie Wilson, then asked the court to rule that they were committing his client as an accessory before the fact and that he had no case to answer as a principal in the conspiracy or the robbery.

The appeals by Hawser and Mathew on behalf of their clients were both rejected.

All counsel for the defence then turned to a different matter. They asked that the referral to the higher court should be at the Central Criminal Court in London. A trial at the Old Bailey would make things easier logistically, and with all the various members of the bar being based in London, the Central Criminal Court would be a great deal less expensive for the public purse than a Buckinghamshire venue. The other factor they argued was the likely length of the trial, which would make it difficult for the everyday business of other Buckinghamshire Assize hearings to take place.

There was another motive for wanting the trial to take place at the Central Criminal Court, although this was not revealed by defence counsel. It was generally agreed that a jury drawn from London would be more diverse and objective. They would be removed from local feelings about the violent crime that had intruded on rural Buckinghamshire. In short, the defendants would get an easier ride with a cosmopolitan London jury.

The request to relocate was also rejected and magistrates ruled that the trial should be held in Buckinghamshire Winter Session of Assize at Aylesbury commencing on 13 January 1964.

The final business of the day concerned bail applications. Mr Richard made the case for Brian Field and Mr Fordham for Goody. After hearing what the counsel had to say the magistrates took a clear line between those charged with receiving, who were granted bail, and those charged with conspiracy and robbery, who were remanded in custody. Finally, Ellis Lincoln (solicitor for Goody) asked that the prisoners be sent to Brixton Prison to await trial, as it would be more convenient for prisoners and counsel. His application was also refused.

As Monday, 2 December drew to a close the story of 'The Great Train Robbery' seemed to have reached a resting point. But just as things appeared to have been neatly tied up ahead of Christmas, the next day brought another dramatic new development.

27

For three weeks Detective Chief Inspector Walker of C11 had been following up inquiries. With Chief Superintendent Tommy Butler's approval, round-the-clock observation had been carried out at 65a Eaton Square, London, SW1. Finally, at 16.00 on Tuesday, 3 December, six carloads of police officers drove the mile from New Scotland Yard to Belgravia. Having parked out of sight, the redoubtable Tommy Butler made his way along the grand, stucco-fronted houses of Eaton Square, accompanied by Detective Inspector Frank Williams, Detective Sergeants Jack Slipper, Jim Nevill, Steve Moore and Bernard Price, and Detective Constable John Estensen.

Slipper and Nevill were sent round to the back of number 65. Officers at the rear entrance of properties were often the ones who apprehended fleeing suspects, and in his biography Slipper explained the particular pressure of his role:

> There's always a special responsibility attached to watching the back of the premises because it's a tradition in the Squad that the worst thing that can possibly happen is to have a suspect escape out of the back. If you ever lose one, you go to any lengths to make an excuse for it, but your story is never accepted. In the Squad it simply isn't on, whatever your reason.

When the two officers got to the rear of the property they discovered there was a twenty-foot-high wall blocking access. With only moments to go before Butler and Williams were due to enter from the front there was no time to go in search of a ladder. If the suspect did sneak out through the rear exit, he could climb in either direction into one of the neighbouring gardens without being seen. Seconds before Butler went into the main entrance, Slipper and Nevill suddenly raced past him and turned into a communal entrance that led to the back garden. Unaware of the problem they were trying to overcome, the methodical and ever-calm Butler was not amused, commenting drily that Slipper 'must be losing his grip, tearing around like that'.

Butler and Williams were let into the property by the caretaker, Bill Farrow. When asked about the occupants of the basement flat, Farrow told them that for the past two months the basement apartment had been occupied by Mr and Mrs R.J. Grant. Farrow said that he had not met or seen Mr Grant. Mrs Grant had told him her husband was in hospital following a heart attack. The caretaker added that Mrs Grant had said she was nervous about visitors. If he wanted her for any reason, he'd been instructed to ring the doorbell using a particular signal of two long rings followed by a short one.

Butler and Williams quietly made their way down the staircase to the basement and along the hallway to Flat A. The walnut-veneered front door looked sturdy and had a spyhole for checking visitors. Butler put his finger on the doorbell and pressed it three times – two long, one short – and the detectives stepped away either side of the door, out of vision of the spyhole.

Seconds later, the door was opened by a woman. Butler and Williams burst in and found a thin man wearing pyjamas and a red dressing gown sitting on a sofa. He jumped up when he saw them.

'You are John Daly,' Butler said, more as a statement than a question.

'No, my name is Mr Grant,' the man replied.

It took Frank Williams a moment to be sure. The slim, bearded man standing in front of him looked very different from the man they had come to arrest. Last time Williams had seen John Daly he was a portly sixteen stone and clean-shaven. But after the initial surprise there was no doubt that the gaunt and hirsute Mr Grant was in fact Daly. Williams reminded him they had met before and insisted he knew who he was.

'Hello, Mr Williams,' Daly responded politely. 'Yes, you've got me.'

When Butler informed Daly that his fingerprints had been found at Leatherslade Farm, Daly told him, 'You're wasting your time. I've never been to that bloody farm. That's the truth.'

While Daly's girth had dramatically decreased, his wife, Barbara, looked considerably larger. She was now almost nine months pregnant and Daly expressed concern that she should not be questioned.

In their biographies, Williams and Slipper offer no explanation as to why the Flying Squad chose that particular day to raid Daly's flat. They had had the building under observation for weeks. In Piers Paul Read's book, he expounds a theory that Daly's minders had betrayed him. Like his brother-in-law Reynolds, Daly was a friend of Mary Manson who had been acquitted only the previous day. Read suggests that Daly 'had been betrayed by Godfrey Green [Daly's minder] – afraid that now Mary Manson had been released he would lose control of John's money'.

According to Read, after apprehending Daly, Butler telephoned Mary Manson and asked her to look after the heavily pregnant Barbara. If true, it is a rare glimpse of a more compassionate side to the uncompromising and dry bachelor detective.

Leaving other officers behind to search the tiny basement flat, Butler and Williams took Daly back to Scotland Yard where he was asked the usual questions from the prepared list. Again, Daly denied knowing Leatherslade Farm and said very little. He was later driven to Buckinghamshire to be formally charged. At Aylesbury police station, Daly refused to allow his photograph to be taken, despite a number of attempts.

Around this time Reynolds, too, came close to being caught when a local police patrol called at his Croydon hideaway. While Franny answered the front door, Reynolds stayed upstairs, listening as the officer told her that he was concerned having noticed a ladder leaning against an upstairs window. When the officer went into the flat to check all was well, he found Reynolds undressed and pretending to be Franny's lover. After the embarrassed police officer had gone, Bruce and Franny Reynolds hurriedly packed their possessions and left immediately. When the flat was later searched, finger marks were discovered confirming that Reynolds had been there as well as John Daly and James White.

According to Bruce Reynolds' version of events, on the day his brother-in-law, John Daly, was arrested, he received confirmation that contracts had been exchanged on a house he had bought in Albert Mews, Kensington, London, W8. Reynolds' trusted friend the Captain, who had acted as front man for the transaction, duly sent word that he had the keys. Reynolds took a circuitous route using several taxis to the Captain's place in Bayswater. Managing to dodge the porter, Reynolds roused the Captain at one o'clock in the morning, got the keys and went straight to his new hideout.

Albert Mews is a small, dog-leg street tucked away in a less fashionable part of Kensington, at the top of Gloucester Road. On the basis that the best place to hide is a city, it was not a bad choice. But Reynolds' latest move raised the question why, with the frenetic activity of the Flying Squad in the metropolitan area showing no signs of abating, had he stayed in London, let alone tied a slice of his money up in a property in Kensington? Was he still clinging to the slim hope that the furore over 'The Great Train Robbery' was just going to go away and he and his family would be able to resume some sort of normal life again?

TRAIN RAID POLICE SEIZE 'QUIET MAN' was the headline on the front page of the *Daily Mirror* on Wednesday, 4 December. The *Daily Express* led with *TRAIN POLICE SWOOP*, and the accompanying article reported that after John Daly was taken away to Scotland Yard a policewoman had stayed at the Belgravia flat with his pregnant wife Barbara. Later in the evening a green Ford Zephyr pulled up outside 65 Eaton Square and two men got out: Barbara's brother, wearing a suede jacket, and a bald man in a fur-lined coat. They pushed past pressmen gathered at the scene without comment, and were quickly admitted through the front door. Shortly afterwards, the men came out of the building leading Mrs Daly with the fur coat over her head. They hurriedly loaded a suitcase into the boot of the Ford Zephyr, got in the car and drove away.

On Wednesday, 4 December, a clean-shaven John Daly appeared before Linslade magistrates. The court heard evidence from Butler and Williams who each gave their account of Daly's arrest. Detective Inspector Hawkins applied for Daly to be remanded in custody pending further inquiries. Daly was asked by the magistrate, Mr J. Warren, if he had anything to say.

Daly replied, 'It's all lies.'

Warren ruled that John Thomas Daly should be remanded until the following Tuesday and Daly was led away. *The Times* reported that the entire hearing had taken just four minutes.

Piers Paul Read offers an insight into what was running through the minds of the bandits who had thus far managed to evade capture when he reveals that James, who was hiding in relative safety and comfort in a flat in St John's Wood, had decided to give himself up when the time came, 'for if he was on the run for the rest of his life, he would never be able to return to motor racing or his mother, the two things that mattered most to him'.

In *No Fixed Address*, Frank Williams, drawing on his close understanding of the criminal world, says that he had formed the impression that those men still wanted for questioning might be persuaded to give themselves up if the circumstances were right. He thought that the first to crack could be Buster Edwards, and he had been trying to make contact with Edwards through an intermediary.

For the robbers on the run there was a simple choice: flee and face the prospect of a lifetime as fugitives, or give themselves up and take their chances. If they waited until after the main trial of the other accused, they would have a better idea of how best to play their respective legal defence. They would know the basis on which their co-conspirators had been acquitted or convicted, and that would allow them to fine-tune their own stories and defence accordingly. Rumours and speculation had been rife about the length of sentences that might be handed out, but once the remaining fugitives had a definite idea of the penalty they could expect to face, that would be another factor to consider. If they gave themselves up, pleaded guilty and returned some of the stolen money, there might be an opportunity for negotiation. If White, Reynolds, Edwards and James were playing a waiting game, it would explain why none of them had opted to leave the country. But their various plans suggest they were also clinging to the vain hope they were somehow going to avoid prosecution.

While Jimmy White had removed himself to Mansfield in Nottinghamshire, his partner Sheree had taken their baby son and gone to stay on an army base in Aldershot with a friend of a friend whose husband had been posted abroad. White had no doubt grown tired of the extortion that every helper had imposed on him. On one occasion, according to his account to Piers Paul Read in *The Train Robbers*, White had been asked to pay £3,000 a week to sleep in an ex-jail mate's garage.

Encouraged by the capture of Daly, Tommy Butler was optimistic that the other men might also still be in London. It galvanised the efforts of the Flying Squad. Over the next five days they continued their inquiries on the damp, overcast streets of the capital.

Chief Superintendent Butler and Detective Inspector Williams were very different kinds of men and their ideas about detective work were equally divided. But they agreed on one thing. If they were going to make any further progress in finding the remaining fugitives or recover the stolen money it was going to be through luck or informants. They needed a break. There was no lack of information coming in from both the public and underworld contacts, prompted by the lure of the £260,000 reward still on offer, but so far they had nothing.

Then, late on the afternoon of Tuesday, 10 December there was not just one break but two in quick succession. The first was an anonymous telephone call to the police from a woman who said that Roy James was living at 14 Ryder's Terrace, St John's Wood (near the world-famous Abbey Road Studios where the Beatles' *Please Please Me* was recorded during 1963).'

At 18.30, while Butler was starting to coordinate his team and plan a raid, Detective Chief Inspector Sid Bradbury took another anonymous call. The voice on the end of the phone said that £50,000 of the money stolen from the mail train was going to be left in a telephone box at the junction of Black Horse Court and Great Dover Street, Camberwell.

'Be there in five minutes,' the caller said, and hung up.

Bradbury told Williams about the call and Williams went to Butler's office. The Grey Fox was sceptical as usual. 'It's another hoax,' he said.

'At least let's go and see,' Williams urged. 'We have been given a time limit of five minutes. If we delay, those concerned might get cold feet and call it off.'

Eventually Williams had his way. Butler put the St John's Wood operation on hold and agreed to go with him to take a look.

The two detectives immediately set off in Butler's Mini, speeding to the rendezvous in the heart of the badlands south of the river. As they approached the telephone box, which was on the main A2 road through Camberwell, surrounded by blocks of public housing, they could make out a dark shape inside. Butler pulled up alongside and the two men got out to investigate. Inside the glass-paned telephone box, in full view of passing pedestrians and traffic, were two bulging sacks tied with string.

Butler, convinced that someone was having a laugh at their expense, was cautious. But with nothing to lose, he and Williams dragged the heavy sacks from the phone box and, with some difficulty, wrestled them on to the rear seats of Butler's Mini.

Williams and Butler then got back in the car and watched. It was possible that if they waited, someone might come forward. For several days Williams had been feeling optimistic that the messages he had been sending out via his contacts would yield something sooner or later. It was conceivable that any minute one of the men wanted for questioning would step out of the shadows and give himself up.

While the two detectives sat in Butler's Mini with the windows steaming up, Williams prodded the sacks on the back seat. They smelled damp and musty and appeared to be full of small packages. It was intriguing and tempting to take a closer look, but they decided not to open them until they got back to the safety of the Yard. After several minutes, Butler had had enough and started the engine. It did not look as though anyone was going to present themselves after all and with the possible capture of another member of the gang in the offing he was eager to get away.

Back at the Yard, Butler and Williams heaved the two sacks up several flights of stairs to their offices. With Bradbury and other members of the team gathered around, Williams untied one of the bags and immediately spotted packets of banknotes inside. He bent down, grabbed the bottom corners of the sack and tipped the contents out on to the floor. In his biography, Williams says he regrets not having looked up to catch the expression on Butler's face as the packages of banknotes tumbled out.

Butler remained tight-lipped. After instructing Sid Bradbury to spend the night in the office keeping guard over the sacks, he turned and without further comment walked back to his office to continue working out the details of the St John's Wood raid. When the money recovered from the telephone box was counted the next day, it amounted to £47,245.

In a Channel 4 television interview in 1999, Freddie Foreman told another version of the sacks of money recovered from the telephone box. He related the story for the camera with his usual beguiling gangster guile, saying that he had acted as an intermediary for one of the three men who were never arrested for their part in the train robbery.

Foreman said he brokered a deal with Williams that, in return for the recovery of two sacks of stolen money, plus an additional ten thousand pounds to be left for Williams at a bookmakers as 'a drink', the police would leave that particular suspect alone.

In Piers Paul Read's *The Train Robbers* it is said that Buster had asked an intermediary to enquire if anything could be done. The offer from the police was that if he gave himself up along with £50,000, they would say he had been brought in purely to clean the farm, which would 'probably' give him a five-year sentence. Edwards haggled and they finally agreed to between £35,000 and £40,000, to be surrendered with a £5,000 'drink'.

Thus there are three conflicting accounts concerning the money recovered from a telephone box on 10 December. The first, told in a biography published ten years after the event, was from Frank Williams, the Flying Squad detective whose close associations with members of the South London underworld were disapproved of by his superiors. The second, in Piers Paul Read's book, was based on unreliable information supplied by some of the convicted robbers fifteen years after the event. The third, from Foreman, was put forward in a television interview thirty-six years later. None of these sources can be entirely relied upon. Williams was a policeman of mixed reputation; the robbers are inclined to say whatever suits them and puts them in the best light; and Foreman is a seasoned criminal and self-confessed murderer. Take your pick.

The search for Roy James had extended to seventy-six countries and he had been on the police suspect list since the end of August. Later in the evening of Tuesday, 10 December, forty detectives including Williams, Nevill and Moore gathered at St John's Wood police station to await the arrival of Tommy Butler for a briefing. Detective Constable Patricia Willey had been added to the team in case there was a woman at the target address. By the time Butler had arrived and issued his final instructions, allocated locations and responsibilities, it was 19.45 when the team left the police station and moved into position.

Initially, Butler and Williams went into a house that backed on to the row of mews cottages at Ryder's Terrace, but it offered no alternative means of entry. There was only one route, through the front door, which offered little element of surprise. Williams was in favour of a quick forced entry giving no time for any occupants to escape. Inevitably, Butler had a different idea. He sent Patricia Willey to the house carrying a shopping bag. Constable Willey was instructed to pretend she had a message for James. She was told to mention certain names in order to make it sound convincing. The Grey Fox wanted to try and trick the occupants into opening the door.

With the team all tucked out of sight and watching from various concealed vantage points, Willey walked casually up to the front door of number 14 and rang the bell. Butler and Williams had hidden in a nearby doorway and Williams began to worry that local residents in the narrow mews would notice the activity and come out to investigate.

There was the sound of music playing and a light on upstairs in number 14. Willey rang the bell again, but no one answered. As Willey stood at the front door, there was the shadow of a man behind the curtains in an upstairs French window. Williams decided to wait no longer. Running over and positioning himself under the window, he beckoned Steve Moore over and lifted him on his shoulders. Moore managed to pull himself up on to a small iron balcony and smashed the glass of the French doors. Williams scrambled up behind Moore and followed him into the room just in time to see the lower half of a man disappearing up a metal spiral staircase and through a skylight. With other officers bursting in through the front door, the two detectives gave chase, climbing up the metal stairs out of the skylight.

Alerted by the noise, some officers in the mews below looked up, scanning the roof. Light from torches flicked back and forth, sweeping the darkness. Suddenly there were shouts as the figure of a small man with a holdall in his hand was spotted running across the rooftops of adjoining cottages with Moore and Williams stumbling in pursuit, their leather shoes slipping on the slate. As the dark figure ahead of them reached the end of the roofline, he threw his bag over the edge and jumped down after it out of sight.

In the mews below, Butler was quiet and motionless, watching all the frantic activity. It had not gone quite as he'd planned, but there was no need to panic. The Grey Fox never left anything to chance. He knew Roy James' daredevil escape attempt would be in vain. When James landed in soft damp earth sixteen feet below he found Detective Sergeant John

Matthews waiting for him. Butler had positioned him before the raid to cover the only possible escape route.

Inside the holdall James had thrown down were bundles of bank-notes. 'That's nothing to do with me,' he said, pointing at it.

James, like Daly, had grown a beard. But there was no mistaking the small wiry man whom the press had dubbed 'The Weasel'. When officers later questioned neighbours, they said that James had been living at 14 Ryder's Terrace for four months. Throughout the extensive investigation of the London metropolitan area, James had been just three miles from Butler's office.

He was taken to Scotland Yard for questioning and, as with all the other members of the mail-train gang that had been apprehended, after Butler's list of questions had been put to him, he was driven to Buckinghamshire and formally charged at Aylesbury police station.

The money found in the bag James was carrying was damp and stuck together. It was later peeled apart, carefully counted by bank clerks and found to total £12,041.

Wednesday's national newspapers were full of the sensational roof-top chase and the latest arrest in the mail-train case. 'The Great Train Robbery' was back in the headlines.

The Times also ran a story about Mary Manson, along with a statement from Lesser and Co., her solicitors:

In view of persistent attempts on the part of less reputable members of the press to gain access to Mrs Manson's house and otherwise pester her, we wish the following facts to be made public:

1) Mrs Reynolds' child is being looked after by Mrs Manson, with the full knowledge of the police. This task was voluntarily undertaken by Mrs Manson, as his grandmother, in whose care he was, is suffering from a severe heart condition.

2) Mrs Daly, who is ill following the shock of her husband's arrest, is expecting a second child. It was with the knowledge of the police that she too has gone to Mrs Manson's care.

3) There is no mystery about this association. John Daly used to work for Mrs Manson's husband and Mrs Daly and Mrs Reynolds are sisters.

It is hoped that the publication of these facts will prevent further intrusion.

Three days after Christmas, on Monday, 28 December, Barbara Daly gave birth to a nine-pound baby boy.

On Thursday, 31 December, a special session was held at Linslade Magistrates' Court sitting in Leighton Buzzard. The purpose was the committal proceedings for John Thomas Daly and Roy John James.

Howard Sabin set out the prosecution's case. When questioned by police officers both men had denied ever having been to Leatherslade Farm. But Daly's fingerprints had been found on a card from a Monopoly game and James' prints on a Pyrex dish and a page of *Movie Screen* magazine. Both items had been found at the farm. In addition, Daly had gone into hiding and changed his appearance, while James had tried to evade capture by police officers and had been caught with over £12,000 in a bag in his possession. James also had £131 in cash in his pocket when he was arrested. Two of the five-pound notes had been identified by cashier's markings as belonging to the National Commercial Bank of Scotland, Inverness. They had been sent to London on 7 August 1963 by registered post via the overnight Glasgow to Euston mail train.

It was a familiar story to the magistrates. The hearing was adjourned until Friday, but the committal proceedings for the two men charged with conspiracy to rob the mail train and stealing 120 mailbags from Frank Dewhurst was already feeling like a formality. Both the police and Mr Sabin were feeling quietly confident that their most recent captives would shortly be joining the other accused and committed for trial in Buckinghamshire Winter Session of Assize at Aylesbury commencing in January.

1964

28

The morning of Monday, 20 January 1964 was damp and misty and grey. A large crowd stood in the rain along the streets of Buckinghamshire's county town and outside the Rural District Council Chamber in Walton Street to watch the mail-train criminals arrive from Aylesbury Prison. Shortly after ten o'clock the convoy came into sight, led by a police Jaguar with its blue light flashing. Close behind was a large, ominous black van with dark slit windows that had been borrowed from the Metropolitan Police. It was followed by a minibus loaded with policemen, and at the rear of the convoy came a grey Morris 1000 van containing police dogs and their handlers.

Newspaper photographers and television crews were in position to capture the moment. Among the crowd on the opposite pavement, several Scotland Yard plain clothes officers in hats and mackintoshes were keeping an eye on who turned up to watch the trial. In the line of people who had been queuing for over an hour to get a seat in the public gallery were wives, sweethearts and relations of the accused who had come to witness the fate of their loved ones. Among them stood Mary Manson.

With all the concerns about security, there was a small army of uniformed police officers standing in front of the onlookers as Charles Wilson, Gordon Goody, Thomas Wisbey, Ronald Biggs, Brian Field, Robert Welch, James Hussey, Roger Cordrey, Roy James, John Daly, Leonard Field, and William Boal with a newspaper over his head, were led from the black Maria in through the entrance. John Wheater walked into the building unescorted in a dark suit, white shirt and tie, carrying a briefcase. He could have been mistaken for a member of the legal team. Although charged with the serious offences of conspiracy to rob the mail train and obstructing the course of justice, Wheater had been granted bail, as had those charged with receiving: Martin Harvey, Robert Pelham, Renee Boal, Arthur and May Pilgrim, Walter and Patricia Smith. After all the months of waiting and questioning and previous appearances at Linslade Magistrates' Court and the committal proceedings, their time had finally come. Soon the seventeen accused men and three women would know what their various involvements with the two-and-a-half-million-pound mail-train raid would cost them.

To complete the sense of occasion, a black chauffeur-driven Humber pulled up outside at the main entrance a few minutes later and the presiding judge, Mr Justice Edmund Davies, stepped out already dressed in his full regalia of wig and crimson gown. Crossing the pavement, Davies made his way into the building with a bearing and dignity befitting the occasion.

Inside the converted Council Chamber the stage was set for the long-awaited trial by jury of those who had been arrested for their part in the 'crime of the century'. After five months in the headlines, both at home and abroad, there was scarcely a person in the developed world who had not heard about 'The Great Train Robbery' and did not have an opinion about it.

Hundreds of police officers had been actively engaged in tracing and apprehending the accused. The legal teams had prepared 2,300 written statements and hundreds of exhibits. Prosecution and defence solicitors, barristers and their clerks amounted to more than fifty men and women, and the press gallery was jammed full to capacity. The sheer scale of the proceedings was unprecedented in British criminal history.

In the centre of the courtroom the barristers, including eight 'silks' or QCs (Queen's Counsel), solicitors and their clerks sat at a long row of desks. A microphone had been set up in the witness box and in the opposite corner, Detective Constable Milner and Police Constable Cullen stood over the exhibits laid out on a wide table. It was a curious and eclectic collection of bric-a-brac and could have been mistaken for a white elephant stall at a church fête. In the dock, which locals had nicknamed the Nuremberg dock because of its size, the twenty accused men and women were seated in two rows on pastel green upholstered chairs.

At 10.30 the court bailiff called, 'All rise.' Mr Justice Edmund Davies entered through the same door from which the accused had come, resplendent in his legal attire. In the few seconds it took him to walk to his desk on the dais, Davies took in the measure of his courtroom: the barristers, public gallery and the prisoners standing in the dock. As he took his seat with the royal coat of arms on the wall behind him, the opening business of the long show trial began.

Davies was a wise choice. In addition to enjoying a reputation for courtesy, high intelligence and shrewdness, his background dispelled any notion of old school privilege or patronage. There was a soft Celtic lilt to his voice that was particularly evident in his pronunciation of certain vowels. He came from a Welsh mining village, and had been educated at Mountain Ash Grammar School, London University and Oxford.

It took over thirty minutes for the clerk of the court to read out all the various charges against the accused and hear their pleas for each one. The indictments were that thirteen of the defendants had conspired to rob the Glasgow to London overnight mail train, and that twelve of the men had also taken part in the robbery at the track. There were charges against Wheater, Brian Field and Leonard Field of conspiracy to pervert the course of justice, and charges of receiving for those who had been found in possession of money knowing or believing it to be stolen.

The cases against Harvey, Pelham, Renee Boal, Arthur and May Pilgrim and Walter and Patricia Smith were 'put down' to be heard at a later date.

Roger Cordrey was next to be dealt with. He had decided to plead guilty to conspiracy and receiving stolen money, but denied taking part in the robbery. Cordrey's plea had been accepted by the prosecution and he too was removed from the dock. Unless called to give evidence, Cordrey would only reappear for sentencing.

The remaining twelve men were seated in two rows of six, placed in the order of the indictment, left to right, Boal, Wilson, Biggs, Wisbey, Welch and Hussey in the front, with Daly, James, Goody, Brian Field, Leonard Field and Wheater at the back. Many of the gang were dressed in smart, fashionable suits and while they may have considered it gave them an air of respectability it also stood out in the county courtroom and invited the question how men of their background and modest trades could afford such expensively tailored clothes.

Before the trial could properly get under way the court heard an objection from Mr Ivor Richard for the defence of Brian Field. Richard explained that Karin Field had reported being approached by a man who told her that for £3,000 he could make sure her husband was acquitted. The Judge decided the issue was sufficiently grave to hear from Karin Field, but when she was called upon to speak no one could find her, although she had been seen arriving earlier. 'Gone shopping,' Davies commented with a wry smile. While court bailiffs searched for her, Detective Chief Superintendent Butler was called to the witness box to give the police view on the matter.

The man's offer had been reported to Butler by Mrs Field and he had asked her to arrange a meeting at Reading railway station. Butler intercepted the man and after questioning him had let him go. Butler was asked if he thought the incident posed a real threat to the impartiality of the jury. He replied, 'I can only express an opinion. I think as he knows very slightly one of the accused, he was trying to get himself into a group of criminals and crime that otherwise he would know nothing about.'

It was a surprisingly oblique response from the usually plain-speaking, no-nonsense Flying Squad chief. Butler was aware that among the associates of the accused and unconnected members of the London criminal world there were many jackals sniffing around for an opportunity to get a share of the spoils.

After twenty minutes, Karin Field appeared and told her side of the story. It was partly corroborated by her neighbour Evelyn Bowsher, the midwife who had delivered Karin's premature baby. Davies listened carefully, considered what had been said, and finally dismissed the challenge but thanked Mr Richard for bringing the incident to the attention of the court. The Judge's wise, unhurried handling of this potentially disruptive incident set a tone to the proceedings and gave everyone in the courtroom the first of many demonstrations of his incisive authority, knowledge of the law and the case before him. By the time the court had dealt with Mr Richard's concerns the hearing was adjourned for lunch.

The twelve members of the jury were sworn in when the court reconvened. The make-up of the all-male jury was drawn from the everyday menfolk of Buckinghamshire: George Plested, William J. Grant, Arthur Edward Greedy, Norman Mace, Richard Thomas Tadman, Terrance Addy, Frederick Freeman, William Mullins, George Edward Pargeter, Alexander Sinclair Watt, Ernest F.M. Smith and Leonard Thane. Their trades and professions included a printer, an architect, a clerk of works, an engineer, a works foreman, a sales manager, an insurance man, a gentleman's outfitter and a jeweller. To help them in their unenviable task, each member of the jury was given a dossier containing documents, photographs, maps and a notebook, even a magnifying glass to help them with smaller details that would be referred to.

It was clear that Davies had been ruminating as he ate alone in his impromptu chambers, a room normally occupied by Mrs Lilith Chambers, chairman of the council. He spoke to the jury about the unusual nature of the trial and warned that it would inevitably be both long and complicated. He finished his remarks with a warning:

> Sometimes evil persons who have unworthy motives are out to wreck a trial and deliberately engage a juror in conversation about the case he or she is trying and then promptly take steps to have the juror accused of improper conduct.

To cement the consequences in the minds of his jurors, Davies explained that if a jury was compromised in this way it would result in an enormous amount of extra time and expense. He concluded that he had no reason to believe that such interference would be attempted, but 'such incidents are by no means unknown in the long history of our law'. Davies, sensitive to the impact of his warning on the jury, ended his remarks by saying cheerfully, 'Let us with good heart embark upon our respective tasks.'

Once the Judge had concluded his advice to the jury, Mr Arthur James QC, the leading member of the four-man prosecution team for the Crown, got up from his desk and took to the floor. After giving a brief outline of the legal implications of the conspiracy and robbery with aggravation charges against the accused, he began his dissection of the mail-train robbery that had taken place near Cheddington on 8 August 1963. It started simply and could have been the opening of a fairy tale.

'There was a train, the Up Postal train, which left at twelve thirty a.m. from Crewe ...'

Mr James, who was later compared to a 'tougher Mr Pickwick' by Malcolm Fewtrell, spoke in a clear, bold voice without hurry or affectation. He set out the details of the robbery to the members of the jury with great ease and erudition, never assuming that they knew anything, although each one of the twelve jurymen had arrived at court with a great deal of foreknowledge and understanding of the story he was telling them. James' command of his tale at first appeared comfortable and fluent, and it was only after he had been on his feet for twenty minutes or so that beads of perspiration began to appear from under his wig and run down his temples. What was no doubt playing in the back of his mind was the rather less certain aspects of the task that lay ahead of him.

Arthur James' opening speech for the prosecution took ten hours and carried over into the second day of the trial. He offered an insight into how the money was divided and referred to a piece of paper that had been found in the holdall belonging to Roy James and the money recovered from the woods at Dorking. Each share, he suggested, amounted to well over £100,000 – a figure that served to remind the court of the huge sums involved.

'Do not think I am suggesting that there is some mastermind sitting somewhere who worked it all out and placed his small men to do this and that,' James said. He explained the prosecution's view that the robbery was conceived by a group of men who decided to rob the mail train and then went about recruiting others to help them. 'Each man had a different role, but each was doing something to further the common design and therefore each was equally a conspirator, though their responsibility in a moral sense may have differed.'

After concluding his narrative and theories about the organisation of the robbery, James said, 'None of the men who were on the train will be able to pick out any individual as being one of the participants in the raid. Mills, the driver, will tell you there were fifteen people involved and that is the way we put the case before you – that there were fifteen people on the track.'

James made this statement with the same unswerving confidence, but it was of course untrue. When Mills had first been questioned immediately after the robbery, he had told the police that he thought there were 'twenty to thirty bandits'. The re-working of such details was plain to see for anyone who remembered those early news reports of what driver Mills had said. But no one appeared to spot the anomaly, or at least no one raised an objection even when Mills was later called as a witness and said something entirely different.

In conclusion, James said:

The second charge, that of robbery with aggravation, includes all the same accused, except Mr Wheater. Robbery itself involves, subject to what my Lord may say, proof of forcible taking of goods or money from the person of another or from his presence against his will by violence or putting that person from whom the goods are taken in fear. Robbery with aggravation, so far as this case is concerned, means that that robbery took place at a time when some of the robbers were armed with offensive weapons. There is no need for all of them to be armed. If it is proved they were acting together, and you may think they were acting together here, whoever boarded the train in furtherance of the one and only purpose of robbing it, then possession by one or more, is possession by all. Now these men were armed with coshes, an axe, and other weapons. Mr Mills, the driver, was beaten up and others were struck and threatened. That is the nature of the second charge and we say those who are connected with the farm are those who went on to the track and committed the offence. Some of the disguises used, you may think, were found at the farm. It is quite inconceivable in a case such as this, is it not, that you would have one party on the railway track committing the robbery and a wholly different party back at the farm? It is quite inconceivable.

James' opening speech was the first indication that the evidence presented by the prosecution in court was, by necessity, not to be solely a scholarly procession of facts but a hypothesis when it came to associating the accused to the robbery. Even after months of extensive police investigation and tireless efforts to obtain hard evidence to directly connect those arrested and accused of the mail-train raid, there was not a single fingerprint or witness to link the men in the dock to the crime scene.

The key to the Crown's prosecution was to tie the accused to being at Leatherslade Farm at the appropriate time and dates. Mailbags and money wrappers had been discovered in the cellar by Sergeant Blackman and Constable Woolley and that was concrete evidence that the farm had been used as a hideout by the robbers. Through fingerprints and paint traces, the men in the dock could be linked to the farm and the prosecution team was hoping to prove beyond reasonable doubt that by association they must therefore have been the men who robbed the mail train. It remained to be seen if they could glue those two things together in the minds of the jury.

Even though Boal and Cordrey had been found in possession of large sums of money, and had admitted that money had come from the mail-train raid, it did not prove they were guilty of the charges of conspiracy and aggravated robbery. Despite the eloquence and pomp and circumstance of the courtroom, the incontrovertible truth remained that the only people who knew beyond speculation who was involved in the robbery were the robbers themselves.

In the dock, Boal, Wilson, Biggs, Wisbey, Welch, Hussey, Daly, James, Goody, Brian Field, Leonard Field and Wheater listened attentively as the case was set against them. They looked respectfully at the Judge when he gave directions and observations and, along with everyone else in the courtroom, they smiled at his occasional asides and laughed at his jokes. It must have given some welcome relief from the intimidating, dry and formal legal procedure. Goody, Wilson and Field, who sat near each other, regularly exchanged looks, whispered comments and appeared at ease with the situation. John Wheater, on the other hand, took no part in it and though sitting among them remained detached and stared into space.

Day three of the trial, 22 January, was the first of thirteen days which saw a seemingly endless procession of prosecution witnesses filing through the courtroom. Jack Mills was the first to be called. A pinched grey man, looking older than his fifty-eight years, the train driver entered and walked unsteadily to the witness box. Gripping the rail of the stand, Mills was sometimes inaudible and after a few minutes he was seated in a chair at the side where the microphone was lowered to him. As he recalled the events of the robbery, he sipped water, wiped his brow and looked pale and strained. He seemed shaken and broken by his experience at the hands of the robbers five months earlier, and his appearance left a profound and enduring effect on the court and the case against the mail-train bandits.

David Whitby, Frank Dewhurst and the members of his sorting team followed one by one and gave their recollections of the raid and spoke of their clearly terrifying ordeal and the violence.

Detective Sergeant Stanley Davies from Bournemouth CID, who had arrested Boal and Cordrey, gave his account. During Davies' account of the events surrounding their arrests, Boal stood up in the dock and shouted, 'It's a lie, a deliberate lie.' Boal continued to stand, the Judge glanced over at him, but nobody appeared to take much notice of the outburst.

When DS Davies had concluded his statement, the portly Mr Sime, QC for the defence of Bill Boal, said he wished to raise a point of law under rule three of Judges' Rules and the jury was asked to retire. In the following discussion Sime pointed out that Boal and Cordrey had been interrogated without the usual police caution. Detective Sergeant Davies' evidence had included a remark allegedly made by Boal – 'fair enough it came from the train job'. It was this quote that had prompted Boal to react. Mr Sime's 'point of law' was an echo of an objection about 'verballing' raised by defence barrister Geoffrey Leach in Linslade Magistrates' Court on 8 October, but the Judge said that he was going to allow the officer's evidence, adding that he recognised the point Sime was making.

When the jury returned, Mrs Lillian Rixon, wife of Bernard Rixon, owner of Leatherslade Farm, was tied in knots by defence counsel Mr C. Lewis Hawser QC over her identification of Leonard Field. When asked to confirm if the man she had identified five months before was in the court she pointed to Jim Hussey and said it might be him and then promptly withdrew it.

Later, Sergeant Blackman and PC Woolley were called to explain their involvement in the discovery of Leatherslade Farm.

On Tuesday, 28 January, day seven of the trial, Detective Sergeant John Swain of Scotland Yard recalled a search he had made of Goody's home in Commondale, Putney. When he called, the only person at home was Goody's mother. Goody's barrister, Mr Sebag Shaw QC, could not conceal his anger when he asked if the officer had a warrant and Swain replied he did not.

'Were you told to search the house without a warrant?' Shaw asked pithily.

'If Mrs Goody had said "you can't come in" we would have got a search warrant,' Swain retorted. But under further questioning he admitted that he had told Mrs Goody that he possessed a warrant. 'It was a mistake, not a lie,' the detective protested. 'I had other warrants to search other houses on me and I was told to go to Goody's home.'

The Judge was also clearly annoyed by Swain's explanation. 'See it never happens again,' he said severely.

Shaw was keen to underline the point he was making and added, 'There was no reason to search the house at that stage. That was why there was no warrant.'

A little later that day, Detective Chief Inspector Vibart gave evidence concerning his questioning of Goody after he was detained in Leicester. Vibart's account was the second of several given by police officers that were challenged under Judges' Rules. Shaw again objected, saying that as Goody was in custody he should have been cautioned before being questioned and therefore any statements attributed to him were inadmissible. It was the same point of law that his learned friend, Mr Sime, had made when hearing evidence about the events in Bournemouth concerning Cordrey and Boal. Justice Davies listened to Shaw's point with concern and said that under Judges' Rules he was not going to admit Vibart's evidence concerning any statements made by Goody during the interviews conducted in Leicester on 23 August and subsequently at Aylesbury prior to him being released on 25 August.

Detective Sergeant Davies, Chief Inspector Vibart and Detective Sergeant Swain had each made unprofessional, careless mistakes and it was a body blow, not just for the case against Boal and Goody, but the perception of the police investigation methods and their professionalism in the minds of the jury.

On Thursday, 30 January, Mr Justice Davies made an announcement to the court that took everyone by surprise. At the start of the trial he had gone to some lengths to warn the jury about outside interference of their duty. But even Mr Davies had not anticipated that he might personally become the focus of 'evil persons who have unworthy motives to wreck a trial'. He told the court that he had received a letter which, as he put it '... claims to instruct me in the manner I should carry out my duties in this trial in certain eventualities'. His response to the intrusion was to say that if such a letter was received by a member of the jury, the writer would be committing a very serious offence. 'I say this not in order to create an incident,' he said, 'but to warn anyone who writes letters of that kind that, if necessary, they will be followed up and action taken.' Mr Davies did not disclose what influence the letter was attempting to exert on him, or if there was any threat attached to him not complying. The most obvious inference was that it was from sympathisers of the robbers, but it might equally have been from a member of the public, or someone affected by the robbery, suggesting that Davies should not be too lenient with the defendants before him.

At the end of the second week, on 31 January, Detective Inspector Harry Tappin was giving evidence when Mr Michael Argyle QC for the defence of Leonard Field made a submission that the evidence about to be given by Tappin regarding Butler's questioning of Leonard Field at Scotland Yard was again not in accordance with Judges' Rules. Argyle explained that his client was in custody at the time but had not been cautioned.

The court was adjourned until Monday, 3 February. On 4 February in a curious reversal of what might be expected, Mr Justice Davies ruled that the oral evidence up to the time that Leonard Field was put into the detention room at Cannon Row would be admitted, but a written statement taken from Field after being in the detention room would not.

What the jury made of all these technical legal wranglings can only be imagined. In his memoirs, Malcolm Fewtrell mentions having overheard two jury members talking as they left the building, 'I can't make head nor tail of it,' one remarked.

The next drama in the painstaking examination of the mail-train robbery and subsequent investigation was to come on Thursday, 6 February, day fourteen of the proceedings. Again a policeman giving evidence made a blunder in the witness box, but this time it threatened to undermine the whole trial.

29

Without saying a word, each of the accused sitting in the dock made an impression on the court. It was difficult not to draw assumptions simply from their manner and appearance. Goody with his roguish good looks. Welch, quiet, thin and nervous. Most of the time, Leonard Field sat sullenly, only occasionally breaking into an engaging smile, albeit with a missing front tooth. Wilson was always ready to see the joke in the proceedings, as was the large, amiable Biggs, who dwarfed diminutive, pensive Roy James. Even in repose, Boal was red-faced and, apart from his outburst, seemed removed from things. As did Wheater, who sat rigidly, clearly out of place and tortured by every passing hour of the long hearing. Daly, who had lost so much weight during his four months in hiding, still looked undernourished. Wisbey had the face of a boxer. Brian Field looked benign and pleasant. Only Hussey had something about the eyes that made him look capable of real violence.

In *The Robbers' Tale*, Peta Fordham makes an interesting observation of the Aylesbury residents' views about the trial:

> I was in contact every day with a cross-section of local people who rep-
> resented exactly the same strata from which the jurymen were drawn.
> There was not the least doubt that all of these, with only one exception
> that I recall, were convinced of the guilt of the accused before the case
> began.

By 5 February, the thirteenth day of the trial, it was going rather well for the prosecution. Dr Ian Holden of the Forensic Science Laboratory presented his evidence even more convincingly than he had at the committal proceedings. He was not only a scientific expert but also an expert witness. Under fierce cross-examination, first from Mr Sebag Shaw QC, for Boal, and then the rotund Mr Sime QC, for Goody, Holden confirmed that after he visited the Windmill pub in Blackfriars on Friday, 23

August and removed a pair of suede shoes belonging to Goody, five days had passed before Detective Constable Milner had gone to Leatherslade Farm to retrieve a tin of yellow paint from Mr Rixon on 28 August. A further four weeks had then gone by before Holden discovered paint on the shoes on Thursday, 19 September, which led him to taking paint samples from the vehicles found at the farm and thought to have been used in the robbery. A further nine days later on 28 September, one month and three weeks after the robbery, Holden had carried out an examination of paint on a shed floor at Leatherslade Farm.

The timetable of Holden's scientific investigations and discoveries could be seen as driven by his colleagues' apprehension of Goody in Leicester on Friday, 23 August and arising from their desire to construct a link between Goody and the crime.

Then there was the question of the small brass winder found in a jacket belonging to Boal at his home in Fulham. Holden said he had extracted some paint traces from the knurled grooves of the winder, carried out the same spectrographic analysis that he had on the other samples – taken from Goody's shoes, the robbers' vehicles, the shed floor at Leatherslade Farm, the squashed tin of paint – and concluded that all the samples of paint he had taken were identical in composition.

Viewed retrospectively, there are only three possibilities concerning the paint in the grooves of the small brass winder found in William Boal's jacket at his home in Fulham. First, that Boal had been at the farm and picked up the winder, or somehow contaminated it with the yellow paint Jimmy White had used in his attempt to disguise the Austin lorry on the afternoon of Thursday, 8 August. Despite the gang having no usable transport in those first hours after the robbery, Boal would then have to have somehow returned home to Fulham and changed his jacket before going to Oxford by train to meet Cordrey at 13.00 the next day. Second, neither the winder nor Boal had ever been to the farm and the results of Holden's analysis were ambiguous and he was mistaken. Third, that the winder had been planted by officers in order to secure the conviction of Boal, not only for having handled money from the train robbery, but also having taken part in the raid by linking him to having been at Leatherslade Farm.

When it came to Goody, the police were nervous that he might try and pull another clever stunt like the one that had secured his acquittal for the London Airport robbery. The paint evidence against him certainly provided a challenge. Goody would not be able to 'nobble' Holden or the science on which his expert opinion was based. But it still left the paint-matching issue open to question. Had the eminent Dr Holden deliberately manipulated his evidence? Had the paint on Goody's shoes been put there after they were taken from the Windmill pub?

There was an exchange between Davies and Shaw about whether the QC was suggesting that paint samples had been planted. Shaw explained himself: 'My Lord, I am not desirous of making any suggestions. I was exploring the situation so far as one could.' It was an eloquent reminder to the jury that the evidence presented in court was for objective scrutiny and consideration and should not be accepted at face value, no matter how articulate, qualified, or authoritative the witness.

Mr MacDermot for the prosecution came to Holden's rescue and asked him to express in terms of mathematical probability the likelihood of finding a match between all the samples he had obtained from the various sources he was connecting. Holden began his reply by saying that it was difficult to assess in numbers and at first it seemed he had missed an opportunity. He paused, thought about the question, clearly turning it over in his mind, and then added, 'But if one took it that there were one thousand different colours of paint – and one particular firm advertises that number – the probability of getting a colour on one's shoes would be one thousand to one. The possibility of picking the right two colours would be one thousand times one thousand which is a million to one.' Holden smiled modestly. 'That is why I said it was highly improbable you would get it from anywhere else.'

MacDermot had given Dr Holden an opportunity to clinch it and the jury did not need a PhD to work it out. The simple arithmetic spoke for itself. Mr MacDermot then asked, 'How confident do you feel in that expression of opinion?'

The consummately confident Holden replied, 'Well, if I had to go out and find another pair of shoes with both paints on, even if my life depended on it, I do not think I would even bother to try. I do not think I could find them.'

Dr Holden's integrity and scientific understanding were left in no doubt, but the fact remained that it was the lives of others that depended on his evidence and there was a margin for doubt even if Holden did not concede it.

Working against the running tide of expert evidence and public opinion, the defence barristers were diligent and undeterred in their task. Towards the end of Thursday, 6 February, Detective Inspector Basil Morris of Surrey police, stationed at Reigate, was the 185th witness called by the prosecution. He gave his account of an interview he had conducted with Ronald Arthur Biggs on 24 August at his home at 37 Alpine Road, Redhill, and said that Detective Sergeant Church was also present at Biggs' house. During the course of his account, Inspector Morris said that he had asked Biggs if he knew any of the men wanted for questioning in connection with the mail-train robbery. He told the court Biggs had replied, 'I knew Reynolds some years ago. I met him when we did time together.'

Mr Justice Edmund Davies' face twitched and he looked uneasy as he glanced across to Mr Wilfred Fordham who was defending Biggs. Fordham let Morris finish and then leapt to his feet. 'My Lord, there is a matter which I think I ought to invite Your Lordship to consider at some convenient moment, arising out of this witness's evidence.'

'Perhaps it would be as convenient as any now,' Davies replied drily.

The jury was asked to retire and were led out of the courtroom looking rather bewildered while Mr Fordham approached the bench and there was an inaudible exchange between defence barrister and Judge.

Returning to his desk, Fordham waited a moment for the court to settle and then said:

My Lord, I am of course inviting Your Lordship to consider the proper course to adopt in view of the officer's grossly improper, I think those are the proper words, observation upon a matter which, not only is not in issue, but was not upon his deposition, about which he was not asked by myself or my friend, to the effect that the defendant, Biggs, was a man who had been serving a sentence of imprisonment.

Davies was clearly worried and for the first time in the trial looked uncomfortable. He said, 'That the inspector who, of necessity, must be a man of great experience in his duties, should have so far forgotten his duties as to bring in a phrase of that kind quite gratuitously is grossly improper and cannot be too strongly condemned.'

'I hoped my words were right,' Fordham said.

'Your words were not a bit too strong,' Davies agreed. 'And I underlined them; quite gratuitously a stupid thing to do. What are you asking me to do? I am hoping, indeed I am doing more than hoping, I am almost praying, that the jury did not pick up on the phrase. Are you making an application that this jury be discharged and we have to start again?'

Fordham paused, absorbing the full consequences of the Judge's question. 'I cannot make such an application as a reality. I entirely leave the matter to Your Lordship to take such course as Your Lordship thinks proper.'

'I must ask you whether you are applying for that course to be adopted,' Davies pressed.

The court sat in stunned silence as Fordham considered his position. 'It places me in an appalling difficulty, between the matter which is of very grave concern to everybody else, including all the accused and all those concerned and my client. I think before I answer Your Lordship in the way that Your Lordship said you almost prayed, I should be able to answer ...' Fordham paused. 'And I almost pray that I shall be able to answer it in that way ...' Fordham paused again. 'I ought to take instruction from my client.'

Davies was still looking strained. 'I think you must. I do not desire to bring any kind of pressure upon you; I hope that I am doing that which is accurate. I hope, and think it is quite conceivably the case, that the jury did not pick up on the phrase, but there it is.'

'If it were an individual trial, I would have no hesitation as to the way my duty lay,' Fordham said, 'but in a case like this with so many accused and multiplicity of witnesses I think I must take instruction.'

Mr Justice Edmund Davies adjourned the court for ten minutes. When it reconvened both Davies and Fordham looked less tense.

After everyone was seated and with the jury still absent, Fordham said, 'At Your Lordship's invitation, I have considered most carefully, with those instructing me and with my client, Mr Biggs, as to the right course to take, in view of the gravely improper evidence that has been tendered. The view of it I have come to, and a view I have communicated to my learned friend, Mr James, is to invite Your Lordship to discharge the defendant Biggs without verdict, of course, from this jury. I have no other course, in my opinion that is open to me in his interest but to ask Your Lordship to do that. I regret deeply having to make this application, but perhaps the defence are wholly blameless as far as the necessity for the application goes.'

'Wholly blameless,' Davies nodded sagely. 'It is most regrettable because it does mean this: that Mr Biggs will have to remain in custody to await his trial.' He went on to explain that the retrial of Biggs would be, 'at enormous additional expense to the country'.

Although the legal language and theatre of the courtroom had left some people rather mystified about what was going on, there was no doubt about the seriousness of the incident and it served to underline that the successful prosecution of the twelve defendants through all the rules and due process of British law was a complex and precarious business.

Legal restrictions on making the details of the incident public ensured that at some future date Biggs would stand trial by a different jury who would not have their opinion of him prejudiced by knowing that he had previously been to prison. But without a full explanation, the public perception was, as the problem had arisen from the evidence given by a police officer, that the police had acted improperly. Along with previous objections about inadmissible evidence under Judges' Rules, it inevitably further coloured the integrity and reliability of all the accounts given by the numerous investigating police officers.

Day fifteen of the trial brought Superintendent Maurice Ray to the witness box. In Fewtrell's opinion, Ray was without doubt the most impressive witness in the long trial. With his thick glasses, tall and imposing bearing, he dominated the courtroom from the witness box like a 'gaunt eagle'. Ray engaged the court with his enthusiasm and beguiling discourse on fingerprints, how they were collected and compared against the 1,800,000 sets of prints held by the Criminal Records Office. It was all no doubt fascinating, but the evidence that was being presented to connect the accused to Leatherslade Farm was also from fingerprint and palm impressions that had been obtained while the accused were being detained and questioned and then matched with marks found at the farm.

Maurice Ray went on to answer questions about the evidence that he and his team had collected at Leatherslade Farm: Jim Hussey's palm print on the tailboard of the lorry, Bob Welch's on a pipkin of ale, Ronnie Biggs' prints on a plate, a bottle of tomato ketchup and Monopoly box, Daly on a Monopoly card, Roy James' print on a glass plate and a copy of *Movie Screen* magazine. Charlie Wilson's prints had been discovered on a drum of Saxa salt, a Johnson's first-aid kit and a window sill. Tommy Wisbey's were on the bath rail. Ray also said that Brian Field's prints had been found on the bags containing money discovered in Dorking woods, and Leonard Field's on a bank mandate that Brian Field had produced from his briefcase while being interviewed at his house by police on 23 August.

There followed many less entertaining witnesses during the relentless days in the Rural District Council Chamber. Much of the evidence concerned the lesser conspiracy between Brian Field, John Wheater and Leonard Field in the acquisition of Leatherslade Farm.

It was not until Thursday, 13 February that the subject of fingerprints found by Maurice Ray and his team came back into focus. The jury had been adjourned since Tuesday while a string of submissions from defence counsel was heard. Mr Walter Raeburn QC had entered the courtroom that Thursday morning with a collection of books under his arm. Like many of his senior colleagues, Raeburn had been absent from the court on a regular basis, leaving the day-to-day work to juniors. After taking his place in the front rank of the defence counsel, he offered a submission on behalf of his client, John Daly. In an astounding challenge, Raeburn announced that there was really no case against his client. He acknowledged that Daly had been unwise to go into hiding but there was absolutely no proof that his client had a case to answer for either the charge of conspiracy or of robbery. Raeburn's supporting argument and those concerning the various other submissions ran throughout the rest of Thursday, and when the Judge adjourned the proceedings he had not reached a decision.

On Valentine's Day, with the jury still out, Mr Justice Edmund Davies rejected all the representations made by defence counsel except for one. Having recalled the jury he made an announcement that surprised them all.

'It is now the stage when I have to decide, as I have decided, that it would not be right for the case against Mr Daly to proceed any further, for suspicion of a crime is quite insufficient.' Davies explained that the decision was a matter of law and therefore his and not the jury's responsibility. He directed them to acquit Mr Daly, which they duly did. No one in the court looked more nonplussed than Daly, who before the trial had considered pleading guilty. He appeared not to have taken in the enormity of the development and sat white-faced while Mr Wilfred Fordham made an application for costs from public funds on his behalf saying that the financial expense of the trial had been an 'immense burden' on his client. The Judge instantly refused the application, which was an indication as to where the injustice of the matter stood in his mind.

Outside the court, Daly was besieged by reporters. There were the inevitable questions about the evidence that had been presented against him in the form of a Monopoly game card and why he had gone into hiding and lost so much weight. In the midst of all the clamour, a prison officer offered Daly a lift back to Aylesbury Prison to collect his possessions, which he eagerly accepted.

Later that day John Thomas Daly drove to Wimbledon a free man to be reunited with his wife and seven-week-old son, who had been born while he was in custody. Daly's brother-in-law, Bruce Reynolds, had often said Daly was lucky. Like Napoleon, who reputedly asked 'Is he lucky?' before appointing a general, Reynolds had always felt Daly would bring his luck to any job they worked on together.

Daly's release was certainly a minor miracle in many ways. He no doubt felt all the money he had spent on solicitors and Queen's Counsel had been worth every penny. Quite where they thought an innocent antique dealer had found the considerable funds to finance such a topflight defence is an interesting question that will be examined in more detail later in the story. The most pressing question that surrounded Daly's acquittal was why none of the other defendants had managed to get off on the same grounds. Mr Raeburn's argument was that as Daly's prints had been found on a Monopoly card and tokens they could have got there at any time and not necessarily while the game was at Leatherslade Farm. The logic was sound. Nevertheless it was never explained why the same simple principle did not apply to the fingerprint evidence presented by Maurice Ray that had been found on other portable objects – Bob Welch's on a pipkin of ale, Ronnie Biggs' on a plate, a bottle of tomato ketchup and Monopoly box, Roy James' on a glass plate and a copy of *Movie Screen* magazine, even Jim Hussey's palm print on the tailboard of the lorry. Only Charlie Wilson's and Tommy Wisbey's prints had been found on fixed objects at Leatherslade Farm – a window sill and on the bath rail.

But the game of cat and mouse was not over. The eminent team of barristers for the defence, including nine Queen's Counsel, had yet to produce their case and give their clients' side of the story.

30

The defence case for William Boal was the most frustrating to pin down. The obvious line to take for Boal's counsel, Mr W.A. Sime QC, was to simply get Roger Cordrey into the witness box and ask him to explain to the jury why and how Boal came to be with him in Bournemouth. However, there was a complication between the charges that had been brought against both men, and those to which Cordrey had since pleaded guilty.

Roger Cordrey and William Boal had been charged with three separate offences. First, that between 1 May and 9 August 1963 they had conspired with others to stop a train in Buckinghamshire with intent to rob the mail. Second, that being armed with offensive weapons they with others had robbed Frank Dewhurst of 120 mailbags. Third, that Cordrey and Boal on a date unknown between 7 August and 15 August had received £56,037, £79,120, £5,060 in money, the property of the Postmaster General, knowing the same to have been stolen. In short, conspiracy to rob, the aggravated robbery of the train and handling some of the proceeds.

By association, Boal did not appear innocent, as he had been arrested in the company of Roger Cordrey and the pair of them had been in possession of a great deal of stolen money. Cordrey had decided to plead guilty to conspiracy and receiving but not guilty to robbery, and this had been accepted by the prosecution. He could not testify that Boal was innocent of taking part in the raid since he claimed he had not been a participant himself. Cordrey may have thought making a statement of any kind declaring Boal's innocence could compromise his own plea and also invite further questions about the other accused, all of whom, like Boal, had pleaded not guilty to both principal charges of conspiracy and aggravated robbery. Nevertheless, it was curious in the circumstances, and a betrayal of whatever friendship had existed between the two men, that Cordrey said absolutely nothing in Boal's defence.

In Cordrey's absence, Mr Sime had to rely on presenting Boal's version of the truth, but like the stories told by other defendants it provided little in the way of conclusive proof. He argued that Cordrey was to blame for Boal's involvement. Boal was a hardworking family man with his own small engineering business. He had been a government aircraft engineer and a chief planning engineer engaged on special work for rockets. Mr Sime said his client had simply gone along with Cordrey in the hope of getting back the £650 he had previously loaned him.

Leaving aside the three men involved in the lesser conspiracy (Leonard Field, Wheater and Brian Field), Boal clearly had a different profile from the other accused. At the age of fifty he was twenty years older, with his own business and, although he had three relatively minor previous convictions, he was not known to the police as an habitual villain.

In the witness box, despite his excitable personality, Boal was able to hold his own against an onslaught of questions from prosecution QCs Arthur James and Niall MacDermot. To prove his whereabouts, he said that on 8 August he had received a National Insurance payment through the post for £8.16s.6d. The payment was made because Boal had been ill with dysentery. A document was produced to prove it, with a stamp dated 7 August when it had been issued. The following day Boal had taken it to the post office where it had been stamped again. The document was passed to the Judge and jury. Davies examined it with a magnifying glass and said there seemed to be a faint stamp dated 8 August on the right-hand side.

At one point Boal protested, 'I have never been anywhere near the train spot. And if you were to offer me my freedom now, I wouldn't be able to find my way there.' It was a rather innocent statement but his claim that he knew nothing about the £140,000 in the bags he had helped Cordrey transport from Oxford to Bournemouth, then hidden in the two vehicles Boal had recently helped to purchase and concealed in rented garages, sounded just too naïve and improbable. It was perhaps overshooting his claim of complete ignorance of Cordrey's involvement in the mail-train robbery that made Boal appear all the more guilty.

The defence case for James Hussey, Robert Welch and Thomas Wisbey was all tied in together. Their story was that on Saturday, 10 August the three of them had met at Hussey's house near Denmark Hill, South London. A friend of Hussey's called Dark Ronnie had turned up in a lorry and said he had to deliver the lorry loaded with fruit and vegetables to Oxfordshire. He asked Hussey to follow him in his car and give him a lift back home. Hussey had said he was not able to help but suggested Wisbey and Welch might like a drive to the country. Before they departed, Hussey claimed that he had reached into the back of the lorry to get an apple, thereby putting his hand on the tailboard.

The next stage of the story was that Welch and Wisbey followed Dark Ronnie without knowing exactly where they were going. Dark rendezvoused with a man at the Lantern Café on the A40 whom they followed to an out-of-the-way house up a long track. They had not made the connection that this house was the farm that had been used by the mail-train robbers. They did not think the place they visited was a farm since there was no farmyard, animals, or farm machinery. After helping to unload the lorry, Wisbey had gone to the bathroom to wash his hands, which was how his hand print came to be on the hand rail. Then, leaving the lorry behind, Dark, Wisbey and Welch had driven back to London.

Welch, with his piercing blue eyes, who was nicknamed by the press 'the man of steel', told the court that he had picked up the large seven-pint pipkin of ale while he was in the farmhouse because, having previously been a licensee, it interested him as he had never seen one before. Wisbey confirmed the whole story concerning the mysteriously named Dark Ronnie.

Hussey also claimed to have been at Dark Ronnie's home at a party until 2 a.m. on the night of the robbery. When asked to provide the man's address so he could be contacted and invited to come and give evidence, Hussey said he could not recall his friend's address.

As far as the jury was concerned it was possible that the events Hussey, Welch and Wisbey described had actually taken place, but without corroboration it all sounded a bit flimsy. In anticipation, the prosecution placed an advertisement in the *Evening Standard*:

The Great Train Robbery Urgent. Will anyone answering to the name of Dark Ronnie, friend of James Hussey, telephone Ellis Lincoln (Solicitor) immediately HOL 221 or SPE 8795.

On the twenty-third day of the trial much to everyone's amazement a short, dark, Cockney man appeared in the witness box and confirmed his name was Ronald Darke of 19 Outward House, Upper Tulse Hill, London, SW2. An equally astonished Mr Justice Edmund Davies explained to Darke, 'It is my duty to tell you that you are not obliged to answer any questions either from Mr Brown [for the defence of Hussey] or the prosecution, or myself if you think the answers have a tendency to incriminate you.'

Darke confirmed the story about delivering a lorry to Oxfordshire on 10 August in every detail. He said they had met a man he knew as Stanley Webb at a roadside café on the A40 who had guided them to a remote farmhouse. They had unloaded the fruit and vegetables and Wisbey and Welch had given him a lift home. He also corroborated Hussey's alibi that Hussey had been at his house on the night of 7/8 August. Under cross-examination by Arthur James QC the rather shifty and nervous Ronnie Darke explained that Stanley Webb had asked him to deliver the lorry, for which he was paid £10. Darke assured the court that he had since tried to trace Webb but without success. After a long and arduous session in the witness box, Ronald Darke was dismissed and it was left to the jury to make up their minds what they made of it all.

It was certainly strange that the alleged trip in the lorry loaded with fruit and vegetables was said to have taken place on 10 August, two days after the robbery. Why did Hussey, Wisbey and Welch pick that day? If they had said it was on 7 August, or some day prior to the robbery, it would have fitted into the chronology of established facts more convincingly. It would have tied in with the lorry found by police at the farm with Hussey's palm print on the tailboard which matched a description of the lorry used in the robbery that witnesses had reported seeing. But if what Hussey, Welch, Wisbey and Darke said had been true, why would the gang of bandits have needed a lorryload of fruit and vegetables so soon after the robbery and so shortly before they left? Given the huge quantity of provisions left behind at Leatherslade Farm, that was unlikely. And if the gang had run out of fresh food and still been at the house, why did Hussey, Welch, Wisbey and Darke not see any of them, or any evidence of their ad-hoc occupation that was strewn everywhere when the Sergeant Blackman and Constable Woolley arrived the following Tuesday?

However tenuous the story may have sounded in court, it was theoretically possible as far as the jury was concerned, given the information that was known at the time. It did at least serve to establish that Maurice Ray's evidence concerning the finger and palm prints of Bob Welch on a pipkin of ale, Tommy Wisbey's on the bath rail and Jim Hussey's on the tailboard of the lorry was not absolute proof of their involvement in either the mail-train conspiracy, or the robbery.

On Wednesday, 19 February a number of witnesses were called in defence of Roy John James. His counsel, Mr Howard, said that although his client had been found in possession of £12,000 in cash, the money could not have come from the robbery as most of the notes were issued after the event. He produced a racing car manufacturer who spoke of James' extraordinary talent on the racetrack. Next to take the stand was a taxi driver named Derek Robert Brown, of 67 Bridge Road, Chessington, Surrey. Brown told the court that on the evening of Wednesday, 7 August he had dropped James at the Bagatelle Club (a familiar name to readers of Arthur Conan Doyle – *The Return of Sherlock Holmes, The Mystery of the Empty House*). The court heard that Derek Brown knew Roy James well and had picked him up again at about 02.30, taken him home, then had coffee with him and they had talked until 04.00 on the morning of 8 August. Under cross-examination from MacDermot, Brown admitted that he had visited James on seventeen occasions at Aylesbury Prison. This last revelation rather undermined Brown's evidence, but like Daly, James' fingerprints had only been found on portable objects – a glass plate and a copy of *Movie Screen* magazine. Perhaps hoping that might work in his favour, Roy James elected not to go into the witness box in his own defence.

Charles Frederick Wilson also elected not to appear in the witness box. The normally high-spirited and jokey Wilson had been dubbed 'the silent man' by the press. After the elaborate and questionable stories given in defence of some of the accused, Wilson had perhaps made a shrewd calculation. The Judge had frequently reminded the court that none of the defendants was obliged to say anything or give an explanation.

What still persisted vividly in everyone's mind was Tommy Butler's claim that, when arrested, Wilson had said, 'I don't see how you can make it stick without the poppy [money] and you won't find that.' Wilson's counsel, J.C. Mathew, told the court that his client denied ever saying that. But although the colourful phrase was excluded from the trial it had been so widely reported in the press that it remained etched in everyone's memory.

Before Goody came to the witness box on 21 February, Mr Sebag Shaw QC for his defence announced that he would produce evidence to show that Goody had been pestered by the press, in particular by Ian Buchan of the *Daily Express*.

The prosecution had reason to believe that Buchan would provide false evidence and at 23.30 that evening the *Daily Express* reporter was interviewed by Gerry McArthur in the presence of two police officers and a colleague of Buchan's named Arnold Latcham. The interview and his subsequent statement took all night. Buchan confessed that he had entered into an agreement with Goody's fiancée, Pat Cooper, to give false evidence on Goody's behalf, but he maintained that he had only agreed to do so in order to get his story. Buchan's statement had been prefaced by the understanding that it was more important to get the truth than prosecute the journalist and the prosecution team had supported the decision. Ian Buchan was not subsequently called as a defence witness.

In the witness box the following morning Gordon Goody, immaculately dressed and wearing a Royal Artillery regimental tie, appeared sharp and intelligent. He openly admitted to having been on trial twice in connection with the London Airport robbery the previous year before eventually being acquitted. He stuck to his alibi that he had been in Ireland at the time of the mail-train robbery and his reason for the trip he had taken with his mother was to smuggle watches. Goody had not been found with, or connected to, any stolen money and had not been identified in either of the two police identity parades in which he had participated. The only evidence against him was the yellow and khaki paint Dr Holden said he had found on Goody's shoes, which had been matched to other paint samples taken from the vehicles found at Leatherslade Farm. It was a subject that was to resurface later in the trial.

*

On Monday, 24 February, Brian Arthur Field stood in the witness box and agreed that two of the four bags found in the woods at Dorking, containing £100,900, belonged to him. He said he had lost the bags some time before. Miss Janet May Marlow, a secretary at the James and Wheater law firm, later gave evidence to confirm that Field had brought two bags into the office and they had gone missing before the robbery. Field offered his opinion that the bags had probably been stolen by one of the many criminals who passed through his office on a daily basis.

Brian Field was an enthusiastic witness and often needed no prompting before elaborating on his answers. He appeared plausible, confident and talked very quickly – on several occasions the Judge asked him to slow down. As Field spoke, he sometimes looked up at the public gallery and smiled at his wife, Karin. He said his boss, John Wheater, was hard-working and conscientious but rather chaotic. When reminded about what he had said at Scotland Yard when asked if he knew Leonard Field – 'he is decidedly like the man, but it's not him' – Brian Field was contrite. He admitted lying to Tommy Butler but said that at the time he had been in custody for forty-eight hours, was mixed up and anxious and concerned only at that stage with saving his own skin rather than helping the police.

Several witnesses followed, including Karin's sister and mother, who was a member of the synod in Hanover, and a journalist friend of Brian's, all extolling his virtues and good character.

There were lighter moments during the implacable dark days. When questioning a woman who kept poodles in an effort to prove that the Fields' poodle, Maxi, had been in her care on 7 August, Mr Arthur James QC for the prosecution asked after the dog's welfare, calling him by name to check the veracity of the witness. 'I trust, madam, that Maxi was in good health. Was he?'

The kennel owner, showing no sign of understanding why the question had been asked, replied primly, 'He is a she.'

Davies, always quick to show a dry sense of humour when the opportunity was right, could not resist commenting, 'Mr James, you must be psychic. I was wondering if we would finish this case without finding out the sex of that dog.'

*

On Friday, 28 February the court turned its attention to the defence case for Leonard Denis Field. His evidence continued on the following Monday, telling the court that he had lied about 'certain matters'. Field admitted that the farm had been bought in his name and that he had been told by Brian Field that he would get a considerable sum of money if he 'just stayed away from the office'. He had subsequently learned from Brian Field on 9 August that Leatherslade Farm had been used by the robbers but that Mr Wheater would take care of things and see that he was not involved. Leonard Field was insistent that he knew nothing about the conspiracy or the robbery and said his only mistake was refusing to tell the police what he knew when first questioned. Explaining his responses to Tommy Butler at Scotland Yard, Leonard Field said, 'I agreed to do what I had been told.' In response to further questions, Leonard Field said that after he was arrested he thought Brian Field would keep to his agreement. While in Aylesbury Prison he had been visited by John Wheater and had asked his solicitor what evidence the police had against him. Wheater told him that he could not make it out. Then in the Magistrates' Court at Linslade he heard a statement that had been made about him by both Wheater and Brian Field. 'I must admit that I was very bitter towards Wheater because I knew that the statement that had been made against me gave me no chance whatever of not being arrested. I never had a dog's chance.'

On Tuesday, 3 March, Mr Graham Swanwick QC called Paul Bryan DSO, MC, Conservative MP and Vice Chairman of the Conservative Party. Bryan had been the commander of an infantry battalion in which John Denby Wheater had served as his intelligence officer in Italy during World War Two. The Right Honourable Paul Bryan gave a favourable account of Wheater's character, although his most pertinent observation was less complimentary. 'He was active, brave and loyal, but he was not outstandingly competent. I would say that he needed supervision.'

Brigadier Geoffrey Barrett OBE, director of Army Legal Services, then came to the witness box and expressed a similar view. Wheater had worked in his department for six years and, Barrett said, he had been a good officer but at times 'a bit disorganised and casual'.

Wheater's army career had not been without its achievements. He had been mentioned in dispatches while in action with the Royal West Kent Regiment and later awarded the MBE for services in the field. It was clear that the first plank of Wheater's defence was to set him apart from the other men sitting in the dock.

Having put his client in context, Mr Swanwick then called John Wheater to give evidence in his own defence. Wheater's normally untidy hair had been cut and his bushy moustache was neater. In a thin, high voice which had changed little since he was at Uppingham School, John Wheater first gave an account of his education, military background in World War Two and later in Japan during the Korean War in 1953 where he had first met Brian Field.

As the questions turned to more recent events and his involvement with Leatherslade Farm, there was a tragic air to Wheater. His voice often died away at the end of sentences and he had a plaintive look about him. There was little he could say in rebuttal of the prosecution's evidence. He had been central to the purchase of Leatherslade Farm. His signature was on documentation. He had handled the deposit and corresponded with his legal counterpart, Mr Meirion-Williams of Oxford solicitors Marshall and Eldridge.

Sensing the impression he was making on the jury, Wheater said when talking about his farcical denial that he knew Leonard Field at Scotland Yard: 'I've seen many identifications go wrong. It may sound somewhat stupid, but in my frame of mind I was over-influenced by Leonard's denials.' Wheater presumably hoped that his explanation, if seen in the context of him being disorganised and forgetful, mitigated the lies he had told Tommy Butler when insisting that he did not recognise Leonard Field at Scotland Yard. Instead, Wheater's attempt invited the conclusion that he was both dishonest and extraordinarily stupid. Nevertheless, the examination of all the witnesses and evidence against John Wheater by Mr Swanwick QC was scrupulous and tireless and stretched over the best part of three days.

A vivid picture of life at the offices of James and Wheater in New Quebec Street was provided by secretary Janet Marlow, who was employed to do general office work, typing, and operate the switchboard. She told the court the law firm operated from three small rooms. There was a main office occupied by herself and Brenda Field (Brian

Field's ex-wife), and two other offices in which Brian Field and John Wheater worked.

Various documents were discussed, including one that had Wheater's scribbled notes concerning the mortgage of 150 Earls Court Road. Marlow said that the office was chaotic and untidy and her boss was unmethodical and very forgetful. He did not keep proper records of what happened, often failed to write letters confirming the instructions he had received, did most of his business on the telephone and was out of the office a lot of the time. She said that she and Brenda would regularly write letters for Mr Wheater. Having been given a file, they would extract key information, compose the letters themselves, sign them and post them. They never used 'pp' John Wheater.

Marlow told the court that the office was very busy with people coming and going and telephones constantly ringing. She remembered two occasions when she had to telephone the police to find out the address of a client who had come to them asking Mr Wheater to represent them, but he had forgotten the details.

The cases in defence of the lesser conspirators, Field, Wheater and Field, were battles fought on several fronts. Whereas Wisbey, Hussey and Welch and their counsel had stuck together, this second triangle of men were divided both in character and in terms of each providing separate and uncomplimentary accounts, in both senses of the word.

On Friday, 6 March, Mr Shaw, for the defence of Gordon Goody, belatedly called two scientific experts to the witness box. Shaw was challenged about why he was only now producing these witnesses, but he argued that he had been obliged to call alternative witnesses as his original expert witness, Dr Grant, had been unavoidably detained in Pakistan.

The additional evidence concerning the paint samples examined by Dr Holden was a long and arduous process that was to consume nearly four days of the trial. Though complex and exhausting, the questions surrounding Holden's samples formed the cornerstone of the case against Goody and had so far gone unchallenged.

31

The first scientific expert to be called was Mr Cecil Hancorn Robins, Bachelor of Science, Fellow of the Royal Institute of Chemistry, chief chemist at Hehner and Cox Ltd, Fenchurch Street, London, consulting and analytical chemists. Robins told the court that he had been doing spectrographic work for sixteen years and he was given permission by the Judge to refer to notes he had with him.

The background to Robins' involvement was then established. Dr Grant, head of Hehner and Cox Ltd and a close associate of Dr Holden, had originally been invited to Scotland Yard in November 1963 to corroborate Holden's findings but Grant was now in Pakistan and had been away longer than anticipated. He had left the country in January, before Holden was called to the witness box, and so his chief chemist Cecil Robins was standing in for Grant. Robins had attended court on 5 February when Holden first presented his forensic evidence concerning paint samples.

In order that Robins could form his own opinions about the paint evidence it was arranged on 15 February that he would visit Holden at Scotland Yard two days later. On 17 February he duly visited Holden's laboratory and was 'shown a number of spectra connected with the case'. Robins reported that during his visit to Scotland Yard Dr Holden had told him how and where he had obtained the samples and that was accepted at face value. Robins said that he had no means of checking how the three spectra he was then shown by Holden had been made or where the samples analysed had originated.

The first spectrum was of khaki paint said to have come from the sole of a suede shoe identified as Goody's (exhibit 120). Next he was shown spectra of khaki paint said to have been taken from a Land Rover found at Leatherslade Farm (exhibit 379). Finally he was shown a third spectrum of a sample of khaki paint which Holden said he had taken from the Land Rover himself (exhibit 383).

Mr Shaw QC asked Robins to state what he had observed.

Robins replied, 'I noticed that the two spectra of the khaki paint from the car were identical in my opinion, but when I compared them with the spectrum taken from the shoes I saw one very important difference. The difference was that in the spectra of khaki paint taken from the car there was a very prominent line and that line was not contained in the spectrum of paint taken from the shoes.'

Mr Shaw asked, 'Given the spectra that you were shown then by Dr Holden, would it be possible, if it were thought right, to demonstrate that difference in this court conveniently?'

Robins said, 'Yes, if a projector were produced or were available, yes, it would be possible and I think something that could be seen and recognised by any person of any intelligence. I think it is apparent.'

'What does that line at that position you saw it in the spectrum indicate?' asked Shaw.

'It is a line given by the metal chromium,' said Robins.

'And that, you say, existed in the two samples of khaki paint which you were told by Dr Holden had been taken from the Land Rover?'

'Yes. I consider it absent in the spectrum of paint taken from the shoes,' Robins confirmed.

'Then what do you say about the suggestion, which we heard from Dr Holden, that all three spectra were identical?'

'I do not agree with him, that all three spectra are identical,' Robins said. 'And I think that the significance of the presence of a chromium line in that paint taken from the Land Rover and the absence of the chromium line in the paint taken from the shoes is sufficient to show that they are not the same paints and they have not got the same composition.'

Robins went on to explain that two days later, on 19 February, he had been invited by Holden to look at further spectra at Scotland Yard. This time another sample of khaki paint said to have been taken from the shoes showed a very faint chromium line.

Robins' opinions and revelations were a significant challenge to Holden's earlier evidence and Shaw was keen to exploit this to maximum effect. But during an excruciating set of questions about dates and times intended to cement the matter, Robins seemed to get confused about what was being asked to establish the distinction between the spectrum taken from the shoes he had examined on 17 February, which had no chromium line, and the second sample taken from the shoes he examined on 19 February with a 'very faint' chromium line. Finally he gave the answer Mr Shaw had been seeking. When asked why he thought there was a faint chromium line in the sample he had seen on his second visit, Robins replied, 'My opinion is that the chromium present in the spectrum from the shoes which I was shown on the nineteenth is the result of contamination from the surface of the shoe from which it was obviously scraped off.'

'And was not a constituent of the paint?'

'No, I do not think it was. I think that is the most reasonable explanation.'

Shaw asked, 'Is that your scientific conclusion?'

'I think the two paints are different in composition,' Robins repeated firmly.

What Robins had presented was not simply that the samples of khaki paint he had looked at differed due to contamination but that the analysis of the khaki paints, said to be identical by Holden, was clearly different.

Content with that, Shaw moved on to 21 February when Holden and Robins went to the Fulmer Research Institute at Stoke Poges to see another expert, Mr Douglas Nicholas, head of the spectrographic department. Nicholas had attempted to undertake his own independent analysis. Robins said he did not think Mr Nicholas managed to obtain a 'pure' khaki paint sample from the shoe. The original amount had been very small and most of it had been scraped off by Dr Holden.

Shaw asked, 'What is your final conclusion – I think perhaps you have stated it already – in regard to the sample of khaki paint you saw as being derived, on the one hand, from the shoe, and on the other hand from the Land Rover?'

'I think they are quite definitely not the same paint,' Robins said again.

Shaw then moved to the matter of samples of yellow paint from the lorry, a squashed tin found at the farm, on the clutch pedal of one of the Land Rovers and a smudge said to have been found on the instep of a shoe belonging to Goody. On 17 February at Scotland Yard Holden had also shown Robins some spectra of yellow paint from the shoe, the lorry and the pedal of the Land Rover.

Robins started by making an astonishing remark:

Of course, it has never been claimed that they are identical spectra, because the paint which came from the shoes is admitted to be contaminated with mineral matter and it has a large amount of silica there; more than one would normally find in paint. The investigation I carried out consisted of trying to see whether there were any lines present in the yellow paint that was taken from the lorry which were not present in other spectra.

After further diversions Robins said, 'I could not find any line present, certainly on this occasion, which was present in the lead paint which was not also present in the yellow paint from the shoe.'

On 21 February, during the visit to the Fulmer Institute, Robins said he watched Mr Nicholas take minute samples of yellow paint. Again, after his analysis there was no element present which differed from samples from the shoes to the lorry. 'It therefore could have come from the same source.'

Shaw was keen to underline the statement, 'It *could* have come from the same source? That is as far as anybody can go?'

Robins said that was the conclusion he came to.

Having got bogged down in questions concerning the khaki paint, Shaw said, 'I want to take this as shortly as possible because it is so easy to obfuscate a simple issue with a lot of scientific talk and I am very anxious to avoid that.'

'Yes,' Robins replied.

'Eventually, looking at the spectra you were shown of the yellow paint taken A) from the shoes B) the paint taken from the lorry, was there some distinguishing feature which appeared?'

Robins hesitated, 'The paint taken from the shoes and the paint taken from the lorry?'

'Yes.'

Robins thought about it, then said, 'I have not mentioned the tin so far.'

Shaw contained his exasperation and clarified his point that the paint from the tin and the paint from the lorry appeared to be from the same source but it was the yellow paint from the shoe that he wished to distinguish from the other two.

Robins said, 'He [Mr Nicholas] could not get a satisfactory pure sample from the shoe.'

After further questions about what was seen on the spectra that were available, Shaw then asked Robins if the similarities in Dr Holden's spectra of the yellow paint led him to the conclusion they had come from the same source.

'Not necessarily, no.'

Justice Edmund Davies, who had at various times tried to help clarify the matter, appeared as confused as everyone else. Looking impatient, he said petulantly, 'Could they have come from the same source or not?'

Robins looked over to the Judge nervously and said, 'I think they could have and they also could not have.'

When pressed, Robins said, 'I think it is a matter which different observers might form different opinions about.'

Although what Robins had told the court had undoubtedly called into question Dr Holden's more emphatic claims, he sometimes seemed muddled. He was less confident and articulate, less accustomed to the rigour and hectoring of the courtroom, and as a result appeared less convincing than the seasoned and assured Dr Holden.

At the start of his cross-examination, Mr MacDermot sought to elucidate the scientific analysis that had been under such fierce and exhaustive debate. He first tried to clarify for the jury the purpose of Holden's spectrographic analysis and the lines produced on the resulting spectra. 'Do you agree that they are lines which are the result of light given out by an element which is being split up by a spectrograph into its component wavelengths? Each particle of light is given a line on the spectrum characteristic of a particular element – comparable to a fingerprint, as Dr Holden put it.'

Robins agreed.

MacDermot, who had clearly been swotting up on the science, suggested that, for example, astronomers use spectrographs to analyse the various minerals present in the combustion of stars. He explained that in forensic science the method is employed to determine all the constituent parts that make up a particular compound or composite. The process determines the qualitative elements but not specifically the quantitative elements – i.e. which elements are present, but not precisely how much of each. 'Minor trace elements come, in the main, from impurities,' MacDermot said, drawing on his newly acquired knowledge. 'They are not, therefore, material that are required in the manufacture to be present in order to produce the product.'

Robins confirmed that was indeed the case.

MacDermot then attempted to dismantle any findings that had been produced at the Fulmer Institute by Mr Nicholas by proposing that his equipment and methods were different from those of Dr Holden.

Robins agreed that it was important to compare the results done using the same methods – like with like. But, he said, with Mr Nicholas' methods and equipment it was possible to obtain *better* quantitative results – thereby pulling the rug from under MacDermot's inference.

Mr Shaw QC got to his feet and raised the point that Nicholas' methods and equipment were not relevant since the inconsistencies Robins had identified in the paints were based on Holden's own spectrographs. And it undermined the point MacDermot had been pursuing.

Undeterred MacDermot changed tack and asked Robins to confirm that even between two samples from the same source that were examined in the same way, there would be minor differences in each result.

Robins said that while minor differences could arise, the main constituents are always present irrespective of, say, how well the paint was mixed. So differences from one sample to another would only be in the trace elements. He said paint manufactures mix ingredients at the manufacturing stage in order to avoid inconsistencies, or in practical terms streakiness, when the paint is applied. The chromium line in the khaki paint from the Land Rover, however, was not a trace element or impurity but a fundamental constituent.

Eventually Robins stood down and it was the turn of Douglas Nicholas of Fulmer Research Institute. Nicholas told the court that he had been in charge of the Department of Spectroscopy for fifteen years and had carried out analysis for a wide range of clients including the Ministry of Aviation, Royal Mint, UK Atomic Energy Authority, Central Electrical Research Laboratory, US Air Research and Development Command.

Nicholas said that he had first been consulted on 20 February. During the visit by Robins and Holden the following day he had attempted to undertake his own spectrographic analysis but there was not enough paint on the sole of the shoe to obtain a 'pure' khaki paint sample. Like Robins, Nicholas' opinion on the difference between the paint from the Land Rover and the paint from the shoe based on Holden's spectra was, 'The paints are probably not the same.'

MacDermot was now faced with two independent experts whose opinion differed from his star witness Dr Holden. Under the guise of establishing Mr Nicholas' qualifications, he asked Nicholas to confirm that he had no science degree and had learned 'by experience' not by 'academic diploma'.

Although academic one-upmanship may have held some sway with the jury, the incontrovertible truth was that Nicholas was the head of Fulmer's spectroscopy department; he had done thousands of analytical studies on a vast range of materials over the fifteen years of his career, whereas spectroscopy was only one aspect of Holden's expertise and experience as a forensic scientist.

Nicholas was a modest and quiet man, sometimes to the point of inaudibility. To begin with the microphone had to be adjusted so he could be heard. But modest though he was, he was clearly well qualified to pass judgement on the findings of the more forthright Dr Holden.

Despite MacDermot's unsubtle attempts to undermine Douglas Nicholas' considerable expertise, the scientist remained calm and cogent. When challenged on his knowledge of paint, he told the court that there was no difference in the examination of paint by spectrographic analysis than any other substance. He repeated that in his opinion the spectra for the khaki paint contained distinct differences and that suggested the khaki paint on the shoes did not come from the same source as paint from the Land Rover. In examining the yellow paint from the tin he said he had found a cadmium line in the spectra which was not present in Dr Holden's spectra of paint from the pedals or the shoes. He concluded all the yellow paint could have come from the same source.

Mr MacDermot was again presented with another variation of mismatching samples and the word 'could'. He countered it by diverting. He explained the basis of the Crown's case in the matter: 'We do not suggest that Mr Goody's shoes caused the yellow paint to get on to the pedals of the Land Rover. The pedal paint is only of narrative interest – demonstrating Dr Holden's arrival at his conclusions.'

In the dogged pursuit of definitive answers MacDermot was also mindful that during Dr Holden's original evidence Shaw had asked Holden if the yellow paint found in the Land Rover could have come about when the vehicle was driven by police from Leatherslade Farm to Aylesbury. Yellow paint had been found on the gravel floor of the shed and that could equally be how the paint was transferred to the pedals. Holden had agreed the point.

Finally Nicholas stood down and Dr Holden was recalled. He repeated his evidence in light of the opinions given by the defence's expert witnesses saying that, while he was certain the khaki paint *had* come from the same source, he conceded the yellow paint *could* be from the same source.

The prosecution may have intended their expert witness, Dr Holden, to have the last word on the matter of paint samples, but with him now saying the yellow paint only *could* be, rather than definitely *was*, from the same source, while the more contentious khaki paint definitely was from the same source, it was a contradiction of his earlier mathematical odds of a million to one chance of two identical paints being found on Goody's shoes.

In reality, despite the obsession with the provenance and scientific details of the paint samples and differences in spectrographs, the defence expert witnesses had not been able to prove conclusively their opinions any more than Dr Holden had. What had been illustrated by the very long-drawn-out questioning, however, was that the science was not exact and was open to the interpretation of the analyst. There were no absolute conclusions to be drawn from the conflicting facts and opinions of different experts concerning spectrographic analysis. But even after all the time that had been devoted to this single aspect of the case, there remained a crucial question about whether the jury had followed all the convoluted twists and turns and mind-numbing debate about Dr Holden's paint samples.

In all the talk of paint in relation to Goody's case, there was no mention of the paint on the brass winder belonging to Boal. The case against Boal was finely balanced between traces of yellow paint on the winder found in a jacket pocket at his home, the circumstantial events of his arrest in Bournemouth and the National Insurance document for sick pay he had produced stamped 7 and 8 August. The Judge had observed there was indeed a faint Post Office stamp on the top-right corner. It seems odd that Sime did not call the Post Office employee who handled Boal's payment that day at his local post office to give evidence as it would have substantiated Boal's alibi. Sime did not call Boal's doctor either, who must have been treating him for his recent and debilitating bout of dysentery and would have signed him off work in order to authorise the National Insurance payment.

The evidence of those two independent witnesses could have added weight to the claim that Boal was not part of the mail-train gang and had never been to Leatherslade Farm.

It remained for the jury to decide whether they found the eminent Dr Holden's scientific analysis of the winder found in Boal's jacket, with all the attendant imponderables, the events in Bournemouth, or Boal's date-stamped National Insurance document convincing. Certainly there was evidence to connect Boal with the stolen money after the robbery, but there appeared to be more than reasonable doubt about the exact nature of Boal's involvement and he and his counsel must have been feeling quietly optimistic about his prospects of being found not guilty of the charges of conspiracy and robbery.

The prosecution then recalled herdsman John Maris, who had first alerted the police to Leatherslade Farm as being the hideout of the bandits. There was an objection from Mr Brown QC for the defence of Hussey, but Davies overruled it. The point Mr James for the prosecution was keen to make soon became clear. Mr Maris said he was milking cows in the sheds at the bottom of the track leading to Leatherslade Farm between 06.00 and 09.00 and again between 15.15 and 17.00 on Saturday, 10 August. If any vehicles had driven up to the farmhouse, as Wisbey and Welch had claimed, he would have seen or heard them, but he had not.

On Tuesday, 10 March the closing speeches for the defence began. They followed the same sequence in which the defence cases had been heard over the preceding weeks. It was a roll-call for the good and the great of the English bar: W.A. Sime QC for Boal; R.K. Brown QC for Hussey; F. Ashe Lincoln for Welch; J.A. Grieves QC for Wisbey; W.M. Howard for James; J.C. Mathew for Wilson; Wilfred Sebag Shaw QC for Goody; C.L. Hawser QC for Brian Field; Michael V. Argyle QC for Leonard Field, and G.R. Swanwick QC for Wheater. Biggs had been represented by Wilfred Fordham. The prosecution counsel consisted of A.E. James QC, N. MacDermot QC, H.W. Sabin and J.D.A. Fennell.

After more than forty days of tragedies and dark humour, endurance, joys, surprises and epic drama, it was the legal equivalent of a curtain call for Wagner's *Ring* cycle, or perhaps by that stage, the longest trial in British criminal history felt more like the nine circles of Hell in Dante's *Inferno*.

By Saturday, 14 March, the closing speeches had finally been concluded. But even before Mr Sime had got to his feet four days earlier, the jury must have known the story inside out. 'The Great Train Robbery' had been a constant topic in the news over the five months leading up to the trial. Before the jury had been sworn in they had already read countless details about the case they were about to hear in the press, seen it reported on television, heard about it on the radio and discussed it with their friends, relations and neighbours. People the world over had been fascinated by the robbery, the police investigation, the arrests, the reporting of the Linslade Magistrates' Court hearings and the committal proceedings. Inside the Buckinghamshire Assize courtroom in the converted Rural District Council Chamber the jury had heard many more particulars from hundreds of witnesses. Written depositions had been read out. They had examined objects, documents, maps, diagrams and photographs and all the while, sitting just a few feet away for the last two months, had been the ten accused men whose fate they alone would shortly decide.

32

As the Buckinghamshire Assize trial of the accused in the mail-train robbery moved into its final act, there was still another surprise to come in the courtroom. On Monday, 16 March, day forty-one of the trial, as the Judge was about to begin his summing up, the proceedings were abruptly halted. Mr Arthur James QC for the Crown announced that he had a matter to bring to the attention of the court concerning one of the jury. The man in question was the modest, bespectacled Terrance Addy from Chalfont St Giles. James said, 'Yesterday a communication from one of the jurymen in this trial was made to the police, as a result of which he was asked to communicate with Your Lordship.'

Davies looked unsurprised and said that he had received a note about the matter. As Mr Addy rose anxiously from his seat among his fellow jurors, Davies looked down at him and said, 'You have been good enough to supply the court with a note relating to an incident which occurred yesterday when a stranger called upon you and made a suggestion to you, that you should for a monetary reward attempt to sway the jury in this case. You forthwith reported the matter to the police. You have acted with absolute rectitude in the matter. It is so important that a jury should be permitted to arrive at its conclusion honestly and fairly, and the administration of the criminal law in this country is vitally dependent on this. So I am going to adjourn this case for a short time.'

Mr Addy was instructed by the Judge to go immediately to a private room and speak to Malcolm Fewtrell in the presence of the clerk of the court and a shorthand writer and tell him everything he knew 'so that the criminal or criminals who are attempting the ancient and still vigorous offence of embracery may be brought to justice'. It was doubtful if anyone other than those legally qualified had the slightest idea of what embracery was, let alone the anxious Mr Addy. (Embracery is an offence in English law, dating back to 1410, of influencing a jury illegally and corruptly.)

The court was reconvened twenty minutes later and the Judge made a short speech to the jury about the matter reminding them of his advice at the start of the trial:

> I was not being melodramatic and that warning was required. We are going to get a verdict in this case. You will, gentlemen, be more than usually punctilious during the next week so that nobody can possibly say there is anything wrong. We are going to arrive at finality in this trial.

A copy of the statement Mr Addy had made was handed to the Judge. There was no doubt in anybody's mind of the possible consequences if the integrity of the jury was compromised. If the defence had grounds for objection, the whole trial would have to start all over again from the beginning with a new jury and that was unthinkable. No one present, Judge, jury, prosecution, defence, or accused, wished to even contemplate that grim possibility. Nevertheless, the defence was duty bound to raise their concerns about how the incident might affect the jury's view of their clients.

The ever-vigilant and astute Mr Justice Edmund Davies was keen to head off any objections:

> Defence counsel are a little anxious, about the matter to which Mr Addy was so outrageously subject. I told you earlier that you will all dismiss the incident utterly from your minds as having no relation to the issue which you have to try. I thought I sufficiently conveyed to you by those words that there is no kind of evidence that the approaches were made on behalf of these accused men, or any particular accused man, and you will entirely dismiss the incident from your minds. It has no bearing on your task which is sufficiently difficult without it.

Despite the Judge's attempt to smooth things over from the legal standpoint, whoever was behind the approach made to Mr Addy had clearly made a foolish move. As the attempted subversion of Mr Addy had been made public it inevitably served to invite the conclusion that at least one of the accused was seeking to wreck the trial and that brought suspicion on them all.

*

In his summing up, Mr Joseph A. Grieves QC, counsel for Wisbey, had warned the jury against falling into what he called the 'Nuremberg mentality'. What Grieves was getting at was that in such a high-profile case there could be a natural presumption by the jury that any person who had been arrested and was now sitting in the dock in such an important case was guilty by virtue of having been brought to trial.

There were other aspects to a group trial too. If the jury concluded that any of the accused was guilty they might, by association, also assume that every man in the dock was. Having endured the many weeks of the trial, the sense of national occasion and feverish public interest, heard about the exhaustive efforts of hundreds of police officers, seen the unprecedented security and rigmarole of transporting the prisoners back and forth from Aylesbury Prison, the jury may have found it impossible not to be drawn to that assumption.

In many ways this problem was at the epicentre of the judicial process in the long trial of this disparate group of men who were in different ways connected to the mail-train robbery. Each had an individual case to answer based on specific evidence against him, and in all the overlapping complexity of the prosecution case and multiplicity of statements, exhibits and hundreds of witnesses, it was asking a great deal of the twelve untrained men of the jury to keep track of it all and keep each man separate in their minds.

It is impossible to encapsulate the many layers of Mr Justice Edmund Davies' summing up of the case against the mail-train conspirators and robbers. His speech lasted for six days, extended to more than a quarter of a million words and was diligently recorded by the court transcription unit from Marten, Meredith & Co. of London, WC2 on 4,815 pages of typed manuscript. A now browning and dog-eared copy of the transcript is held at the National Archives in Kew and is freely available to any member of the public who cares to read it in full.

Davies prefaced his summing up by saying to the jury, 'You will be relieved to know that I do not propose to review every bit of evidence which has been presented to you over so many weeks. We have explored not only the highways but the by-ways and country roads. And sometimes we have even gone up cart tracks.'

The Judge described the mail-train robbery as a 'diabolical crime'. In framing the Crown's case he said, 'According to prosecution witnesses, the loss was £2,500,000. It has also been suggested by the prosecution that the gang used Leatherslade Farm, near Oakley, Buckinghamshire, as their operational base and hiding place.'

Mr Davies said that the crime had involved the most careful planning and the most careful assigning and allocating of tasks to a variety of people. 'It is terribly easy, is it not, for an accused person who had left his tell-tale marks at the scene of the crime – in this case Leatherslade Farm the hideout of the criminals – to assert he arrived there only after the crime was committed.'

Despite Davies' intelligence, wisdom, knowledge of the law and the lengths he had gone to demonstrate the fairness of his court, the statement that the scene of the crime was Leatherslade Farm and not Sears Crossing was obfuscating if not misleading – at least to members of the jury who were without legal training. From the start of the trial the principal challenge facing the Crown prosecution was to convince the jury that Leatherslade Farm was linked to the robbery and that any man who had been at the farm between certain dates must have taken part in the mail-train raid. That assertion contained a flaw that had been clearly demonstrated in court: it was theoretically possible that a person might have been at the farm while the mail-train robbers were there who had no part in the robbery or conspiracy. Davies would go on to make clear later in his summing up when talking about the charge of conspiracy, 'no matter what part a person played after the robbery, unless he had something to do with the planning beforehand he is not guilty, even though he may greatly have assisted the robbers to make their getaway'.

Yet the basis of the charges of conspiracy was that any person proved to be at the farm had participated in the conspiracy to rob the mail train.

In reality there had been no crime committed at Leatherslade Farm; it was simply a means to an end, a place where the gang had stayed before and after their raid. And though they had masqueraded as builders, it was by prior arrangement with Mr Rixon, the existing owner. The conspiracy and planning by necessity had been done long before the gang arrived at the farm, and the theft of 120 mailbags from Frank Dewhurst had taken place twenty-eight miles away from a train at Bridego Bridge. And yet here was Mr Justice Edmund Davies conflating it all together in his summing up as if it was a seamless and incontrovertible matter of fact.

Leatherslade Farm was simply the place where evidence of the crime had been found in the form of empty mail sacks and money wrappers. The prosecution had produced no evidence to link any of the accused to the scene of the robbery and had for the most part only provided evidence connecting the accused to movable objects found at the farm, with only a few cases involving fixed objects: a bath rail and window sill in the case of Hussey and Wilson. Cordrey and Boal had been found in possession of some of the stolen money. Although most of the accused had denied any association when first interviewed by police officers, none of it proved that these were the men who had planned the robbery or had ambushed the mail train at Sears Crossing in the early hours of 8 August 1963.

Davies went on to say that there was no direct evidence that any of the vehicles found at the farm were used in connection with the robbery. This was significant in Hussey's case as the principal evidence against him was his palm print on the lorry and that print could have got there by innocent means, for example if he had put his hand on the lorry while it was parked elsewhere, as he had claimed.

In dealing with the paint samples Davies suggested since there were no traces of khaki paint found at the farm, the repainting of the stolen Land Rover from blue to khaki was done somewhere other than Leatherslade Farm.

In explaining the charge of conspiracy to the jury Davies went to some lengths:

From all I have been telling you about conspiracy several things emerge. Firstly, a person who played no part in the planning of this robbery beforehand cannot be a conspirator within count one (conspiring to rob the mail train). As regards count one no matter what part a person played after the robbery, unless he had something to do with the planning beforehand he is not guilty, even though he may greatly have assisted the robbers to make their getaway. If his first connection with the robbery was after its perpetration he cannot, I repeat, be found guilty of the first count, and still less of the second count (aggravated robbery of the mail train), for a person who merely assists a felon after his crime in order to shield him from justice is an accessory after the fact and no one of these accused men is charged with that. You cannot convict a person who appears on the scene for the first time after the robbery and has no contact with the case otherwise with being a robber.

On Tuesday, 17 March, day forty-three, the Judge began his résumé of the principal prosecution evidence against each of the accused. Looked at retrospectively, the case of William Boal is the most deserving of closer scrutiny.

Boal's hopes of disassociating himself from the conspiracy and the robbery looked promising. The Judge had already made a point that concerned Boal's defence against conspiracy in his general observations: 'no matter what part a person played after the robbery, unless he had something to do with the planning beforehand he is not guilty, even though he may greatly have assisted the robbers to make their getaway'.

The second charge of aggravated robbery against Boal was also looking less than convincing. As Davies began his summary of the allegations against Boal, he reminded the jury that there was no fingerprint or other evidence to connect Boal to Leatherslade Farm. Boal had taken part in two police identity parades and had not been picked out. He told the jury that if the Crown had only proved that Boal was Cordrey's stooge then he should be acquitted of both conspiracy and robbery.

In relation to the two charges of receiving, Davies said if the Crown had not proved that Boal knew the origin of the money, he should be acquitted of the charges of receiving. When Cordrey had bought a Rover car in Oxford he was in the company of another man – but that man was not Boal.

But just as things were looking hopeful for Boal, the Judge began to talk about further circumstantial evidence. Boal had acted as front man throughout the majority of the events in Bournemouth. He did most of the arranging, talking, and negotiating when renting the flat in Wimborne Road, buying two cars and renting two garages. He had also paid the car salesman, Mr Nabney, with a five-pound note that had come from the robbery. The police had unlocked the Austin car in the garage at Mrs Clarke's house in Tweedale Road with a key they had found on Boal. They had unlocked a suitcase containing a large sum of money with a key they found on Boal. All six suitcases and bags found in the Rover at Miss Saunders' garage in Ensbury Avenue were unlocked with keys found on Boal. The briefcase found in the bedroom of the flat in Bournemouth, which contained another large of sum of money, also held four engineering blueprints belonging to Boal, as well as the log book for the Rover car bought by Cordrey in Oxford. Cordrey had registered the car at Boal's address. It had been posted there and brought along by Boal. Boal had later denied that he was in possession of the keys and suggested it was a mix-up by the police. Davies was dismissive of the £8.18s.6d. National Insurance payment that Boal had offered as his alibi, despite the fact that he had cashed it at the post office and it had been date-stamped 8 August.

It all amounted to a pretty damning indictment of Boal, although the Judge did downgrade the importance of the yellow paint analysed by Dr Holden. 'Can any reliability be placed upon the yellow paint which Dr Holden says he found on the knob? Mr Sime says, "No. It is a yellow herring," as he puts it. The Crown say that is not right and do not invite you to regard the paint evidence in Mr Boal's case as anything like as strong as the paint evidence which they have adduced in the case of Mr Goody.'

On day forty-six of the trial, Friday, 20 March, the Judge broke off from his summing up to say there had been some speculation about where the jury's 'hideout' would be when they retired to consider their verdict. Davies praised the press for their restraint and loyalty in not revealing in past weeks legal matters that had come to light in court when the jury had been adjourned and many newsworthy events had occurred but had not been reported. He warned reporters that it would not be in the public interest or in the interests of concluding a fair trial for them to report the location of the jury's place of retirement.

Davies also gave some reassurance to the jury about their homes and families. They had expressed understandable concern about further interference and intimidation following the approach that had been made to Mr Addy. 'So far as it is within my power,' Davies said, 'I direct the police authorities that protection will be provided for twenty-four hours a day. It may be a matter of difficulty, for I know the police force are extended and taxed to an almost impossible extent, but that will be done, I am sure.'

While the Judge's announcement allayed the jury's fears, the most exciting part of his diversion to everyone in the court was that he told the jury that he would conclude his summing up on Monday:

> We will assemble here as usual at 10 a.m. You will each bring with you your night cases. How long you will be in retirement I don't know, but you must come fully prepared. That means everything you require you will bring with you. If I may embark on a homely topic: if you are smokers bring your smokes; if you are sweet eaters bring your sweets. Nothing may be sent out for. You will have no wireless, no television, no newspapers. No messages can be delivered to you, either by note or telephone, and in no way can you communicate with people outside. There have been cases in our legal history where it has been said that juries have improperly taken into their retirement documents which ought not to have been taken. You will be taking all the documents you are in receipt of and I hope you will not mind, in case legal representatives want to examine them, making available for inspection your night cases as well as your documents before you retire. You will be completely incommunicado immediately you leave this court on Monday until you have intimated to us you are ready to return.

By the middle of the afternoon on Monday, 23 March, day forty-eight of the trial, Mr Justice Edmund Davies had concluded his marathon thirty-two-hour-and-thirty-minute summing up. At 15.36 the twelve men of the jury, carrying their night cases and thick dossiers of documents, diagrams, maps and photographs, were led out of the courtroom and taken by coach to the Grange Youth Club on the outskirts of Aylesbury to consider their verdict.

The Buckinghamshire Assize court continued other business while the jury was in retirement. On Tuesday, 24 March Justice Edmund Davies agreed to four separate trials for the four men and three women, Martin Harvey, Robert Pelham, Renee Boal, Arthur and May Pilgrim, Walter and Patricia Smith, accused of receiving money from the mail-train robbery. Defence counsel had submitted that it would be prejudicial to the accused if they were all tried together. The trials were set to begin on 8 April.

The prospect of the forthcoming Easter weekend focused the jury's discussions and at 20.15 on Wednesday, 25 March, after sixty-five hours of discussion and deliberation, the longest retirement in British legal history, they had finally reached a unanimous verdict. The court was reconvened on Thursday, 26 March, the morning before Good Friday. At seven minutes past ten, James Hussey was the first of the accused to be led into the packed courtroom, followed by Welch and the eight other accused men flanked by prison officers. Ranks of uniformed policemen stood around the dock while other officers had been placed strategically at courtroom entrances. Waiting patiently for the arrival of Mr Justice Edmund Davies, the prisoners sat quietly, barely moving, some occasionally glancing up towards relatives in the public gallery.

At 10.29 Davies entered, took his seat on the dais and made a solemn announcement: 'No one is to enter or leave this court until the proceedings are over. I want no stampede. But if the prison officers prefer to move each individual accused as his case is over, then that may most certainly be done.'

Looking tired and pale after their long hours in retirement, George Plested, William J. Grant, Arthur Edward Greedy, Norman Mace, Richard Thomas Tadman, Terrance Addy, Frederick Freeman, William Mullins, George Edward Pargeter, Alexander Sinclair Watt, Ernest F. M. Smith and Leonard Thane, the twelve men of the jury, walked back into a silent courtroom and took their seats. The foreman was asked to stand. The clerk read out the charges against each defendant and the foreman announced the jury's unanimous verdicts.

In response to the seven men charged with robbing Frank Dewhurst, a GPO official, of 120 mailbags while armed with offensive weapons:

Douglas Gordon Goody – Guilty.
Roy John James – Guilty.
Robert Welch – Guilty.
James Hussey – Guilty.
Charles Frederick Wilson – Guilty.
Thomas William Wisbey – Guilty.
William Boal – Guilty.

The seven men were also found guilty of charges of conspiracy. And then it was the turn of the remaining three men in the dock to hear the jury's verdict on the charges of conspiracy against them.

Brian Arthur Field – Guilty.
Leonard Denis Field – Guilty.
John Denby Wheater – Not Guilty.

Field, Wheater and Field were all found guilty of conspiring to obstruct the course of justice. The jury were dismissed from returning charges of receiving against Roy James and William Boal.

To a man, the guilty in the dock remained impassive apart from the odd nervous shrug or twitch of the mouth.

Davies thanked the jury for 'the unbearable burden of many weeks', adding: 'Not only is this county, but the whole country is grateful to you. Your services are enormously appreciated.' After telling the jury that they would be exempted from further jury service for the rest of their lives, the Judge said, 'You and I have been sitting here together for so long life will never seem quite the same without you.' Subdued laughter and relief rippled through the courtroom.

The prisoners were taken from the Rural District Council Chamber for the last time, loaded into the large Black Maria and driven in a convoy of police vehicles with blue lights flashing, the mile along the A418 back to Aylesbury Prison.

The case against Ronald Arthur Biggs was still to be heard on 8 April. For Bruce Reynolds in his mews house off Gloucester Road, West London, Buster Edwards in his Thames-side hideout in Wraysbury, and Jimmy White, who was by now living the life of a hill farmer in Derbyshire, the verdicts confirmed that they too would struggle to be found not guilty if they were arrested and went to trial.

Inside the prison van Wisbey, Hussey, Wilson, Welch, James, Goody, Wheater, Field and Field were now all facing terms of imprisonment. But for the men found guilty and those still on the run, the next big question remained unanswered – how long would each of them get?

33

Following the Easter weekend, just under two weeks after the verdicts, the trial of Ronald Arthur Biggs opened on Wednesday, 8 April. The hearing took place in the eighteenth-century red-brick-and-stone, Palladian building of Aylesbury Crown Court with Mr Justice Edmund Davies presiding. Biggs was charged with conspiracy to stop the mail train and robbery of 120 mailbags armed with offensive weapons. He pleaded not guilty to both charges.

In front of a new jury of nine men and three women the evidence against Biggs was presented all over again, including the discovery of his fingerprints at Leatherslade Farm on a plate, a bottle of tomato ketchup and a Monopoly box. This time a much-chastened Detective Inspector Basil Morris of Surrey police did not mention that when Biggs was asked if he knew any of the men wanted for questioning in connection with the mail-train raid he replied that he had met Reynolds in prison. Morris simply stated that Biggs had said 'he had known Reynolds some years ago'. Biggs had given the police permission to search his home and had explained that the £510 found in his possession had been won at the races in Brighton. It was later confirmed that Biggs had won money at Brighton Races the previous week.

The prosecution called their witnesses over the following three days and by the end of Friday, 10 April the hearing reached a swift and concise conclusion of the Crown's case against Ronald Arthur Biggs.

The following Monday, Biggs stood in the witness box wearing a smart sports jacket and cavalry twill trousers and gave his side of the story. He explained to the court that a man called Norman Bickers, whom he had known for thirteen to fourteen years, had put a proposition to him about a 'job'. Bickers had given Biggs no details other than saying that it was going to be carried out in the countryside. Towards the end of June, Bickers telephoned him to make arrangements and then visited him at home on Saturday, 4 July. He told Biggs that the job was going to take place during the August Bank Holiday but gave no details, saying that the people were very concerned about security.

Following the meeting with Bickers, Biggs said he had told his wife that he would be going tree-felling in Wiltshire on 6 August. When the day arrived, Bickers collected Biggs from his home and they drove to a place he now knew as Leatherslade Farm. After seeing army uniforms at the farm, Biggs told the court he had expressed his concern to Bickers. 'It looks as though the raid might be planned on an army camp or depot, and if that is the case I want to get out here and now,' he recalled saying. Early the next day Biggs told the court that he and Bickers had left the farm and driven first to Oxford and then to Bickers' flat in London, where he had stayed for two days. On their return journey Bickers had said, 'They are thinking of stopping a mail train.' On the evening of the robbery they had stayed up until after midnight discussing tropical fish and Biggs returned home to Redhill, Surrey on Friday, 9 August.

The story was possible, but despite Biggs' claim of a long-standing association with Bickers he did not appear as a defence witness to corroborate Biggs' story so it was left open to doubt.

The closing statements and the Judge's summing up were heard on Tuesday, 14 April, and the jury retired to consider their verdict. It took them just ninety minutes to arrive at a unanimous decision. They found Ronald Arthur Biggs guilty of both charges.

On Wednesday, 15 April, Biggs and the ten men previously found guilty at the main trial were all brought before the court for sentencing. Mr Justice Edmund Davies spent the day hearing details of their previous convictions from the prosecution and pleas of mitigation were offered by their defence counsel.

Detective Chief Superintendent Tommy Butler was called to provide the court with information about the criminal records of each of the accused.

Boal had three previous convictions, and had served a term of eighteen months imprisonment fourteen years earlier in 1949 for receiving stolen property.

Welch had two convictions. In 1958 he was sentenced to nine months imprisonment for receiving stolen goods (the 'goods' in question comprised coffee, tea and custard powder, but that was not mentioned by

Butler). Welch had also received a fine for selling intoxicating liquor outside permitted hours.

Wilson had been previously found guilty of criminal offences on four occasions. The most serious had been four years earlier, in 1959, when he was sentenced to thirty months imprisonment for conspiracy to steal.

At the age of seventeen, Wisbey had been fined £5 for shop-breaking. In 1958 he had been sentenced to four months in prison for receiving stolen goods, and before his arrest in August 1963 he had been fined £5 for assault on a police officer.

Hussey had six offences on his record. In 1950 he was sentenced to eighteen months for causing grievous bodily harm. In 1952 he was fined £6 for causing grievous bodily harm. In 1958 he was sentenced to three and two years consecutively for warehouse-breaking, larceny, and causing grievous bodily harm.

Roy James had six prior convictions, five connected to stealing cars or bits of cars; the most serious was a charge of shop-breaking in 1958, as a result of which he was sentenced to three years corrective training.

In March 1948, at the age of nineteen, Goody had been sentenced to twenty-one months imprisonment and twelve strokes of the birch for robbery with violence. In 1956 he had been given a three-year prison sentence for shop-breaking and larceny.

Leonard Field had just one prior conviction: in May 1951 he had been fined £2 for loitering suspiciously with intent to steal from motor vehicles.

Mr Geoffrey Leach pointed out that Cordrey's only conviction had been twenty-two years earlier and the Judge said that he would ignore it.

Mr Graham Swanwick QC for John Wheater said, 'I am able to place him before Your Lordship in a different category from all others.' He pointed out that Wheater was a person of hitherto excellent character. More importantly, he had no foreknowledge of the crime.

Brian Field also had no previous convictions.

As is customary in British law the clerk of the court asked each of the men, 'Have you anything to say why judgment should not be passed on you according to the law?'

In reply, William Boal said, 'I am not guilty of this charge. I can only beg mercy.'

Roy James replied, 'I had no part in the robbery. I went to the farm and I knew that I was doing wrong, but I got involved and that is why I ran away. I have never hurt anybody in my life.'

Brian Field was contrite but as usual chose his words carefully. 'I very much regret that I am in such a position and I ask you to exercise such mercy as you can.'

The other nine convicted men remained silent.

The court was adjourned until the following day, which left the prisoners to endure one further night of waiting to hear their fate.

On the morning of Thursday, 16 April 1964 the overnight rain still lay in puddles and the sky was streaked with dark clouds as the large Black Maria containing those found guilty of taking part in the mail-train robbery turned into Aylesbury Market Square under heavy police escort. Judgment Day had arrived for Roger Cordrey, Bill Boal, Tommy Wisbey, Bob Welch, Jim Hussey, Gordon Goody, Roy James, Ronnie Biggs, Leonard Field, Brian Field and John Wheater. They were taken from the van down to the holding cells in the basement of Buckinghamshire's Crown Courthouse.

Over two hundred interested parties had managed to squeeze themselves into the 1774 courtroom, including police detectives, wives, sweethearts, relations and friends of the prisoners, pressmen and local people. Tucked into a corner, train driver Jack Mills sat grim-faced. It was hard to distinguish the members of the bar who had become well-known figures about the town during the three months of the Special Winter Assize Court hearing. All of them looked alike in their wigs and black gowns as they entered and huddled in groups at the front of the court, like crows gathering to pick at the last remains of a carcass.

The restless crowd suddenly hushed when the bailiff barked 'silence', then 'all rise' and a scene from what could have been a historical pageant began. The ranks of barristers stood in line at their desks as Mr Justice Edmund Davies entered. He moved more slowly than usual and his face was graver and more statesmanlike beneath his short wig. Cloaked in his crimson gown, flanked by the sheriff of the county in ceremonial attire and carrying a sword, Davies was the very embodiment of the State and all the more impressive and splendid set against the sombre interior of wood panelling and the royal coat of arms above his bench.

Roger Cordrey was the first prisoner to be called up from the cells. The Judge began straight away, reading from his prepared notes. He spoke with more urgency and gravitas than he had during the fifty-one days of the trial. Gone was the paternal tone, the asides and the dry wit. Mr Justice Edmund Davies was the vehicle of British law and though his voice was soft and measured it carried the full authority and weight of it.

You are the first to be sentenced out of eleven greedy men whom hope of gain allured. You and your co-conspirators have been convicted of complicity in one way or another, of a crime which in its impudence and enormity is the first of its kind in the country. I propose to do all in my power to ensure that it will also be the last of its kind. Your out-rageous conduct constitutes an intolerable menace to the well-being of society. Let us clear out of the way any romantic notions of dare-devilry. This is nothing more than a sordid crime of violence inspired by vast greed. All who have seen that nerve shattered engine driver can have no doubt of the terrifying effect on the law-abiding citizen of a concerted assault by armed robbers. To deal with this crime leniently would be a positively evil thing. When a grave crime is committed it calls for grave punishment, not for the purpose of mere retribution but that others similarly tempted will be brought to the realisation that crime does not pay, and the game is not worth the most alluring candle. Potential criminals who might be dazzled by the enormity of the prize must be taught that the punishment they risk is proportion-ally greater. I therefore find myself faced with the unenviable task of pronouncing grave sentences. You and the other accused vary widely in intelligence, strength of personality, antecedent history, in age and in many other ways. Some convicted of this indictment have absolutely clean characters up to the present. Some have previous convictions of a comparatively minor character. Others have previous convictions of gravity which could lead to sentences of corrective training or preven-tative detention. To some, the degradation to which all of you have sunk now will bring consequences vastly more cruel than to others. I have anxiously sought to bear in mind everything that has been urged on behalf of all of the accused by your learned Counsel, to whom I am so greatly indebted, but whatever the past of a particular accused and whatever his position, all else pales into insignificance in the light of his present offences. Furthermore, the evidence, or rather lack of it, renders it impossible to determine exactly what part was played by each of the eleven accused convicted of the larger conspiracy or the eight convicted of actual robbery. I therefore propose, after mature deliberation, to treat you all in the same manner, with two exceptions.

You Cordrey, are the first of the exceptions. On your own confession you stand convicted of the first count of conspiracy to rob the mail train and on counts three, four and five of receiving in all nearly one hundred and forty-one thousand pounds of stolen money, but when arrested you immediately gave information to the police which enabled them to put their hands on nearly eighty thousand pounds and the remainder was eventually recovered. Furthermore, at the outset of this trial you confessed your guilt and I feel I should give recognition of that fact in determining your sentence. I do this because it is greatly in the public interest that the guilty should confess their guilt. This massive trial is the best demonstration of the truth of that proposition. In respect of the four counts you must go to prison for concurrent terms of twenty years.

It took a moment for the implications of the sentence to sink in. In those fleeting seconds, with Cordrey still frozen in the dock, the minds of barristers, press and the public raced with shock and calculation. If Cordrey was an exception and had got twenty years for pleading guilty to conspiracy and receiving, what would the others get?

Cordrey was taken down and put in a cell away from the other prisoners still waiting. Boal was the next to be brought up. Unaware of Cordrey's sentence, he stood in the dock blinking as he took in the sight of the courtroom through the thick lenses of his horn-rimmed spectacles.

Without hesitation, Davies launched straight into his next speech.

William Gerald Boal, you who are substantially the oldest of the accused, have been convicted of conspiracy to rob the mail and of armed robbery itself. You have expressed no repentance for your wrong doing, indeed, you continue to assert your innocence; but you beg for mercy. I propose to extend to you some measure of mercy and I do it on two grounds. Firstly, on account of your age, you being a man of fifty, and secondly because, having seen and heard you I cannot believe that you were one of the originators of the conspiracy or that you played a very dynamic part in it or in the robbery itself. Detective Superintendent Fewtrell has confirmed me in that view of you which I had already formed, but your participation in any degree nevertheless remains a matter of extreme gravity. In the light of these considerations, the concurrent sentences you will serve are, upon the first count, twenty-one years and upon the second count, twenty-four years.

As the sentence was passed, Boal's head swayed slightly on his shoulders as if he had been hit from behind. He was taken down by a prison officer and replaced by a sharply dressed Charlie Wilson.

'No one has said less than you throughout this long trial,' Davies began.

Indeed I doubt if you have spoken half a dozen words. Certainly no word of repentance has been expressed by you. If you or any of the other accused had assisted justice, that would have told strongly in your favour. The consequence of this vast booty of something like two and a half million pounds remains almost entirely unrecovered. It would be an affront to the public weal that any of you should be at liberty in anything like the near future to enjoy those ill-gotten gains. Accordingly, it is in no spirit of mere retribution that I propose to secure that such an opportunity will be denied all of you for an extremely long time.

Everyone in court, public, press, counsel and police officers alike was aware this was the defining moment in the sentencing of the principal participants of the mail-train robbery and the tension was palpable as Edmund Davies looked up from his papers to pronounce Wilson's fate.

On the first count you will go to prison for twenty-five years and on the second you will be sentenced to thirty years.

Despite the many months of speculation, the likely prison terms had been the silent ingredient in the unfolding story of 'The Great Train Robbery'. The enormity of the sentence was incredible. Never before in the history of British justice had such a sentence been passed for robbery.

Trying to make sense of it and put it into context, some recalled the trial of former British spy George Blake in 1961. He had been found guilty of being a double agent for the Russians and sentenced to forty-two years. Although the maximum sentence for an offence under Section One of the Official Secrets Act was fourteen years, Blake had been charged with five separate offences. In May 1961 his trial at the Old Bailey, under Lord Chief Justice Lord Parker of Waddington had ended with Blake being found guilty on three counts of espionage. The three fourteen-year maximum sentences had been consecutive.

Biggs was next to be brought up from the basement cells. Like the others, he stood in the dock looking pale in the muted light, unaware of what had gone before. The Judge reiterated his remarks: 'I do not know when you entered the conspiracy or what part you played,' he said; but his observation of Biggs was uncompromising: 'What I do know is that you are a specious and facile liar and you have this week, in this court, perjured yourself time and again, but I add not a day to your sentence on that account.'

In the public gallery, sitting under the clock, Charmian Biggs looked on. She was later described by Fewtrell as dressed like an Impressionist painter's model. As the thirty-year sentence was passed, Biggs looked up at his wife and gave her the flat smile of a man already resigned.

The next three in the succession of prisoners, whose failed defence had been intertwined, were Wisbey then Welch then Hussey. Wisbey, looking crisp in a dark blue suit, was told that he had thrown no light on the crime or his involvement in it. Accordingly he got thirty years and was promptly taken down. Welch bowed as the sentenced was passed but otherwise displayed no emotion.

Davies went into more detail before sentencing Hussey, reminding him that he had previously been convicted of 'grave crimes' including two involving violence. Despite his record, Hussey had a reputation for being warm-hearted and courteous. When his sentence was passed, the big man bowed like a courtier and without a hint of sarcasm said, 'Thank you, My Lord.'

Next to face the consequences of his actions was Roy James. Davies told him, 'You are the only one of the accused in respect of whom it has been proved you actually received a substantial part of the stolen money. You still had twelve thousand pounds when you were arrested and I have no doubt the original sum far exceeded that figure.'

Although James had been found with £12,000 in his bag when he was arrested after a rooftop chase in St John's Wood, the prosecution had not 'proved' that the money came from the train. Most of the notes had been issued after the raid. But the time for such argument and detail had passed and James' guilt had been decided by the jury.

'In a short space of time,' Davies continued, 'you had what your counsel described as a brilliant and meteoric success as a racing driver. I strongly suspect it was your known talent as a driver which enabled you to play an important part in the perpetration of this grave crime.'

There was nothing brilliant or meteoric about the small, quiet man who was led back down to the cells after learning that his involvement in the mail-train raid had cost him not only thirty years of his life but his dreams of becoming a professional racing driver.

The smooth-talking, ruthless Gordon Goody was next to face reality. 'In some respects you present this court with one of the saddest problems,' Davies told him. 'You have manifest gifts of personality and intelligence which could have carried you far had they been directed honestly. I have not seen you in the court for three months without noticing that you are a man capable of inspiring the admiration of your fellow accused.' The Judge left Goody in no doubt that he also considered him to have played a major part in the conspiracy and robbery. Davies said Goody was 'a dangerous menace to society' and despite all his personal gifts he too must be removed from presenting any further threat and go to prison for thirty years.

Brian Field was next to receive the benefit of Mr Edmund Davies' penetrating observation:

> Your strength of personality and superior intelligence enabled you to obtain a position of dominance in relation to your employer John Wheater. I entertain no serious doubt that you are in no small measure responsible for the disastrous position in which this wretched man now finds himself. Whether it was simply a coincidence that two of the four bags found in Dorking woods containing over one hundred thousand pounds were your property or whether that fact is an indication

of further complicity in the main conspiracy, again I have no means of knowing. That you played an essential role in the major conspiracy is clear.

For his role in the conspiracy and obstructing the course of justice, Brian Arthur Field was sentenced to twenty-five years in prison.

In dealing with Leonard Field, Davies said, 'You are a dangerous man.'

A woman's voice called out from the public gallery, 'No!' But the Judge took no notice, and carried on: 'Not only have you perjured yourself repeatedly in this trial to save your own skin but on your own showing you perjured yourself at one stage in an endeavour to ruin Brian Field. I sentence you not for perjury. I sentence you solely for conspiracy.' Davies told Leonard Field he had made a 'vital contribution to the enterprise', for which he would go to prison for twenty-five years.

A woman's Cockney voice wailed from the gallery and for a moment the solemn proceedings descended into music hall. 'He's innocent, sir. I'm his old mother,' she cried. A policewoman moved to eject Mrs Field, but she had not finished her plea for her son. 'I'm seventy-three,' she shouted, as if that might make a difference. 'Justice is not right.'

As Mrs Field was edged towards the door, her son looked up at the commotion from the dock. 'Never mind, Mum,' he called. 'I'm still young.'

With Leonard Field and his mother removed, the mood subdued quickly and the court was silent again by the time Wheater was brought up. There was a different tone to Davies' review of the final man, who stood ashen and straight-backed in the dock, waiting for justice to be done: 'You have served your country gallantly in war and faithfully in peace. There is no evidence that you contributed to your present position by profligate living of any kind. Indeed, your standards seem to have been distinctly lower than your managing clerk's.' Davies said that he would treat Wheater as if he had no knowledge until after the robbery of the purpose of Leatherslade Farm. When that became clear he could have contacted the police 'as a decent citizen would have' and volunteered the information they needed. Instead he had professed his incompetence and inability to help and the jury had concluded that was false. He was a solicitor and that made his offence graver. 'I have come to the conclusion that you must go to prison for three years.'

There were still the trials of the six who stood accused of receiving, but the slow grinding wheels of British justice had done their principal job and eleven men had gone to prison, as the Judge had promised, 'for an extremely long time' for their part in 'The Great Train Robbery'.

Detective Superintendent Malcolm Fewtrell was finally in a position to take his retirement, seven months later than he had planned, and the Buckinghamshire Constabulary could return to their everyday rural police work. But for several men it was far from over. The amount of money stolen had been calculated from the start but the price of the crime was only now apparent and plain for all to see. Reynolds, Edwards and White might have escaped so far, but they knew the heat was still on and that they had not been forgotten. The Grey Fox was not going to rest until he had found all those still on the run and brought every last one of them to justice.

34

Mr Justice Edmund Davies had one last job to do. After dispatching eleven guilty men to prison for up to thirty years there was time before lunch to hear Mr Arthur James QC's opening prosecution speech in the cases against those arrested for receiving stolen money believed to have come from the mail-train robbery.

First in the dock were Cordrey's brother-in-law and sister, fifty-two-year-old Alfred Pilgrim and his forty-nine-year-old wife, May. They had been charged with receiving £860. With them was the fifty-two-year-old wife of William Boal, Renee, who had been found in possession of £330. They all pleaded not guilty and elected to be tried together.

When the court resumed after lunch, Mr James seemed to have lost his appetite for criminal prosecution and made an unexpected announcement. 'In all the circumstances I think the proper course for the Crown to take here would be not to call any evidence before the jury.'

The Judge agreed and on his direction the jury returned verdicts of not guilty. The prisoners were discharged and such was the relief that Alfred Pilgrim collapsed on the pavement outside the court and was taken to Aylesbury hospital. He was later allowed to go home.

There is a story that Alfred Pilgrim was on medication and had been denied it while being held in custody at the court and that was the reason for his sudden collapse, but there is nothing in public records or published accounts to confirm or deny it.

Next into the dock was Roy James' mechanic, Robert William Pelham. He pleaded guilty to receiving £545 between 9 and 24 August 1963. After hearing his plea, Davies said, 'I am disposed to think that no public good will be served by sending you, a man with no previous convictions of any kind, to prison, despite the gravity of this offence.' Pelham was given a conditional discharge.

Walter Smith and his wife Patricia were then put in the dock. Walter Smith was charged with receiving two sums of £2,000 between 2 and

10 October 1963. His wife was charged with receiving £470. She had concealed the money in her dress when the police were searching their home. Mr Smith pleaded guilty and Mrs Smith pleaded not guilty. Without further ado Davies discharged Patricia Smith and remanded her husband in custody to await sentencing. Walter Smith was later given three years imprisonment.

Finally it was the turn of Martin Harvey. He admitted to receiving £518 and was sent to prison for twelve months.

Before adjourning the court, Davies spoke from the bench to the Chief Constable of Buckinghamshire, Brigadier John Cheney, who was due to retire the following year:

> I cannot mention individually all those members of your county force who partly by inspiration, partly by endlessly patient work, have brought to justice some, but unhappily not all, of the criminals who embarked on the dreadful enterprise. It may be that I fail in justice to many by mentioning some. If so I ask forgiveness.

Davies spoke of the unstinting efforts of Detective Chief Superintendent Gerald McArthur and Detective Sergeant Pritchard from Scotland Yard who had worked closely with Detective Superintendent Malcolm Fewtrell. He also commended the work of Detective Superintendent Tommy Butler and his Flying Squad team in London under Commander George Hatherill. He thanked Chief Inspector Reginald Ballinger of Buckinghamshire Police, who had been in charge of the court arrangements, for his 'efficiency, patience and endless courtesy', and he praised Detective Constable Keith Milner and Detective Sergeant William Collins for their 'dazzling mastery' over more than six hundred exhibits. The Judge concluded his speech and the hearing by saying, 'I leave this county with feelings of deep appreciation for the signal work of your force.'

And so it was that Mr Justice Edmund Davies brought his involvement with the trials of those greater and lesser participants in 'The Great Train Robbery' to a close. He had presided over nearly sixty days of hearings and spent countless hours outside the courtroom contemplating the difficult task that had befallen him.

It is not possible to say with any degree of certainty how events, great or small, both inside and outside his courtroom influenced Mr Justice Edmund Davies' decision to pass unprecedented penal sentences for those men found guilty of conspiracy and robbery of the overnight mail train on 8 August 1963. Across the nation the balanced and fair-minded British public were at first shocked and then disapproving. Some of the criticism turned to outrage, even among the most law-abiding and conservative. The long sentences were the main topic of discussion in national newspapers. The argument was a simple one. Terms of imprisonment for crimes of violence were normally between fifteen and twenty years; the sentences of thirty years were greater than those imposed for rape or murder. Even with full remission, those men with thirty-year terms would not be released until they had served twenty. A murderer jailed for life was unlikely to serve more than fifteen years. Was stealing banknotes regarded as more wicked than murder? Was the legal system taking a sterner view of crimes against property than crimes against people? Was it retribution? Was it merely to deter others? Was it panic? And was spending thirty years in prison likely to reform any criminal?

An alternative view expressed by the *Daily Telegraph* was that killers are less susceptible to deterrents than thieves and that the heavy sentences had matched 'the exorbitance' of the offence.

Away from the intense publicity, complexities of the law and debate in the courtroom, the British nation in whose name justice had been done felt privately unsettled and uneasy. Justice had been done and seen to be done, but somehow crime and punishment seemed to have been misjudged.

In his secluded Kensington mews hideout, Bruce Reynolds learned on the six o'clock news of the thirty-year sentences that had been given to his fellow gang members. He was stunned and bewildered. Then came a final realisation that, if he was to escape the clutches of the law, and more particularly Tommy Butler, he would have to leave the country. Reynolds and his wife Franny had been on the run and prisoners in their own house for months. Despite having shaved his head and grown a moustache, Reynolds had rarely ventured out. When he did, it inevitably involved elaborate planning and the help of others. Their son, Nick, was still being looked after by Mary Manson in Wimbledon, and the thought of reuniting his family and starting a new life abroad had its attractions, but how could it be done and where would they go?

Reynolds could, and no doubt should, have made the decision to leave the country a long time earlier, certainly after he had seen the determination of the hunt to find the robbers and the evidence stacked against them. Realistically, he should have made plans for life after the robbery long before he took part in it. But Bruce Reynolds had never been a realist. Like other members of the mail-train gang, he had been slow to think things through, and then he had procrastinated. He had ducked and dived, spent a great deal of his stolen money on minders and safe houses. With the Captain's help, he had eventually bought his small house in Albert Mews, but even that was an indication of his limited scope. Despite his taste for fast cars and expensive suits, his dreams for his son to attend Harrow School, his big ideas of adventure and more romantic horizons, Reynolds seems to have remained a man of narrow vision, reluctant to be parted from his native London, let alone the country he knew.

Over the next few days he got in touch with contacts, arranged a false passport, and started planning his escape.

Edwards was faced with a similar dilemma. If he had seriously considered giving himself up, as Detective Inspector Frank Williams had been trying to persuade him to do for months through intermediaries, the prospect of a thirty-year sentence had changed that. He too would have to get out. But unlike Frances Reynolds, Edwards' wife June initially refused to leave her friends and family and everything she knew for a life in another country with all the attendant uncertainties, unknowns and isolation.

Like the others, Jimmy White, his partner Sheree and their baby son Stephen had been constantly on the move for eight months. They had vacated their home at 66 Woodlands, Beulah Hill, which they rented in the names of Mr and Mrs James Edward Patten, and narrowly avoided being apprehended after the discovery of £30,440 behind panelling in their cream-and-fawn, four-berth caravan at Clovelly Caravan Site, Boxhill. White and Sheree decided they would be less conspicuous if they split up. White went first to Clapham for a short time and then passed through a string of places around London. While his harbourers were initially only too happy to fleece him for money they soon became nervous and asked him to move on. Eventually, White left London and fled to Nottinghamshire, where refuge had been arranged with a couple called Alfred and Jean Place on a council estate. Then he rented a room at 60 Maltby Road, Mansfield, Nottinghamshire. The safe house had been arranged by an old associate of White's called Henry Isaacs of 10 Saddleton Road, Whitstable, Kent. Isaacs and his wife, Joanna, also organised for Sheree and her baby to stay in Hampshire on the army base in Aldershot with a friend whose husband had been posted overseas.

For a time during the autumn of 1963 it appears the Places and or the Whites moved to a rented bungalow called Edbury's in Nursery Lane, Whitstable, which was again arranged by the Isaacs. During the later part of 1963, White, who was using the name Bob Lane, was seen there by Henry Isaacs' son, Michael.

When the tenancy of Edbury's came to an end in January 1964, Jimmy White decided to make more permanent plans. With Henry Isaacs' help, he bought Crown Edge Farm on the outskirts of Glossop in Derbyshire. Alfred Place acted as the purchaser and Isaacs installed his son Michael (who had no idea that White, aka Bob Lane, was a fugitive) at the farm.

Henry Isaacs' and Jimmy White's complex network of associates included Albert Milbank, a known receiver and fence of stolen goods and money. Milbank was under observation and had regularly been seen coming and going at 69 Belsize Park Gardens, London, NW3. The address was occupied by a German woman called Mrs Heller, who was believed to be in touch with Reynolds. Both Milbank and Isaacs were observed by police visiting a flat at 85 Hermatage Court in Wanstead, owned by Miss Edith Simons. The significance of that address was that both Isaacs and Milbank had been seen at the flat when solicitor's clerk George Stanley was also present.

Stanley's firm, Lesser and Co., represented many of the mail-train gang and his association with London's most notorious criminals dated back to the early 1950s. The Flying Squad were of the opinion that Stanley was a 'very shrewd' and 'cunning' operator; for years detectives had suspected that his involvement with his clients extended beyond his role as legal clerk, but they had yet to pin anything on him.

There has been a good deal of speculation about George Stanley and his possible role in the mail-train conspiracy and robbery. He was certainly closely involved in the defence of most of the train robbers who stood trial. Despite being diabetic and having only one lung (he had suffered from tuberculosis as a child), Stanley was a solidly built man of about 5'8". Even among his family, he had a reputation for being ruthless when it came to money. After Stanley died in a car crash in 2008 at the age of ninety-seven, his nephew, Lee Sturley, claimed in May 2009 that George Stanley had helped launder mail-train money through property deals in Southend and swindled many of the robbers in the process. It is too late now to reliably establish Stanley's actual involvement, but it is certain that he benefited handsomely from the mail-train robbery. He probably had a wider influence too, in that it seems likely the ambitious young Brian Field decided that his income could be similarly augmented if he followed Stanley's example.

For the men who had been caught and convicted, their last remaining hope was that the severity of their sentences would be reduced on appeal. The prison authorities decided to split the men up after sentencing. The camaraderie they had established during the long trial was at an end and they were soon scattered far and wide. Biggs was taken to Lincoln and then to Chelmsford, Goody to Pentonville, Cordrey to Stafford, Wilson to Winson Green in Birmingham, Welch to Canterbury, Hussey to Liverpool, James to Winchester, Brian Field to Oxford, Leonard Field to Bedford and Wheater to Wormwood Scrubs.

After the sentencing, Wisbey was taken to Oxford Prison. When his wife Rene visited him she said their telephone at home had been ringing continuously with enquiries from the press. Wisbey told her to move away and make a new life for herself and their children, as thirty years was too long to wait. Rene, however, refused to give up hope or turn her back on their relationship.

The main group, assumed to be the hard core, were kept under Rule 43 (now Rule 45), which confined them to their cells twenty-three hours a day. They were allowed no contact with other prisoners, no radio or newspapers, and were only allowed to exercise under close supervision alone in prison yards. When visited by loved ones, they were forbidden to embrace.

*

By early June 1964 Reynolds' arrangements to leave the country were at last in place. His pal Terry Hogan, whom he refers to publicly as Harry Booth, had done a dummy run the week before to check the plan would work.

Early on the morning of Thursday, 4 June, Hogan picked up Reynolds from Albert Mews and they drove to Elstree Aerodrome in Hertfordshire where a pilot and a Cessna light aircraft were waiting. From Elstree, Reynolds was to touch English soil one last time at Gatwick while the plane was refuelled and the pilot lodged his flight plan. The single-engine aircraft then took to the summer skies once again, headed high above the Sussex fields for the coast and finally out over the English Channel. It was a relief from the self-imposed imprisonment of his small mews house in Kensington, but being a fugitive was only a freedom of sorts. After ten gruelling months, Reynolds was leaving it all behind, or at least putting some distance between himself and his pursuers. But he was also leaving behind the life he knew, his friends, his wife and his son.

When the Cessna landed at a small private airfield near Ostend, Reynolds slipped out through a gate while the pilot went to register their arrival. Waiting in the car park was his friend the Captain, dressed in a pale buff mackintosh and standing by a hired black Mercedes. For a moment, the Captain and Reynolds lost themselves in the fantasy of a cloak-and-dagger adventure and the cold prospect of a future forever on the run was transformed into something less limiting and bleak.

The following day, after a night in Brussels, Reynolds' false passport, in the name of Keith Clemens Miller, was stamped by Belgium Immigration. He then boarded a scheduled Sabena Airlines flight bound for Mexico via Toronto. At 19.00 on 6 June 1964 Reynolds arrived alone in Mexico City, 5,556 miles from home.

Meanwhile, Jimmy White's new life at Crown Edge Farm in Derbyshire was under threat. In June his associate Henry Isaacs was sent to prison for fraud and his affairs came under scrutiny. Alfred Place was implicated; what's more he had a brother-in-law, Alan Dare, who was a policeman. Realising that his rural idyll was at an end, White found himself with no alternative but to abandon his investment, pack up his family and go on the run once again.

*

On Monday, 6 July the cases of those convicted for their part in the mail-train robbery were brought before the Court of Criminal Appeal at the Royal Courts of Justice in London with Mr Justice Fenton Atkinson, Mr Justice Lawton and Mr Justice Widgery presiding. For the Crown the team was once again Mr A.E. James QC, Mr N. MacDermot QC and Mr H.W. Sabin and Mr J.D.A. Fennell.

First to be heard were the appeals of Wilson, Biggs and James. Wilson seemed to believe that going to court again was a waste of time and chose not to attend. On 7 July it was the turn of Hussey and Wisbey, and on 8 July the appeals of Welch, Biggs and Goody were heard.

All the appeals of these principal players were dismissed. Atkinson said when reviewing their sentences that the train robbery was of enormous and quite exceptional gravity, differing from the ordinary type of case, not only in degree but also in kind. There was the number of men engaged, the extent of the planning and preparation, and the object of attack. To stop and rob a mail train was an act of organised banditry directed at a vital public service and it had the character of an act of warfare against the community, touching new depths of lawlessness. He concluded:

> in our judgement, severely deterrent sentences are necessary. The maximum sentence on count two was imprisonment for life and such a sentence might well have been imposed. In our view sentences approximating to the maximum are fully justified because of the grave threat that such crimes as this present to the public as a whole.

The purpose of the sentence, Aitkinson said, was to be 'punitive', to 'deter others' and to 'safeguard this country'. They were, concluded Atkinson, wholly exceptional sentences for a wholly exceptional crime for which the type of sentence normally imposed for armed robbery was inadequate.

When the case of Brian Field came before the Court of Appeal on Thursday, 9 July, and Leonard Field and John Wheater on Friday, 10 July, they must have all been feeling gloomy about their prospects. But in a surprise verdict by the jury, Brian Field was acquitted of robbery and receiving, which left little basis for a conviction for conspiracy. With only a guilty verdict for obstructing the course of justice, Atkinson pronounced when sentencing Brian Field the following week that Field's twenty-five year sentence would be revoked and he would serve a term of just five years.

John Wheater's appeal was dismissed and his three-year sentence remained unchanged. The appeal of Leonard Field, who was facing twenty-five years in prison having been found guilty of taking part in both the robbery and conspiracy, was allowed. As with his namesake, his sentence was reduced to five years for obstructing the course of justice.

On Monday, 13 July, Cordrey and Boal appeared before the Court of Appeal. 'This is a difficult case,' Atkinson said. 'There is a possibility that the case of one particular accused has become obscured by the totality of the weight of evidence against the others.' He recognised that Boal did not fit the profile of the other men convicted of robbery and that he was neither temperamentally nor physically disposed to have taken part in the raid. Boal was found not guilty of robbery and a charge of receiving was substituted. The appeal against his sentence for conspiracy was dismissed and Boal's concurrent sentences were reduced from twenty-four years to fourteen.

All the lawyers for the defence made an application for leave to appeal to the House of Lords and all were refused by Atkinson on the grounds that 'there is no point of law of general or public importance'.

So that was it. Eleven months after the mail-train robbery, the legal process had run its course for the twelve men who had been found guilty. Brian Field, who had been instrumental in the conception of the crime, was lucky to have been cleared of conspiracy on appeal. That in turn had led to the collapse of his conviction for robbery and the grave prospect of a twenty-five-year sentence was reduced to a mere five.

Leonard Field, who had only ever been a pawn in the bogus purchase of Leatherslade Farm, had been acquitted of the larger conspiracy to rob the mail train. His five-year term for obstructing the course of justice, though harsh given his actual involvement, was the best he could have hoped for.

The case of William Boal had not only, as Atkinson put it, 'become obscured by the totality of the weight of evidence against the others', but had resulted from the same critical factors in the prosecution's case against all the accused men. In all proabability the jury would not have arrived at the verdicts they did if the case against each of the accused men had been heard separately. To reach a unanimous guilty verdict the jury had been persuaded to accept that the often questionable circumstantial evidence found at the farm connected men to the crimes of conspiracy and robbery beyond reasonable doubt. And the jury may not have reached that verdict so readily if they had entered the courtroom without a great deal of foreknowledge, preconception and received opinion about the accused men and the crime. That influence cannot be disregarded.

Although not entirely innocent, Boal had been more foolish than deeply criminal. At worst, he had been an accessory after the fact, but he had not been charged or found guilty of that offence. Boal had allowed himself to be manipulated by Roger Cordrey and was certainly guilty of poor judgement. His true involvement was both incidental and largely unwitting. But in small incremental steps in his actions and statements, and through the grinding process of law, Boal had moved inexorably towards catastrophe and was to be punished for crimes in which he had played no part.

Whatever their individual circumstances, for the convicted men no last glimmer of hope now remained of reversing their destiny. In their own solitary ways, they were each going to have to resign themselves to their fate and somehow find ways to live with it.

But that was not the end of the tale or of the men who had been dubbed the Great Train Robbers and who, by association, or circumstance, had been catapulted into the public arena.

In less than a month, a year and four days after the mail-train ambush, the story of 'The Great Train Robbery' was to have another extraordinary twist. The next chapter was smaller in scale but equal in impudence to the original crime – if not more so, because the forces of law and order thought they had anticipated and prepared for it. Just as the attention of the nation was turning towards an autumn General Election there was another act of criminal defiance, another scandal for the press, another exciting instalment for the public and another painful jab in solar plexus for an already bruised and ailing establishment.

35

After his conviction in the main trial, Charlie Wilson had been taken to Winson Green Prison, three miles north-east of Birmingham city centre. Wilson was kept under close supervision on the maximum-security C-Wing on Landing No. 2 in a cell that had previously been used for Soviet spy, Gordon Lonsdale.

In 1961 Lonsdale, alias Konon Trofimovich Molody, born in Moscow in 1922, was intercepted by Special Branch officers in London. He was holding a carrier bag containing copies of four British Admiralty test documents and a tin of undeveloped film which was later found to show details of HMS *Dreadnought*, Britain's first nuclear submarine. Found guilty of conspiring to pass classified information, Lonsdale was sentenced to twenty-five years – five years less than Wilson.

Lonsdale had vacated the cell at Winson Green in order to be traded at the Glienicke Bridge in Berlin on Wednesday, 22 April 1964 for British businessman Greville Wynne, who had been apprehended by the KGB in Moscow.

Most of Charlie Wilson's time was spent confined to his cell, where a single bare light bulb burned twenty-four hours a day. Prison warders checked on him every fifteen minutes and he was stripped of his clothes at night.

Shortly after 03.00 on Wednesday, 12 August, while C-Wing warder William Nicholls was making his routine checks, three men propped a ladder against the wall of a nearby builder's yard and climbed over into the grounds of a mental hospital neighbouring Winson Green Prison. Using grappling irons, they scaled the twenty-foot prison wall and swung down on a rope ladder to the exercise yard below. Keeping to the shadows, the men ran across twenty yards of open ground and up the steps to the rear of cell block B. One of the men took a key from his pocket, opened the heavy, studded oak door, and then used a second key to unlock the steel grille just inside.

According to various accounts later given by Wilson, at 03.15 he woke to the sound of keys rattling in his cell door. Three masked men entered silently, dressed in everyday clothes. One of them said to Wilson, who was naked apart from his vest under a thin prison blanket, 'You're coming out.'

Wilson said he was not going anywhere and the man drew a revolver from his pocket. Another man tossed Wilson a bundle of clothes. Still not knowing who the men were, or how they had managed to get to him, Wilson quickly pulled on a pair of dark trousers, a black roll-neck sweater, plimsolls and a balaclava.

The men manhandled Wilson out of his cell and past a bound-and-gagged Nicholls lying unconscious in the corridor. They led Wilson quietly down metal stairs to the ground floor, where they opened a series of gates and doors with keys, closing and relocking each one as they made their way back towards B block. Exiting the building as they had entered, and locking the prison door behind them, they crossed the yard, climbed back over the prison wall, hauled up the rope ladder and dropped down to the neighbouring mental hospital and retraced their route into the builder's yard. Clambering out over an opposite wall, they reached the towpath running beside the Birmingham and Wolverhampton Canal. After a short run they arrived at two waiting cars and seconds later they were driving away. Wilson's escape had taken under three minutes.

It was not until 03.50, half an hour later, that the first call to the police was made from Winson Green Prison. Over the following hours, Detective Chief Superintendent Gerald Baumber, head of Birmingham CID, was alerted and began to assemble a special team. When the news reached Tommy Butler in London, he was predictably taciturn and said he was 'not in the least surprised'. But with his team still working hard on finding and capturing Reynolds, Edwards and White, it must have been sobering news for the milk-drinking bachelor. As if tracking down and arresting the fugitive mail-train robbers wasn't already difficult enough, he was now going to have to start all over again with Wilson.

There are two theories about the escape of Charlie Wilson. One is that he masterminded the whole thing himself, which may explain why he did not attend his appeal hearing in London. The other is that he was effectively kidnapped. While the men behind the jailbreak remain unnamed, their motives were no doubt driven by the fact that Wilson, with his share of the stolen train money still intact, would be in a position to reward his rescuers handsomely. Either theory is perfectly possible. Wilson had his own network of underworld associates and contacts and was known to be well connected with the gangsters who ran protection rackets in London's West End.

Understandably, the audacious escape of 'Great Train Robber' Charles Frederick Wilson sparked a frenzy of press headlines and media interest. On BBC Television a thirty-five-year-old reporter called Magnus Magnusson (later of *Mastermind* fame) stopped and interviewed people on the streets of London to test the public mood.

He asked the first passer-by, 'Which side are you on, the escaper or the police who are trying to catch him?'

A man in a suit with pair of dark glasses, holding a dog, replied in a camp and fruity upper-class voice, 'Well, I think, speaking loosely, at this moment of time, the escaper, with certain reservations, of course, depending I would think, on the crime.'

'Why are you on his side?'

The man sighed and put the dog down. 'Er, well, in so many regards, one thinks, jolly good luck. One is again speaking loosely, and let's hope the police are not watching,' he said with a wry smile.

'Would you think so if he had had to murder a warder to get out?'

The interviewee pursed his lips. 'Certainly not. No. Certainly not.'

'Would you give any help to the police at all to catch him?'

'Again, under certain circumstances, seeing the man perhaps passing in the street, I wouldn't like to commit myself as to what I would really do. One's first reaction is, yes, of course I would. On measured thought, perhaps one wouldn't.'

'Do you think the public as a whole tends to identify with the escaper rather than the police?'

'Yes, I would think that we do, if I may speak for the public. I think one is always concerned that there but for the grace of God go I. I would hate to sit in judgement upon any other person.'

With that Magnusson moved on to a young woman and asked, 'In an escape like this, whose side are you instinctively on, the escaped man or the police?'

'Oh, the escaped man, I think,' the young woman replied

enthusiastically. 'I like to encourage the police, but I'd like him to have a good run for his money.'

'So it's just a game?'

'I think it is as far as I'm concerned, yes.'

'Is this an instinctive sympathy?'

'Yes. As a hunted animal or a hunted man, it's the same thing.'

The third interviewee was a conservative-looking man in his mid-thirties. At first, he appeared more public-spirited, saying, 'I'd sympathise with the police, I think, generally speaking. But I'd be sympathetic towards anybody who actually has escaped.'

'Why?'

'Well, somebody who can go as far as escaping, it's a little bit romantic and, well, I'd just be slightly sympathetic towards him.'

'Do you hope that they don't catch him?'

'Oh no. No. I think they should catch him.'

The next interviewee was a large woman with a lot of dark frizzy hair. 'In a case like this, are you on the side of Wilson or the police?' said Magnusson.

'The police, of course,' the woman answered sternly. 'I think it's dreadful. I think thieves ought to get what's coming to them.' She paused and then added, 'Besides, I'm a policeman's wife.'

What happened to Wilson after he was driven away from Winson Green Prison is open to interpretation. The only accounts come much later from either Wilson, other criminals or associates 'in the know'.

Piers Paul Read's version, told to him by some of the gang fourteen years after the escape, claims that Wilson stayed hidden in Britain until the end of 1964 before crossing the Channel under the name Ronald Alloway 'on an ordinary ferry from Dover to Calais'. In *No Fixed Address*, Frank Williams says Wilson 'was subsequently flown out of England by light aircraft'. More recently, in *Killing Charlie*, author Wensley Clarkson has Wilson immediately heading for 'a deserted landing strip' and flying off in a small private plane to a barren airport in northern France.

What is known is that Wilson ended up in Canada the following year, having first visited Reynolds in Mexico City. Some time later he bought a two-acre plot near the shores of the St Lawrence River and built a ranch-style house in Hudson Heights, about forty-three miles west of Montreal.

After Bruce Reynolds' departure, his wife Frances walked into Scotland Yard and asked to see Tommy Butler. Butler questioned her at length about her husband, but there was no basis to detain her and he let her go.

Free at last from her ten-month close confinement, and reunited with her son, Franny Reynolds went on holiday to Ireland with Mary Manson. The alternative version of Franny's movements, told by Reynolds in his 1995 biography, is that his wife went on holiday to the South of France. Whatever the location, Franny was well aware that her movements would be closely watched and she made no attempt to contact her husband. In the late summer of 1964 Franny and Nick went to stay with her sister and brother-in-law, John and Barbara Daly in Sutton, Surrey.

Daly had been under scrutiny since his Valentine's Day acquittal. Although fortunate to have been set free, 'lucky' John Daly had not been able to enjoy the fruits of his crime.

Against Reynolds' advice, Daly had entrusted his money to a man called Green who had offered to invest it for him. But while Daly was being held in custody, Green vanished along with the money. According to the robbers' account in Piers Paul Read's book, Green moved to Brighton, changed his name to Hugget and shortly afterwards died, leaving no chance of Daly ever recovering his loot from the mail-train raid.

That may be true, but a different version of what happened to Daly's share of the money appears in a Post Office Investigation Branch report held in the GPO archive at Mount Pleasant in London.

Immediately after the robbery John Daly went with a man called Michael Black to a house in Boscastle, on the north coast of Cornwall, where he hid his share in the garden. The house was occupied by a man Daly knew called Bill Goodwin, his niece Kathleen Audrey Sleep, and Goodwin's eighty-year-old mother.

After Daly was arrested, Michael Black went to Boscastle, dug up the money in Goodwin's presence and took half of it and fled to Spain. Black subsequently returned to England and later died.

After Black had taken half the money, Goodwin bricked the remaining cash into the wall of the kitchen in the presence of his niece, Kathleen Sleep. Not long afterwards, Bill Goodwin died.

After his acquittal, Daly went to Boscastle with associate Billy Still to collect his money. He accepted Kathleen Sleep's explanation that Black had taken it. It is not clear if Miss Sleep told Daly about the remainder of his money hidden in the wall, but that is where the other half remained.

Cornwall police knew that Daly and Still had visited the area, as they had been stopped for a traffic offence. When Tommy Butler was informed his view was that Daly was probably unaware of Black's death and was looking for him.

In September 1965, Butler went to Cornwall and spoke to Miss Sleep. She admitted that Daly and Black had buried about £150,000 in the garden, and told Butler that Black had subsequently taken half the money and her uncle had then bricked the other half into the kitchen wall. During a subsequent visit from Butler, Miss Sleep produced a biscuit tin containing £9,349 in one-pound notes, which she said her dog had unearthed in the garden beside the garage. Both the tin and banknotes showed signs of having been buried for some time. Miss Sleep explained that when her landlord had told her of his intention to install central heating and make alterations to the kitchen, she had removed the money from the wall, burned the five-pound notes, because she thought they could be traced, and buried the remainder in the garden. Tommy Butler, presumably satisfied he had reached the end of that trail, brought no charges against Kathleen Sleep.

The facts were reported to the Director of Public Prosecutions, suggesting that Daly be prosecuted for receiving, but the DPP decided not to proceed on the grounds that further evidence might come to light when Reynolds or Edwards was arrested. However, no further charges were ever brought against the lucky John Daly.

In September 1964, Jimmy White and his family again found some measure of refuge when, with the help of Joanna Isaacs, they moved to a rented farmhouse called Pett Bottom Farm near Folkestone in Kent.

By October 1964, public attention was focused on the forthcoming General Election. Both parties had new leaders. Following the retirement of Harold Macmillan, the Conservative Party had appointed Alec

Douglas-Home to take over. Although Douglas-Home had served as Parliamentary Private Secretary to Neville Chamberlain and participated in the famous negotiations with Adolf Hitler before the outbreak of World War Two, the sixty-two-year-old was a curious choice to lead his party into the next election, given the country's appetite for reform. Although he had renounced his peerage when moving to the House of Commons, with his modest, patriarchal tone and understated good manners, Douglas-Home had an indelible stamp of a bygone era about him.

Following the sudden death from a heart condition of the Labour Party leader Hugh Gaitskell on 18 January 1963, pipe-smoking Harold Wilson, a Huddersfield-born, former head boy of Wirral Grammar School, had been chosen to take his party to the polls. Wilson was viewed as being on the Labour Party's centre-left so the decision seemed to embrace the domestic thirst for social reform. In the General Election of 15 October 1964 the Labour Party ousted thirteen years of Tory government, but only just. Harold Wilson won by four seats.

It was in the shadow of such towering events that Frances Reynolds obtained a false passport in the name of Angela Green. Accompanied by her son Nick, and with a modest collection of suitcases, they boarded an overnight ferry at Harwich to the Hook of Holland. Not long after, the Reynolds family were reunited in Mexico City, where they were free to spend their money and live the 'good life' that Reynolds had always dreamed of.

Bruce Reynolds still had a large amount of stolen money at his disposal, but without management and investment even that sizable sum was finite. He later commented that he was not concerned about spending his loot from the train job and had never worried about the cost of his lavish lifestyle. He said that he always remained 'supremely confident' that something would turn up. How Reynolds realistically thought that any kind of major opportunity would fall his way in a country where he had no contacts, and no knowledge of the country, its culture or the language is a mystery. The bravado and delusion of gangsters often seems to run close to that of compulsive gamblers.

With four men now on the run, Tommy Butler was as determined as ever, but the trail was growing steadily colder. After a spate of press headlines and renewed public interest following Wilson's escape, attention quickly dwindled along with the pressure from both the media and higher powers.

Throughout 1964 the health of Jack Mills had continued to deteriorate. He had not returned to his prestigious job of driving Travelling Post Office trains; instead British Railways had assigned him light duties, working in the stores at his local Crewe depot.

Although Mills had not been forgotten, his health problems remained unexplored or at least undiagnosed. His initial head injuries had been nasty and required fourteen stitches, but after the abrasions to his scalp had healed only his family could see the deeper, longer term effects.

His son, John Mills, later said, 'He got shingles, which the doctor said was delayed shock coming out. And from then on his right hand shook, it never stopped until the day he died. And he started to sway. It was terrible. From that day he went downhill. He was not my dad of old.'

1965

36

In January 1965 Jack Mills was given a payment of £250 by the newly appointed Postmaster General, Tony Benn. In February, Mills received a second payment of £250, this time from the clearing banks. The payments were some recognition of his debilitated condition, but the story of Jack Mills has never been anything more than a marginal component in the train-robbery saga.

Whenever 'The Great Train Robbery' is mentioned by the media, there's always a glib and generic mention of the injured train driver Jack Mills. Popular misconceptions abound, which include Mills being shot during the raid and/or dying on the spot, to being absolutely fine afterwards and glossed over altogether. While the robbers and policemen have been glamorised and written about, the story of Mills has remained both oversimplified and polarised.

On one side the robbers' insistence that the violent attack on Mills was an isolated incident is clearly nonsense. The year before they had knocked unconscious two of the three security guards they attacked during the BOAC London Airport robbery. And in the mail-train raid the statements of the men on the HVP coach all report being physically attacked and seeing others being hit with coshes and an iron bar.

The gang also maintain that Mills overplayed his injuries and subsequent poor health. He was accused of being a 'fucking good actor' by Charlie Wilson, who maintained that the blow to his head with an iron bar on the night of the robbery was really nothing of any consequence. This callous remark is in the context of some of the mail-train gang having habitually used violence in the past and previous victims having recovered – at least, so far as they knew. But it ignores, either by convenience, denial or ignorance, that even minor head injuries can produce permanent damage and trauma often triggers long-term ill-health.

The flipside of the Jack Mills story is that he was not adequately supported by his employers British Railways, manipulated by the prosecution to support their case and used by the authorities to dismiss

Robin Hood notions about the train robbers and justify the long prison sentences.

The personal and private tragedy of this ordinary working man and his family has in various ways been skirted over, misrepresented and exploited. Among the many portraits of the robbers, the police and establishment figures, Jack Mills, the only genuine victim, has remained a pawn. His family doctor in Crewe treated him until his death in 1970. He had known Mills before the robbery and saw the effect the attack had on him in those following years. It is clear from medical records and recollections of Mills' family that, following the night of 8 August 1963, Jack Mills was never the same man. He never returned to driving trains and continued to be dogged by a legacy of health problems for the remaining seven years of his life.

On Saturday, 30 January, thousands of people attended the state funeral of Winston Churchill, countless more lined London streets, witnessed by millions of television viewers watching live around the world. The revered wartime leader had suffered a severe stroke on 15 January. Having never fully recovered, he died nine days later, aged ninety. Over the three days leading up to the funeral 321,000 people filed past the coffin of Sir Winston Leonard Spencer-Churchill, lying-in-state in Westminster Hall and draped with the Union flag.

Crime stories in the British media had moved on from 'The Great Train Robbery' to the arrest of identical twins Ronnie and Reggie Kray in the basement bar of the Glenrae Hotel on Seven Sisters Road on suspicion of running a protection racket. Despite applications for bail, the Kray brothers were remanded in custody to await trial. The case for their prosecution revolved around the claim by Soho club owner Huw Cargil McCowen that the brothers had demanded a percentage of the club takings in return for supplying two door attendants. When the case came before a jury in March, they were unable to reach a verdict; after a retrial, the Krays were acquitted. Within weeks of being released, the twins had taken over McCowen's club and renamed it the El Morocco. Ronnie and Reggie Kray would not be arrested again until 1968.

One story that attracted no headlines but generated a flurry of memoranda between government officials was the forthcoming publication of Peta Fordham's *The Robbers' Tale*. A copy of the manuscript had been read by C.G. Osmond, Controller of the GPO's Investigation Branch and circulated to senior civil servants and politicians at the Home Office.

The focus of concern was not that the author attempted to portray the criminal actions of the thieves as romantic or admirable, although that might have been considered ill-judged for the wife of one of the defence counsel. Any fears aroused by Mrs Fordham's claim that 'through her unique contacts she was able to obtain direct and extraordinary information' were allayed by her pronouncement that such information was 'far too dangerous to print'. The primary worry for the GPO Investigation Branch had more serious consequences and was outlined in a memorandum from Osmond and marked 'Strictly Confidential':

> One of the features of Mrs Fordham's manuscript is that it describes in some detail the part played by Reynolds, Edwards and White in the planning and carrying out of the great train robbery. As a layman it seemed to me that publication of this account would make it difficult for anyone who had heard of it, or read it, to serve as a juryman at the trial of these men if they should be caught, since he could hardly be in any doubt of their guilt before the trial began. This raises the question whether publication would obstruct the justice and if so whether the Post Office, having had the manuscript in its hands had any responsibility in the matter.

Before fleeing the country, Reynolds had met with Edwards and the two men had agreed to meet in Mexico. It is not possible to pin down exactly when Buster Edwards left Britain as there are several conflicting accounts. Leaving aside the elaborate details as to exactly how Edwards' escape plan was implemented, he seems to have crossed to continental Europe hidden aboard a cargo ship that set sail from St Katharine's Dock, next to Tower Bridge. Before being joined by his wife and daughter, Edwards underwent plastic surgery in Cologne. The initial surgery was not entirely successful and Edwards spent several painful weeks suffering from an infection.

The various accounts suggest that Edwards, travelling with his wife and daughter under the name Ryan, arrived in Mexico City in April 1965. But the Edwards family, particularly June, did not take so readily as the Reynolds to their feckless foreign lifestyle. Stealing a large amount of money had presented practical problems, evading capture had tested their ingenuity to the limit, and now the tantalising promise of 'the good life' was proving elusive.

By summer 1965 'The Great Train Robbery' was old news. Even Detective Superintendent Tommy Butler took a break from New Scotland Yard and travelled to the South of France. According to Jack Slipper, Butler spent a fortnight scanning the beaches with his binoculars hoping for a sight of Wilson, Edwards, White and Reynolds.

Shortly after three o'clock on 8 July, prison officer's wife Winifred Williams was at the front window of her staff bungalow at the rear of Wandsworth Prison when a green Ford Zephyr drove slowly past and parked next to the prison wall. A few minutes later a shabby dark red removal lorry drew up behind the Zephyr. As she went about her housework, Mrs Williams wondered why none of her neighbours had mentioned that they were moving.

The other side of the twenty-five-foot-high prison wall, fourteen prisoners had been exercising in E Yard for the past half-hour. Their prison uniforms bore a yellow flash to indicate that they were on the 'A-escape list' and under special watch.

When Mrs Williams next glanced out of her window she saw a heavily built man with a stocking over his head get out of the Ford Zephyr. A masked man in blue overalls then emerged from the lorry holding a gun.

At 15.05 one of the four prison officers on duty in the exercise yard saw a man in a stocking mask appear over the top of the wall. Before the officer had time to react, the man shouted something, threw down a rope ladder and a second tubular steel ladder. Three prisoners started running to the wall but when prison officers attempted to pursue them, they were blocked and dragged to the ground by other prisoners. The officers watched helplessly from the exercise yard as convicted train robber Ronnie Biggs climbed up the ladder and over the wall, along with Robert Anderson (serving twelve years for conspiracy to rob a sub-postmaster), Eric Flower (twelve years for armed robbery) and Patrick Doyle aka Anthony Jenkins (four years for conspiracy to rob).

A petrified Mrs Williams, realising what was going on, bolted her front door and hurried to her bedroom: 'I looked out through the bedroom window and saw two prisoners coming over the wall. I only saw two. They were dressed in blue overalls and striped shirts, prison uniform. I took down the number of the car.'

Having scrambled up the ladders, Biggs, Anderson, Flower and Doyle jumped down on to the top of the lorry and disappeared through a hole that had been cut in the roof. The escaped prisoners then ran to three waiting cars which sped off down the service road on the north side of the prison. As they were nearing the main road they met a prison work party with a dustcart coming the other way. Unaware who was inside the vehicles speeding towards them, prison warders ordered their work party to move out of the way and waved the cars through.

A dark green Zephyr matching the description and AYX 470B index number given to the police by Mrs Williams was later found abandoned just over a mile away at Wandsworth Common railway station.

According to the various accounts of the criminals and their associates, the escape was organised by Paul Seaborne, a convict who had been released from Wandsworth in June 1965. Seabourne, who was allegedly paid £10,000 by Charmian Biggs, purchased rope ladders (Biggs, being a builder by trade, had apparently calculated the height of the prison wall by counting the number of brick courses), axes, a shotgun and an old red removal lorry which he converted for the plan. He also engaged the services of two men at £2,500 apiece, though others must have been involved because five men were subsquently found guilty of assisting in Biggs' escape: Henry Holsgrove, George Ronald Leslie, George Albert Gibbs, Ronald Brown and Terrance Mintagh.

Immediately after his escape Biggs was taken to a house six miles away in Dulwich. He stayed there for six weeks before going to Bognor Regis where he was visited by Charmian. It seems extraordinary that the wife of an escaped prisoner was not under twenty-four-hour police observation.

In July 1965 Jimmy White and his family left Pett Bottom Farm and moved into to a flat at Claverly Mansions, overlooking the beach at Littlestone-on-Sea.

After the escape of Charlie Wilson and Ronnie Biggs the authorities were taking no chances. In September, Goody, Wisbey and James were moved to the newly opened high-security E Block at HMP Durham. Like all those imprisoned for their part in the mail-train ambush, they were kept under close observation and were often moved at short notice to different cells and sometimes to different prisons.

The Chief Constable of Durham, Alec Muir, got into a tangle with the press after expressing concerns that 'atomic weapons' might be used to help Gordon Goody escape. Though he later issued an apology, saying that his statement had been extravagant, 'in cold blood I would use the term military weapons'. Muir's atomic weapons remark has been repeated ever since as one of the many extraordinary 'facts' of Great Train Robbery folklore. Nevertheless, security at the prison was stepped up and reinforcements were brought in from Catterick army base: an officer, a sergeant and sixteen soldiers of the 1st Battalion, Lancashire Regiment.

In December 1965 Wisbey's wife was interviewed by ITN having just visited her husband in Durham Prison. She told the reporter, 'They are shut up on their own so long, you just wouldn't treat an animal like that.' When asked how her husband was, she said, 'His spirit is gradually, you know, going. He's trying to take it like any man, but I think they are trying to break them down.'

William Boal's teenage son David was also interviewed on television. The reporter asked, 'When you go and see him, does he rely on you to bring him news and look after everything for him?'

His face frozen by nerves, David replies in a hesitant, newly broken voice, 'Well as I'm the oldest ... he expects me to look after Anthony and Deborah of course. He puts me in charge of them to see they don't run around the streets too much. He expects me to give them some sort of tuition the way he gave me.'

'What sort of things do you teach them that he taught you?'

'Well, just ... erm ...' David swallows. His eyes are glassy, his bottom lip trembles and the corners of his mouth turn down. The teenager's face expresses not self-pity but a sense of injustice and anger. Though he is unable to say what he is feeling in words, David Boal has made his point about his devoted father, who used to whistle bird impressions and tap dance to amuse his three children.

The marital relationships of the men convicted for their part in the train robbery proved less enduring. In April 1965, Roger Cordrey divorced on the grounds of his wife's adultery, and later that month Brian Field followed suit. Karin had returned to Germany shortly after the trial ended; while collaborating on the series of articles which were later published in *Stern*, she began a relationship with journalist Wolfgang Löhde. By April 1965 she was pregnant with Löhde's child. Divorce proceedings were concluded without delay.

In October, Biggs was smuggled out of England on a boat that sailed from Tilbury Docks to Antwerp. He was then driven to Paris. Freddie Foreman claims to have helped him and says he 'took nothing for it'. In the Clinique Victor Massé in Paris, Biggs underwent plastic surgery. On 29 December 1965, using the name Terence Flurminger, he caught a flight from Orly to Sydney, via Zurich.

1966

Solicitor John Wheater was released from prison on 11 February 1966, having served two years of his three-year sentence for conspiracy to obstruct the course of justice. On 6 March a newspaper article by Wheater appeared in the *Sunday Telegraph* in which he insisted that there was no mastermind, that some of those involved in the robbery had not been named by the police, and that there was a link between the gang and an insider in Post Office security. Wheater claimed that the Post Office employee had made contact with one of the gang via a relation acting as intermediary. It was not an earth-shattering revelation but corroberated the theory as to how the robbers had come by details of the procedures and the sums of money transported on the Travelling Post Office train they ambushed.

Although the search for an inside man had continued to be pursued by GPO investigators, Tommy Butler's team had never considered it a fruitful avenue. Butler remained sceptical that a Post Office insider was necessary to the plan. He was of the opinion that simple observation would have been sufficient.

After his brief reappearance on the public stage, John Wheater moved to Harrogate to run a family laundry business and quietly slipped into obscurity.

On 4 April, Detective Superintendent Tommy Butler received a telephone call from a man in St Albans. The caller was a weekend sailor who claimed that during a trip to Romney Marsh he had met a man called Bob Lane, engaged in renovating boats at Littlestone on the Kent coast. He said that Lane bore a striking resemblance to the fugitive train robber Jimmy White.

Scotland Yard had received many such calls over the years and Butler was inclined to be rather dismissive of them. But on this occasion he immediately dispatched two local detectives to investigate the claim. Either there was something convincing about this particular tale, or perhaps Butler had become so desperate he was ready to follow up any lead. However, despite the fact that White was going by the name of Bob Lane and living at Littlestone, the Kent policemen reported they were unable to locate him.

On 12 April the St Albans informant made contact again, and supplied Bob Lane's address. He had been invited for a drink at Lane's flat and had noticed that all the furnishings were brand new. He also provided the registration number of Lane's car and a Land Rover.

A week later Tommy Butler received a telephone call from a *Sunday Mirror* journalist called Victor Sims. Sims explained that, at the request of the London correspondent for *Stern* magazine, Peter Wickham, he had met two men in a car in Cockfosters on Sunday, 17 April. He believed one of the men was fugitive Jimmy White and that he wanted to sell the manuscript of his life story to the German magazine.

When the document came into police possession some time later, it was clear that it was indeed an authentic, and in many ways remarkable, account by Jimmy White of his life, his involvement in the mail-train robbery and his subsequent years on the run. It was also clear that the lengthy document had been written by a professional, most likely Peter Wickham.

It is not clear why Wickham involved Sims in the charade at Cockfosters, other than perhaps to authenticate White's consent and authorship. The account subsequently appeared in *Stern* magazine, who hold the copyright on Jimmy White's story.

Kent police called Butler on 18 April to say they had received information that White was living in Littlestone under the name of Bob Lane.

Despite information concerning White's whereabouts coming from two independent sources it was not until nearly three weeks later at 12.20 on Thursday, 21 April that Flying Squad officers Slipper and Hyams arrived at Claverley, a large Victorian building on Grand Parade, overlooking the beach at Littlestone. The detectives went to flat 4 on the ground floor and Slipper knocked on the door.

37

W hen Jimmy White answered the door, Detective Sergeant Jack Slipper said, 'You are James Edward White.'

'Yes, that's right,' White replied. 'I am glad it's all over. How did you get on to me?'

Jimmy White and his family had been on the run for two and a half years. He had spent most of his share of the mail-train robbery and with dwindling resources and options his arrest came as a relief in many ways.

After being searched by Slipper, White was taken to a police car outside. On the way up to London he said, 'I might as well tell you, I've got some money in my dressing gown in the bedroom.' After a long pause, he added, 'And there is some more money under the drawer in my garage. I am telling you this because I think the world of my wife and boy and will do anything to save them any harm.'

Police officers later found two bundles of notes in White's dressing gown; each amounted to £1,000. In the garage was another bundle, this time amounting to £250.

White was taken to Hammersmith police station and interviewed by Tommy Butler. Allegedly he admitted that he was 'on the job, in the mail-train coach as the money was taken and at the farm afterwards'. When Butler told him he was going to be driven to Aylesbury and charged, White said nothing and shrugged his shoulders. James Edward White was formally charged at 17.15.

Inevitably there are other versions about the information that led to White being located in Littlestone. One was that a member of Dover lifeboat crew, where White was working as a volunteer, gave the police the tip-off having seen photographs of the men still wanted for questioning in a newspaper. Another was that a local landlord in Littlestone was asked to get White's fingerprints on a glass to confirm his identity.

Jimmy White had a total of £2,250 in his possession when he was arrested. While being held at Hammersmith police station, he told

Butler there was another £4,800 hidden behind the panelling of his caravan which the police had not found. White appeared before Linslade
magistrates on 22 April and was remanded in custody until committal
proceedings on 6 May.

After a four-day hearing at the lower court, White's assize trial
opened on 16 June. It was a brief and perfunctory affair. The resourceful ex-paratrooper had initially pleaded not guilty to both the charges
of conspiracy and robbery, hoping that he might get away with being
found guilty of receiving. But when he was made aware of the prosecution case against him he changed his mind and pleaded guilty to
robbery and not guilty to conspiracy. With the pleas accepted by the
prosecution and a swift verdict by the jury, it only remained for Justice
Nield to pronounce sentence. This time there were no lofty speeches
about the crime 'striking at the heart of the nation'; Nield gave White
eighteen years, just over half the terms given to many of the gang.

Three thousand miles away in Mexico City, Reynolds and Edwards
read of Jimmy White's arrest and trial in a British newspaper. Edwards
was encouraged by the reduced sentence, and with growing pressure
from his wife June to leave Mexico and go home, his thoughts returned
to the idea of giving himself up.

On 30 July 1966 something truly remarkable happened. As with 'The
Great Train Robbery', it was a defining moment of the decade and BBC
sports commentator Kenneth Wolstenholme's words in the closing seconds of extra-time have become immortalised: 'And here comes Hurst.
He's got... some people are on the pitch, they think it's all over. It is
now!' Watched by a TV audience of thirty-two million, Geoff Hurst
scored three goals and Martin Peters kicked one. England had beaten
Germany 4–2 at Wembley to win the World Cup.

By the summer, Edwards had resigned himself to returning to
England and taking his chances with the British legal system. Through
an intermediary, he contacted Detective Inspector Frank Williams,
who was by then Butler's deputy at the Flying Squad, and arranged the
time and the place.

Despite Butler's usual scepticism that it was all a hoax, in the early
hours of 19 September Frank Williams arrived at the appointed rendezvous near Elephant and Castle, London, to find Edwards waiting for
him with a written statement.

'I came here tonight to give myself up,' Edwards said. 'I am doing it for a number of reasons. I was never on that train, and it's about time the truth was told. I have read that man Peter Fordham's book, it is full of childish lies.'

Edwards was cautioned and told that a warrant had been issued for his arrest. He handed Williams a piece of paper that seemed to have been torn from a school exercise book, saying, 'I have written something here which I would like to give you. It is the truth, I didn't get to the farm until after the robbery.'

Williams read the statement:

For a long time now I've been going to give myself up.

I was definitely going to come in, in a few weeks time but now I'm glad that I've made it now.

I didn't do the train robbery like people say I did.

That's why I'm writing this because I want a fair deal.

I didn't go up the farm until after the robbery had happened.

My job was to clean it down and burn the rubbish.

I did do a bit of this and you can call it panic if you like, but something happened at the farm and I got the wind up. This was because the job was so big that I could hardly believe it.

Some money was left in the kitchen for me and I was to get more afterwards.

I never did get it.

Although people think I had a lot more, the truth is I didn't get very much.

I have nothing left now that's one of the reasons I've given myself up.

At Williams' request, Edwards signed the statement R.C. Edwards.

As with all the other convicted men, there was no direct evidence to connect Buster Edwards to the crime scene. But his prints had been found at Leatherslade Farm on one of the Land Rovers and on a bank wrapper that came from the HVP coach. In addition there were several other pieces of minor circumstantial evidence against him: groups of men had been seen coming and going from his Twickenham flat in Margaret's Road, and a Land Rover had been parked outside his home shortly before the robbery.

Edwards was taken from Elephant and Castle to Scotland Yard. At about 02.15 Tommy Butler saw him in the presence of Frank Williams. Butler read out the warrant and cautioned Edwards again, then ran through a pre-prepared questionnaire. During questioning, Edwards carefully thought about each question and in many cases re-read it before offering his answer.

After initialling each answer and signing the completed document, Buster Edwards was detained at Cannon Row police station. Later the same day he was taken to Aylesbury, where he was formally charged. He made no reply.

The trial of Ronald Christopher Edwards took place at Nottinghamshire Assize on 8 and 9 December with Mr Justice Milmo presiding. Edwards' defence counsel, Bernard Caulfield QC, argued that his client was not a master criminal and that his role was simply peripheral. Jack Mills appeared for the prosecution; he appeared pale and unwell as he explained that, up until the robbery, he had always enjoyed good health, 'But since then I have felt pretty awful.' Mills' right hand trembled constantly as he stood in the witness box giving his account of the raid. He went on to tell the court that he had been unable to return to his job and had been restricted to light duties and shunting work at his local Crewe depot on and off for the last year and a half.

After a short retirement, the jury found Edwards guilty of both conspiracy to rob and robbery. Before passing sentence, Justice Milmo said,

You have been convicted on overwhelming evidence of a crime which shocked every person in this country ... You played for high stakes and punishment must, in the public interest, be severe. I deal with you on the footing that you were in on this at a very early stage indeed, but nevertheless that you were not one of the leading planners, or a leader in the matter at all. I deal with it on the footing that you were in the hierarchy, if that is the proper word to use, somewhere below White.

The sentence was shorter than Jimmy White's: twelve years for conspiracy and fifteen for robbery to run concurrently. Nevertheless it was a lot more than Edwards had been hoping for and perhaps been led to believe. The eleventh member of the mail-train gang was led back down to the cells facing the prospect of a very long and arduous incarceration.

*

Six months earlier, Charlie Wilson had been joined in Canada by his wife Pat and two daughters, Cheryl and Tracy. They were living a respectable middle-class life in Hudson Heights, about forty miles west of Montreal, under the name of Alloway.

The Reynolds family had decided to move from Mexico. Bruce had made various attempts to become a legitimate businessman, including investment in a Dunhill concession, with little success. And there was no realistic opportunity of going back to thieving without contacts and a knowledge of the way things worked. The highlife in Mexico City was surprisingly expensive and without creating any significant income from his remaining money he was constantly draining his resources. The family crossed into the United States in their Cadillac and drove north.

Piers Paul Read's account has the Reynoldses driving up the Pan-American Highway, but that would have taken them through Las Vegas, Salt Lake City, Calgary and ultimately to Alaska, not to Toronto where the Reynolds family ended up. Perhaps they went a very long way round, but it would have made more sense for them to follow the chain of interstates via Washington and New York, which apparently they visited. Even that route is a drive of over 3,000 miles.

While Franny stayed in Toronto, Bruce went to visit Wilson. The Reynoldses then headed to Vancouver and attempted to gain official residence using false passports. Faced with long delays, ever-shrinking funds and the growing anxiety that the authorities might be on to him, Reynolds decided to return to Europe.

1967

At the start of 1967 the family flew to the South of France.

British culture was a world export and domestic developments reflected a confident, optimistic future and the changing times. The first gas from the North Sea arrived onshore on 4 March. On 8 April Sandy Shaw won the Eurovision song contest with 'Puppet on a String'. On 11 May Britain applied for membership of the European Economic Community. An armada of small boats greeted Sir Francis Chichester on *Gipsy Moth IV* arriving back in Plymouth Sound on 29 May, having completed the first single-handed sailing voyage around the world with just one stop in Sydney Australia in nine months and one day.

In April 1967 Brian Arthur Field, who had been sent to prison for obstructing the course of justice, was released after serving four years of his five-year sentence. Despite being the instigator of the crime and instrumental in its execution, the solicitor's clerk walked away, changed his name to Brian Carlton and disappeared.

On 1 June The Beatles released their acclaimed LP, *Sgt Pepper's Lonely Hearts Club Band,* and at the end of the month Keith Richards of the Rolling Stones was sent to prison for possession of illegal drugs. Mick Jagger was also given three months for a similar offence.

In July the Wimbledon Lawn Tennis Championships were broadcast in colour by the BBC and a new Sex Offences Act decriminalised homosexuality in England and Wales.

On 27 July the new Criminal Justice Act was passed to amend the law relating to:

the proceedings of criminal courts, including the law relating to evidence, and to the qualification of jurors, in such proceedings and to appeals in criminal cases; to reform existing methods and provide new methods of dealing with offenders; to make further provision for the treatment of offenders, the management of prisons and other institutions and the arrest of offenders unlawfully at large; to make further provision with respect to legal aid and advice in criminal proceedings; to amend the law relating to firearms and ammunition; to alter the penalties which may be imposed for certain offences; and for connected purposes.

The act was to lead to the establishment of a Parole Board the following year. The new board would consider whether a prisoner should be eligible for release after serving one-third of their sentence. For convicted members of the mail-train gang who had received long sentences, the news offered a beacon of hope. Even those sent down for thirty years had the prospect of being released after serving ten, provided they had kept out of trouble.

On 20 September the Cunard passenger liner *QE2* was launched by Queen Elizabeth II who used a pair of gold scissors to cut the tape that her mother had used to launch the *Queen Elizabeth* and her grand-mother had first used launching the *Queen Mary*. And at the end of the year in a typical paradox of Anglo-French relations the first supersonic passenger aircraft Concorde was unveiled in Toulouse just a month after President Charles de Gaulle had vetoed British entry into the EEC.

1968 and Aftermath

At 08.00 on Thursday, 25 January 1968 Charlie Wilson was about to leave home to take his daughters to school when the doorbell rang. Now feeling settled and safe in his new life Wilson opened to the door to find Tommy Butler standing there with fifty officers of the Royal Canadian Mounted police behind him.

After extradition proceedings, Wilson was flown back to London handcuffed to Butler – one of the rare occasions the Grey Fox was seen smiling – before being taken under armed guard to HMP Parkhurst on the Isle of Wight. The nineteenth-century prison had a newly con-structed high-security wing known as 'The Cage'. Although Wilson was not to be reunited with his old comrades immediately, among other high-risk criminals the Cage held Gordon Goody, Roy James, Jim Hussey, Roger Cordrey and Tommy Wisbey.

Having postponed his retirement, Tommy Butler did not rest. Not only would his life be empty without police work but before claiming his pension he wanted to capture Reynolds and recapture Biggs.

The Yard had received a tip-off that Bruce Reynolds was in the South of France. The information was correct: the Reynolds family had rented a villa in St Maxime on their return from Canada. But despite Butler's extensive reconnaissance he could not find his man, even though Reynolds had been in touch with known contacts such as his old part-ner in crime Terry Hogan.

With his cash running out fast, Reynolds decided to move back to England in August 1968. To begin with the family stayed in their old house in Albert Mews. The sale of the property might have provided much-needed funds had it not been lost by the Captain in a card game. As a result, Reynolds was reduced to renting the property he had pur-chased with some of his mail-train loot five years earlier.

Finding himself back in his old hideout, eking out dwindling finances, the reality of his circumstances was inescapable. To add to the pressure, Reynolds was unable to find the criminal work he had been counting on. He had convinced himself that he enjoyed an unrivalled reputation as a master criminal and that he would have his pick of the best jobs around. However, none of the serious London players would work with Reynolds, especially when it was widely known that Tommy Butler was as determined as ever to catch him.

According to Reynolds' account, he tried to trace Brian Field in the hope he might put him in touch with the Ulsterman. There had been the promise of an even bigger job after the mail train. But Reynolds' efforts were in vain; he could find no trace of Field.

After two months scratching around in London the Reynoldses moved again. This time to a house at 14 Braddons Hill Road in Torquay, Devon, called Villa Cap Martin. Reynolds still continued to travel up to London looking for opportunities but the only offers came from the lower orders of the underworld.

At 06.00 on Friday, 8 November the doorbell rang. Reynolds was fast asleep in bed, but even in his dreams he must have known what it meant. When his son Nick saw Tommy Butler and his team on the doorstep he turned and ran upstairs and the Grey Fox followed him. Butler entered the bedroom and said, 'Hello, Bruce. It's been a long time.'

Reynolds' reply was '*C'est la vie*'. His time had come, but like White and Edwards it was a relief after the stressful years of life on the run. The longed-for El Dorado that he'd chased throughout his adult life had proved a catalogue of vain hope, misconception and disaster.

Following in the footsteps of the other robbers, Reynolds was taken to Aylesbury and charged with conspiracy to rob and robbery. Butler persuaded him to plead guilty on the understanding that no further charges would be brought against Franny, Terry Hogan or the many others who had, in one way or another, harboured and helped him.

Two months later, on 14 January 1969, the trial of Bruce Richard Reynolds was held in the old courthouse in Aylesbury's Market Square. The last time Reynolds had appeared in court had been in less auspicious circumstances: two months before the mail-train robbery, on 30 May 1963, Reynolds had received a fine from a court in Ongar for poaching.

On this occasion there was a great deal more at stake, but little to argue about. His fingerprints had been found at Leatherslade Farm on a bottle of tomato ketchup and the now famous Monopoly board game. Making no attempt to invent an elaborate story as to how they got there, Reynolds pleaded guilty to both charges. His defence pleaded that their client had expressed remorse for his crime and that he had handed back £5,500.

Reynolds had spent around £140,000 – about £2,000,000 in today's money – in five years. He had had his chance at the good life and quite literally blown it.

Before pronouncing sentence, Mr Justice Thompson said, 'It would be wrong for me to give any encouragement to the idea that successful avoidance of arrest for a period entitles a criminal to a reduction in sentence ... I shall make the same kind of reduction in sentence (for pleading guilty) as I believe would, in like circumstances, have been made by the judge at the main trial. I sentence you to twenty-five years imprisonment.'

Outside the court, the press crowded around Tommy Butler. 'Does this mean that this is the end as far as the train robbery is concerned?' a reporter asked.

'No,' said Butler, with a trace of a smile on his thin lips. 'Got to catch Biggs first.'

Ronnie Biggs' life on the run ballooned into a saga all of its own. His face is indelibly etched in the memories of millions of people worldwide. Having been a fugitive in Australia and Brazil for thirty-six years, he finally returned voluntarily to Britain in 2001 aboard a private jet hired by the *Sun* newspaper. He was seventy-two, in poor health and still had twenty-eight years of his original thirty-year sentence to serve.

Having been returned to prison and served a third of his sentence a Parole Board hearing on 23 July 2009 recommended that Biggs be released. On 4 July, Labour Home Secretary, Jack Straw, refused Biggs parole on the grounds he was 'wholly unrepentant'.

Having been admitted to Norfolk and Norwich University Hospital with pneumonia on 28 July, and after tireless petitioning by his Brazilian-born son Michael, Ronald Arthur Biggs was officially released from prison custody on 6 August on 'compassionate grounds' – two days before his eightieth birthday and forty-five years, three hundred and sixty-three days after 'The Great Train Robbery.'

38

Various loose ends were left unresolved in the long aftermath of the mail-train robbery. The identities of various gang members, including the Ulsterman and an alleged Post Office insider have never been revealed. Who were the men that got away? What happened to all the money?

In the British Postal Museum and Archive at Mount Pleasant, London, there is an extensive collection of documents concerning 'The Great Train Robbery'. The GPO Investigation Branch conducted an independent inquiry which ran parallel to that of the police. Whereas the Buckinghamshire CID and the Flying Squad concentrated their efforts on apprehending the criminals who ambushed the mail train, the Post Office investigation team also focused on the possibility that the bandits had help from inside their organisation. As Postmaster General Reginald Bevins had promised on the day of the raid, there was a full inquiry, and it continued for many years after the mail-train ambush.

Among the documents in the Post Office archive, some of which remain 'closed', there are a few in particular which offer insights and contain information that is not mentioned in the numerous accounts of 'The Great Train Robbery' or police documents held in the National Archive in Kew. The contents of one file contain two lists of possible suspects. The first is a confidential list of names drawn up by Tommy Butler on 16 August 1963. The second is a list compiled by Head of Scotland Yard, Commander George Hatherill on 27 August.

The origins of Butler's list began twenty-four hours after the robbery when various names were put forward by informants to John Cummings of C11. Along with other names Butler gathered from his own inform-ants, they were cross-checked against details of convicted offenders held by the Criminal Records Office and two unofficial indexes assem-bled by Scotland Yard. One index listed known nicknames of criminals; the other was referred to as 'the girlfriend index'. Using information from all these sources, just eight days after the robbery Tommy Butler assembled a list of eighteen names:

Gordon Goody
Charles Wilson
Bruce Reynolds
James White (aka Patten)
Robert Welch
Roy James
John Daly
Harry Pitts
Michael Kehoe
Terry Sansom
George Sansom
Frederick Robinson
Jack Cramer
Henry Smith (aka Wade)
Charles Lilley
Billy Ambrose
Kenneth Shakeshaft

On Thursday, 29 August 1963 there was a special conference for Great Train Robbery detectives held at Scotland Yard. Hatherill was in the chair; also present was his deputy Chief Superintendent Ernie Millen. Hatherill announced that on the previous Tuesday he had seen an informant who gave him a list of fourteen names. Hatherill said that he was satisfied that those named criminals were the 'certain offenders' who made up the mail-train gang. He had also been told that the money was divided into eighteen lots: as well as the gang who carried out the raid, there were shares for the Post Office insiders and for the man who had bought the farm. Hatherill revealed that his informant had told him Brian Field had made contact with one of the insiders from whom he obtained information about 'HVP mails' carried on the Up Special TPO. Field first put the plan to another gang who rejected it before putting it to Gordon Goody who agreed to take it on.

Millen's autobiography, published after his retirement from the force, gives further details of how Hatherill came by the suspect list and extraordinarily accurate information about the crime. Millen reveals that he was approached by a barrister acting for a client currently serving a prison sentence. Millen and Hatherill subsequently went to visit the man in a provincial prison (assumed to be Dartmoor) on 14 August.

In his 1971 autobiography, Hatherill doesn't elaborate on where he obtained his information but does say that his list was based on more than a single informant:

> ... I began to receive information from various sources which, when put together, gave a fairly comprehensive picture of the crime and those who had been involved. From what we knew already, it was quite clear that this information was substantially accurate ...

Hatherill's list is as follows:

Gordon Goody
Charles Wilson
Bruce Reynolds
James White
Roy James
John Daly
Ronald Edwards (Buster)
Thomas Wisbey
James Hussey
Roger Cordrey
Brian Field
Henry Smith
Dennis Pembroke
Fair-haired man, 25 years old – well spoken, not named
Nondescript man – not named but may be Jimmy Collins
Post Office Man 1
Post Office Man 2

Butler's and Hatherill's suspect lists are astonishing. With the exception of Biggs and the gang's train driver all the men arrested and successfully prosecuted for their part in the mail-train raid and who have subsequently admitted to being part of the gang, appear on these two lists.

It is possible that Michael Kehoe was the informant that John Cummings of C11 named as Mickie. But what of these other men:

Billy Ambrose
Jack Cramer
Charles Lilley
Dennis Pembroke
Harry Pitts
Frederick Robinson
Terry Sansom
George Sansom
Kenneth Shakeshaft
Henry Smith

Pembroke, sometimes also referred to as Daniel or Danny, was an associate of Robert Welch and is known to have been at a farm near Beaford, Devon with Welch when he was in hiding after the train robbery. Pembroke is listed in 'Group B' of a GPO Investigation Branch master list of suspects as 'strongly suspected'.

Another name on Butler's list, Charles Lilley, a printer born 11 January 1921, was also observed staying at the farm in Beaford. He too was a known associate of Welch. Lilley's file at the National Archives will remain closed until 2021.

In May 1964, the name Ronald Harvey was added to the combined list. Harvey is another of those known to have been at Beaford. Ronald Harvey's brother Martin was charged and convicted after being found in possession of £518 which he admitted had come from the mail-train robbery.

The men who were known to have been at Beaford with Welch were: Dennis Pembroke, Charles Lilley, Ronald Harvey and John Phillip Strum.

Terry and George Sansom were brothers who lived in Hove, near Brighton. Terry Sansom was acquitted of a £9,400 payroll robbery in the early 1960s. He was also cleared of being part of a drug-smuggling conspiracy at Brighton Crown Court in the late 1980s. At the time he

Leatherslade Farm
(Mirror Pix)

Stores and some of the items left behind at Leatherslade Farm
(Buckinghamshire Police/National & Postal Archives)

Mail sacks found in the cellar by PC John Woolley
(Buckinghamshire Police/National & Postal Archives)

Robbers' vehicles being taken away from Leatherslade Farm by police
(Press Association)

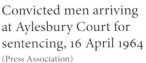

Convicted men arriving at Aylesbury Court for sentencing, 16 April 1964
(Press Association)

Mr Justice Edmund Davies
(Getty Images)

(Left to right) Pritchard, McArthur and Fewtrell arriving at Aylesbury Assizes
(Press Association)

Karin Field
(Daily Telegraph)

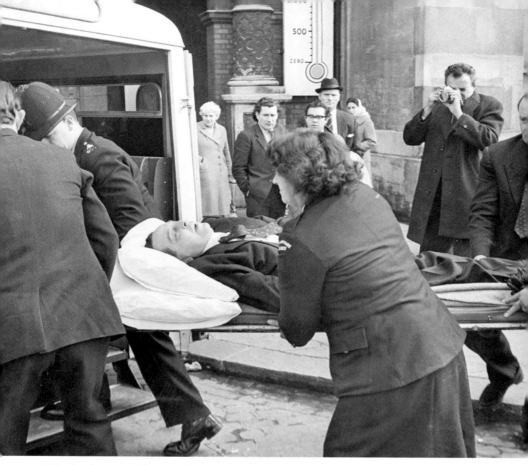

Alfred Pilgrim collapses after being discharged from Aylesbury Assizes, 16 April 1964

(Getty Images)

Mary Manson

(Daily Telegraph)

Jack Mills

(Press Association)

Mail-train gang arriving at the Court of Criminal Appeal, The Strand, London, July 1964

(Rex Pictures/Daily Mail)

Wandsworth Prison, Ronnie Biggs' escape, 8 July 1965

(Mirror Pix)

Charles Wilson handcuffed to Tommy Butler flying back to the UK after his arrest in Canada, 2 January 1968
(Getty Images)

Bruce Reynolds outside Linslade Court, Buckinghamshire, 18 November 1968
(Getty Images)

(Left to righ
Bruce Reynolds, Frances Reynold
Barbara Daly and John Da
(Press Associatio

Buster Edwards at his flower stall outside Waterloo Station in London, 1975
(Mirror Pix)

Charlie Wilson, 1979
(Press Association)

James White, 1978
(Press Association)

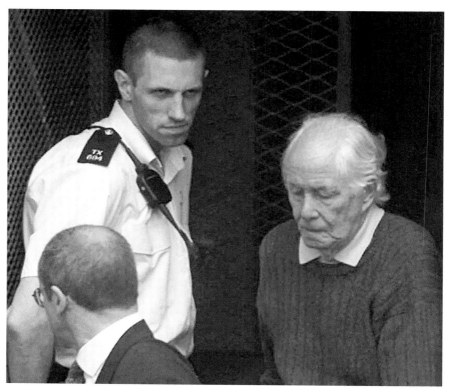

Ronnie Biggs after finally returning to the UK, 2001
(Press Association)

Bruce Reynolds, 2003
(Jiri Rezac/Eyevine)

lived at Court Farm, at the top of King George VI Avenue, also known locally as Snaky Hill, in Hove. George Sansom was the father of the England and Arsenal footballer Kenny Sansom.

The only man who appears on both Hatherill's and Butler's lists is Henry Smith. Henry Thomas Smith, born 20 October 1930, was 6'1½" inches tall and lived at 22 Provost Dwellings, Provost Street, London, N1. He had two distinguishing tattoos on his arms – a bird scroll and the word 'Mother'. Henry Smith and Walter Smith are named in another GPO Intelligence Branch list of persistent offenders. Walter Smith and his wife Patricia were charged in connection with receiving money from the mail-train raid. When questioned, Walter admitted he had been purchasing £5 postal orders in order to launder the money. Walter Smith was later convicted of receiving £2,000. It is not known exactly how Henry and Walter Smith are connected. It seems likely they were related and could be brothers. Their homes in Shoreditch were one hundred yards from each other. Henry Smith's file in the archive is to remain closed for seventy-one years and will not be available until 2036.

Are three of these other men on Butler's and Hatherill's roll-call of suspects the mysterious Messrs One, Two and Three? The accuracy of the lists is self-evident: all the gang members who were caught and convicted are named. It is reasonable to assume that the three men never charged with conspiracy and robbing the mail train are on those lists too.

Given the extensive police investigation, why were three of the gang never prosecuted? Was there a deal done with Detective Superintendent Frank Williams behind the scenes, as Freddie Foreman later claimed? Williams said in his autobiography that these men were not phantoms but known to the police and questioned but could not be charged because of lack of evidence. The robbers who were sent to prison claimed that the evidence used to convict them was fabricated or manipulated. If this was true, why did the police not 'fit-up' the three that got away?

Another unanswered question concerns the identity of the gang's alleged Post Office insider. The man nicknamed 'The Ulsterman' because of a tailor's label in his jacket, who was introduced to Goody and Edwards by Brian Field, claimed that his information came from his brother (according to some sources, his brother-in-law or stepbrother). Theories about the identity of 'The Ulsterman' continue to the present day. In a Channel 4 programme broadcast on 9 January 2012, author Andrew Cook promised to reveal 'The Great Train Robbery's Missing Mastermind'. Allegedly, Channel 4 lawyers became nervous at the eleventh hour, which could explain why the programme did not name anyone who had not been implicated before and left the 'missing mastermind' unidentified.

According to the information received by Hatherill in August 1963, inside knowledge had been given to the gang by an Irishman. This may refer to the Ulsterman or his brother who he said worked on the railways. The GPO Investigation Branch developed this line of inquiry and established there were sixteen officers on the Up Special TPO who could be regarded as Irish. Of these, only ten have one or more brothers. Three officers who were working on the mail train on the night 7/8 August 1963 had criminal records, but the police could find no evidence to connect any of these men to known members of the gang.

A possible lead to the identity of the inside man came from a telephone call to Helston Police in June 1965. The caller was a Miss Mallahian, a WRN serving in the Royal Navy. She reported that a family named Reilly living at Townview, Rathdrum, County Wicklow in Ireland had been involved with the train robbers. She also mentioned a man named John Reilly.

The GPO Investigation Branch, following up this lead, discovered that a man named James Patrick O'Reilly, who was one of the Post Office employees working on the TPO on the night of the robbery, had family connections in Rathdrum. His father was called John. O'Reilly was unmarried and drove a Vauxhall Victor index number THM462 and lived alone at 87 Napier Road, Tottenham, London, N17. At the time of the robbery O'Reilly had a girlfriend who worked in Lloyds Bank.

James O'Reilly was placed under observation for several months and the matter was raised with the Irish police, but investigators were unable to find any evidence of his involvement. Although O'Reilly was observed as living modestly, he and his brother, who went by the name of Thomas Edward Reilly, were later in negotiations to buy a substantial three-storey Victorian house at 205 Church Street, Edmonton, London, N9. Were the O'Reilly brothers the mystery informants behind the mail-train robbery? Part of James Patrick O'Reilly's file at the British Postal Archive is to remain closed until 1 January 2030.

Another TPO officer who came under suspicion was Englishman Frank Stockwell, who had joined the train at Crewe. By that stage there were ninety-one white mailbags containing 531 HVP packages on board, so he would have got a good idea of the amount being transported that night. Immediately after the raid, Stockwell volunteered to join colleague Leonard Lotts in summoning help.

Stockwell resigned from the GPO on 6 June 1966 and was reported to have opened a greengrocer's at 71 Richmond Street, Brighton. Some time later he gave up the shop and moved to a caravan at Wyneham, Henfield, Sussex. He was later traced to 'an isolated dwelling' known as The Cottage, Cowfold, Horsham, Sussex. The Post Office Investigation Branch was unable to establish the source of Stockwell's livelihood, but he was alleged to have said that he had won a lot of money and was emigrating to Australia. By 12 October 1967, Frank Stockwell's fortunes had changed dramatically and he was applying for 'public assistance'. Post Office investigators lost interest in Stockwell as he displayed no further 'signs of affluence'. But in the context of those who were known to have had a share of the loot, it's worth bearing in mind that Daly was swindled out of the bulk of his share almost immediately and Jimmy White lived modestly for nearly three years while most of his money was extorted from him in return for shelter from the law. Showing no obvious signs of affluence was not necessarily proof of innocence.

Although the search for an 'inside man' by the Post Office Investigation Branch was extensive and exhaustive, their inquiries were confined to GPO employees with a working knowledge of TPOs. However, the idea that inside knowledge had come from a Post Office employee is built on shallow foundations. Gordon Goody and Buster Edwards were the only members of the gang to meet the Ulsterman, but it was never confirmed how he came by his information. It was said the Ulsterman's brother worked on the railways but it is equally possible that his information came from a different source, such as an employee of one of the banks who regularly dispatched banknotes via registered post to head offices in London. O'Reilly's girlfriend worked in Lloyds Bank. Whereas GPO employees might be aware of the volume of registered mail, a bank employee would have greater insight into the timing and amounts of money being sent to London. There is nothing in the archives to show that either the police or the GPO Investigation Branch followed that line of inquiry.

The third perennial question about the train robbery is what happened to all the money? Only £358,408 has ever been recovered from the haul of an estimated £2,595,997.10s.

In the appendix of *The Train Robbers*, Piers Paul Read sets out his theories based on the incorrect total amount of £2,631,684. The figure seems to originate from the charge sheets of Cordrey and Boal and has been replicated in various official documents and books ever since. Read suggested each of the seventeen main players – fifteen men on the track, plus Brian Field and the Ulsterman – received £150,000. That would give a total of £2,550,000. According to Read, the remaining £45,997 was distributed as follows:

> £20,000 was given to Biggs to pay Stan/Peter the train driver. [Allegedly, Biggs never did pay him.]
>
> £12,500 was paid to Leonard Field. [Although Field said that he was only offered £5,000 for his services. Moreover he was never found in possession any of the stolen money.]
>
> £2,000 to Roy James to buy vans in London after the original vehicles used for the robbery had been compromised and the search for a hideout became known. [That amount seems excessive for two second-hand vans at 1963 prices.]
>
> £8,000 was paid to a friend of Wilson's. [No explanation is given as to what this sum was for.]
>
> £38,500 was paid to two men called Mark and Joey Gray, who were employed to clean up the farm. [As discussed earlier, it is debatable there was ever a plan to clean up the farm, as its discovery was not originally anticipated.]
>
> £684 was left behind at the farm in Scottish and Irish banknotes.

These lesser amounts all conveniently add up to £81,684. But given the doubtful provenance of these claimed payments, it is unconvincing. The gang could have spent £81,684 on various smaller payments, overheads and helpers, but that is a huge amount, equivalent to about £1.2 million in today's money.

While Piers Paul Read suggests the main participants each got £150,000, Biggs claims in one his many 'autobiographies' that the figure was more like £145,000. George Hatherill's 1971 autobiography asserts that 'the whole lot was divided into eighteen shares, each of them totalling about 140,000'. That sum, like his remarkably accurate suspect list, was based on information he had received.

Perhaps the best way to estimate how much each main share amounted to is to add up what was spent by Roger Cordrey and what was recovered after his arrest in Bournemouth:

Rover 105R, registration number TLX279 – £380
Grey Austin A35 van registration number UEL937 – £210
Ford Anglia, registration number RHJ383 – £273.14s.
Sent to Cordrey's sister May Pilgrim via Renee Boal and later found in her possession – £860
Found in Renee Boal's possession – £325
Found in Mrs Clarke's garage in a bag in the Austin A35 van – £56,047
Found in Miss Saunders' garage in six suitcases in the Rover – £78,982
Found at the rented flat in Wimborne Rd – £5,910

TOTAL: £142,987.14s.

If each main share amounted to £143,000, that would allow for an additional equal share to have been paid to another unknown member of the gang.

£143,000 multiplied by eighteen gives a total of £2,574,000; plus £20,000 for the train driver; plus £684 in Scottish banknotes abandoned at the farm; plus £1,313.10s. for sundry expenses; adds up to the total amount stolen from the mail train of £2,595,997.10s.

What provides more solid ground for concern about the way all the stolen money was disposed of is the tens of thousands of pounds that was paid to solicitors and barristers in legal fees. While some of the defendants claimed legal aid, or 'poor person's relief' as it was then called, many did not. On page 281 of *The Train Robbers*, Read estimates the expenditure on legal fees as follows:

Jim Hussey   33,000
Tommy Wisbey   28,000
Gordon Goody   30,000

Bob Welch	30,000
Roy James	10,000
Brian Field	49,000 (legal and other expenses)
Total:	180,000

William Boal claimed he did not know the money he was handling was stolen, but it didn't save him from being sent to prison for fourteen years. How much greater a crime was it that the many learned counsel for the defence pocketed fees that in all likelihood came from the train robbery, given that none of their clients had that kind of money before 8 August 1963.

A number of lives were blighted by the robbery, but none more so than Jack Mills'. When Charmian Biggs had her story published in the *Sunday Mirror* in October 1969 and was allegedly paid £30,000, it prompted an article on Jack Mills in the *Daily Mail*. On 26 October 1969 a Jack Mills Appeal Fund was set up at the Nantwich Road Social Club. By 10 November 1969 the fund had reached £26,715.

At the time, Mills was retired and housebound, living in a house with an outside lavatory. His home was due to be demolished and Mills and his wife had been offered a new council house. It was hoped that the Appeal Fund would give them the opportunity to buy a bungalow with a view, so that Mills could spend his remaining days in comfort. But for Jack Mills the appeal money came too late. On 4 February 1970 he died from lymphatic leukaemia, with a further complication of bronchial pneumonia.

David Whitby, the fireman who had been in the locomotive with Mills, died of a heart attack on 6 January 1972. He was thirty-four.

On 8 May 1970, Tommy Butler died of cancer aged fifty-seven, just sixteen months after finally retiring. A memorial service was held at St Margaret's Westminster, attended by Butler's mother and hundreds of Scotland Yard colleagues, including many who had worked with him on the Great Train Robbery investigation.

Seven years into his fourteen-year sentence, Bill Boal was admitted to hospital on 29 May 1970 and diagnosed as suffering from a brain tumour. He died on 8 June. Many years later, and too late for Boal, Reynolds stated publicly that he had never met or heard of William

Boal and that he was never part of the mail-train gang.

Roger Cordrey, whose sentence had been reduced to fourteen years on appeal, was released in April 1971 after serving eight years.

Jimmy White and Buster Edwards were released from prison in April 1975. White went to live in Sussex; although he occasionally gave media interviews, he never courted public attention and was never connected with further crimes. Edwards was charged with shoplifting from Harrods in October 1975 and returned to prison for six months. After being released a second time Buster Edwards ran a flower stall outside Waterloo station. *Buster*, the feature film starring Phil Collins as Edwards, premiered in the UK in 1988. Six years later on 28 November 1994 Edwards, aged sixty-two, hanged himself and was discovered in his garage near Waterloo by his brother. Although the coroner recorded an open verdict due to the level of alcohol found in Edwards' system, two possibilities have been suggested as a reason for his suicide. First, that Edwards was implicated in a fraud investigation and he could not face the prospect of going back to prison. Second, a Sunday newspaper was about the print an exposé on his private life.

Of the men sentenced to thirty years, Roy James was released in August 1975. He returned to motor racing, and in 1976 suffered a broken leg while racing at Silverstone. In March 1994 James was sentenced to two years in prison for attacking his wife and shooting his father-in-law. While in prison he had a triple bypass operation and shortly after being released, on 20 August 1997, he died aged sixty-one following a heart attack.

Jim Hussey was released in November 1975, and Gordon Goody's prison term ended in December. Goody went back to live with his elderly mother in Putney for a while; after she died he moved to Mojácar in southern Spain, where he ran a bar.

Tommy Wisbey was released in February 1976 and Bobby Welch in June.

Hussey and Wisbey were convicted of cocaine trafficking on 26 July 1989 and sentenced to seven and twelve years respectively.

When James Hussey died on 16 November 2012 the report in the *Sun* newspaper about his deathbed confession was followed by a *Daily Mail* article the next day. The headline more or less told the whole story: '*Great Train Robber finally admits to coshing engine driver in deathbed confession that solves 49-year-old mystery of who was behind attack during notorious 1963 raid.'*

It invites a question. Was the confession genuine or did 'Big Jim' Hussey see it as an opportunity to generate some final cash for his surviving family? In the *Sun* article Jack's son John Mills aged seventy-one, said, 'My dad told me who he thought did it – and it wasn't James Hussey. I won't divulge who he said. I wasn't there so I guess we will never know for sure.'

The last two convicted members of the mail-train gang came out of prison in 1978: Bruce Reynolds on 6 June and Charlie Wilson on 18 December. On 24 April 1990 Wilson was shot dead by a professional hit man next to the swimming pool at his villa in Marbella. His body was flown home to England and buried on 10 May.

At the time of writing, eighty-one-year-old Bruce Reynolds is living alone in Croydon, having lost his wife Franny in 2011. He has built a reputation as the leader of 'The Great Train Robbery' gang and perhaps in some ways this has fulfilled his boyhood dream to be someone. It remains debatable, however, whether Reynolds' role was any more significant than that of other participants. In a rare interview for the ITV's *Real Crime* series broadcast on 13 June 2001, Gordon Goody said of Reynolds:

> ... you hear all these stories about Mr Big, and this one was the leader and all that, you know, there are no leaders in The Great Train Robbery, this was a group of determined criminals ... he played as much a part as I played, or Tommy played, or anything else ...

Solicitor's clerk Brian Field, who had been adopted as a child and whose ambitions had led him to instigate the most famous robbery of the twentieth century, met his end at the age of forty-four in a head-on collision while driving his Porsche in May 1979. He had changed his name to Brian Carlton. His third wife, Sian, died in the car with him.

Although not the most talked about or notorious names connected to the mail-train robbery, Brian Field and Gordon Goody were the principal initiators and architects of the whole enterprise. It was Goody, accompanied by Edwards, who met the contact put forward by Field to gather the crucial information on which the robbery was conceived and planned. It was Goody who received the call from the Ulsterman that the raid was to be postponed by twenty-four hours. On the night of the robbery, Goody led the attack on the cab. When the gang's train driver failed to get the train moving, Goody salvaged the situation by having Mills move the train to Bridego Bridge. He was almost certainly in charge of the attack on the HVP.

After the decision was made that the gang needed to abandon Leatherslade Farm sooner than planned, Goody orchestrated the 'evacuation' to Brian Field's house.

When it came to the capture and prosecution of Goody, the police went to great lengths to construct and cement the case against him. They were cautious that Goody would be resourceful in his attempts to refute or undermine any evidence presented. Dr Holden's forensic evidence ensured there could be no tampering with exhibits or manipulation of witnesses. However, the 'million to one chance' of a match between two paint samples allegedly found smeared on the instep of Goody's suede shoes was challenged in court by expert witnesses and cannot be said to have been proven beyond reasonable doubt.

Goody's greatest public accolade came from the perceptive Mr Justice Edmund Davies who said when sentencing him, 'You have manifest gifts of personality and intelligence which could have carried you far had they been directed honestly.'

In June 1967, Gordon Goody sued the *People* newspaper for libel after an article referred to him as one of the mail-train robbers. Although Goody was three years into his thirty-year prison sentence at the time, in British law, conviction is not proof of guilt.

While in prison Goody maintained his association with his defence barrister Wilfred Fordham, who made repeated representations to the Home Office on his behalf. Peta Fordham continued to correspond with Goody for many years and visited him regularly. A model prisoner, he took Spanish lessons and learned Italianate calligraphy, which he used in some of his correspondence, now stored in the National Archive.

Some time after Gordon Goody was finally released on 23 December 1975, having served ten and a half years, he moved to Mojácar in southern Spain and opened a bar called Chiringhuito Kon Tiki on the Paseo del Mediterraneo. Although he later publicly admitted he was one of the mail-train gang, while others bragged about their role and sought money or notoriety Goody lived quietly; he seldom gave interviews, never sold his story to a newspaper or wrote a biography. While the rest of the gang spent or lost their money, Goody's was reputedly 'well looked after'. Of all the men who took part in the mail-train robbery, he is the only known member of the gang who appears to have enjoyed any long-term benefit from his involvement.

The English Electric Class 40 locomotive that Mills was driving on the night of the robbery was involved in a series of accidents and mishaps during its twenty-two-year service. On Boxing Day 1962 it was hauling the 'Midday Scot' when, due to driver error, it collided with the rear of the 16.45 Liverpool to Birmingham express between Winsford station and Coppenhall Junction, Cheshire, killing eighteen passengers and seriously injuring thirty-three. On 8 August 1963 it became embroiled in 'The Great Train Robbery.' In 1964 a fireman was killed after climbing on top of the nose of the engine to clean the front windscreens when he made contact with the overhead wires and was electrocuted. In 1965 the engine suffered a total brake failure on the approach to Birmingham New Street; luckily, quick-thinking signalling staff diverted the train to another platform at the last minute. Although it smashed into the back of a freight train, only the guard was injured.

A last photograph of the English Electric Class 40 locomotive D326 that Mills had been driving on the night of the robbery was taken in April 1984. Severe scrapes are visible down the side of its body panelling. To avoid souvenir hunters cashing in, three months after being withdrawn from service D326 was dismantled and cut up for scrap.

On 7 May 2001, Biggs arrived back in the UK and was returned to prison to serve the remainder of his sentence. Due to ill-health, he was released on compassionate grounds on 7 August 2009, aged seventy-nine, following the campaign by his Brazilian son Michael. After suffering several strokes Biggs is unable to speak and wheelchair bound. At the time of writing he is living at the Carlton Court Nursing Home in Barnet, north London. His last brush with the law was in December

2010, when Biggs reported that £100 had disappeared from the savings box he keeps close to his bed.

Jack Slipper died at the age of eighty-one on 24 August 2005. Malcolm Fewtrell died three months later, aged ninety-six.

The fiftieth anniversary of the Buckinghamshire mail-train ambush on Thursday 8 August 2013 will fall on the same day of the week as the 1963 robbery.

To understand fully the long saga of 'The Great Train Robbery', Britain in the early 1960s must be placed as a backdrop to all the events that took place. The criminals, investigation teams, lawyers and politicians were men and women of their time and that is the inescapable launching point of the story.

Whatever the shortcomings of British Railways, the Post Office, the police investigation, the legal system and the hundreds of men and women involved in bringing the criminals to justice, they believed they were acting in the interests of society. Despite the myths and the folklore, the criminals never did fit the image of the working-class hero, so potent in those restless years of social change. Exaltation of their crime was misplaced; regardless whether their actions were seen as daring and clever, or foolish and callous, the mail-train robbers were only ever out for themselves.

Was 'The Great Train Robbery' great? There was a great deal of money stolen. There were a great many people involved and it took a great deal of police effort to bring the criminals to justice and public money to pay for the trial and the time the robbers spent in prison. After the longest criminal trial in British history the convicted men were sentenced to a great many years – 307 in total.

For the criminals, great plans were made and great dreams were lost. The press got a great deal of copy out of it and the public followed the story day by day with great interest and sometimes amusement. There were a great number of mistakes made by the criminals, but also by British Railways, the GPO, the banks, the police and the legal system. Over the last fifty years a great many lies and half-truths have been told, and there has been a great deal of manoeuvring and covering up. The robbery offers a great lesson in human nature. It also provides an illustration of how, when the great and noble ideas and principles on which a civilised society is run are put to the test, they can be greatly compromised or even subverted. In that sense, the mail-train robbery could be considered great in many ways.

Folklore is a continually shifting story that evolves through constant retelling. Written narratives have a way of evolving too, when they are told and retold over many years. Each version adds something new to what has already been said. The real story of 'the perfect crime', 'the crime of the century' is a tapestry of ambition, complacency, naivety, vanity, avarice, incompetence, good fortune, bad judgement and of half-remembered events. It contains inadvertent as well as intentional misrepresentations born out of ego, self-preservation and self-interest. In the life stories and legacies of the many people whose fates converged in the train robbery of 8 August 1963 there are no winners, no heroes and only one completely innocent victim: train driver Jack Mills. The truth has always been too fragmented to ever completely reassemble. And in any case, real-life stories are never made of a single truth or perspective but many divergent viewpoints.

The unrecovered money has all been spent and most of the lives of the participants – the robbers, the robbed, police, victims, legal teams, journalists and many others – have run their course. Some of the participants have found a small place in history. They will be remembered. And in the end, isn't that what every human being most desires?

I hope Jack Mills would forgive me if I give the last word to a great British film. It is not a direct comment on the violent criminal deeds carried out at Sears Crossing in August 1963, more a wider observation about two things that are central to 'The Great Train Robbery'. First, how large institutions mitigate their losses and how it is always the small man who pays for it. And second, it astutely illustrates the mindset of the criminal in trying to pass off their wrongdoing as something admirable or even noble.

One truth is certain. We all – by which I mean the British public – paid for 'The Great Train Robbery' in monetary terms. We each inadvertently bought a tiny slice of it, and that was the cost of the diversion it brought to our otherwise ordinary lives.

The Ladykillers is a 1955 British black comedy made by Ealing Studios, directed by Alexander Mackendrick starring Alec Guinness, Cecil Parker, Herbert Lom, Peter Sellers and Katie Johnson. An American, William Rose, wrote the screenplay. He claimed to have dreamt the entire film and merely had to remember the details and write them down when he woke up.

Katie Johnson (born 1878) plays Mrs Wilberforce and Alec Guinness a gentlemanly con-man and thief, Professor Marcus. Marcus and his associates pull off a meticulously planned and ingenious robbery, stealing sixty thousand pounds from a railway station. Towards the end of the film Marcus is rumbled by his elderly landlady, Mrs Wilberforce. Undeterred, he attempts to justify the crime to her (for reference, in pre-decimalised British currency a farthing was worth one tenth of 1p):

MARCUS: Mrs Wilberforce, I don't think you quite understand the intricacies of this particular situation. Let me try to explain, Mrs Wilberforce. You see in this case it would do no good to take the money back. Strange as it may seem to you, nobody wants the money back.

MRS WILBERFORCE: Don't expect me to believe that.

MARCUS: But it's true Mrs Wilberforce. You see, this particular shipment of money was insured, so now the insurance company simply pays to the factory sixty thousand pounds and then in order to recover its money it puts one farthing on all premiums, on all the policies for the next year. You see? So how much real harm has been done to anybody? One farthing's worth, Mrs Wilberforce, one farthing's worth. Now you hadn't thought about it like that, had you?

Daily Mail, Thursday, 5 February 1970

JUST AS LIFE WAS LOOKING ROSIER FOR DRIVER MILLS ...

By Rhona Churchill

'I prayed hard on the night Jack died that he would go,' Mrs Florence Mills told me yesterday at her son's home in Crewe.

'So did Pat my daughter-in-law. We had been spending every afternoon with him in hospital. We had been there for four weeks and we'd watched him deteriorate and could see how he was suffering.

'We just couldn't bear to see him suffering any more.

'He is better off out of his suffering. He never complained but on his last day alive, he said to me, "Flo, I don't think I can bear it any longer." They were almost his last words. His voice was only a whisper. I had to lean down over him to hear him.'

So ended the long, patient suffering of Driver Mills, who never recovered from being coshed by the Great Train Robbers six and a half years ago and who never lived to see the £5,000 bungalow or enjoy the income from the £34,387 fund to which the *Daily Mail* readers so generously contributed.

Mrs Mills said: 'He was so looking forward to moving into it at the end of this month.

'We had great plans. There was a sun lounge at the back and a small lawn and flower beds and we were going to buy Jack one of those swinging round chairs so that he could move it when he wanted a change of view and we planned to buy him a little wicker table.'

'There is a carpet on the sun lounge floor that looks just like growing grass and central heating and built in wardrobes. It's a beautiful bungalow. I told Jack all about it and he was ever so excited. It was just right for him and the garden was full of roses. Now he will never see it. Now there is no point in buying anything for it.'

Jack Mills' final illness started with 'flu on Christmas Eve. After watching football on television on the Saturday night after Christmas, Florence Mills undressed him, put on his pyjamas and dressing gown and said, as usual: 'We'll go to bed now, Jack.'

'Then I tried to lift him and found I couldn't,' she said. 'The use had gone right out of him. So we sat up all night together.

'Every now and then he would say, "Try and get me to bed, Flo."

'In the morning he said, "Don't let them take me to hospital, Flo. If I go I won't come out again. You'll manage me. You've got me better before." But this time I couldn't.

'When the doctors knew he was dying they asked if I'd like to take him home. If I could have taken him to the bungalow I'd have had him home there with a private nurse just to give him a bit of pleasure before he died, but it wasn't to be, was it?

'Now I've got to move in alone. I know it will be awful at first. But I must get used to being on my own and I've lots of friends and relations near me.'

Florence Mills asked me to thank the thousands of *Daily Mail* readers who sent money and letters to her after my article about her and Jack Mills last October.

'I have two sacks full of letters in the back parlour of our old home,' she said. 'Jack and I tried to read them all but we couldn't. We were so moved by them we'd start crying. But I'll always keep them. I couldn't destroy any of them. I'll take them with me to the bungalow and some day there I'll read them all.

'Please thank all your readers who were so kind to Jack and me and tell them I won't waste their money. I haven't the heart to. A lot of it came from old aged pensioners like Jack and me.

'In fact, it is still coming in. I had a letter today saying a cheque for £237 had just arrived from railway men in Australia.

'What a pity Jack never knew about it.

'The money will buy me comfort but I would much rather have Jack alive and well.'

APPENDIX – MAPS

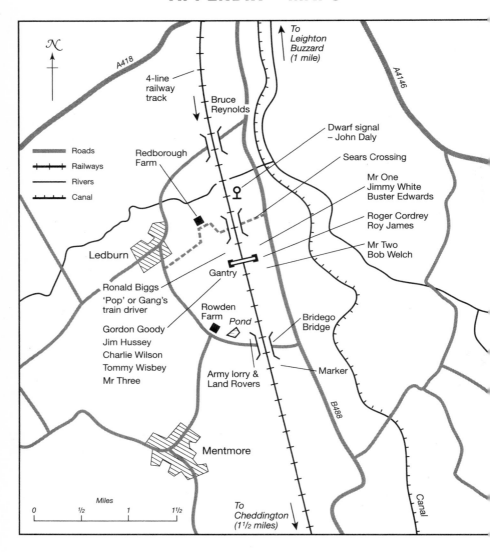

N

To Leighton Buzzard (1 mile)

A418

A4146

4-line railway track

Bruce Reynolds

Dwarf signal – John Daly

Sears Crossing

Redborough Farm

Mr One
Jimmy White
Buster Edwards

Roads
Railways
Rivers
Canal

Roger Cordrey
Roy James

Ledburn

Mr Two
Bob Welch

Gantry

Ronald Biggs
'Pop' or Gang's train driver

Rowden Farm

Pond

Bridego Bridge

Gordon Goody
Jim Hussey
Charlie Wilson
Tommy Wisbey
Mr Three

Marker

Army lorry & Land Rovers

B488

Mentmore

Miles

0   ½   1   1½

To Cheddington (1½ miles)

Canal

Crime scene

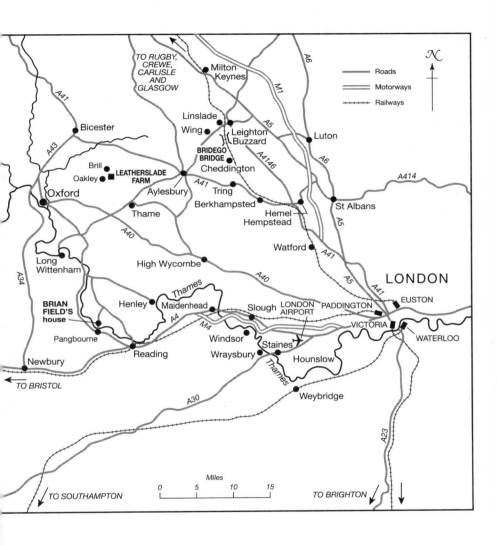

Thames Valley: key locations associated with the robbery

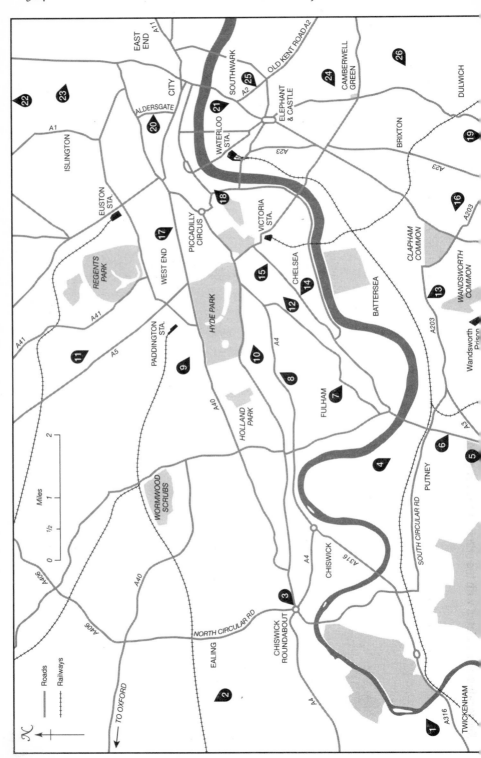

Key locations associated with the crime and investigations

1   Buster Edwards' flat at 214 St Margaret's Road, Twickenham

2   Terry Hogan's flat at 10 Walpole Lodge, Cumlington Road, Ealing, w13

3   Chequered Flat garage, Chiswick, where Reynolds purchased Austin Healey, registration number REN22, for £800

4   Gordon Goody's mother's house at 6 Commondale, Putney, sw15

5   Mary Kazih Manson, Wimbledon Close, The Downs, Wimbledon, sw19

6   Bruce Reynolds' home at Flat 1, 40 Putney Hill, sw15

7   William Gerard Boal, Burnthwaite Road, Fulham, sw6

8   Address given for Leonard Field by solicitor John Wheater: 150 Earl's Court Road, w8

9   Reynolds stayed at 'The Captain's' flat in Queensway, Bayswater, w2

10 Reynolds' final hideout in Albert Mews, Kensington, before departing to Mexico

11 Roy James' refuge in a mews house at 14 Ryder's Terrace, St John's Wood

12 Roy James' flat, 907 Nell Gwynne House, Sloane Avenue, sw3

13 Reynolds' grandmother's flat at 38 Buckmaster Road, Battersea, sw11

14 Jimmy White purchased an Austin Healey, registration number REN22, for £900 from Allery & Bernard Ltd, 372-4 King's Road, Chelsea

15 65a Eaton Square, SW1, the flat where John Daly was in hiding when arrested

16 Charlie Wilson's home , 45 Crescent Lane, Clapham, sw11

17 Eastcastle Street, w1, where Billy Hill planned 1952 robbery

18 Scotland Yard

19 Reynolds and his wife Franny moved to a one-bedroom flat above a dry cleaning shop at 71 Handcroft Road, Croydon

20 Jimmy White's Café, Aldgate, ec1

21 Thomas Wisbey's betting shop, 1 Red Cross Way, ec1

22 Leonard Denis Field of Green Lanes, Haringey, n8

23 Robert Welch's home, 30 Benyon Road, n1

24 Wisbey's home, Ayton House, Camberwell, se5

25 Fifty thousand pounds of the money stolen from the mail train was left in a telephone box at the junction of Black Horse Court and Great Dover Street, Camberwell, se1

26 James Hussey's home, Eridge House, Dog Kennel Hill, East Dulwich, se22

Crime scene showing layout and distance between signals

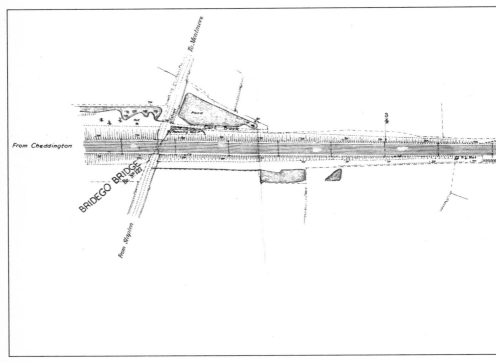

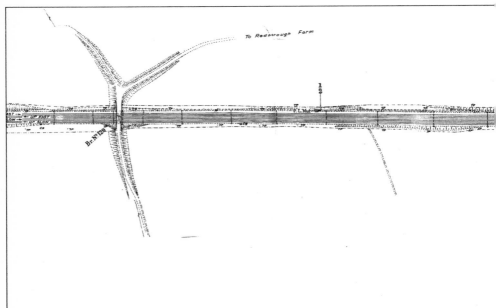

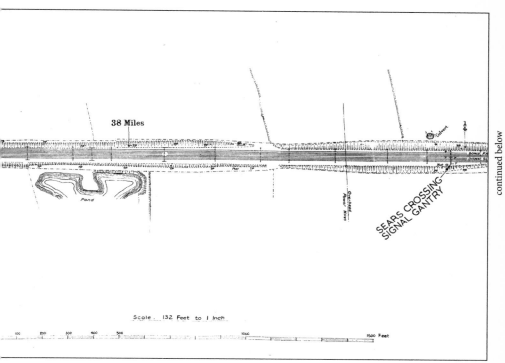

38 Miles

SEARS CROSSING
SIGNAL GANTRY

Pond

continued below

Scale . 132 Feet to 1 Inch

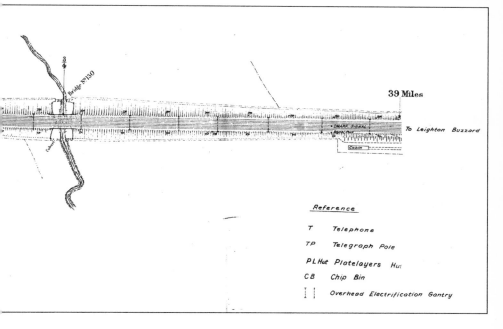

Bridge Nº 130

39 Miles

To Leighton Buzzard

Cabin

Reference

T   Telephone

TP   Telegraph Pole

PL Hut   Platelayers Hut

CB   Chip Bin

| | Overhead Electrification Gantry

APPENDIX – THE ROBBERS

Total Gang: 21
Trackside: 16
Non-trackside 5
(Unnamed Gang: 5)

The Gang (Trackside)
Ronnie Biggs
John 'Paddy' Daly
Ronald 'Buster' Edwards
Gordon Goody
Jimmy Hussey
Roy James
Bruce Reynolds
Jimmy White
Charlie Wilson
The Train Driver
Mr One
Mr Two

South Coast Raiders
Roger Cordrey
Bob Welch
Tommy Wisbey
Mr Three

Other Gang Members
Brian Field
Leonard Field
John Wheater
The Ulsterman
Informant

Also implicated and convicted but not a participant in the
conspiracy or robbery: William Boal.

Ronald Arthur Biggs

Age: 34
Born: 8 August 1929
Occupation: Carpenter and builder

Born in Lambeth, London. His mother died when he was fourteen and shortly afterwards he embarked on a career as a small-time petty criminal, making his first appearance in court at the age of fifteen. He joined the R AF in 1947 and was dishonourably discharged two years later after receiving a six-month prison sentence for robbery. Over the next ten years he was in and out of prison for a variety of offences and it was during one of these spells that he met Bruce Reynolds.

In 1960 he married Charmian Powell, the daughter of a headmaster, and they had three sons. By 1963, he had virtually retired from his life of crime, having established a small building firm in Redhill with his business partner Raymond Stripp. However, it was in the early summer of 1963 that he made contact with his old friend Bruce Reynolds and asked if he might borrow £500.

Biggs' escape from Wandsworth prison on 8 July 1965 and the story of his life as a fugitive for 45 years and 363 days before returning to the UK in 2001 has become a media saga in its own right. In many ways, although Biggs played a minor role in the robbery, he has been a key factor in continued media attention and reference to 'The Great Train Robbery' over the last fifty years.

Train Robbery:

Arrested: 4 September 1963
Sentenced: 30 years
Escaped: 8 July 1965 – HMP Wandsworth
Re-arrested: 7 May 2001
Released: 7 August 2009

Previous Convictions:

9 February 1945
Lambeth Juvenile Court – Stealing lead pencils from a shop – DISMISSED.

8 June 1945
Lambeth Juvenile Court – Stealing radio parts from church store – BOUND OVER 12 months & 10 shillings surety.

16 November 1945
Lambeth Juvenile Court – Stealing a watch – BOUND OVER 12 months & £1 surety.

17 February 1949
County of London Sessions – Shop-breaking & larceny; housebreaking & larceny; False representation of national registration card – IMPRISONED 6 months.

28 July 1949
North London Magistrates' Court – Taking & driving away motor car. Use of motorcar. No certificate of insurance. Misuse of motor fuel – IMPRISONED 2 months. Fined 40 shillings. Disqualified driving 12 months.

30 November 1949
Essex Quarter Sessions – Shop-breaking & larceny – BORSTAL TRAINING. Escaped Borstal institution 4 February 1950 and recaptured.

28 March 1950
Central Criminal Court – Robbery (six other cases taken into account) – IMPRISONED 3 years.

24 March 1953
County of London Sessions – Garage-breaking & stealing motorcar. Value £1,000 (one other case taken into account) – IMPRISONED 3 years.

30 March 1953
Buckinghamshire Quarter Sessions – Burglary & stealing property value 18 shillings. House-breaking & stealing property value of £5, £164.15s., £22.12s. respectively (three cases and three further cases taken into account) – IMPRISONED 4 years, concurrent with sentence 24 March 1953.

15 June 1956
Surrey Appeals Committee – Stealing paint from a building site.
Stealing a pedal cycle. – PROBATION 2 years.

2 April 1958
Dorset Quarter Sessions – Taking a motor vehicle without consent.
Receiving stolen toilet goods. Receiving stolen car rug – IMPRISONED
12 months.

25 April 1958
Surrey Appeals Committee – Stealing paint. Stealing cycle. (Original
offence 15 June 1956.) – IMPRISONED 18 months & 18 months.
Concurrent with sentence 2 April 1958.

John 'Paddy' Thomas Daly

Age: 32
Born: 6 June 1931
Occupation: Antique dealer

Born in New Ross, Republic of Ireland, John Daly was widely known
as 'Paddy'. A quiet man despite his imposing size – 5' 11" and weighing
in at 16–17 stone with a scar on the right side of his forehead – he had
the complete trust of Bruce Reynolds, who liked working with him as
he considered him to be lucky. He was also Reynolds' brother-in-law,
having married Barbara Allen, the sister of Reynolds' wife, Frances.
Daly was the only member of the gang to be acquitted during the trial,
which was ironic because he had considered pleading guilty. A close
friend of Mary Manson and her live-in partner J.S. MacDonald, who
was also Daly's employer at Mac's Antiques. When he went on the run
after the robbery, MacDonald took over his mortgage and paid the
mooring fees for his cabin cruiser *Trap Six*, which was moored at the
Strand Shipyard in Chiswick.

Train Robbery:
Arrested: 3 December 1963
Sentenced: Found not guilty on direction of the judge
Released: Acquitted 14 February 1964

Previous Convictions:

7 August 1948
Woking Petty Sessions – Stealing £1 from a shop – BOUND OVER.

23 December 1948
West London Magistrates' Court – Unauthorised taking of motorcar –
POLICE DETENTION 1 day.

24/26 January 1950
County of London Sessions – Burglary & larceny (two cases) –
BORSTAL TRAINING.

15 October 1952
County of Middlesex Sessions – Shop-breaking, larceny, burglary &
unauthorised taking of a motorcar – IMPRISONED 15 months & disqualified for 3 years.

19 November 1953
South Western Magistrates' Court – Suspected person loitering with
intent to steal from motorcars – FINED £10 or 6 weeks imprisonment.
He was committed 25 February 1954.

13 January 1954
Bow Street Magistrates' Court – Suspected person loitering with intent
to steal from motorcars. Assault on police – IMPRISONED 3 months,
3 months consecutively.

31 December 1954
Kingston Borough Magistrates' Court – Stealing three pairs of trousers,
value £11, from a shop display stand – IMPRISONED 6 months.

28/29 March 1960
Northampton Borough Quarter Sessions – Attempted shop-breaking.
Estreating bail (1957) – IMPRISONED 1 year. To estreat £50.

Ronald Christopher 'Buster' Edwards

Age: 32
Born: 27 January 1931
Occupation: Florist

A short man (5'6"), and inclined to be corpulent, Edwards was a former boxer with a reputation for being aggressive and violent. He spent part of his childhood as an evacuee in Devon. After leaving school at fourteen his first job was as a fitter's mate in a garage. This was followed by a series of jobs including working for a coal merchant, a waste-paper business, and a sausage factory, before he was conscripted. During two years service in the RAF he spent 56 days in detention for stealing cigarettes from the sergeants' mess. He met June Rothery in 1947 when she was only fifteen; they married at Lambeth parish church and had two children. Their first child Perry died after six weeks, and June suffered two further miscarriages before giving birth to their daughter Nicolette in 1960. From 1956–59 Buster was part of a firm run by Freddie Foreman and it was during this time that he met Tommy Wisbey. In August 1959, Buster opened a drinking club called the Walk-In with Mike & Johnny Prince. He became a heavy drinker, and after one particularly heavy session he was arrested outside his flat, sitting in a stolen motorcar. Facing a prison term, he was advised by his friends to contact solicitor's clerk Brian Field. Edwards was acquitted of the charge, although he was sent to Brixton Prison for fourteen days for driving while disqualified. By this time he was working with Gordon Goody and Terry Hogan. He met Bruce Reynolds at the Shirley Ann, a club owned by the Richardson brothers. In her autobiography, Marilyn Wisbey suggests that he was homosexual. Along with Gordon Goody, Edwards was the only one of the robbers to meet the Ulsterman. He was also the main link with Roger Cordrey and the South Coast Raiders. He was one of the last of the robbers to be arrested, having been on the run for three years. The police thought he was not particularly sharp-witted in the criminal sense, unlike Gordon Goody and Bruce Reynolds.

The real character of Buster Edwards has been eclipsed by the 'cheeky chappie' portrayal of him in the 1988 feature film *Buster* in which Edwards was played by Phil Collins.

Train Robbery:

Arrested:	19 September 1966
Sentenced:	15 years
Released:	1975
Died:	29 November 1994. Suicide.

Previous convictions:

18 July 1950

RAF Court Martial, Newark – Breaking & Entering. Stealing cigarettes. Wilful damage – IMPRISONED 42 days.

3 November 1960

Lambeth Magistrates' Court – Selling intoxicating liquor without a justice's licence – FINED £50.

4 January 1961

Old Street Magistrates' Court – two charges of driving without insurance – FINED £10 and disqualified.

11 May 1961

West London Magistrates' Court – Attempted larceny from a van & assault on police – FINED £15 & £20.

21 November 1961

County of London Sessions – Driving a motor vehicle while disqualified – IMPRISONED 14 days & disqualified 2 years.

Gordon Goody

Age:	33
Born:	11 March 1930
Occupation:	Hairdresser

Of Irish descent, Goody was the most charming and charismatic of the robbers, with a reputation for dedication and reliability. He was also a powerful and vicious individual. His first brush with the law was for robbing and beating up a homosexual man, who he said had made advances to him; in addition to a prison sentence, he received twelve strokes of the birch.

Goody, who had a legitimate job in a ladies hairdressing salon called Courtneys, was popular with women. He enjoyed the high life that the proceeds of his criminal activities brought him. Despite his playboy image, he lived in a small cottage in Putney with his mum.

In 1960 he teamed up with Bruce Reynolds, Buster Edwards, Charlie Wilson, Roy James and Terry Hogan to rob an armoured van. This was followed by a series of wage snatches. Ernest Millen, former head of the Flying Squad, considered Gordon Goody to be the cleverest of the robbers – a 'criminal sergeant-major'.

Goody is the only known member of the mail-train gang to have enjoyed any long-term benefit from the crime.

Train Robbery:

Arrested: 3 October 1963
Sentenced: 30 years
Released: 1975

Previous Convictions:

22 June 1945
Lambeth Juvenile Court – Stealing two lamps from a boathouse and a pedal cycle – BOUND OVER for 12 months.

18 January 1946
Lambeth Juvenile Court – Receiving stolen jersey – BOUND OVER for 12 months.

21 January 1948
County of London Sessions – Shop-breaking and stealing coat value £18.18s. Stealing cigarettes and clothing, value £15. Throwing stone at plate-glass window – BOUND OVER for 2 years & fined £10.

2 March 1948
Central Criminal Court – Robbery with violence – IMPRISONED 21 months & 12 strokes of the birch.

20 October 1949
Bow Street Magistrates' Court – Suspected person. Intent to steal from motorcars – IMPRISONED 3 months.

8 November 1949
County of London Sessions – Shop-breaking & larceny – IMPRISONED 9 months.

18 May 1955
Surrey Quarter Sessions – House-breaking with intent – CONDITIONAL DISCHARGE 12 months.

6/15 March 1956
Shop-breaking & stealing jewellery. Taking & driving away motorcar – IMPRISONED 3 years. Disqualified from driving 7 years.

20 February 1961
Richmond Magistrates' Court – Possessing a firearm while a prohibited person. Possessing ammunition while a prohibited person – FINED £8 and ordered to pay 3 guineas costs. Weapon & ammunition confiscated.

Roy James

Age: 28
Born: 30 August 1935
Occupation: Silversmith

A small man at 5'4", in the press he was mistakenly attributed the nickname 'Weasel'. James represented the new breed of criminal: non-smoking, non-drinking and a fitness fanatic. At the time of the robbery, he was on the brink of success as a world-class racing car driver, at the wheel of a Brabham BT6 he'd bought with his share from the London Airport wages robbery. A friend of Graham Hill (World Champion in 1962), he became a pupil of John Cooper, the creator of the F1 Cooper and the Mini Cooper, who taught him how to drive fast cars and thought he had the makings of a champion.

The police never succeeded in catching up with his Jaguar Mk II 3.4 litre (the most popular getaway car among villains). Bruce Reynolds described a stunt pulled by James during their escape from the London Airport job, where he steered the car into the middle of an exceptionally busy intersection, then spun it 180 degrees and brought it to a perfect halt. This stopped all the traffic crossing their path, so Reynolds and the others were able to drive through the section at high speed without stopping. James was arrested for the London Airport robbery, but was later released due to lack of evidence.

He joined the mail-train robbery gang in May, and was responsible for cutting the telephone wires and uncoupling the coaches.

Train Robbery:

Arrested: 10 December 1963
Sentenced: 30 years
Released: 1975

Previous convictions:

3 May 1956

West London Magistrates' Court – Larceny. Stealing vacuum cleaner, value £10. Stealing cine projector, value £87.10s. – PROBATION 12 months.

2 July 1956

Police Court, Jersey – Larceny from motorcars. Stealing sunglasses, value 16 shillings – HARD LABOUR 3 days.

18 October 1956

Middlesex Quarter Sessions – Receiving. Stolen motorcar, tools, etc., value £12 – IMPRISONED 3 months.

27 February 1957

West London Magistrates' Court – Taking & driving away without consent; No insurance. Larceny. Stealing spare wheel, radio set, value £30.12s.6d. – FINED £5, £1, £5.

8/11 July 1958

County of London Sessions – Shop-breaking & larceny (two cases) value £478. Value £188.9s. – IMPRISONED. Corrective Training 3 years.

13 June 1963

County of London Sessions – Dangerous driving – FINED £15 & ordered to pay £15 costs.

Bruce Reynolds

Age: 31
Born: 7 September 1931
Occupation: Antique dealer/car dealer

The most complex character of the gang. Formative influences included the death of his mother when he was four; evacuation during the Second World War; his poor relationship with his father and stepmother; his good relationship with his grandmother (Reynolds) and 'Cobby', a boy he met at Claud Butler's bicycle company in Clapham who introduced him to the opportunities and rewards of crime.

At his trial in 1969 Reynolds played down his role in the mail-train robbery and distanced himself from the violence, particularly the assault of Jack Mills. Since his release from prison in 1978 he has claimed to be the unofficial leader and/or brains behind the robbery, although much of his current image and reputation are built upon his own stories. Reynolds clearly had a part in organising the raid, as well as being a 'cut above' most of his criminal contemporaries in ambition and intellect, and that gave him an edge. He considered himself to be a career criminal and had aspirations to be the best, imagining himself as a gentleman thief. As well as violent smash-and-grab raids, he was a house-breaker and jewel thief who approached his work with a sense of style. Reynolds had a taste for fast cars and the trappings of wealth; he claims to have driven his Aston Martin to the South of France where he mingled with rich locals (apparently his lack of French and strong London accent didn't prevent him blending in) and stole their valuables. He likens himself to Cary Grant in *To Catch a Thief*, and has also compared himself with T.E. Lawrence.

Reynolds' conversation is peppered with references to the 'good life', 'El Dorado' and 'derring-do'. An aspirational, narcissistic and insecure man, he would buy handmade shoes and suits from Savile Row and dine out at top restaurants. Largely self-taught while in prison, he is fond of quoting from books (particularly Hemingway) in order to establish his credentials. In later life Reynolds wanted to become a writer and his *Autobiography of a Thief* (1995) is the best of the train robber biographies, although the penetration and writing is considerably more accomplished than the few articles Reynolds has since penned for national newspapers.

Ever the romantic, in old age Reynolds remains an inveterate fantasist, seeing himself as a Raffles-type figure. His most persistent fantasy was the claim to have been 'the youngest major in the British army', even though when he was called up for real military service he deserted on his second day. He certainly likes to be thought of as a 'leader' and his criminal reputation is very important to him.

If Reynolds was the brains behind the 1963 mail-train robbery he demonstrably lacked the ability to conceive of a plan that would have brought about its overall success. He has never taken responsibility for the gratuitous violence or the catastrophic failings of Leatherslade Farm and the 'exit' strategy. Despite having received considerable proceeds from the mail-train robbery, he was unable to derive any long-term income or benefit from it.

Train Robbery:

Arrested: 8 November 1968
Sentenced: 25 years
Released: 1978

Previous convictions:

17 September 1948
South Western Police Court – Assault on police and riding a cycle without lights – FINED 20 and 30 shillings.

20 April 1949
South Western Magistrates' Court – Larceny of cigarettes and money valued at £70.3s.2d. – BOUND OVER for 12 months.

1 June 1949
County of London Sessions – Shop-breaking & larceny – BORSTAL TRAINING.

21 March 1950
County of London Sessions – House-breaking & larceny; Workshop-breaking & larceny; Shop-breaking & larceny; Factory-breaking with intent – BORSTAL TRAINING.

25 October 1950
County of London Sessions – two counts of shop-breaking & larceny (handbags valued at £15; eight pairs of slippers valued £59; Garage-breaking & larceny; Office-breaking with intent and two charges of larceny – IMPRISONMENT 18 months & BORSTAL TRAINING.

29 October 1952
South Western Magistrates' Court – Using motor vehicle without insurance – FINED £10 & disqualified for 2 years.

18 November 1952
County of London Sessions – two counts of shop-breaking & larceny (five wireless sets value £89; two overcoats value £97); Unauthorised taking of motor vehicle – IMPRISONMENT 3 years & IMPRISONMENT 9 months (concurrent).

26 January 1955
Lambeth Magistrates' Court – Larceny from shop display (portable wireless set value £18) – IMPRISONMENT 6 months.

17 May 1956
South Western Magistrates' Court – Receiving a stolen heat lamp – FINED £25 or 3 months. No record of option chosen.

16 January 1958
Central Criminal Court – For malicious wounding with intent and assaulting peace officer (two cases) – IMPRISONMENT – 1) 2 years & 6 months; 2) 6 months; 3) 6 months (all consecutive).

30 May 1963
Ongar Magistrates' Court – Poaching – FINED £10.

Jimmy White

Age: 43
Born: 21 February 1920
Occupation: Café proprietor

The oldest member of the gang, White had fought with the Royal Artillery Regiment and the Army Air Corps during the Second World War. Although under-age when deployed, he saw active service in North

Africa and Italy. He claimed to be one of seven successful candidates out of four hundred volunteers for the Parachute Regiment. On 7 June 1944, the day after D-Day, he was invalided out of the army due to a duodenal ulcer. Initially he was given a pension of 18 shillings, but felt betrayed by his country when this pension was cut to 9 shillings and then stopped altogether. White was a hard worker and tried his hand at a number of legitimate businesses, but was seduced by the rewards of crime when, as the owner of a small garage, he became involved in 'ringing' stolen cars.

At the time of the robbery he ran a small café in Aldersgate Street, near Smithfield. It has been suggested that it was White who introduced Mr One into the gang. Although not one of the main conspirators, he played a key role in the robbery. He was responsible for acquiring the three vehicles that were used and appears to have undertaken the role of quartermaster, looking after supplies.

Jimmy White was known for his ability to melt into the background, merging with his surroundings and becoming almost invisible. This talent enabled him to remain undetected for nearly three years after the mail-train robbery.

Train Robbery:
Arrested: 21 April 1966
Sentenced: 18 years
Released: 1975

Previous convictions:

7 July 1955
Hendon Magistrates – Receiving cigarettes & tobacco valued at £900 and furniture at £16 – PROBATION 3 years.

14 May 1958
Acton Magistrates – Receiving jewellery valued £40. Stealing by finding a wallet valued £2.10s. – IMPRISONMENT 6 months and 3 months (consecutive).

23 June 1958
Bedfordshire Quarter Sessions – Shop-breaking & stealing photographic equipment. value £377.9s.3d. – IMPRISONMENT 18 months (to run consecutive to the previous term).

Charlie Wilson

Age: 31
Born: 30 June 1932
Occupation: Greengrocer

A big, cheerful man with piercing blue eyes and a quick sense of humour. Ex-pupil of Honeywell School, Battersea, he left school at fourteen. Wilson was a late starter as a thief but very quickly forged friendships with a number of violent gangsters and adopted their unorthodox methods. One of the principals in the planning and organisation of the train robbery, he was by all accounts an intimidating presence, the archetypal heavy. Yet despite being the most powerful and feared villain in the gang, he was a devoted family man with a happy marriage and three young daughters.

He was a close associate of Bruce Reynolds (the two men had been childhood friends) as well as Roy James. It was Wilson who put forward the idea for the London Airport robbery, having met a man who worked in the BOAC administration offices. Wilson had an extensive network of underworld contacts, hence his sensational escape from a top-security prison a few months after being sentenced to thirty years for his part in the mail-train robbery. When he was eventually traced and recaptured in Canada, he had made himself so popular with local residents that they petitioned the Canadian government to allow his wife and daughters to remain in the country. In 1990 he was shot dead by a hitman as he relaxed by his swimming pool on the Costa del Sol (Marbella), where it was alleged he had become involved in drug dealing.

Train Robbery:

Arrested: 22 August 1963
Sentenced: 30 years
Escaped: 12 August 1964
Recaptured: 25 January 1968
Released: 1978 (the last of the train robbers to be released from prison)

Previous Convictions:

20 January 1954
South Western Magistrates – Theft of petrol – FINED £5.

20 December 1956
South Western Magistrates – Suspected person. Intent to steal from motor cars – CONDITIONAL DISCHARGE – 12 months.

7-16 January 1958
County of London Sessions – Receiving stolen property (two counts) – IMPRISONED 12 months.

26 May 1959
Central Criminal Court – Conspiracy to steal – IMPRISONED 30 months.

Tommy Wisbey

Age: 33
Born: 27 April 1930
Occupation: Bookmaker

A minor player in the robbery, but a very colourful character – with an even more colourful wife and daughter. He was a big fan of Frank Sinatra and Tony Bennett and was reputed to have a very good singing voice. He would often entertain the family using the vacuum-cleaner pipe as a pretend microphone. After leaving school at fourteen he worked as a messenger boy at the *Star & News Chronicle* then as a porter at Covent Garden Market. During his National Service he was a driver for the Royal Army Service Corps and was discharged with a good character. He then worked for his father in the family wholesale bottle business.

Wisbey was the link between the main group of robbers (Reynolds, Wilson, Goody and Edwards) and Roger Cordrey and the South Coast Raiders. Buster Edwards knew Wisbey from the mid-1950s when they had worked for Freddie Foreman. Wisbey's father-in-law was a cousin of the infamous Billy Hill, who dominated the London crime scene in the 1950s. Wisbey's wife had been a bridesmaid at Freddie Foreman's wedding, and Foreman was to become godfather to Wisbey's eldest daughter Marilyn. In later years, Marilyn was involved in a long-term relationship with 'Mad' Frankie Fraser.

A self-confessed 'heavy', Wisbey's principal job in the mail-train robbery was to frighten the train staff and help unload mailbags.

Train Robbery:

Arrested:	11 September 1963
Sentenced:	30 years
Released:	1976

Previous convictions:

30 July 1947
Essex Quarter Sessions – Shop-breaking – BOUND OVER 12 months. £5 surety. £1 to prosecution costs.

28 October 1958
Lambeth Magistrates – Receiving stolen wireless sets – IMPRISONED 4 months.

14 August 1963
Highgate Magistrates' Court – Assault on police – FINED £5 and costs of 42 shillings.

Roger Cordrey

Age:	42
Born:	30 May 1921
Occupation:	Florist and antique dealer

As the leader and brains behind the South Coast Raiders, by 1963 Cordrey had already successfully stopped and robbed six trains on the South Coast line. Buster Edwards had heard of Cordrey's reputation for being able to stop trains through his old friend Tommy Wisbey, himself a South Coast Raider. Cordrey immediately insisted that the rest of the Raiders be brought in on the job, principally as heavies. It is likely that Mr Three, one of the men who was never named or captured, came as part of the Cordrey package and hailed from the Brighton area.

A compulsive gambler with an encyclopaedic knowledge of the

winners of the Grand National, Cordrey also enjoyed angling and went fishing around Oxford prior to the robbery (he was in possession of fishing tackle when arrested). His wife had left him and his sons a few days before the robbery.

His sister Florence May (Maisie) and brother-in-law Alfred Pilgrim, were arrested and charged with receiving stolen money from the train robbery. And it was down to Roger Cordrey that Bill Boal became involved.

The first robber to be apprehended and the only one to plead guilty to conspiracy, Cordrey's plea of not guilty to robbery was accepted by the prosecution. He received a much lighter sentence than the others.

Train Robbery:

Arrested:	14 August 1963
Sentenced:	20 years
Appeal:	14 years
Released:	1971

Previous Convictions:

16 December 1941
Surrey Sessions – two counts of embezzlement. Six counts of falsification of accounts. Larceny as a servant – BORSTAL TRAINING.

James (Big Jim) Hussey

Age:	31
Born:	8 April 1933
Occupation:	Painter and decorator

An unmarried professional villain who lived with his elderly parents in a small flat in Dog Kennel Hill, described by a probation officer as 'a warm cohesive unit', Big Jim was a huge man who came across as tough but dim-witted. His first brush with the law was in 1946 when he was caught stealing pencils and sports equipment from his school at the age of thirteen. His reputation as a strong-arm 'heavy' stemmed from his first spell in prison, after being sent down for GBH at the age of nineteen. By 1958 he had graduated to assaulting policemen. On emerging from a job with a night watchman clamped under each arm, he allegedly told police, 'I'll be honest with you, I was on the unders the other night with a team of dippers and the line bogeys surprised us and we all had it in our dancers. I got away and I thought you were nailing me for that.'

A childhood friend of Charlie Wilson's, Hussey was meant to be part of the London Airport job, but he was in Munich picking pockets at the time. He joined the train-robbery gang as a heavy and was picked out during an identity parade by a hotel receptionist as one of five men, including Bob Welch, who had come to stay at the Flying Horse Hotel in Nottingham a few weeks before the robbery. His girlfriend, Gill, a feisty redhead whom Hussey married after his release from prison, became very close friends with June Edwards and Rene Wisbey. Wisbey and Hussey subsequently teamed up together and were convicted for smuggling cocaine in 1989.

Train Robbery:

Arrested:	7 September 1963
Sentenced:	30 years
Released:	1975

Previous Convictions:

23 August 1946
Lambeth Juvenile Court – three counts of stealing sports equipment, pencils etc., from a school – DISMISSED.

18 November 1949
Lambeth Juvenile Court – Unauthorised taking of motor vehicle. No Insurance – FINED £4. Disqualified for 12 months.

9/16 May 1950
Central Criminal Court – Causing grievous bodily harm with intent. Assault occasioning actual bodily harm – IMPRISONED 18 months.

13 June 1952
Lambeth Magistrates – two counts of causing grievous bodily harm – FINED £12.

5 September 1953

Bow Street Magistrates' Court – Suspected person loitering with intent to steal from motorcars. Rogue & vagabond – PROBATION 12 months.

25 June 1956

Lambeth Magistrates' Court – Tampering with the mechanics of a motorcar – FINED £5.

2/17 December 1958

Manchester Crown Court – Warehouse-breaking & larceny of cigarettes and tobacco valued £10,820.1s.10d. – two counts of causing grievous bodily harm with intent to resist arrest – IMPRISONED 3 years & 2 years (consecutive).

18 December 1962

Munich Court – Picking pockets – IMPRISONED 5 months. Local banishment order – Deported and arrived in UK 19 December 1962.

Robert (Bob) Welch

Age: 35
Born: 12 March 1929
Occupation: Club proprietor & betting shop owner

Bright, intelligent and very strong, Welch's undoing was his addiction to gambling. He ran the New Crown Club, a drinking establishment in Elephant and Castle, but it was closed down by the police after he was convicted of selling alcohol outside permitted hours. Most of the money he'd made from the club was gambled away. He divided his time between his wife and girlfriend, often spending three or four nights a week with the latter. His wife was apparently too frightened to question him about his regular absences from home.

A member of Roger Cordrey's gang, the South Coast Raiders, Welch was the first name mentioned in connection with the train robbery by the men from Scotland Yard's C11 branch.

Train Robbery:

Arrested:	25 October 1963
Sentenced:	30 years
Released:	1976

Previous Convictions:

1 October 1958

County of London Sessions – Receiving stolen coffee, tea and custard powder. Value: £2,616.13s.2d. – IMPRISONED 9 months.

21 March 1963

Bow Street Magistrates' Court – four counts of selling intoxicating liquor outside permitted hours – FINED £210.

Brian Field

Age:	29
Born:	15 December 1934
Occupation:	Solicitor's managing clerk

Brian Field was put up for adoption as soon as he was born. After leaving elementary school he worked as an office boy in a solicitor's office before serving two years as a private in the Royal Army Service Corps, where he saw active duty in Korea in the early 1950s. It was here that he first met John Wheater, who at that time was working in the Army Legal Service. Discharged from the army with 'a very good character', in April 1959 he became a clerk at G.P. Voss & Son, 247 Bethnal Green Road, E2. In May 1960 he became a managing clerk (legal executive) with the firm James & Mallors, which later became James & Wheater, with John Wheater as the sole solicitor. Handsome and ambitious, Brian Field met his second wife Karin in 1961, when she was working as a hostess at Winston's nightclub in Mayfair. The couple married in January 1962 and moved to a house in Pangbourne which they named Kabri (an amalgam of Karin and Brian). Described by the GPO Investigation Branch as a man of lively intelligence but deeply insecure; they believed he sought security through the acquisition of material wealth, and that this had resulted in him getting out of his depth socially. Bruce Reynolds considered him to be the weakest link in the chain, and was certain that, if caught, Field would quickly cooperate with the police. He had no previous convictions.

Train Robbery:

Arrested:	15 September 1963
Sentenced:	25 years
Appeal:	Sentence reduced to 5 years
Released:	1967
Died:	May 1979. Car crash.

No Previous Convictions

Leonard Denis Field

Age:	31
Born:	1931
Occupation:	Merchant Navy seaman

At the time of the robbery he was working as a steward for P&O and was about to join the SS *Canberra* in Southampton when he was arrested. One of seven children, when not at sea he lived with his mother in North London. It was through his brother Harry Field, a convicted horse doper and bank robber, that he came into contact with the solicitor John Wheater and his clerk Brian Field (no relation).

Train Robbery:

Arrested:	14 September 1963
Sentenced:	25 years
Appeal:	Sentence reduced to 5 years
Released:	1967

Previous convictions:

17 May 1951
Clerkenwell Magistrates' Court – Suspected Person. Intent to steal from motorcars – FINED 40 shillings.

John Wheater

Age: 41
Born: 17 December 1921
Occupation: Solicitor

Educated at Uppingham School, Wheater saw active service during the Second World War in Italy where his bravery saw him mentioned in dispatches and put forward for a Military Cross. Described as a man of undoubted 'honour and integrity', if somewhat 'scatty' and 'disorganised', he left the army in 1946 to train as a solicitor. He rejoined the army in 1949, working for the army legal service, retiring in 1955 with the rank of major.

He took over the solicitor's practice of James & Mallors in 1961, where he employed Brian Field as his managing clerk. It was a busy, chaotic and untidy office and by his own account he was not a good solicitor being unmethodical, forgetful and failing to keep proper records. Married with two young daughters.

Train Robbery:

Arrested: 17 October 1963
Sentenced: 3 years
Released: 1966

No Previous Convictions

William Gerald Boal

Age: 49
Born: 22 October 1913
Occupation: Precision engineer. Proprietor of Unity Precision Engineering.

Originally from Durham, he came to London at the age of fourteen. A small man with a ruddy complexion and poor eyesight (his eyes were burned in a workplace accident that left him requiring thick-lensed glasses and rendered him unable to drive). Boal was an emotional man, prone to sudden outbursts; in the words of Detective Sergeant Pritchard: 'he tended to gabble on. His words would sort of come out in a rush at times and then he would go quiet.'

Boal met Roger Cordrey after the war when they both lived in Kingston and used to play snooker together. It is widely agreed that he took no part in either the conspiracy or the robbery. Although there might have been a successful appeal if all the jailed mail-train robbers had spoken out against Boal's conviction, curiously none of them did. In his 1995 biography, Bruce Reynolds said that he had never met the man or even heard of him before his arrest. Detective Superintendent Fewtrell said that he had never been convinced by the case against Boal.

A devoted family man, William Boal's wife and three young children were left stranded by his imprisonment, and struggled to live with the stigma, hardship and injustice of his sentence. Seven years after being jailed, he was diagnosed with a brain tumour and died shortly after.

Train Robbery:

Arrested:	14 August 1963
Sentenced:	21 years
Appeal:	14 years
	Died in prison 26 June 1970

Previous convictions:

2 September 1947
Feltham Magistrates – Found on enclosed premises for unlawful purpose – FINED £20.

24 January 1949
Surrey Quarter Sessions – Two counts of receiving stolen property. Fraudulently extracting electricity – IMPRISONED 18 months.

19 April 1963
Mortlake Magistrates' Court – Assault on police – FINED £10 & BOUND OVER for 12 months.

APPENDIX – POLICE ORGANISATION

Ranks

PC
Sergeant
Inspector
Chief Inspector
Superintendent
Chief Superintendent
Commander
Deputy Assistant Commissioner
Assistant Commissioner
Deputy Commissioner
Commissioner

The Metropolitan Police

Commissioner
Sir Joseph Simpson (1958–68)

Asst Commissioner 'A' (Operations and Administration)
Sir John Waldron (1963–66)

Asst Commissioner 'B' (Traffic)
Andrew Way (1963–68)

Asst Commissioner 'C' (Crime)
Lieutenant-Colonel Ranulph (Rasher) Bacon

Asst Commissioner 'D' (Personnel and Training)
Tom Mahir

'C' Department – CID

Commander George Hatherill

C1 Murder squad, forgery, drugs, passports, illegal immigrants, Art &
   Antique squad, Industrial espionage, Government liaison
C2 Crime correspondence

C3 Fingerprints
C4 Criminal Records Office
C5 CID Policy
C6 Company Fraud Squad
C7 Laboratory Liaison, Explosive Officers, Technical Support
C8 Flying Squad, Robbery Squad
C9 Provincial Crime Branch
C10 Stolen Car Squad
C11 Criminal Intelligence
C12 Regional Crime Squad (No. 9 Region)
C13 Anti-terrorist Squad

Police personnel involved in the main investigation
Flying Squad (Mail Train)
Det. Chief Superintendent Ernie Millen – Head of the Flying Squad
Det. Chief Superintendent T. Butler (Head of the Flying Squad Sept '63)
Det. Chief Inspector P. Vibart
Det. Inspector Frank Williams
Det. Superintendent G. McArthur
Det. Sergeant J. Pritchard
Det. Sergeant Steve Moore
Det. Sergeant Jack Slipper
Det. Sergeant Jim Nevill
Det. Sergeant Lou Van Dyck
Det. Sergeant Tommy Thorburn

Incident Post at Brill police station until 16 August 1963
Buckinghamshire Constabulary
Det. Inspector V. Hankins
Det. Sergeant R. Baldry
Sergeant. G. Salmon
Det. Constable F. Wright
Det. Constable P. Frost
Det. Constable B. Hone
Police Constable J. Woolley
Miss E. Broughton (Typist)

Metropolitan Police
Det. Sergeant L. Read
Det. Sergeant R. Gorton
Det. Constable J. Kemp

HQ Central (Aylesbury)
Buckinghamshire Constabulary
Det. Sergeant L. Bishop
Det. Constable P. Jones
Det. Constable F. Wright
Police Constable D. Bennett
Police Constable A. Smith
Police Constable A. Jenkins
Police Constable W. Hazlewood
Police Constable W. Price
Police Constable A. Paddy
Police Constable P. Collins
Police Constable D. Pritchard
Police Constable D. Carter
Police Constable D. Addison (Driver)
S/Cadet N. Walpole
Metropolitan Police
Det. Inspector D. Chitty
Det. Constable J. Kemp
Typists
Miss U. Grace
Miss J. Martin
Miss E. Broughton
Miss E. Galbraith
Miss M. Reynolds
Miss P. Keene
Miss B. Jarratt
Mrs L. Carter
Mrs I. Williams
Mrs J. Milson

Outside Inquiry

Buckinghamshire Constabulary

Det. Inspector R. Coles

Det. Inspector V. Hankins

Det. Sergeant P. Fairweather

Det. Sergeant J. Driver

Det. Sergeant R. Baldry

Sergeant. G. Salmon

Det. Constable P. Frost

Det. Constable B. Hone

Metropolitan Police

Det. Sergeant L. Read

Det. Sergeant R. Gorton

Exhibits Officers

Buckinghamshire Constabulary

Det. Constable K. Milner

Police Constable W. Cullen

Photography Department

Buckinghamshire Constabulary

Det. Sergeant G. Gaunt

Det. Constable J. Bailey

Metropolitan Police

Mr K. Creer

Fingerprint Department

Buckinghamshire Constabulary

Mr S. Clark

Det. Sergeant G. Gaunt

Det. Constable J. Bailey

Det. Constable D. Letherington

Det. Constable M. Stallworthy

Metropolitan Police

Det. Superintendent M. Ray

Det. Inspector G. Lambourne

Det. Inspector J. Chaffe

Forensic Science Laboratory
Metropolitan Police
Dr I.G. Holden
Det. Chief Inspector J. McCafferty
Det. Chief Inspector H. Faber
Det. Sergeant N. Brown

Metropolitan Police
Det. Chief Superintendent J.W. Godsall

Det. Superintendent R.A. Anderson
Det. Superintendent J. Cummings
Det. Superintendent Osborne

Det. Chief Inspector S. Bradbury
Det. Chief Inspector Walker
Det. Chief Inspector Mesher
Chief Inspector W. Knight
Chief Inspector W. Baldock
Chief Inspector Favour

Det. Inspector J. Barker
Det. Inspector Bond
Det. Inspector F. Byers
Det. Inspector R. Chitty
Det. Inspector J. Hensley
Det. Inspector K. Jones
Det. Inspector D. Neesham
Det. Inspector R. Roberts
Det. Inspector H. Tappin
Det. Inspector Trodd
Det. Inspector W. Wright
Inspector Mason
Inspector Chase

Det. Sergeant P. Bird
Det. Sergeant Burdett

Det. Sergeant G. Day
Det. Sergeant D. Dilley
Det. Sergeant C. Dracott
Det. Sergeant W. Hughes
Det. Sergeant M. Hyams
Det. Sergeant Maidment
Det. Sergeant Marshall
Det. Sergeant J. Meyrick
Det. Sergeant P. Jones
Det. Sergeant J. Mathews
Det. Sergeant B. Price
Det. Sergeant N. Reid
Det. Sergeant J. Swain
Det. Sergeant B. Tredwell
Det. Sergeant J. Vaughan

Det. Constable Cooper
Det. Constable J. Estensen
Det. Constable Lloyd-Hughes
Det. Constable Purchase
Det. Constable K. Rogers
Det. Constable Simmons

Woman Det. Constable Willey
Woman Police Constable James

Police Constable C. Bartlett
Police Constable Fisher
Police Constable Gilley

Buckinghamshire Constabulary
Chief Constable – Brigadier John Cheney
Assistant Chief Constable G.H.W. Wilkinson
Chief Inspector R. Ballinger

Inspector B. Barrett
Inspector G. Matheson

Inspector J. Mellows
Inspector J. Schofield

Sergeant R. Blackman
Sergeant Maydon
Sergeant Plested
Sergeant Potter

Det. Constable M. Eeles
Det. Constable G. Lake
Police Constable Atkins
Police Constable Bell
Police Constable Lewis
Police Constable Milne
Police Constable P. Stephens
Police Constable Webb
Police Constable Whiteman

Bournemouth Police
Chief Constable Donald Lockett
Det. Superintendent H.J.H. Ballard
Det. Chief Inspector Tilling
Det. Sergeant S. Davies
Det. Sergeant P. Southey
Police Constable R. Archer
Police Constable C. Case

Leicester Police
Det. Sergeant H.J. Strong
Det. Constable A. Brown

Surrey Constabulary
Det. Inspector B. Morris
Det. Inspector B. West
Inspector G. Cork
Det. Sergeant Church
Det. Constable A. Illing

Police Constable R. Searle
Police Constable G. Bixley
Police Constable D. Cooper

GPO Investigation Branch
C.G. Osmond OBE – Controller
F. Cook
R. Darke
J. Johnson
T. Spires
A. Moriarty
R. Woodward
H.M. Eilbeck
Det. Sergeant Frost

British Transport Police
Chief Constable W.O. Gay
Det. Superintendent J. Ward
Det. Inspector T. Harrop
Det. Inspector Armstrong
Det. Constable M. Keighley
Det. Constable R. Morton
Police Constable V. Saunders

RAF SIB
Sergeant R. Sutcliffe

Other Police
Det. Chief Superintendent Elwell (Hertfordshire Police)
Det. Sergeant Cooke (Hertfordshire Police – Incident Room)
Det. Inspector Densham (Oxford County CID)

Her Majesty's Inspector of Constabulary
Sir Edward Dodd CBE

Peter Brodie OBE
Det. Chief Superintendent Fisher

Det. Chief Inspector Jones

Buckinghamshire Constabulary – August 1963:
The county of Buckinghamshire at the time covered 479,411 acres with a population of 508,000. There were 1,012 miles of classified roads and 1,024 miles of unclassified roads totalling 2,036 miles.

The Buckinghamshire Constabulary in 1963 was made up as follows:

1 chief constable
1 assistant chief constable
2 chief superintendents
6 superintendents class 1
7 chief inspectors
38 inspectors
99 sergeants
537 constables
1 woman police inspector
3 women police sergeants
21 women police constables
196 civilians

Authorised male establishment: 691. Actual male establishment 8 August 1963 was 683.

Buckinghamshire constabulary police vehicles totalled 132:

16 traffic cars
9 criminal investigation cars
1 car for officer at C9
1 Ford Anglia training car
1 Austin A60 driving instruction
34 general purpose cars
1 relief Anglia
1 Morris 1000 Traveller, Road Safety
1 A55 photography van
1 Morris Minor stores van
4 5cwt dog vans

1 light removal van

5 general purpose mini buses

1 Land Rover

4 traffic motorcycles

45 general purpose motorcycles

2 Training motorcycles

1 relief motorcycle

The strength of the force on duty in the county of Buckinghamshire at the time of the robbery at 03.30 on 8 August 1963 was fifty-four men and a dog:

6 constables in 3 wireless cars

9 constables and 1 sergeant in modified patrol cars

1 constable on cycle patrol

5 sergeants and 32 constables on beat patrols

1 sergeant with a dog patrol

The principal area of the county related to the robbery was the Linslade sub-division where the train was stopped. Linslade, at the north-eastern border of the county was 43,600 acres with a population of 13,000. In this area there were 207 farms and smallholdings, two disused RAF airfields and the small railway station at Cheddington.

In the neighbourhood of Leatherslade Farm, twenty-eight miles away on the opposite side of the county near the Oxfordshire border, there was a police 'out station' in the market town of Brill. Due to the low crime rate in the area – nine reported crimes in 1963 – the previous police strength of a sergeant and two constables had been reduced to one constable (PC545 John Woolley) in 1962. The constable's beat covered five parishes – Brill, Oakley, Boarstill, Wormington and Dorton – an area of 12,000 acres, 52 farms, with a population of 2,500.

APPENDIX – SENIOR POLICE OFFICERS

Commander George H. Hatherill OBE

Promoted to Commander (Crime) at New Scotland Yard in 1954, Hatherill was known to his colleagues as 'Uncle George'. He spoke eight languages and had carried out seventeen successful murder investigations; among those he arrested were John Christie (10 Rillington Place) and Kenneth Haig (the Acid Bath Murderer). Hatherill was the model for John Creasey's best-selling fictional detective 'Gideon of the Yard'. Considered the most formidable detective to emerge from London's CID in many years, he was famed for his comment, 'There are only about 20 murders a year in London and many not at all serious – some are just husbands killing their wives.' He had a reputation for never raising his voice and solving problems sitting in his chair while never taking his cigar out of his mouth.

Detective Chief Superintendent Ernie Millen

At the time of the robbery Millen was head of Scotland Yard's Flying Squad, but during the course of the investigation he was promoted to Deputy Commander under George Hatherill. On Hatherill's retirement in October 1964, Millen took over as Commander of 'C' Department with 2,850 detectives under his command.

Regarded as one of the finest detectives at Scotland Yard, he described himself as 'overlord' at the Yard during the hunt for the Great Train Robbers. He maintained in his autobiography that there was no 'mastermind' involved, that most of the brains were supplied by Goody and Reynolds, and that three separate London gangs had been involved. He dismissed the claim that four of the robbers were still free as 'sheer bunkum' and that the entire gang was brought to justice 'without exception'.

Detective Chief Superintendent Tommy Butler

PC965, Butler's first years were on the beat in Canning Town. A squadron leader during the war, he was a secretive single man who lived with his aged mother, whom he had supported since the age of fourteen, in a small house near Hammersmith Bridge. At the time of the robbery he was in charge of the CID, Metropolitan Police District. Known as the (Old) Grey Fox he worked very successfully with fellow detective and 'terrible twin' Peter Vibart.

A traditional, old-style copper, Butler lived and breathed the Flying Squad and worked seven days a week. He had terrible handwriting and spoke very fast, often asking questions very quickly, one after the other. A shrewd, serious man who was never impulsive, Butler's investigations were always thorough and based on experience with a degree of intuition. His approach where criminals were concerned was to 'pick him up, lock him up and interrogate him – and don't place too much reliance on forensic evidence'.

In the early sixties, while observing the inexorable rise of the London gangs, and the Kray twins in particular, he wrote a highly confidential report for his bosses pointing out that '... their [the Krays] arrest will probably be achieved only by unorthodox policing, or by very good fortune'. It was this very combination that was to bring him success in his investigation into the mail-train robbery, allied with his ruthless determination to capture and put away every single one of the robbers. Towards the end of his career, the GPO Investigation Branch noted that Butler had become so obsessed with catching the remaining train robbers that he would spend his days off and his weekends travelling down to Margate, Ramsgate and Southend to spend the day scouting the beaches in hope of a bandit sighting.

Detective Inspector Frank Williams

A tough, grim-looking man with a pitted, pudgy face, Williams was generally disapproved of by his Scotland Yard superiors for his unorthodox methods. He was known as the 'best informed' officer in the Yard, having developed a complex network of informants and grasses, but he also had the reputation of being an undisciplined detective and regularly faced accusations of bribery, blackmail and corruption. Although he eventually reached the rank of detective chief superintendent, he was overlooked as Butler's replacement as head of the Flying Squad.

Detective Superintendent Gerald McArthur

An Old Etonian who had flown Sunderland flying boats for Coastal

Command during the war, McArthur also served as the Queen's bodyguard on several state occasions. Along with Detective Sergeant John Pritchard, he was the first officer from Scotland Yard to arrive at Aylesbury on the afternoon of the robbery. Within a week, Tommy Butler had taken over the running of the investigation while McArthur was put in charge of the preparation of evidence and compilation of reports for the Director of Public Prosecutions. Later he was to become known for breaking up the Richardson gang at a time when many London-based detectives were known to be corrupt and in the pay of the London gangs.

Detective Superintendent Ernest Malcolm Fewtrell

Born in Ryde, Isle of Wight, where his father was a policeman, Fewtrell joined Buckinghamshire police as a cadet in 1927. He was an able and conscientious policeman who led the investigation into the train robbery until the arrival of Scotland Yard. Bruce Reynolds said of him, 'One does not impugn the integrity of Malcolm Fewtrell or the Buckinghamshire CID. It is certain that whatever other conspiracies Scotland Yard might have hatched "to get the bastards" (Chief Superintendant Butler's words), Malcolm and the boys from Buckinghamshire CID were not involved.' Fewtrell retired immediately after the trial in 1964 and published *The Train Robbers*, one of the first books on the robbery.

APPENDIX – ITEMS FOUND AT THE FARM

1 Austin Load Start drop-side lorry (pickaxe handle found under near-side seat)
2 Land Rovers
Squashed tin of yellow paint

Evening Standard (Friday, 2 August 1963)
Buckinghamshire Advertiser (Friday, 9 August 1963)

Pickaxe handle
Wood saw
Hacksaw blades
Wire cutters
Bolt cutters
Screwdriver
Sweets

116 outer white mailbags
236 green inner mailbags
38 small white canvas bags
109 linen bags
43 canvas bank bags
13 bank belts from National Provincial & Midland Banks
A collection of string and sealing wax
A large number of bank and GPO labels, paper and wrappings

£628 cash in Scottish banknotes

A partially burnt khaki balaclava helmet
A partially burnt jacket with a nylon stocking in the pocket

Lieutenant's jacket
Corporal's jacket
Badge of the Parachute Regiment

6 khaki denim jackets
6 khaki denim trousers
3 balaclavas
Black hood with eyeholes
Nylon stocking mask
Single leather glove (its partner was found on the rail track)
Various waterproof and cold-weather jackets
Various blue denim overalls and jackets
Pair blue denim trousers
Bib-and-brace overalls
Blue jacket
Shirt
Pullover

Instructions for the use of handcuffs
4 batteries (6 volt) – same size as those found on the gantry
40 torch batteries

6 sleeping bags
13 blankets
11 air beds
5 air cushions
20 towels

Set of chess pieces
Ludo
Snakes & ladders
Monopoly

Camping gas stove
Gas cylinder
9 pipkins of ale (2 full, 6 empty)
15 complete sets of cutlery
15 brown mugs
16 metal plates
Pyrex plate
40 candles

Kraft Dairylea spread in small boxes
Sifta table salt
Saxa table salt
18 one-pound packets of butter
Maxwell House coffee (catering size)
16 two-pound packets of sugar
Batchelor's garden peas (box)
18 tins of Senior's pork luncheon meat
9 tins Fray Bentos corned beef
38 tins of Campbell's soups
Lyons coffee
Prince's peaches
Armour Star baked beans
40 tins of Heinz baked beans
15 tins of Fussell's condensed milk
38 tins of Heinz soups
20 tins of peas
34 tins of fruit salad
Tins of creamed rice
Heinz Ideal Sauce
2 crates fruit – apples and oranges
Sack of potatoes
200 eggs
34 toilet rolls

APPENDIX – FINGERPRINT EVIDENCE

Established in 1901, the fingerprint department at Scotland Yard by 1963 housed over 1,800,000 sets of prints. During an investigation these would have to be examined and compared by hand. It is worth noting that at that time the identification of finger and palm prints on paper had only recently been perfected. The train-robbery case involved the deepest and most concentrated fingerprint probe ever tackled.

When Leatherslade Farm was discovered, a team of four civilian searchers and two detective inspectors from the fingerprint branch (C3) went to the farm to deal exclusively with crime marks. A further two officers were dispatched to process the bank envelopes discovered at the farm. As each print was discovered, Detective Superintendent Maurice Ray was called in; he would then develop the prints himself.

Millen's autobiography describes:

…the finger print boys performed 'the biggest finger-print exercise on the scene of the crime ever known in the history of crime detection'. They worked round the clock for three days and during this time a police cordon around the farm prohibited anyone except forensic experts and high ranking officers getting through.

Between 200 and 300 mailbags and over 1,000 other items were examined and rejected by the Forensic Science Laboratory. Forensic Laboratory staff accompanied Flying Squad officers to the homes of fourteen suspects. At the trial, 325 forensic exhibits (some divided into as many as six sub-exhibits) were produced in evidence.

During the train-robbery investigation approximately 750,000 comparisons were made, 1,534 bank envelopes were examined, 243 photographs of prints were taken which were determined to show 311 finger and 56 palm prints. In addition, 793 sets of elimination prints were taken and 164 suspects were put forward.

Of the robbers arrested, nine were identified by fingerprints found at Leatherslade Farm, three by fingerprints found elsewhere and two by forensic evidence found at the farm.

Fingerprints found at Leatherslade Farm:
Ronnie Biggs
John Daly
Buster Edwards
Jim Hussey
Roy James
Bruce Reynolds
Bob Welch
Charlie Wilson
Tommy Wisbey

Fingerprints found elsewhere
Brian Field (briefcase)
Leonard Field (bank authority)
Jimmy White (caravan)

Forensic evidence connected to Leatherslade Farm
Gordon Goody (khaki and yellow paint)
Bill Boal (yellow paint)

APPENDIX – ARRESTS, CHARGES AND PRISON SENTENCES

	Date of Arrest	Bail	Charges
William Boal	14 August 1963		Conspiracy to Rob Robbery Receiving (3 counts)
Roger Cordrey	14 August 1963		Conspiracy to Rob Robbery Receiving (3 counts)
Renee Boal	15 August 1963	Bailed	Receiving (2 counts)
Alfred Pilgrim	15 August 1963	Bailed	Receiving (2 counts)
May Pilgrim	15 August 1963	Bailed	Receiving (2 counts)
Mary Manson	21 August 1963	Bailed	Receiving
Charles Wilson	23 August 1963		Conspiracy to Rob Robbery
Robert Pelham	24 August 1963	Bailed	Receiving (2 counts)
Ronald Biggs	4 September 1963		Conspiracy to Rob Robbery
James Hussey	7 September 1963		Conspiracy to Rob Robbery
Thomas Wisbey	11 September 1963		Conspiracy to Rob Robbery
Leonard Field	14 September 1963		Conspiracy to Rob Robbery Conspiracy to obstruct Justice
Brian Field	15 September 1963		Conspiracy to Rob Robbery Receiving Conspiracy to obstruct Justice

Verdict	Sentence	Release
Guilty	21 years	Died in prison 1970
Guilty	24 years	
Jury Discharged from giving verdict		
PLEADED Guilty	20 years	Released 1971
NOT Guilty		
PLEADED Guilty	20 years	
NOT Guilty on instruction of Judge	Acquitted	
NOT Guilty on instruction of Judge	Acquitted	
NOT Guilty on instruction of Judge	Acquitted	
Case DISMISSED		
Guilty	25 years	*Escaped 1964*
Guilty	30 years	Released 1978
PLEADED Guilty	Conditional Discharge	
Guilty	25 years	*Escaped 1965*
Guilty	30 years	Released 2009
Guilty	25 years	Released 1975
Guilty	30 years	
Guilty	25 years	Released 1976
Guilty	30 years	
Guilty	25 years	Released 1967
Jury Discharged from giving verdict	5 years	
Guilty		
Guilty	25 years	Released 1967
NOT Guilty		
NOT Guilty		
Guilty	5 years	

	Date of Arrest	Bail	Charges
Martin Harvey	1 October 1963	Bailed	Receiving
Gordon Goody	3 October 1963		Conspiracy to Rob Robbery
Patricia Smith	10 October 1963	Bailed	Receiving
Walter Smith	10 October 1963	Bailed	Receiving (2 counts)
John Wheater	17 October 1963	Bailed	Conspiracy to Rob Conspiracy to obstruct Justice
Robert Welch	25 October 1963		Conspiracy to Rob Robbery
John Daly	3 December 1963		Conspiracy to Rob Robbery
Roy James	10 December 1963		Conspiracy to Rob Robbery Receiving (2 counts)
James White	21 April 1965		Conspiracy to Rob Robbery
Alfred Place	2 September 1965		Harbouring James White
Jean Place	2 September 1965		Harbouring James White
Henry Isaacs	2 September 1965		Harbouring James White
Joanna Isaacs	2 September 1965		Harbouring James White
Buster Edwards	19 September 1965		Conspiracy to Rob Robbery
William Green	9 November 1967		Harbouring Buster Edwards
Bruce Reynolds	8 November 1968		Conspiracy to Rob Robbery

NB: Sentences for more than one offence were concurrent

Verdict	Sentence	Release
PLEADED Guilty	12 months	
Guilty	25 years	Released 1975
Guilty	30 years	
NOT Guilty on instruction of Judge	Acquitted	
Guilty	3 years	
NOT Guilty		Released 1966
Guilty	3 years	
Guilty	25 years	Released 1976
Guilty	30 years	
NOT Guilty	Acquitted	
NOT Guilty	Acquitted	
Guilty	25 years	Released 1975
Guilty	30 years	
Jury Discharged from giving verdict		
NOT Guilty		Released 1975
Guilty	18 years	
Guilty	4 years	
Guilty	9 months	
Guilty	2 years	
Guilty	Bound Over (3 years)	
Guilty	15 years	Released 1975
Guilty	12 years	
Guilty	2 years	
Guilty	25 years	Released 1978
Guilty	25 years	

APPENDIX – APPEAL COURT HEARINGS

Court of Criminal Appeal 6–20 July 1964

	Counsel	Original Counts		Original Appeal	Sub. Sentence
CORDREY Heard 13.7.64 Jud'mnt 14.7.64	Mr Leach	1. Conspiracy to Rob 3. Receiving £56,037 4. Receiving £79,120 5. Receiving £5,060	20 years 20 years 20 years 20 years	Allowed Allowed Allowed Allowed	14 Years 14 Years 14 Years 14 Years
BOAL Heard 13.7.64 Jud'mnt 14.7.64	Mr Slme QC Mr Eyre	1. Conspiracy to Rob 2. Robbery 6. Receiving £56,037 7. Receiving £79,120 8. Receiving £5,060	21 years 24 years - - -	Dismissed Allowed Substituted Substituted Substituted	14 Years - 14 Years 14 Years 14 Years
WILSON Heard 6.7.64 Jud'mnt 8.7.64	Mr Hutchinson QC Mr Mathew	1. Conspiracy to Rob 2. Robbery	25 years 30 years	Dismissed Dismissed	
BIGGS Heard 6.7.64 Jud'mnt 8.7.64	Mr Fordham	1. Conspiracy to Rob 2. Robbery	25 years 30 years	Dismissed Dismissed	
JAMES Heard 6.7.64 Jud'mnt 8.7.64	Mr Durand QC Mr Richardson	1. Conspiracy to Rob 2. Robbery	25 years 30 years	Dismissed Dismissed	
HUSSEY Heard 7.7.64 Jud'mnt 8.7.64	Mr Brown QC Mr Freeman	1. Conspiracy to Rob 2. Robbery	25 years 30 years	Dismissed Dismissed	
WISBEY Heard 7.7.64 Jud'mnt 8.7.64	Mr J. Platts-Mills QC Hon. P.M. Pakenham	1. Conspiracy to Rob 2. Robbery	25 years 30 years	Dismissed Dismissed	
WELCH Heard 8.7.64 Jud'mnt 8.7.64	Mr Elwyn Jones QC Mr Gamgee	1. Conspiracy to Rob 2. Robbery	25 years 30 years	Dismissed Dismissed	
GOODY Heard 8.7.64 Jud'mnt 9.7.64	Mr Sebag-Shaw QC Mr Fordham	1. Conspiracy to Rob 2. Robbery	25 years 30 years	Dismissed Dismissed	
BRIAN FIELD Heard 9.7.64 Jud'mnt 13.7.64	Mr Hawser QC Mr Richard	1. Conspiracy to Rob 12. Conspiracy to obstruct Justice	25 years 5 years	Allowed Dismissed	20.7.64 – No Variation in Sentences
LEONARD FIELD Heard 10.7.64 Jud'mnt 13.7.64	Mr Argyle QC Mr Jowitt	1. Conspiracy to Rob 12. Conspiracy to obstruct Justice	25 years 5 years	Allowed Dismissed	20.7.64 – No Variation in Sentences
WHEATER Heard 10.7.64 Jud'mnt 13.7.64	Mr Swanwick QC Mr Waley	12. Conspiracy to obstruct Justice	3 years	Dismissed	20.7.64 – No Variation in Sentences

APPENDIX – LAWYERS

Trial Judge:	Mr Justice Edmund Davies
Prosecuting Counsel:	Arthur James QC
	Niall MacDermot QC
	J.D.A. Fennell
	H.W. Sabin
Appeal Court Judges:	Mr Justice Widgery
	Mr Justice Fenton Atkinson
	Mr Justice Lawton

Defendents	Solicitors	Trial – Counsel	Appeal – Counsel
Ronnie Biggs	Lesser & Co.	Wilfred Fordham C. Salmon (2)	Wilfred Fordham
William Boal	Malcolm Davis & Co.	W.A. Sime QC E. Eyre (2)	W.A. Sime QC E. Eyre (2)
Roger Cordrey	Hardcastle, Sanders & Armitage	J.G. Leach I.T.R. Davidson (2)	J.G. Leach
John Daly	Lesser & Co.	W.A.L. Raeburn Wilfred Fordham (2) J.N. Speed (3)	
Brian Field	Lipson, Rumney & Co.	C. Lewis Hawser QC I.S. Richard (2) G.C. Hesletine (3)	C. Lewis Hawser QC I.S. Richard (2)
Gordon Goody	Lesser & Co.	Sebag-Shaw QC Wilfred Fordham (2) C. Salmon (3)	Sebag-Shaw QC Wilfred Fordham (2)
Roy James	Sampson & Co.	W.M. Howard J.N. Speed (2) J.C. Mathew	Victor Durand QC K.A. Richardson
Charlie Wilson	Sampson & Co.	J.C. Mathew J.N. Speed (2) W.M. Howard (2)	Jeremy Hutchinson QC J.C. Mathew (2)

Jimmy Hussey	Lincoln & Lincoln	R.K. Brown QC R.G. Freeman (2)	R.K. Brown QC R.G. Freeman (2) Mr Salts (2)
Bob Welch	Lincoln & Lincoln	F. Ashe Lincoln QC J.L. Gamgee (2)	Elwyn Jones QC MP J.L. Gamgee (2)
Tommy Wisbey	Lincoln & Lincoln	J.A. Grieves QC Hon. P.M. Pakenham (2)	J. Platts-Mills QC Hon. P.M. Pakenham (2)
John Wheater		G.R. Swanwick QC A.F. Waley (2)	G.R. Swanwick QC A.F. Waley (2)
Leonard Field	Lesser & Co.	Michael V. Argyle QC E.F. Jowitt (2)	Michael V. Argyle QC E.F. Jowitt (2)

Later Trials:

Jimmy White	Lesser & Co.		Mr Justice Nield
Buster Edwards	Lesser & Co.		Mr Justice Milmo
Bruce Reynolds	Lesser & Co.		Mr Justice Thompson

APPENDIX – THE TRAVELLING POST OFFICE

Mail had been transported on the railways since 1830, with the first purpose-built sorting carriage appearing in 1838. These were known as railway post offices until 1928 saw them renamed Travelling Post Offices (TPO). They collected and delivered mail from all over the country and were normally manned by a team of seventy postal workers, mostly Postman Higher Grade: experienced mail sorters drawn from the larger sorting offices of London and the provinces. They were expected to sort up to 2,000 letters per hour at 99 per cent accuracy.

Prior to the First World War there were over 130 fully staffed mail trains travelling the network each night. By 1963 this had been reduced to around 40. The last mail train ran on 9 January 2004.

The 'Up' Special or 'Up' Postal that was ambushed at Sears Crossing on 8 August 1963 was typical of most TPOs in that it was a composite train, setting off from Glasgow with five carriages and collecting additional carriages as it made its journey south.

When complete, the TPO consisted of (in order):

1 diesel locomotive
1 bogie brake van
6 Post Office sorting vans
2 Post Office tenders
2 Post Office sorting vans
1 Post Office tender (+ guard)

The diesel engine and twelve coaches had a combined weight of 368 tons and would travel at speeds averaging 70 mph.

The majority of Post Office staff on the train would have been working in the sorting vans. All the coaches were easily identified by the 'Royal Mail' lettering and were generally painted red. Post Office tenders were used as a store for transporting mailbags containing sorted mail. They looked the same as the Post Office sorting vans, bearing the same livery and royal cipher. After 'The Great Train Robbery' it was considered necessary for trains carrying mail to be less obvious as to their contents.

The High Value Packets coach was normally the second carriage behind the engine, just after the bogie brake van. A High Value Packet was one that had been registered and posted by a bank. It was in the HVP coach that registered mail and packages containing valuables or large quantities of money were sorted (prior to the 1963 robbery, some TPOs even carried bullion). Inside this sorting van there were four sliding doors, two mailbag cupboards and seven counters at which the men could work. As the mail was sorted, HVP packages were separated from the ordinary mail and passed forward to the men in the HVP coach, who in turn would sort and stack the mailbags inside padlocked wooden cupboards.

On the night of the robbery there were 128 sacks, each containing one or more mailbags, which in turn held 636 High Value Packets.

The packets contained:

£5 notes	£1,191,030.0s.od.
£1 notes	£1,210,901.0s.od.
10 shilling notes	£174,199.10s.od.
Scottish and Irish notes	£19,692.10s.od.
Miscellaneous	£174.10s.od.

(Best estimated) TOTAL £2,595,996.10s.od.

The build-up of HVP mailbags during the journey south was as follows:

21.45 Carlisle	30 sacks on board containing 141 HVPs
22.56 Preston	41 sacks on board containing 247 HVPs
23.36 Warrington	46 sacks on board containing 247 HVPs
00.12 Crewe	91 sacks on board containing 531 HVPs
01.23 Tamwoth	125 sacks on board containing 647 HVPs
02.12 Rugby	128 sacks on board containing 663 HVPs

At the time of the robbery there were seventy-seven Post Office employees on board, including an inspector and an assistant inspector. In the HVP carriage there were five Post Office employees.

*

British Railways staff consisted of a train driver, a second man (known as the fireman) and a guard at the rear of the train. There were no policemen or security guards on board as there had not been a robbery on a TPO for 125 years.

APPENDIX – BOOKS

Andrew Cook, *The Great Train Robbery: The Untold Story from the Closed Investigation Files*, The History Press, 2013

Ronnie Biggs & Christopher Pickard, *Odd Man Out – The Last Straw*, M. Press Media Ltd, 2011

Robert Ryan, *Signal Red*, Headline Review, 2010

Len Woodley & John Bailey, *The Man Who Photographed the Great Train Robbery*, Armadillo, 2010

Brenda Haugen, *The Great Train Robbery*, Compass Point Books, 2010

Mike Gray, Tel Currie, Michael Biggs, *Ronnie Biggs – The Inside Story*, Apex Publishing, 2009

Peter Guttridge, *The Great Train Robbery (Crime Archive)*, The National Archives, 2008

Wensley Clarkson, *Killing Charlie: The Bloody, Bullet-riddled Hunt for the Most Powerful Great Train Robber of All*, Mainstream Publishing, 2004

Tim Coates, *The Great British Train Robbery, 1963 (Moments of History)*, Tim Coates, 2003

Michael Biggs & Neil Silver, *The Biggs Time: Ronnie & Michael – Man and Boy*, Virgin, 2002

Marilyn Wisbey, *Gangster's Moll*, Warner Books, 2002

Bruce Reynolds, Nick Reynolds, Alan Parker, *The Great Train Robbery File*, Abstract Sounds, 2000

Bruce Reynolds, *The Autobiography of a Thief*, Bantam Press, 1995

Ronald Biggs & Christopher Pickard, *Odd Man Out*, Bloomsbury, 1994

Ronald Biggs & Geoff Deane, *Biggsy's Bible: The Gospel according to Ronnie Biggs*, Virgin, 1988

Ronnie Biggs, *Ronnie Biggs: His Own Story*, Sphere, 1981

Jack Slipper, *Slipper of the Yard*, Sidgwick & Jackson, 1981

Piers Paul Read, *The Train Robbers – Their Story*, W.H. Allen/Coronet 1978

Anthony Delano, *Slip-Up: Fleet Street, Scotland Yard and the Great Train Robbery*, Quadrangle/New York Times Books, 1975

Colin Mackenzie, *The World's Most Wanted Man: Story of Ronald Biggs*, Hart Davis, 1975

Frank Williams, *No Fixed Address: The Great Train Robbers on the Run*, W.H. Allen, 1973

Ernest Millen, *Specialist in Crime*, Harrap & Co., 1972

George Hatherill, *A Detective's Story*, André Deutsch, 1971

Peta Fordham, *Robbers' Tale: Truth About the Great Train Robbery*, Hodder & Stoughton/Penguin, 1965

Malcolm Fewtrell, *The Train Robbers*, Arthur Barker, 1964

John Gosling & Dennis Craig, *The Great Train Robbery*, W.H. Allen, June 1964

Ross Richards, *The Great Train Robbery*, Consul Books, 1964

APPENDIX – TV & FILM

Television Documentaries

The Great Train Robbery, ITV Studios/ITV 2012

The Great Train Robbery's Missing Mastermind, Lion Productions/ Channel 4, 2012

The Great Train Robbers Secret Tapes Revealed, Crime Network/ Channel 5, 2011

Buster – Movie Connections, BBC Television, 2009

Master Crime Museum – Great Train Robbery, Crime Network/Brighter Picture/Endemol, 2008

Ronnie Biggs – The Last Escape, North One Television/Sky One, 2005

Kidnap Ronnie Biggs, IWC Media/Channel 4, 2005

Days That Shook The World – The Great Train Robbery, Lion Television/ BBC Scotland/History Channel, 2004

The Legend of Ronnie Biggs, Meridian TV/MMTV Production/Channel 5, 2002

I Was a Great Train Robber, Carlton TV/Fulcrum Productions/ITV 4, 2001

Secret History – The Great Train Robbery, Blakeway/Ten Alps/Channel 4, 1999

'I Married a Great Train Robber', *Cutting Edge*, Channel 4, 1996

'Once a Thief', *Everyman*, BBC Television, 1995

Underworld, BBC Television 1994

'The Great Train Robbery', *Great Crimes & Trials of the 20th Century*, Uden Associates, 1993

'The Great Train Robbery', *Man Alive*, BBC Television, 1978

'The Great Train Robbery', *World in Action*, ITV, 1964

Television Drama

Mrs Biggs (5 episodes) ITV Studios, September 2012

The Great Paper Chase, BBC Television 1989

Films

Buster (1988), Director: David Green; Starring: Phil Collins & Julie Walters, Hemdale Film Corp.

Prisoner of Rio (1988), Director: Lech Malewski; Starring: Steven Berkoff, Paul Freeman & Peter Firth, Palace Pictures

Die Gentlemen bitten zur Kasse (1966), Director: Claus Peter Witt; Starring: Horst Tappert, NDR

Robbery (1967), Director: Peter Yates; Starring Stanley Baker & Frank Finlay, Paramount Pictures

INDEX